ALIGNING
FACULTY REWARDS
WITH
INSTITUTIONAL MISSION

ALIGNING
FACULTY REWARDS
WITH
INSTITUTIONAL MISSION
Statements, Policies, and Guidelines

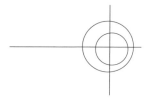

Robert M. Diamond
Syracuse University

ANKER PUBLISHING COMPANY, INC.
Bolton, Massachusetts

Aligning Faculty Rewards with Institutional Mission
Statements, Policies, and Guidelines

ISBN 1-882982-26-6

Composition by Lyn Rodger, Deerfoot Studios
Cover design by Boynton Hue Studio

Anker Publishing Company, Inc.
176 Ballville Road
P.O. Box 249
Bolton, MA 01740-0249

www.ankerpub.com

ABOUT THE AUTHOR

ROBERT M. DIAMOND is Research Professor and Director, Institute for Change in Higher Education, Syracuse University. Formerly he was Assistant Vice Chancellor, Director of the Center for Instructional Development, and Professor of Instructional Design, Development and Evaluation, and Higher Education at Syracuse, and Director of the National Project on Institutional Priorities and Faculty Rewards funded by the Lilly Endowment and the Pew Charitable Trusts.

Diamond coauthored the 1987 National Study of Teaching Assistants, the 1992 National Study of Research Universities on the Balance between Research and Undergraduate Teaching, and was responsible for the design and implementation of Syracuse University's award-winning high school/college transition program, Project Advance. Diamond is author of numerous books, including *Serving on Promotion and Tenure Committees: A Faculty Guide* (Anker, 1994), *Preparing for Promotion and Tenure Review: A Faculty Guide* (Anker, 1995), *Designing and Assessing Courses and Curricula: A Practical Guide* (Jossey-Bass, 1997), and, with Bronwyn Adam, *Recognizing Faculty Work: Reward Systems for the Year 2000* (Jossey-Bass, 1993), and he is a consultant to colleges and universities throughout the world.

CONTENTS

PREFACE

Discussions of faculty priorities abound, with a growing number of institutions claiming an increased emphasis on the quality of teaching and on their role in the community. In practice, however, faculty reward systems at these institutions often convey a different emphasis, giving more weight to publications and scholarship than to teaching and community service, thus creating a mixed message for faculty. Disparity between an institution's mission statement and its reward system (what it says and what it does) undercuts the effectiveness of each: If these goals are to be reached, the institution must reward behaviors that best support its mission.

PURPOSE OF THIS BOOK

Developing a high-quality faculty reward system that supports the mission and priorities of the institution and is fair to the individual is not a chance activity: It must be developed over time through a process that actively involves faculty and administrative leaders. And while it is not an easy process, it is, however, one that is essential to the long-term health of the institution.

Policies and procedures that describe the review process, establish priorities, and describe the roles of individuals and committees must be articulated in integrated statements at various levels of the institution. The more care that is taken to develop statements that are in concert and mutually reinforcing, the more effective and fair the system of faculty hiring, orientation, and review will be. A thorough and well-planned development process lessens the likelihood of confusion as to priorities, roles, procedures, and requirements and the extra work, frustration, and—in some cases—poor decision-making that can result.

Fortunately, there is a growing body of literature on academic scholarship: its nature, the forms it takes in various academic disciplines, and strategies for its effective documentation, with significant energy devoted to thinking about post-tenure review. However, less attention has been paid to the documents themselves. What information concerning the faculty reward and review process should be included in institutional, school/college, and department statements and collective bargaining agreements? What guidelines should be provided to faculty preparing for review and to those serving on committees? There is a dearth of document models on which to build.

While there is no single model for a guiding document, this book presents numerous samples of documents that various institutions have developed at various levels. Institutions are different, priorities vary, and what is appropriate for one school or college may not be appropriate for another. But there are certain key elements that should be included in any institution's documents and certain questions that should be addressed. This book attempts to highlight those.

THE BOOK'S ORGANIZATION

Aligning Faculty Rewards with Institutional Mission identifies the issues that should be considered and presents examples from many different institutions, large and small, private and public. These have been selected to demonstrate how the same issues can successfully be addressed in a number of ways and to provide some good examples that you may want to build on, taking into consideration your own institution's mission, history, and culture.

Since the promotion, tenure, and faculty reward system must be addressed in a number of different documents, the book is structured around the specific documents themselves. Chapter One provides an overview of a faculty reward system; then Chapter Two addresses strategies for getting review of that system onto the institutional agenda. Since the communication and presentation process affects the scope of the discussion that follows, care must be taken to approach this organizational change in an open and positive manner and to communicate the importance of the work to be undertaken. Chapter Three discusses the need for a quality institutional mission and vision statement upon which the priorities of a faculty reward system must be based.

Chapters Four, Five, and Six focus on the operational policy documents of the institution, school, and college (Chapter Four); the department (Chapter Five); and the collective bargaining unit (Chapter Six). These chapters describe procedures, anticipate specific requirements, and articulate functional priorities. In all chapters, we have tried to be specific and to present as many examples from a diversity of institutions as possible. Following Chapter Six is an annotated bibliography of resources on promotion and tenure systems.

I would like to express my appreciation to the many authors and contributors of the excerpts that have been used throughout this book. These examples are the result of hard work by many talented and dedicated faculty and administrators. Use them well!

Robert M. Diamond
Jamesville, NY
January, 1999

INSTITUTIONAL PRIORITIES
AND THE
PROMOTION AND TENURE PROCESS

The closer the match between the mission of an institution and the priorities as described in the tenure and promotion system, the more productive the faculty will be in helping the institution reach the goals that have been identified. All too often what are articulated as the priorities of a college or university are not supported by the faculty reward system. This gap can create problems for the institution, its administrators, and the dedicated faculty who work there. The present criteria for rewarding faculty work at many institutions, based primarily on the scientific model of research and publication, are often counterproductive to reaching larger academic goals that most campuses agree are both central to the institution and vital to the development of a quality educational experience for students. In 1987, Ernest Boyer reported that "conflicting priorities and competing interests . . . appeared with such regularity and seemed so consistently to sap the vitality of the baccalaureate experience" (Boyer, 1987).

In his follow-up publication, *Scholarship Reconsidered: Priorities for the Professoriate* (1990), Boyer argued that "a wide gap now exists between the myth and the reality of academic life. Almost all colleges pay lip service to the trilogy of teaching, research, and service, but when it comes to making judgments about professional performance, the three rarely are assigned equal merit. . . . The time has come to move beyond the tired old 'teaching versus research' debate and give the familiar and honorable term 'scholarship' a broader, more capacious meaning, one that brings legitimacy to the full scope of academic work."

Boyer's position seems to be shared by many in academe. Over 50,000 faculty, chairs, deans, and administrators at research universities (Gray, Froh, & Diamond, 1992; Gray, Diamond, & Adam, 1996) indicated that even those most directly involved with the present reward system—the faculty, chairs, and deans—often consider the balance between research and teaching on their campus inappropriate. One young faculty member lamented: "As a new junior professor, I have come into the profession with a strong interest in research, but an equally strong interest in serving students by helping them learn both in and outside of the classroom. The attitude I'm receiving from all levels . . . is that research is what counts. If the other areas of service and teaching are lacking, but research is strong, then promotions will follow. Unfortunately, I think this is the wrong message to be sending faculty."

Most significantly, the results of these studies indicate that efforts to modify the promotion and tenure system to recognize and reward teaching are supported by a majority of faculty, chairs, deans, and central administrators at research, doctoral, and master's level institutions. On the positive side, results from a more recent study have indicated that on a number of campuses, efforts to place increased importance on teaching is underway and that priorities are viewed as changing (Diamond & Adam, 1997).

CHARACTERISTICS OF AN APPROPRIATE AND EFFECTIVE PROMOTION AND TENURE SYSTEM

How might we think differently about faculty rewards in a time of tight resources, multiple demands, and changing technologies? We propose that a faculty reward system appropriate for these dynamics must have the following characteristics:

THE FACULTY REWARD SYSTEM IS ALIGNED APPROPRIATELY WITH THE INSTITUTION'S MISSION STATEMENT

All colleges and universities are not alike. State and private institutions, church-related colleges, and urban and rural institutions, large and small, all have their own agendas. Some institutions have a distinct research mission, while others focus primarily on teaching and/or service. An effective promotion and tenure system must be sensitive to these differences and build and support the mission statement of the institution. In order to support change in reward systems, the institutional mission and vision statements must be realistic, operational, and sensitive to the unique characteristics and strengths of the institution. Such is not always the case: All too many institutional mission statements are vaguely articulated, employing nonspecific language open to a variety of interpretations, while others express lofty ideals which are difficult to attain and impossible to assess. Samuel Hope, executive director, National Office for Arts Accreditation in Higher Education, made the following observation, "From my perspective in accreditation, it is not unusual to see tremendous rhetorical emphasis on the mission-goal objectives equation within institutions and programs. It is also not unusual to see failure to work the real meaning of this concept in various operational areas. The assessment of faculty work is one of these areas . . . an institution cannot claim to have a unique mission . . . if it does not also have a unique approach to assessing the quality of faculty" (Hope, 1992).

THE FACULTY REWARD SYSTEM IS SENSITIVE TO DIFFERENCES AMONG THE DISCIPLINES

Several years ago, Syracuse University, with support from the Lilly Endowment and the Fund for the Improvement of Post-Secondary Education, began a series of projects focused on the faculty reward system. As part of this initiative, a number of professional associations established task forces to develop statements articulating the range of activities that could be considered scholarly. As this project has progressed, significant differences among the disciplines have become clear. There are differences in what faculty do across disciplines, as well as in the language they use to describe what they do. It is important that reward systems acknowledge and honor the inherent functional differences among the humanities, the social sciences, sciences, and professional schools. While some fields are comfortable with the traditional terms of research, teaching, and service, others find the model developed by Eugene Rice more comfortable. In his important article, "The New American Scholar" (1991), Rice divides "scholarly work" into four components.

1) The advantage of knowledge: essentially original research

2) The integration of knowledge: synthesizing and reintegrating knowledge, revealing new patterns of meaning, and new relationships between the parts and the whole

3) The application of knowledge: professional practice directly related to an individual's scholarly specialization

4) The transformation of knowledge through teaching: including pedagogical content knowledge and discipline-specific educational theory

For many of the disciplines, a review of the work of Rice, Boyer, and others has been an excellent place to begin. Ultimately, however, a model uniquely molded to the values and language of the particular discipline usually emerges. Statements from the professional associations are likely to facilitate generative dialogue in their fields. A single model or process is simply not realistic given the differences among the disciplines. What we see evolving is a set of standards and criteria that are functional at the institution, college, and department levels and comprehensible to those outside the discipline who have key roles to play in the promotion and tenure process.

The work of the professional associations to date reveals that one thing is common across disciplines: Important faculty work is not being rewarded. Service, teaching, and creativity are risky priorities for faculty members seeking tenure or promotion at many institutions. The report from the Task Force to Redefine Scholarly Work of the American Historical Association (1992) reflects this concern:

This debate over priorities is not discipline-specific but extends across the higher education community. Nevertheless, each discipline has specific concerns and problems. For history, the privilege given to the monograph in promotion and tenure has led to the undervaluing of other activities central to the life of the discipline—writing textbooks, developing courses and curricula, documentary editing, museum exhibitions, and film projects to name but a few.

Similar problems appear in drama departments with the production of a play; in English or writing departments when a faculty member works in the community to develop a literacy program; and in management, economics, sociology, or retailing when a professor's skills are used to help a community group address a significant problem. To put it bluntly, the focus on research and publication and the mad dash for federal funds and external grants has diverted energies away from important faculty work and has had a direct and negative impact on the quality of classroom instruction and the ability of institutions to provide support for and involvement in their communities. It also diverts energies from types of research that do not fall within the traditional publication realm. Real limitations exist for faculty who want to ensure recognition for their scholarly pursuits. The choice is often between research that intrigues and excites them and the type that can be represented in a publication and will appeal to the prestige journals or publishers. The result has been a proliferation of what might be called "establishment research."

THE FACULTY REWARD SYSTEM IS SENSITIVE TO THE DIFFERENCES AMONG INDIVIDUALS

We each bring to our work different strengths, interests, and perspectives. Establishing an identical set of criteria for all faculty, as we have tended to do, is unrealistic and can undermine the quality of an academic unit. The truth is that outstanding researchers are not necessarily great teachers, and great teachers are not always exceptional researchers. The goal for each department, school, or college should be to bring together a group of talented individuals who can work together in a synergistic manner to reach the goals of that unit. A department needs the great teacher who can motivate and excite entering students as much as it needs the quality researcher or author who can break new ground in the discipline. The reward system must also recognize that faculty, at different times in their careers, will focus their attention in different areas. This may at one time be the result of a departmental assignment, while on another occasion it will be inherent to the discipline. In some fields, a faculty member's major research accomplishments are early in his or her career; in others, a scholarly focus occurs later, when the individual has had the opportunity to expand his or her perspectives.

THE FACULTY REWARD SYSTEM INCLUDES AN ASSESSMENT PROGRAM THAT IS APPROPRIATE, PERCEIVED TO BE FAIR, AND WORKABLE

To reach this goal, we are proposing a selected professional portfolio that is tailored around the specific responsibilities of an individual faculty member. This system would permit an in-depth evaluation of representative items and activities rather than the more customary quick review of often overlapping and redundant studies and publications. It should be a system that stresses, where appropriate, process as much as product and incorporates the expert judgment of peers or colleagues. It should also be a system that separates exceptional and innovative teaching, software and curriculum development, and significant research about teaching from those activities that all faculty perform in their classrooms and laboratories.

THE FACULTY REWARD SYSTEM RECOGNIZES THAT MOST ACTION TAKES PLACE AT THE DEPARTMENTAL LEVEL AND THE MOST SPECIFICITY IN DOCUMENTATION IS REQUIRED THERE

One of the more challenging issues that the chair will face is ensuring that there is an appropriate mesh between how a faculty member spends his or her time and the priorities of the department. Since faculty have different strengths, the process should ensure the best possible match between individual talents and departmental needs. While some faculty may spend a great deal of their energy improving the introductory courses and developing good pedagogy, others, based on the needs of the department and their personal strengths, may be asked to focus their energies on graduate teaching, on basic or applied research, or in discipline-related work in the community. The combination of a wide range of activities involving faculty with different strengths is essential if a department is to reach its maximum potential.

As Carla Howery, deputy executive director of the American Sociological Association, stressed in a presentation at the 1997 summer Minnowbrook conference, when a quality match between the talents and interests of an individual and the needs of the department does not exist, action then becomes necessary (see Figure 1.1).

The goal is to use the faculty reward system in a fair way to support the priorities of the unit and to recognize and utilize more effectively the strengths of individuals. This will require planning, development, and evaluation at both the departmental and individual level (see Figure 1.2).

FIGURE 1.1

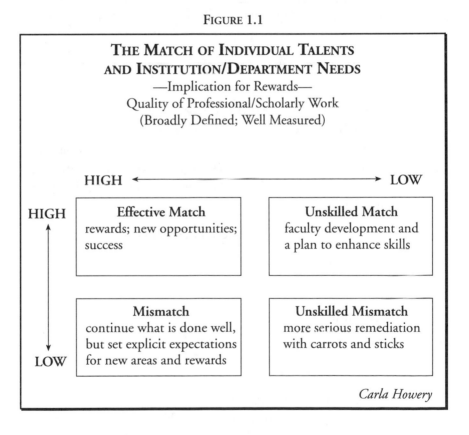

THE MATCH OF INDIVIDUAL TALENTS
AND INSTITUTION/DEPARTMENT NEEDS
—Implication for Rewards—
Quality of Professional/Scholarly Work
(Broadly Defined; Well Measured)

HIGH ⟵——————⟶ LOW

HIGH

Effective Match
rewards; new opportunities; success

Unskilled Match
faculty development and a plan to enhance skills

Mismatch
continue what is done well, but set explicit expectations for new areas and rewards

Unskilled Mismatch
more serious remediation with carrots and sticks

LOW

Carla Howery

FIGURE 1.2

THE PARALLEL PROCESS FOR DEPARTMENTS AND INDIVIDUALS IN PLANNING, DEVELOPMENT, ASSESSMENT, AND REWARDS		
Process/Purpose	Individual	Department
Planning	Personal Goals	Strategic planning/ mission statements
Development (formative)	Formative pre- and post-tenure	Retreats, committee meeting
Evaluation	Annual review: P&T	Program review
		Carla Howery

THE FACULTY REWARD SYSTEM ARTICULATES THE CHARACTERISTICS OF SCHOLARLY WORK

Our work with the disciplinary associations suggests that seeking a single definition of scholarship may be less productive than identifying a set of characteristics that typify scholarly endeavors. Most disciplines will agree that scholarly work:

- Requires a high level of discipline-related expertise

- Breaks new ground or is innovative

- Can be replicated

- Can be documented

- Can be peer reviewed

- Has significance and impact

In *Scholarship Assessed,* a 1997 report from the Carnegie Foundation for the Advancement of Teaching, Glassick, Huber, and Maeroff proposed a slightly different approach that focuses more on process. Their six characteristics of scholarship include:

1) Clear goals

2) Adequate preparation

3) Appropriate methods

4) Significant results

5) Effective presentations

6) Reflective critique

It is best left to the individual institution, school, college, or department to determine which combination of features or characteristics is appropriate for their use. Using such a model eliminates the many problems associated with definitions of scholarship where disciplinary differences are most apparent. Faculty reward guidelines focused on a set of characteristics that can be applied across the disciplines and represented and documented variously respect the real differences inherent in the academic disciplines.

POST-TENURE REVIEW AND PART-TIME FACULTY

While our primary focus is on full-time, tenure-line faculty, many of the basics that we will be discussing will also apply to those faculty who are in part-time positions or who already have tenure. In all instances, the review of individuals must relate to mission and priorities of the institution, the units on which they work, and their individual assignments.

For post-tenure review, the process should be perceived as part of an ongoing professional development effort where the focus is on helping each faculty member reach his or her full potential as a productive member of the academic community. The review should be seen as a positive activity designed to benefit the institution and the individual. Unfortunately, too many institutions establish a process that is perceived more as a threat than as an integral element for professional growth. Ideally, the post-tenure review should be simply a continuation of a support and evaluation system that began when that faculty member first came to the college or university.

DOCUMENTATION OF THE PROMOTION AND TENURE SYSTEM

On each campus, there are a number of statements and policies that together combine to provide the working base for the faculty reward system. They include:

- The institutional mission statement

- Institutional guidelines

- The school or college promotion and tenure or merit pay guidelines

- The departmental promotion and tenure or merit pay guidelines

- The collective bargaining agreement (on unionized campuses)

In addition, there are two external documents that may play a role in the development of these guidelines:

- Disciplinary statements

- Accreditation standards

Within any context, the goal is to develop statements that are both supportive and consistent (Figure 1.3). When conflicts arise, in a tenure case, for example, it is often the result of poorly articulated policies, inconsistencies, or contradictions among the campus-produced documents. Later chapters in this book will address the structure, design, and content of campus statements guiding faculty rewards. It should also be noted that, as Figure 1.3 demonstrates, policy statements become more specific as they move from the level of institutional documents to the discipline-focused guidelines at the department level.

The closer the statement is to departments and faculty, the more detailed and specific it becomes. The statement at each level will directly affect the statements above or below it.

FIGURE 1.3

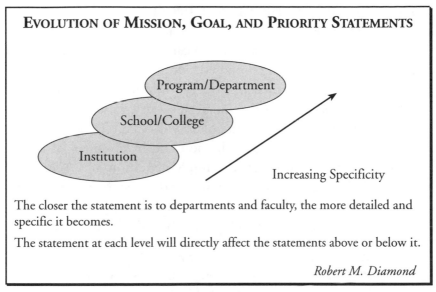

EVOLUTION OF MISSION, GOAL, AND PRIORITY STATEMENTS

Program/Department

School/College

Institution

Increasing Specificity

The closer the statement is to departments and faculty, the more detailed and specific it becomes.

The statement at each level will directly affect the statements above or below it.

Robert M. Diamond

NECESSARY CONDITIONS FOR DEVELOPING A NEW PROMOTION AND TENURE SYSTEM

RECONCEIVING FACULTY PRIORITIES REQUIRES A GENUINE COMMITMENT TO CHANGE

All too often, major institutional initiatives have been characterized by extensive rhetoric and little action. In announcing the first American Association for Higher Education-sponsored Forum on Faculty Roles and Rewards (1992), Russell Edgerton, former president of AAHE, cautioned:

> As in the case of assessment, the aroused interest in clarifying and shifting faculty priorities could unfold in different ways. We can envision a scenario in which there is a growing respect for dimensions of excellence beyond research, and a new appreciation for the "practice" of one's discipline ... a culture in which all dimensions of professional and scholarly work are honored and peer reviewed. But we can also envision a nightmarish scenario ... more reporting requirements, piles of evaluation data no one uses, prizes and rewards that have more to do with public relations than actual faculty motivation or improved performance.

THE ENTIRE ACADEMIC COMMUNITY MUST BE
ACTIVELY INVOLVED IN THE CHANGE PROCESS

Unless the central administration, deans, chairs, and individual faculty members have ownership of any modifications in the promotion and tenure process that are being proposed, adoption and implementation will be problematic. This ownership can come only from giving faculty an active role in setting priorities, establishing criteria, and determining how revised promotion and tenure plans will occur. To be successful, the change process requires participation and involvement of faculty from initial planning through the implementation and assessment stages. One important factor to keep in mind is that, based on the data gathered in the Syracuse and state of Virginia studies, a successful effort will have the support of most college faculty and administrators.

THE PROCESS OF CHANGING THE PROMOTION
AND TENURE CRITERIA WILL BE FAR MORE DIFFICULT
IN SOME ACADEMIC AREAS THAN IN OTHERS

Data from both a National Study of Research Universities on the Balance Between Research and Undergraduate Teaching (Gray, Froh, & Diamond, 1992) and a National Study on the Relative Importance of Research and Undergraduate Teaching at Colleges and Universities (Gray, Diamond, & Adam, 1996) suggests that faculty in the sciences, engineering, and some of the social sciences tend to be more comfortable with the status quo than faculty in some other academic areas. In some fields or disciplines, the need for change is more strongly felt. It is no accident that the National Science Foundation has, as a result of a number of commissioned studies, begun to place increased emphasis on teaching in its grant programs. As federal support for research continues to decline and as institutions recognize that the number of research programs they support must be reduced to those that are of the highest quality, there will be increased pressure on many departments to reestablish priorities and reassess the criteria by which faculty will be recognized and rewarded.

Other disciplines, particularly the humanities, performing arts, most professional schools, and some of the social sciences, will face a different problem. Over the last decade or so, these disciplines have focused more and more attention on publishable research in order to gain "academic respectability." They will now be asked to refocus their efforts on activities that, until now, have received little attention. Younger faculty in these programs have been hired and rewarded as traditional researchers. The change that we are discussing may be most stressful on our newest faculty if, at a key time in their professional careers, the criteria by which they will be judged change. For faculty who have received little support or training in teaching, this change may be particularly difficult to make. William Laidlaw, in a statement from Defining Scholarly Work in Management Education, a task force report for the American Assembly of Collegiate Schools of Business (now the International Association for Management Education) (1992), addresses these issues:

> In the late 1950s and early 1960s, major reports on the field of management education were sponsored by the Ford and Carnegie Foundations. Among the findings of those reports were that business schools were too vocational, lacked academic rigor, and taught subjects that were not founded in basic research. The Ford Foundation followed up its report with an investment of more than $30 million to upgrade the quality of doctoral programs, to incorporate research capability from other disciplines, and to create an environment that valued research as the basis for the development of the disciplines in management education. Our field has spent the last 30 years seeking academic respectability among university colleagues by emphasizing research and scholarship, often narrowly defined.

Members of another task force expressed concern that supporting a broader range of scholarly activity might brand their faculty as academic lightweights, thus dooming them to an academic underclass. However, this same report claims that the benefits of such change would outweigh the negative implications by bringing greater congruence between the university mission and faculty priorities. In addition, the committee members argued that these changes would both encourage greater diversity among faculty and support professional activities that benefit society and reduce faculty stress.

CONCLUSION: IT ISN'T AN OPTION—THE FACULTY REWARD SYSTEM MUST CHANGE

Those of us in higher education must modify what we do and where we invest our energies. A chorus of voices from the public and private sectors are calling for change, and our most important clients—our students—are demanding it. The question is how significant a role we, as faculty and administrators, will play in this process. We can sit back and mildly protest the status quo until frustrated governmental and external accreditation agencies define for us what we will do and how we will do it, or we can take a proactive role in shaping our future. If we are to do the latter, administrators and faculty must direct the process and participate actively in the many conversations that will be necessary to negotiate this change.

The initial stage of this process must be to address faculty priorities as determined by the promotion and tenure system. Unless the criteria by which faculty are recognized and rewarded are modified, what faculty do will remain constant. Administrators must encourage and facilitate this change process, and they must understand the key role they play in establishing a receptive climate for change in the priorities of their institutions. For too long, higher education has been able to establish its own agenda. This is simply no longer possible.

REFERENCES

American Historical Association Task Force to Redefine Scholarly Work. (1992, November). *Redefining scholarly work*. Washington, DC: American Historical Association.

Boyer, E. (1987). *College: The undergraduate experience in America*. New York, NY: HarperCollins.

Boyer, E. (1990). *Scholarship reconsidered: Priorities of the professoriate*. Princeton, NJ: Carnegie Foundation for the Advancement of Teaching.

Diamond, R. M., & Adam B. E. (1997). *Changing priorities at research universities (1991-1996)*. Syracuse, NY: The Center for Instructional Development, Syracuse University.

Edgerton, R. (1992, September). AAHE's new Forum on Faculty Roles and Rewards launches its first conference. *AAHE Bulletin, 45* (1), 14-15.

Glassick, C., Huber, M., & Maeroff, G. (1997). *Scholarship assessed: Evaluation of the professoriate*. Princeton, NJ: Carnegie Foundation for the Advancement of Teaching.

Gray, P., Diamond R. M., & Adam, B. E. (1996). *A national study on the relative importance of research and undergraduate teaching at colleges and universities*. Syracuse, NY: Center for Instructional Development, Syracuse University.

Gray, P., Froh, B., & Diamond, R. M. (1992). *A national study of research universities on the balance between research and undergraduate teaching*. Syracuse, NY: The Center for Instructional Development, Syracuse University.

Hope, S. (1992). *Assessing faculty work: Administrative issues*. Conference paper. Syracuse, NY.

Howery, C. (1997, Summer). Presentation at the Minnowbrook Conference on Institutional Priorities and Faculty Rewards. Blue Mountain Lake, NY.

Laidlaw, W. (1992). *Defining scholarly work in management education,* draft report. St. Louis, MO: American Assembly of Collegiate Schools of Business.

Rice, E. R. (1991, January). The new American scholar: Scholarship and the purposes of the university. *Metropolitan Universities Journal, I* (4), 7-18.

ROLES AND RESPONSIBILITIES: PLACING THE ISSUE ON THE INSTITUTIONAL AGENDA

The faculty reward system can either deter significant change and institutional improvement, or it can facilitate the process. If faculty efforts to redesign courses, improve their teaching, or spend more time in the community are not rewarded and recognized as important, most faculty will be unwilling to donate the time to these activities that they require. All too often, those who do place emphasis in these areas do so at their own risk. At the same time, institutional leaders must recognize that if the goals of their college or university are to be reached, the faculty reward system must support these initiatives, and it is their role to place this issue on the agendas of their institutions.

STATE AND BOARD INITIATIVES

EXAMPLE: THE ARIZONA BOARD OF REGENTS

The promotion and tenure and faculty rewards system will play a major role in determining whether or not any state initiative on the academic side of the enterprise will have the impact that is desired. For example, in 1997, the Arizona Board of Regents (Arizona Board of Regents, 1997) established seven priorities for the system:

1) Improving undergraduate education

2) Strengthening graduate education

3) Enhancing research and impacting economic development

4) Capitalizing on new and emerging technologies to improve teaching, learning, research, and service outcomes

5) Strengthening relationships with governmental, educational, and constituent groups

6) Improving efficiency and demonstrating accountability

7) Assuring access to public university education for all qualified residents of Arizona

It was apparent from the start that extensive faculty effort and support would be required if the majority of these goals were to be reached. The board's work plan for implementation included the following requirements of faculty:

Improving Undergraduate Education

- Promote the active involvement of students in learning

- Assure coherence and global perspective in baccalaureate curricula

- Place greater emphasis upon excellence in teaching and advising of undergraduates

Strengthening Graduate Education and Research

- Increase support for research from state appropriations and from state, private, and federal grants and contracts

- Attract outstanding graduate students and faculty

Extending Access to Public University Education and Improving Underrepresented Student Achievement

- Improve the participation and achievement of ethnic minority groups

- Conduct research that will assist the state in identifying and alleviating the impact of societal factors that reduce ethnic minority education participation rates in Arizona

- Promote access to education for rural, time-, and place-bound students (particularly through collaboration in educational telecommunications)

Enhancing Economic Development and Public Service

- Contribute to the development of high quality primary and secondary schools

- Increase the rate at which research and technology are transferred to both public and private applications

- Provide important cultural activities and access to cultural resources

This led the board to a statewide survey on faculty load and to a major study review of the promotion and tenure system. It also became apparent that a broadening in the way that scholarly activity was defined could increase the amount of energy that faculty devoted to these activities. For example, if a goal is to assure coherence and global perspective in a baccalaureate curriculum or to help develop the quality of pre-college education, faculty will have to devote extensive energies to these projects . . . areas of faculty work that in the past have not been regarded as either scholarly or important. What the Arizona Board of Regents recognized is without a solid relationship between what was said to be important and what was rewarded, their goals would be impossible to reach. This is the rule, not the exception. On most campuses, if change is to take place, early initiatives must focus on the promotion, tenure, and resource issues.

PLACING THE PROMOTION AND TENURE SYSTEM ON THE INSTITUTIONAL AGENDA

In the example just described, the Board of Regents was instrumental in placing a review of the existing promotion and tenure system on the agendas of the faculty and administrators of the three public institutions in the state. In state systems, this approach to change is not uncommon. What is essential, as those involved in the Arizona experience learned, is that if faculty are to be involved, the criteria used in promotion and tenure must be addressed.

EXAMPLE: THE FLORIDA BOARD OF REGENTS

As part of its effort to improve the quality of teaching in the state of Florida, the regents, following a series of discussions on tenure, generated a series of recommendations that led to specific actions in each of the institutions in the system.

Tenure Recommendations, May 16, 1995

Recommendation 1) It is recommended that Florida Gulf Coast University be encouraged to pilot faculty appointment procedures that represent alternatives to the traditional tenure system. Such procedures might include multiyear contracts which would not be tenure-earning but would entail a multiyear commitment and perhaps other incentives. It is recommended further that all other universities in the state university system be encouraged to explore these options.

Recommendation 2) It is recommended that consideration be given to establishing an assessment program for tenured faculty members. Such a program would include a comprehensive evaluation on a periodic basis of the professional contributions of these faculty members. Tenured faculty members who have achieved the rank of professor would be eligible for financial rewards and other recognition based on contributions determined through the assessment program to be highly distinguished over a significant period.

Recommendation 3) It is recommended that each university examine its tenure criteria which exist at the university, college/school, and/or departmental level to ensure that the appropriate emphasis is placed on teaching and teaching-related scholarship. The criteria should be reviewed with respect to the mission of the university and its various academic units.

Recommendation 4) It is recommended that each university review the manner in which teaching is evaluated for purposes of tenure, including the criteria and procedures governing such evaluations, to ensure that such processes adequately address evaluation of teaching by peers, students, administrators, and the candidates themselves. The experience gained in assessing teaching for purposes of the Teaching Incentive Program should be particularly helpful in this review.

Recommendation 5) It is recommended that each university consider the use in one or more of its academic units of a formalized program which provides faculty members with the opportunity to consider workload options with respect to teaching, scholarship, and service. These options would recognize faculty strengths, interests, and goals, and provide for appropriate rewards and recognition based on performance criteria which reflect the emphasis placed on each area of assigned activity.

Recommendation 6) It is recommended that the universities review their current efforts to provide academic administrations with the resources necessary to effectively administer state university system and university policies addressing faculty assignments and evaluation of performance. These resources, designed to assist administrators in assessing and enhancing faculty performance, should include ongoing training, written materials, assistance from appropriate staff members, and employee assistance programs.

EXAMPLES: OREGON STATE BOARD OF EDUCATION AND ILLINOIS INSTITUTE OF TECHNOLOGY

In Oregon, the legislature not only expanded the responsibility of the State Board of Higher Education to "ensure that state needs are met in an integrated fashion" but charged the board with more planning and oversight responsibilities. In turn, the board (Oregon State Board of Higher Education, 1993) proposed giving the institutions more latitude in program development and the faculty more responsibility.

Faculty will have additional responsibility and opportunity to develop and employ pedagogies that acknowledge a new role and responsibility, incorporate emerging technologies, and effectively recognize and serve student needs; faculty commitment, development, and success in these matters are central to the success of the vision (p. 9).

The same is true at the Illinois Institute of Technology, where the Board of Trustees established a national commission to address the future of the institution. Here, too, many of the recommendations called for the development of a "new curriculum and innovative pedagogy," greater involvement of its faculty and students in the urban environment, and increased monitoring of the effectiveness of its programs. In both these instances, the initiatives to meet these goals had to turn to review of their promotion and tenure policies.

INTERNAL INITIATIVES

The top academic leadership can also place the issues of priorities and rewards on the institutional agenda. Unless the president and chief academic officer address these issues and demonstrate their importance to the institution, the topic of faculty rewards will not be addressed. This requires careful planning and a long-term commitment, so that the faculty does not feel that the initiative is from the top down with little faculty involvement. It is essential that faculty at all levels be actively involved in developing revised tenure and promotion guidelines for their programs. The role of administration is to facilitate the process while supporting the concept that different departments will and should develop statements that are appropriate for their units. Many administrators have found that reporting the data from A National Study of Research Universities on the Balance Between Research and Undergraduate Teaching (Gray, Froh, & Diamond, 1992; and Gray, Diamond, & Adam, 1996) has proven to be an excellent way to begin a campus-wide conversation about institutional priorities and the faculty reward system. As noted earlier, data from these studies have shown that most faculty want to spend more of their time on the very activities that most initiatives call for and that they believe the present promotion and tenure system needs revision: It's always nice to know before you begin that the campus community is positively inclined to support the initiatives you hope to implement. The instrument used in this survey (Figure 2.1) can be easily modified, as was done by the Council for Independent Colleges, to meet the needs of different types of institutions.

FIGURE 2.1

FACULTY SURVEY
ON UNDERGRADUATE TEACHING
AND RESEARCH

A. Even if you do not teach undergraduates, please circle the number on each scale below that best represents your perception of the relative importance of research and undergraduate teaching. For example, a 4 would indicate that one is of utmost importance to the exclusion of the other, and a 0 would indicate that they are of equal importance. All responses will be confidential. Only group data will be reported.

In relation to each other, currently how important are research and undergraduate teaching to:

a. you personally

teaching				equal importance				research
4	3	2	1	0	1	2	3	4

b. the majority of other faculty in your department

teaching				equal importance				research
4	3	2	1	0	1	2	3	4

c. your department chair

teaching				equal importance				research
4	3	2	1	0	1	2	3	4

d. your dean

teaching				equal importance				research
4	3	2	1	0	1	2	3	4

B. Please circle the number on each scale below that best represents your perception of:

a. the direction that you think our university is going

teaching				equal importance				research
4	3	2	1	0	1	2	3	4

b. the direction that you think our university should go

teaching				equal importance				research
4	3	2	1	0	1	2	3	4

c. the direction that you think you should go based on your interests

teaching				equal importance				research
4	3	2	1	0	1	2	3	4

C. Please comment on the similarities and differences in the above ratings. (Use back of form if necessary.)

D. Demographics (This information will be used to report group data only.)

   a. your major academic area:

   ❏ Agriculture & Env. Sci.   ❏ Engineering   ❏ Medical/Health
   ❏ Architecture   ❏ Fine & Performing Arts   Related Studies
   ❏ Business/Management   ❏ Human Dev/Home Econ   ❏ Science & Math
   ❏ Communication   ❏ Humanities   ❏ Social Sciences
   ❏ Computer Science   ❏ Info & Lib Science   ❏ Other
   ❏ Education   ❏ Law

   b. your department

   c. faculty rank

   d. no. of years at institution

   e. % of teaching devoted to undergraduates

   f. gender (optional)   M   F

Another useful instrument you can use is the Administrative Checklist (Figure 2.2). Used by trustees, president, provosts, and deans, this instrument can provide information about the perceptions of your faculty reward system. We have found that not only does the data tend to show where problems exist, but that the process of completing the checklist can itself be highly educational to faculty and academic staff. Data on most campuses show that faculty have little idea of what the priorities of their institution are, that departmental mission and priorities statements are fairly rare, and that the reward system is not seen as supporting the priorities that have been identified. "Yes" answers are not too common for most of the questions on most campuses.

A president or chief academic officer can place the issues of priorities and rewards on the agenda of his or her campus by taking direct action. The key here is making sure that everyone hears the message, providing appropriate resources, and ensuring that action will follow. Words alone are never enough.

FIGURE 2.2

INSTITUTIONAL PRIORITIES AND FACULTY REWARDS An Administrative Checklist				
	Yes	No	To Some Degree	Don't Know
1) Does the institution's mission clearly identify its priorities and unique characteristics?				
2a) Do administrators, faculty, and staff believe in and support the statement?				
b) Were they actively involved in its development?				
3) Do individual units or departments have clearly articulated mission statements that identify their specific priorities?				
4) Do such statements mesh with and support the institutional mission statement?				
5a) Do the members of the unit support its mission statement?				
b) Were they involved in its development?				
6a) Are the priorities of the institution and the department understood by new faculty?				
b) Are they clearly articulated at every point in the hiring process?				
7a) Are units evaluated on how well they meet the specific goals defined in their mission statement?				

	Yes	No	To Some Degree	Don't Know
7b) Are resources and awards allocated accordingly?				
8a) Does the faculty reward system (promotion, tenure, and merit pay) actively support the articulated mission statements of the institution and of the unit in which faculty work?				
b) Is good teaching important in the equation?				
c) Are there clearly defined requirements for determining good teaching?				
9a) Do faculty understand the criteria by which they will be judged?				
b) Are they assisted in preparing the necessary documentation of their work?				
c) Are faculty provided with a clear statement addressing faculty rewards procedures, requirements, and criteria?				
10) Is there a mentoring system for new faculty?				
11) Is the faculty reward system sensitive to the differences among the disciplines?				
12) Is the faculty reward system sensitive to the differences in the strengths of individual faculty?				
13) Is the faculty reward system sensitive to the differences in departments?				

	Yes	No	To Some Degree	Don't Know
14) In the faculty reward system, are the weights given to the same activity different among individual faculty?				
15) In the faculty reward system, are the weights given to the same activity different among units?				
16) Does the system recognize the range of important activities that faculty in specific units perform?				
17) Does the system allow individual faculty reward criteria to be modified based on assignment?				
18) Do faculty and unit heads consider the evaluation process fair?				
19a) Are data provided to faculty throughout their careers to help them identify areas of strength and areas in need of improvement?				
b) Is a formal procedure in place to provide assistance and support when needed?				
20) Do faculty who are assigned specific instructional or service projects (curriculum design, community support), receive guidance about how these activities will be reviewed and recognized within the faculty reward system?				

Robert Diamond
November 1998

EXAMPLE: SYRACUSE UNIVERSITY

In his initial address to the faculty at Syracuse University, Chancellor Kenneth Shaw charted a new course for the institution and introduced a restructuring plan that was to lead to Syracuse developing "a more learning- and student-centered culture" (Shaw, 1992).

One focus of his comments was on the faculty reward system. Actions were requested and very specific deadlines established.

Faculty Reward System

It is essential that we improve our faculty reward system to create a more effective balance among teaching, research, and service. At the same time, we will expand the definition of what scholarly work involves. I ask that each school and college review its policies and procedures for evaluating faculty performance and incorporate changes as needed to reflect an increased emphasis on teaching and advising; an improved set of procedures for both formative and summative annual evaluation of teaching and advising for tenured and nontenured faculty; and a description of the appropriate balance, with teaching holding equal emphasis with research, scholarship, and professional activities. These statements as applied to merit salary increases will be submitted to the vice chancellor by April 1, 1992. To further demonstrate our commitment to excellence in teaching, advising, mentoring, and integration of research into the classroom, we will institute a series of annual awards. Initial funding will come from the Chancellor's Fund for Innovation. We will also seek endowments for this purpose through targeted, high-priority naming gift opportunities. A task force to implement creation of these awards will report by April 15, 1992.

Integrating Research into Teaching

To give our students the fullest benefit of attending a university where new knowledge is created every day, we seek ways of integrating discovery into the classroom and into the broader learning environment. One of the best ways is to make students themselves active partners in the research process, in class and out. The vice president for research and computing will consult with faculty and offer a set of initiatives by April 15, 1992.

Improving the Faculty Reward System

1) Policies and procedures. Each department, school, or college will review its policies and procedures dealing with evaluation of faculty performance and incorporate changes, as needed, to reflect:

a) an increased emphasis on teaching, academic advising, and the integration of research into teaching

b) an improved set of procedures (i.e., self-review, student evaluations, peer review, teaching "portfolio" review, etc.) for both "formative" and "summative" evaluation of teaching and for the evaluation of academic advising

c) annual evaluation of all faculty, nontenured and tenured, in the areas of teaching and advising

d) an appropriate balancing of emphasis on the three traditional areas of teaching, research, and service, with teaching accorded at least equal emphasis as research, scholarship, and creative professional activity

e) an explicit response to an expanded definition of research, including the relative weighting of the scholarship of discovery, the scholarship of integration, the scholarship of application, the scholarship of teaching, and where appropriate, creative professional activity.

Statements of policies, standards, and procedures, modified as suggested above, regarding annual merit salary review, will be submitted to the vice chancellor for academic affairs for approval by April 30, 1992 . . . upon approval of an acceptable plan for merit salary review (to be implemented in 1992–93), each unit will be permitted to award its salary increases for 1992–93. (Activity will start in Spring 1992 and continue in 1992–1993).

Corresponding statements concerning tenure, promotion, annual review of nontenured faculty, and appointment and reappointment of nontenured faculty will be submitted to the vice chancellor for academic affairs for approval by November 15, 1992.

2) *Teaching evaluation.* In Spring 1992, the teaching of all faculty—tenured and nontenured—will be evaluated, according to the procedures of the department, school, or college.

3) *Teaching awards.* To further demonstrate an increased institutional commitment to excellence in teaching, advising, and mentoring, and the integration of research into teaching, a series of annual awards will be made to faculty. Endowment of these awards will be designated a leading fundraising priority and naming gift opportunity. In order to implement the program promptly, a proposal for start-up funding should be submitted to the Chancellor's Fund for Innovation. Criteria for these awards and procedures for nominations and selection will be recommended to the chancellor and vice chancellor for academic affairs by a task force report and will be submitted by April 15, 1992.

4) *Development of modified policies and procedures.* These policies and procedures will give greater emphasis to teaching and advising in the annual merit salary review for faculty. Statements from deans of the schools and colleges are due by April 30, 1992.

EXAMPLE: **UNIVERSITY OF GUELPH**

While procedures may vary, the care taken in the planning and the support from the top is consistent with successful initiatives. At the University of Guelph, President Mordechai Rozamski took a somewhat different approach when he established an institution-wide Strategic Planning Commission to develop a vision and long-term plan for the university. Early in the process, the commission actively sought input from individuals on- and off-campus (alumni, retirees, and community leaders in the public and private sector). The final report (University of Guelph, 1995) included the following:

> The University of Guelph recognizes that the most successful universities of the next century will be more efficient, more flexible, and more intensely interactive than the universities of the past. To achieve our goal of ever-increasing excellence in scholarship, this community will act on that recognition with energy, imagination, and a sense of common purpose. We embrace as our primary strate-

gic directions an increasingly learner-centered approach to education and the fostering of research-intensiveness. We believe that these two strategic directions are largely aspects of one another, and that to succeed in one we must succeed in the other. Together, they reflect the mission of the university with respect to lifelong learning. We embrace three additional strategic directions—collaboration, internationalism, and open learning—that will enhance flexibility and interaction, extend the university's reach, and support our highly ambitious, learner-centered, research-intensive agenda.

As in a number of earlier instances, it will be the role of the president and the chief academic officer to ensure that the faculty reward system is modified to actively support this agenda.

EXAMPLE: TOWSON STATE UNIVERSITY

As noted previously, the top academic leadership is also responsible for ensuring that momentum is maintained and that initiatives are carried through. In 1989, Towson State University began an initiative to review its promotion and tenure policies. In 1991, a Task Force on Promotion and Tenure was established by the university senate, along with a second task force on Incentives and Disincentives to Improving Teaching. While support had been developing for these efforts, adaptation of the reports from these task forces by academic units was inconsistent, and it was apparent that the effort required revitalization for a revised faculty reward system to become fully operational.

Building on what had already been accomplished, Robert Caret, Provost and Executive Vice President, used his fall address (Caret, 1993) to the university senate as the means of informing the faculty as to the importance of this effort and what it would mean to them, their students, and the institution. In his 1993 remarks to the faculty senate, as part of this ongoing initiative, he focused on the interrelationships of the work of faculty, the priorities of the institution, and the faculty reward system.

In my 1992 address to the university senate, I tried to provide, from a national perspective, some flavor of the criticism aimed at higher education today, some insight into the reasons for that criticism, and some of the steps I felt should be taken to address it. The academy continues to be under attack [I said] and much of the criticism is deserved. Clearly, we are not making the education of students a top priority in our classrooms and on our campuses. This criticism has been aimed at the professors/the faculty, but the blame needs to be shared.... Many faculty who came to our institutions to teach now feel that teaching is not valued. Many of them, as a result, have dug in their heels, refusing to be really involved in the institution; refusing to be truly involved in their teaching, scholarship, and research; and sadly, often to be truly involved with their students. But at Towson State University, I can assure you that such criticism is wrong. This institution does value teaching and we, the faculty, must do what is necessary to assure that value is reflected in our mission, our decisions, and in our priorities....

The question is, how do we avoid creating a faculty who have given up on their institution—faculty who may be doing more harm to the institution and its students than good? How do we maximize the potential for success for all of our faculty? One major component to help in assuring that success is a faculty role and reward structure that really works.

At Towson State, we have been working to evolve such a role and reward structure—a system that is flexible, realistic, and humanistic, a system that provides a continuity of vision for the faculty so that they can maximize their momentum toward shared and desired goals, and a system that provides accountability.

The models we have been discussing, though not yet formalized, have been accepted here and there on the campus. Many of the annual reports coming forward to my office already embrace these models, in whole and/or in part, for faculty evaluation. We need to build on that acceptance. To begin, we should ask what kind of characteristics should we be seeking in a successful model or set of models for this campus adapted to departmental cultures, as well as faculty needs and institutional mission?

Characteristics of Successful Models

- Give control to the faculty member himself/herself
- Give real guidance and direction to the faculty

- Are simple, flexible, and adaptable

- Allow variance from evaluation period to evaluation period, so that no label is attached to the faculty member on a permanent basis; the faculty member is not "labeled" in perpetuity

- Allow the faculty member to choose the model which he/she wishes to be measured against at the time of the evaluation. After putting together their portfolios for consideration, they determine which yardstick best applies to them. They send their portfolios forward with that yardstick attached.

- Make it possible to work in advance with the department to determine which model is most appropriate, from their perspective, for the time period under discussion. That is not a necessity, though it is desirable.

- Philosophically "fit" this campus, adhering to the principles of shared governance, and based on all of the dimensions of the faculty role—not just research and scholarship.

To help assure that the momentum we have gained continues and that we develop a model or models—I am open to using any model(s) that will work—that become a formal part of our evaluation process, I have established, for the next academic year, a task force (Task Force on Faculty Roles and Rewards) involving key individuals from across the campus to serve as a communication link to assure that we are talking with each other and are taking appropriate steps relative to these initiatives.

... Faculty and their institution must set a common agenda; they must develop a shared vision together. As part of this effort, the institution must provide appropriate recognition and appropriate rewards, and these must become part of the campus culture.

... We need to develop a role and reward system that works for our institutions and our faculty. We must maximize the overlap in the needs which I described at the beginning of this paper, the needs of the student, the needs of the institution, and the needs of the faculty. When the overlap is maximized, we all thrive.

Modifying the faculty reward system at a college or university is no easy task. The process will take time and involve extensive input from the faculty. One of the key questions any administrator must face is where to begin and who to involve. Two entirely different approaches were taken at the University of Memphis and St. Norbert College...approaches that were both appropriate and with differences that showed sensitivity to the very nature of the institutions involved. In each instance, the steps were carefully planned and structured to facilitate extensive faculty input.

EXAMPLE: THE UNIVERSITY OF MEMPHIS

In the fall of 1993, Provost J. Ivan Legg of the University of Memphis (formerly Memphis State University) established a task force to assess the current faculty roles and reward system and to make recommendations for changes. Three elements in establishing this committee were to play a major role in determining the long-term success of the initiative:

1) **Its membership.** The committee was carefully selected to include outstanding faculty leaders from departments throughout the university and included several deans, chairs, and representatives from the board of visitors and the community.

2) **Its charge.** The committee was provided with a clear charge (see Figures 2.3, 2.4).

3) **The resources.** In addition to providing each member of the task force with a number of references, representative members of the committee attended the American Association of Higher Education's Conference on Faculty Roles and Rewards on a regular basis.

It would be 18 months later—after extensive input from individual faculty and academic units; after months of carefully reviewing new publications and other initiatives on promotion and tenure; and after a number of formal meetings with top administrators, chairs, student leaders, and the board of visitors that the final recommendations of the task force would be made. This led to a major revision of the faculty handbook and the establishment of a committee to formally integrate the report into a revised handbook. In addition, task forces were formed to address each of the primary recommendations that required future development. For example, the report from the task force dealing with assessment is leading to a major overhaul of how faculty are evaluated at the university and to a significant revision in the form of curricula vitae which would be consistent with the revised procedures for faculty roles and rewards.

FIGURE 2.3

LETTER OF INVITATION AND ISSUES FOR CONSIDERATION

September 21, 1993

Dear _____

I am inviting you to join the Provost's Task Force on Faculty Roles and Rewards. Linda Bennett, Professor of Anthropology, will serve as chair and Ralph Faudree, Professor and Chair of Mathematics, will serve as co-chair.

The objective of the task force will be to help Memphis State University fulfill its mission as set forth by President Lane Rawlins. A copy of the mission statement is enclosed. The task force will focus on the heart of the university: its faculty.

The need for the task force is based on the premise that it is time for higher education to reevaluate its role. The needs of society have changed significantly over the past 30 years. During this period, our universities have evolved from highly respected, isolated ivory towers, to highly visible and vulnerable institutions.

During this transition, accountability for the roles of faculty has become a major issue. I elaborated on this concern in the faculty convocation presentation I made on April 28, 1993. In particular, the role of faculty in outreach and the education of our students needs to be reevaluated. Closely tied to these two missions is our understanding of what is meant by research and scholarship.

I am asking the task force to review the criteria and processes used for rewarding faculty, in the context of the university mission. I am asking you to recommend not only possible changes but ways in which change can be brought about. In your deliberations, it is important to note that bringing about change is the collective responsibility of the faculty and administrative leadership.

I will meet with the task force to discuss its mission and to provide you with additional information. I would like to have the task force report by July 1994.

I hope that you will be able to join the task force. Please contact my administrative assistant, Iris LaGrone, by October 1 to confirm your participation.

President Rawlins and I will use the recommendations of the Task Force on Faculty Roles and Rewards to empower the faculty to carry out our mission. With your help, we can establish Memphis State University as one of the nation's leading comprehensive urban universities.

Sincerely,

J. Ivan Legg
Provost
Memphis State University
(University of Memphis)

FIGURE 2.4

ISSUES FOR CONSIDERATION
BY THE TASK FORCE
ON FACULTY ROLES AND REWARDS:
UNIVERSITY OF MEMPHIS

1) The mission for a comprehensive doctoral institution has traditionally been defined as research, teaching, and service. Are we fulfilling this mission to the best of our abilities?

2) Do we reward faculty equitably for their contributions within this mission?

3) The term "outreach" is now commonly used when discussing service to the community. Should our mission be research, teaching, outreach, and service?

4) Does our presence in an urban environment place a special emphasis on our mission? On the nature of our research, teaching, and outreach?

5) Does our presence in an urban environment place a special emphasis on the times and places where our programs are offered? Do we need to expand on the mini-college concept?

6) As the only major comprehensive university in the region, do we have an obligation to reach out to the communities around us, or should we limit our outreach to the greater Memphis area?

7) What faculty roles that may be receiving secondary recognition need more emphasis?

8) What is the relative importance of service on committees (departmental, college, university); service on the senate; service to professional societies; and service to the community?

9) How closely related are research/scholarship and teaching?

10) How closely related are research/scholarship and outreach/service?

11) Is lecturing in two to four courses a week sufficient to define the role of a full-time faculty member? Can a faculty member function effectively in this capacity over a 20- to 30-year period?

12) Is teaching primarily a classroom activity? What about working with graduate students? Research with undergraduates? What about innovations? Radical innovations? (e.g., new ways to teach science).

13) Teaching evaluation is an important but sensitive issue to many faculty. If we are to recommit ourselves to the mission of providing our students with a quality education, we must address the issue of teaching evaluation. Processes for evaluation range from highly decentralized with minimum requirements (the situation at MSU) to centralized operations where all faculty are evaluated in all courses and the information is provided to all those involved in faculty review. How should we deal with teaching evaluation at MSU?

14) The quality of research in a discipline is measured by publication in leading journals, success in grants, invitations to speak, awards, and invitations to serve on review panels and editorial boards. These measures are based on peer review. What kind of measures are needed to document excellence in teaching and outreach?

15) Is internal peer review sufficient, or should external national/international peer review to be used in evaluating faculty performance? At all ranks—assistant, associate, full professor?

16) What special attention, if any, should be given to tenure-track faculty?

17) Can common norms be defined for faculty performance? How important are discipline-specific issues in faculty evaluation? What should be the relationship between departments, colleges/schools, and the central administration in assessing faculty performance? Can a common tenure and promotion guideline be used for faculty at MSU?

18) Is there justification for a university-wide tenure and promotion committee? Would such a committee help focus the mission of the university and bring about consistency in quality?

19) What should be the role of a university tenure and promotion appeals committee? Assessment? Advocacy?

20) How well prepared are new faculty to perform research, teaching, and outreach in the institution? Should we be involved in faculty development? What approaches could be used? How important are leaves of absence/sabbaticals?

21) What about group/interdisciplinary efforts in research, teaching, and outreach? Departmental commitments rather than individual faculty commitments? Can these contributions be recognized and, at the same time, can we reward individual faculty who participate in group efforts?

22) Are there departments/programs at MSU that can serve as models for what we want to do in faculty roles and rewards?

EXAMPLE: ST. NORBERT COLLEGE

While the approach taken to address the issues of the faculty reward system also involved the establishment of a college-wide task force, the initial focus of the initiative at St. Norbert was on defining scholarship in an institutional context. The decision by Dean of the College Robert Horn to take this approach was a direct result of his early review of the work of Ernest Boyer on defining scholarship and his understanding of the culture of the college.

Chaired by the director of faculty development (a faculty member), the task force included two faculty representatives each from the natural sciences, the social sciences, and the humanities and fine arts.

The charge to the committee and the timeline for action were clearly stated in the charge to the committee by the dean. Building on Ernest Boyer's *Scholarship Reconsidered*, the task force reviewed the literature on scholarship and developed a faculty survey (Figure 2.5) on scholarship at the college that was distributed to all faculty.

FIGURE 2.5

FACULTY SURVEY DEFINITION OF SCHOLARSHIP AT SAINT NORBERT COLLEGE (SNC)		
1 = Strongly Agree 2 = Agree 3 = Disagree 4 = Strongly Disagree 5 = No Opinion		
ITEMS	*NR*	*COMMENTS: Use this space to explain or elaborate upon your numerical rankings.*
1) A definition of scholarship at SNC should be consistent with the college's "mission statement" and its stated "goals and objectives."		
2) A definition of scholarship at SNC should be congruent with our liberal arts tradition.		
3) A definition of scholarship at SNC should reflect the college's emphasis upon teaching.		

1 = Strongly Agree 2 = Agree 3 = Disagree 4 = Strongly Disagree 5 = No Opinion		
ITEMS	*NR*	*COMMENTS: Use this space to explain or elaborate upon your numerical rankings.*
4) A definition of scholarship at SNC should recognize the differences between a liberal arts college and a research university.		
5) A definition of scholarship at SNC should reflect our uniqueness as an institution.		
6) My perception is that the definition of scholarship at SNC has become increasingly narrow.		
7) My perception is that the definition of scholarship at SNC has become increasingly more capacious.		
8) Publication should be the primary yardstick by which scholarly productivity is measured at SNC.		
9) I am in favor of a definition of scholarship broader than the definitions presently included in the Faculty Handbook.		
10) A definition of scholarship should include scholarly investigation resulting in the discovery of new knowledge (i.e., Ernest Boyer's "Scholarship of Discovery").		
11) A definition of scholarship at SNC should include "serious, disciplined work that seeks to interpret, draw together, and bring new insight to bear on original research" (i.e., Boyer's "Scholarship of Integration").		
12) A definition of scholarship at SNC should include the application of knowledge to "consequential problems" (i.e., Boyer's "Scholarship of Application").		

ITEMS	NR	COMMENTS: *Use this space to explain or elaborate upon your numerical rankings.*
1 = Strongly Agree　2 = Agree　3 = Disagree　4 = Strongly Disagree　5 = No Opinion		
13) A definition of scholarship at SNC should include the creation or discovery of new or innovative pedagogical techniques and the transformation and extension of knowledge through teaching (i.e., Boyer's "Scholarship of Teaching").		
14) A definition of scholarship at SNC should include "classroom research" (i.e., the systematic study of teaching and learning).		
15) A definition of scholarship should take into account the distinctive talents of individuals.		
16) The SNC definition of scholarship need not conform to a particular mold or style simply because that is what "everyone else" is doing.		
17) Activities "relat[ing] directly to the intellectual work of the professor and carried out through consultation, technical assistance, policy analysis, program evaluation, and the like" should be considered scholarship.		
18) An effective preparation and periodic modification of a course are evidence of scholarly work.		
19) Reading about the latest developments in the field and sharing them with students are examples of scholarly activities.		
20) Multidisciplinary work is soft and should not be considered scholarship.		
21) Certain services to the college and the community—those services directly related to one's special field and professional background, such as serving on some committees or advising student clubs—should be considered scholarship.		

Within a month, results were tabulated, disseminated, and discussed. One of the major findings of the report was that the majority of faculty supported the effort to expand the current definition of scholarship and to include the four forms of activity developed by Ernest Boyer and Eugene Rice. The survey also provided the committee with insight into where there was and was not faculty agreement.

A significant result of this initiative was that the task force provided the faculty with a common understanding of how scholarship would be defined at St. Norbert College. Once the faculty assembly approved the definition, it was sent to the board of trustees for their endorsement. It was acted on first by the faculty in December and then the trustees. The second phase was to apply the approved definition to the current criteria for promotion and tenure and to make any appropriate and necessary changes. It was the dean's expectation at that time that within 18 months the trustees would be able to approve any changes in institutional policies.

Chair of the committee Kenneth Zahorski observed that the process itself was not—and could not be expected to be—smooth.

The process had gone smoothly up to this point. However, it soon became painfully clear that gathering faculty opinions and speaking about scholarship in rather general terms was not nearly the same as setting down words that locked a definition into place. The task force, which had earlier discovered that their colleagues' views on scholarship represented a broad spectrum of perception and understanding, now discovered—with some surprise—that the same broad spectrum of opinion existed within the task force itself. Indeed, there was enough dialectical tension involved in each discussion to make Hegel proud. From one side of the table would come an impassioned "Any broadening of the definition represents a watering down of quality!" and from the other an equally ardent "Counting publications is the wrong way to go!" From one end of the table would come an eloquent plea for all classroom preparation to count as scholarship, and from the other a vehement rejoinder that "Publications and presentations are the only true tests of scholarship." Good will, good humor, and collegiality characterized the sessions, but there were still impasses aplenty. Debates ensued, and although some compromises were forthcoming, there seemed to be philosophical ground which some members simply would not relinquish.

There were times when the goal of a consensus definition seemed beyond reach. However, 13 sessions (many of them epic in scope and substance) and four drafts later, the task force completed a four-page document with accompanying rationale and sent it to Dean Horn. The chair and members of the task force felt pleased and relieved, but apprehensive. If it had been so difficult for seven faculty to arrive at a fragile consensus, what would happen when the entire faculty assembly debated the document? What could the task force do to prepare the way for approval of the new broadened definition of scholarship? Would all of its work go for naught? The members prepared for the fateful December 3rd faculty meeting.

The definition that the task force proposed was built upon six tenets, all of which proceeded from the premise that the key to maintaining the integrity of the scholarly process is the documentation, sharing, and evaluation of scholarly endeavors:

- The definition aims at being consistent with the goals and mission of the college. In particular, its underlying philosophical principles are intended to nurture the college's spirit of community and to help foster the "atmosphere of mutual respect and trust" central to its mission statement.

- The definition seeks to be broad enough to encompass, encourage, and nurture the creative and varied talents of the faculty at St. Norbert College, but not so broad as to compromise academic rigor and the integrity of the scholarly process.

- The definition recognizes scholarship as both process and outcome. Built upon the premise that the essence of scholarship is a pattern of intellectual and professional growth, the definition views scholarship as a continuous, lifelong process.

- The definition seeks to recognize and nurture those qualities and characteristics considered institutional strengths (e.g., teaching, interdisciplinary courses and programs, and collaborative learning partnerships).

- The definition acknowledges not only those who push back the frontiers of knowledge, but also those who help to explain and apply this knowledge.

- The definition recognizes the need for St. Norbert College to respond not only to the needs of its own academic community, but also to the needs of the nation and world. The definition recognizes that as a humane and responsible community of scholars, we must relate to the world beyond our campus.

As the following segment from the definition clearly shows, the committee developed a statement that was appropriate to the institution and sensitive to its history and culture.

A Definition of Scholarship at St. Norbert College

Scholarship at St. Norbert College is not an abstract term, but rather a way of life. It is a shared philosophy that deeply values the idea of a community of teacher-scholars learning and growing together—a community where cooperation rather than competition is the norm; a community where faculty-student learning partnerships are the goal; a community enfleshing the "mutual respect and trust" to which our mission statement refers.

The concept of scholarship at St. Norbert College recognizes the value of all who strive to bring light into the corners of darkness, of all who join the struggle to push back the boundaries of ignorance that surround us. This includes not only the explorers who expand the frontiers of knowledge, but also the pioneers who help define the boundaries, construct the maps, and build the roads connecting the various provinces in the new realm. And while our definition reflects our individuality as a small liberal arts college whose reason for being is to help undergraduate students learn, it also recognizes the traditional concept of scholarship informing the wider realm of academia.

In essence, scholarship at St. Norbert College is the bringing to bear of a trained mind on a problem or questions and the public sharing of the results of those labors. It is what academics do. It demands training, clear and objective thinking, synthesis, creativity, and an ability and willingness to communicate. It implies originality, discovery, testing, convincing, and debating. It explores new territory, builds upon what is known, or interprets what is given. It may be seminal, or add a simple footnote. It can be done alone or in teams, but it is done; there is a result, an offering.

At the very heart of the St. Norbert College definition of scholarship is the concept of intellectual vitality and growth. A scholar is an active learner, not a person who passively rests on past accomplishments. In effect, scholars manifest the best qualities of exemplary students: They ask questions, seek answers, look for connections, engage in problem solving, and apply what they have learned. Good scholars, like good students, demonstrate a lifelong commitment to continuing self-education.

The definition of scholarship that resulted from this initiative was approved by the faculty and the board and is now an integral part of the faculty handbook. As a result of this action, the promotion and tenure guidelines and criteria for review at the college have also been modified to support the document. These actions have led to changes in the range of activities being considered as scholarly, which has had a direct and positive impact on the lives of many faculty.

EXAMPLE: OREGON STATE UNIVERSITY

A somewhat different approach to describing scholarship was taken by the task force at Oregon State University. Conrad J. Weiser, who played a major role in the initiative, described the results of this effort as follows:

> The definition of scholarship developed and adopted by Oregon State University (OSU) differs from that proposed by Ernest Boyer. Specifically, Boyer described characteristics of scholarship but did not define scholarship per se. He proposed "four separate but overlapping functions" of the professoriate as: "the scholarship of discovery, the scholarship of integration, the scholarship of application, and the scholarship of teaching." In proposing these four

functions as forms of scholarship, Boyer in effect classified virtually all important faculty activities as scholarship.

In contrast, the OSU guidelines consider that a university, and its faculty, perform essential and valuable activities that are not scholarship. Scholarship is considered to be creative intellectual work that is validated by peers and communicated, including: *discovery* of new knowledge; *development* of new technologies, methods, materials, or uses; *integration* of knowledge leading to new understandings; and *artistry* that creates new insights and understandings. (See Figure 2.6.)

FIGURE 2.6

THE NATURE OF SCHOLARSHIP	
Scholarship is creative intellectual work that is validated by peers and communicated. Forms of scholarship include discovery, development, integration, and artistry.	
Forms	Discovery, development, integration, artistry
Character of scholarship	Generates, synthesizes, interprets, and communicates new knowledge, methods, understandings, technologies, materials, uses, insights, beauty
Audiences for scholarship	Peers, students, users, patrons, publics
Means of communicating scholarship	Publications, presentations, exhibits, performances, patents, copyrights, distributions of materials or programs
Criteria for validating scholarship	Accuracy, replicability, originality, scope, significance, breadth, depth and duration of influence, impact or public benefit
Means of documenting scholarship	Present evidence that creative intellectual work was validated by peers; communicated to peers and broader audiences; recognized, accepted, cited, adopted or used by others; that it made a difference

Conrad J. Weiser,
1998

CONCLUSION

As with any other campus-wide initiative, a review of the promotion and tenure system can become a major item on an institutional agenda in many ways. However, whether the need is first identified by state legislatures, board members, trustees, administrators, or faculty, it is the responsibility of the president or chief academic officer to take the steps necessary for successful implementation.

Administrative leadership must:

1) Formally initiate activity by establishing and changing task forces on committees.

2) Ensure that the process that will be followed will actively involve the faculty as a whole.

3) Provide initiative moral and financial support.

4) Allow the faculty to own both the process once it begins and the recommendations that are made.

It is a time for effective leadership and appropriate delegation. Without these two elements, success will be impossible to achieve.

REFERENCES

Arizona Board of Regents. (1997). *Governance in action.* Phoenix, AZ: Arizona Board of Regents.

Arizona Board of Regents. (1997, May 30). *Charters, missions, and mandates: Historical context for discussion of faculty workload at Arizona's public universities.* Board meeting.

Boyer, E. (1990). *Scholarship reconsidered: Priorities of the professoriate.* Princeton, NJ: Carnegie Foundation for the Advancement of Teaching.

Caret, R. L. (1993, September). *The role of the faculty at Towson State University.* Address to the senate. Towson, MD: Towson State University.

Florida Board of Regents. (1995, May 16). *Tenure recommendations.* Tallahassee, FL: Florida Board of Regents.

Gray, P. J., Froh, R. C., & Diamond, R. M. (1992, March). *A national study of research universities on the balance between research and undergraduate teachers.* Syracuse, NY: The Center for Instructional Development, Syracuse University.

Gray, P., Diamond, R. M., & Adam, B. E. (1996, February). *A national study on the relative importance of research and undergraduate teaching at colleges and universities.* Syracuse, NY: The Center for Instructional Development, Syracuse University.

Oregon State Board of Higher Education Committee on Academic Productivity. (1993, October). *Academic responsibilities and productivity.* Salem, OR: Oregon State Board of Higher Education.

Shaw, K. (1992, February 17). *Restructuring Syracuse University.* Report to the university. Syracuse, NY: Syracuse University.

University of Guelph. (1995). *The final report of the strategic planning commission.* Guelph, Ontario: University of Guelph.

Weiser, C. J. (1998, October). *The value system of a university: Rethinking scholarship.* Handout, Scholarship Unbound workshop.

THE INSTITUTIONAL MISSION AND VISION STATEMENT

Vision—*an ideal and unique image of the future . . . a vision is
an ideal and unique image of the future for the common good.*
James M. Kouzes and Barry Z. Posner,
The Leadership Challenge

In January 1994, 50 faculty members representing all colleges and
most departments at a state institution met to "examine the role of
faculty in the contemporary American university" and in their institution, in particular. Nominated by their chairs, this two-day meeting
made a number of recommendations regarding significant changes in
the promotion and tenure system at the institution. The focus of the
meeting was the relationship between the mission statement of the institution and what was practiced. The following paragraphs are ex-
cerpted from the report issued by meeting participants.

EXAMPLE: **PART A. THE MISSION STATEMENT**
This institution's faculty are primarily concerned with the quality of
education offered to students; that concern is manifested through
personal contact and accessibility. Integral to (the institution's) teaching function is its obligation to provide a climate in which professors
and students pursue scholarly activities or creative endeavors together. These activities enhance the teaching mission of the university. This blend of research and teaching not only contributes to the

advancement of knowledge in specific disciplines, but also offers practical applications as faculty members find new ways to use their research discoveries in working with off-campus practitioners. Faculty members are expected to remain active in their professional activities and organizations and to provide service to the university, community, and state.

EXAMPLE: PART B. THE REALITY

How is all of this accomplished when faculty, students, administrators, and, increasingly, the tax-paying public, believe that our ideals do not match troubling realities? Students tire of passive learning, of testing that emphasizes mere recall, of faculty who must isolate themselves in order to "get their publishing done." There is a conflict between the rhetoric—calling for balanced vitae—and the reality that promotion and tenure files heavily emphasize publications, sometimes of the pedestrian variety. Administrators and public officials tire of hearing faculty plead for more released time *away* from students purportedly to further scholarship and research. Taxpayers and politicians are just as upset with the alleged "12-hour faculty work week" as faculty are exhausted from the 50-hour work week they actually endure, as documented in an article in the campus paper. . . .

The current reward system at this institution officially recognizes teaching as the primary mission of faculty, with research and service as important and necessary components of every professor's job description. However, the relative weight given to these three missions of the faculty is ambiguous. Many faculty find that a productive research program is mandatory in order to advance at this institution, irrespective of teaching contributions. Also, while lip service is often paid to the importance of service to the university and professional organizations, it is widely perceived that these contributions carry little or no weight in promotion and tenure decisions. Hence, while we tout ourselves as a "premier teaching institution," we actually practice a reward system that is not all that different from a research university. The main difference seems to be that faculty who are rewarded at the university have heavy teaching loads while also maintaining a productive research program. As faculty struggle to attain some balance among these competing demands, there is constant pressure to reduce contributions through service and to limit time spent with students. An increasingly skeptical public and government ask us to justify our activities and to document our contributions to society. In this societal context, it does not serve us well to have or actual policies contradict our official policies.

While "supporting" the recommendations of this meeting, the chief academic officer suggested that the different academic units take the actions required for implementation. The results were uneven across campus: Some units made no changes while others developed and implemented a totally revised promotion and tenure system.

This problem is not unique. The issue between what institutions say is important and how faculty are rewarded is apparent at colleges and universities throughout the country. While there are major differences on how faculty spend their time at various types of institutions, the data from the Syracuse and Carnegie studies show increasing demands on the faculty with few serious attempts being made to equate the importance of the activity to the reward system.

THE INSTITUTIONAL MISSION AND VISION STATEMENTS

Ideally, institutional mission and vision statements should be clear and concise and should identify the unique characteristics and priorities of the institution. In addition, the statements should be known and supported by administrators, faculty, and staff.

Unfortunately, on many campuses, neither of these conditions are being met. In a recent review of the mission statements of more than 20 small colleges, the only significant difference among them tended to be in the area of church affiliations. A review of statements from larger institutions also reported more of a boilerplate approach to mission statements, rather than an attempt to identify the particular strengths and priorities of the institution.

And yet, institutions are different. Some serve rural areas, others urban; some have more of a research focus than others; and some have strengths in particular programs that should be emphasized. We have other institutions that have developed an approach to learning as their hallmark or a particular relationship to a segment of their communities. What is important is that the mission statement of an institution is appropriate and specific enough to provide clear guidelines for the establishment of program priorities.

John P. Kotter (1996, pp. 69–70) describes several reasons why a quality vision statement is essential to any institution:

- It can help clear the decks of expensive and time-consuming clutter.

- It serves to facilitate major change by motivating action that is not necessarily in people's short-term self-interests.

- It acknowledges that sacrifices will be necessary but makes clear that these sacrifices will yield particular benefits and personal satisfactions that are far superior to those of today or of the tomorrow that would exist without the attempt to change.

- It helps align individuals, thus coordinating the actions of motivated people in a remarkably efficient way.

In short, without quality mission and vision statements, significant and long-lasting change is almost impossible.

Recognizing the need for details and direction, a number of institutions have worked to develop mission and vision statements that have these characteristics. Those involved in writing more detailed statements have found that the traditional one-paragraph mission statement could not provide the texture and scope that they felt was essential. As a result, many institutions devote one or more pages to their mission statements and often attach to it supportive vision statements that provide additional depth. While there is no single approach or format that is appropriate to all institutions, notice how the following examples address the issues of priorities and unique characteristics of this university.

EXAMPLE: UNIVERSITY OF WISCONSIN, WHITEWATER

The University of Wisconsin, Whitewater seeks wide recognition as a premier regional university committed to the goal of achieving "Excellence for the 21st Century." Through the strategic planning process and the application of Total Quality Management, the university will seek excellence by establishing clear goals and objectives for each unit of the university which are complementary to the university-wide goals and objectives. The adoption of a client-centered approach to all that the university does will necessitate a recommitment by each member of the University of Wisconsin, Whitewater family to achieving the university's goals. The university will utilize the benefits of decentralization but guard against fragmentation.

The University of Wisconsin, Whitewater is and will continue to be primarily an undergraduate university serving career-oriented students from southeastern/south central Wisconsin. Although the overwhelming majority of students will come from the region adjacent to the university, diversification of the student body will be accomplished by:

1) The continuation of the university's unique mission to serve the needs of disabled students

2) An increase in the proportion of students from the top 10% of high school graduating classes

3) The recommitment to recruit and retain minority students so that the Whitewater campus of the university system continues to have the largest minority enrollment in the university cluster

4) An increase in the number of international students

Mission

In addition to the system and core missions, the University of Wisconsin, Whitewater has the select mission to:

1) Offer an extensive range of undergraduate programs and degrees including interdisciplinary programs in letters, sciences,

and the arts, as well as programs and degrees leading to professional specialization

2) Offer graduate education built clearly upon its undergraduate
   emphases and strengths with particular emphasis in the fields of
   business and education

3) Expect scholarly activity, including research, scholarship, and
   creative endeavor, that supports its programs at the associate
   and baccalaureate degree level, its selected graduate programs,
   and its special mission

4) Provide supportive services and programs for students with disabilities

5) Recruit minority and nontraditional students and provide support services and programs for them

6) Serve as a regional cultural and resource center

7) Provide continuing education and outreach programs as integrated institutional activities

EXAMPLE: UNIVERSITY OF NORTH CAROLINA, WILMINGTON

The University of North Carolina, Wilmington is a community of
scholars dedicated to excellence in teaching, research, artistic
achievement, and service to local and global communities. It is an
evolving comprehensive university of moderate size that values
close relationships among students, faculty, and staff in a diverse,
supportive, and challenging intellectual environment.

As the only public university in southeastern North Carolina,
this institution bears a special responsibility for education and service. The university is committed to providing lifelong learning opportunities, assisting with the improvement of public school education, and enhancing the personal, cultural, and economic health
of the region.

EXAMPLE: HOPE COLLEGE

The mission of Hope College is to offer academic programs with
recognized excellence in the liberal arts, in the setting of a residential,

undergraduate, coeducational college, and in the context of the historic Christian faith.

Expanded Statement of Institutional Goals and Objectives for the Academic Program in Terms of Student Achievement

Goal 1: Students will have an ability to understand, communicate, and critically appraise differing ways of knowing.

Objective 1: Students will possess fundamental skills which enable them to:

a) Read, listen, and view with sensitivity and with critical acumen

b) Express themselves clearly, correctly, and succinctly in writing and speaking

c) Apply mathematical principles and procedures effectively

d) Use research facilities and library resources competently

e) Use a studio or performance space to create or perform a work of art satisfactorily

Objective 2: Students will be able to make critical judgments about a fundamental body of knowledge.

Goal 2: Students will become more aware of and sensitive to a variety of disciplines, culture, and religions.

Objective 1: Through direct experience, a student's awareness of and sensitivity to a variety of aesthetic, historical, theoretical, technological, cultural, and religious perspectives should become increasingly broad and deep, as well as coherent.

Objective 2: Students will have a heightened awareness of and sensitivity to gender issues, diverse cultures, international perspective, and a variety of issues calling for social justice.

Objective 3: Students will understand historical Christianity and the roles of religion in the world.

Goal 3: Students will demonstrate an ability to engage in intensive study.

Objective 1: Students will explore in depth an academic discipline or an interdisciplinary area of study.

Objective 2: Students will be active learners, learning through collaborative research, performance, and experience.

Objective 3: Students will have opportunity to become familiar with current practices and issues through internships or other forms of experiential education.

Objective 4: Students will have opportunities for professional and preprofessional education.

Goal 4: Students will demonstrate a sense of the interrelatedness of knowledge, experience, and responsibility.

Objective 1: All graduates will show an understanding of how a personal philosophy of life provides meaning and coherence in one's learning, experiencing, and decision-making. In particular, the student will understand how the Christian world view can inform a philosophy for living and how it can shape one's response to contemporary issues.

EXAMPLE: PORTLAND STATE UNIVERSITY

The mission of Portland State University is to enhance the intellectual, social, cultural, and economic qualities of urban life by providing access, throughout the life span, to a quality liberal education for undergraduates and an appropriate array of professional and graduate programs especially relevant to the metropolitan area. The university will actively promote the development of a network of educational institutions that will serve the community and will conduct research and community service to support a high quality educational environment and reflect issues important to the metropolitan region.

EXAMPLE: DREXEL UNIVERSITY, COLLEGE OF BUSINESS AND ADMINISTRATION

The primary mission of the college of business and administration is to provide men and women with the skills, knowledge, conceptual understanding, and ethical sensitivity to become innovative, responsible, and accountable managers and leaders in the organizations they will join. In our desire to educate tomorrow's managers and leaders at all levels of society, we want to ensure the proper balance between technical skills and humanistic concerns so that our graduates will understand that they have an obligation to serve as well as to lead.

EXAMPLE: FLORIDA INTERNATIONAL UNIVERSITY

The mission of this state university is to serve the people of Southeast Florida, the state, the nation, and the international community by imparting knowledge through teaching excellence, creating new knowledge through research, and fostering creativity and creative expression. The continued globalization of the world's economic, social, and political systems adds to the importance of FIU's mission and combines with our subtropical environment and our strategic location to strengthen Southeast Florida's role as an information and transportation center. From this unique setting, we have derived four key strategic themes that guide the university's development: international, environmental, urban, and transportation and information systems.

EXAMPLE: EMPORIA STATE UNIVERSITY

Emporia State University is a comprehensive Regents university primarily serving residents of Kansas by providing leadership in quality instruction, related scholarship, and service. A student-centered institution, its central mission is to develop lifelong learning skills, impart society's cultural heritage, and educate and prepare for both the professions and advanced study. Faculty, staff, and students interact in a collegial atmosphere that fosters freedom of inquiry and expression.

EXAMPLE: SACRED HEART UNIVERSITY

Sacred Heart is a coeducational, independent, comprehensive institution of higher learning in the Catholic intellectual tradition whose primary objective is to prepare men and women to live in and make their contributions to the human community.

The university aims to assist in the development of people who are knowledgeable of self, rooted in faith, educated in mind, compassionate in heart, responsive to social and civic obligations, and able to respond to an ever-changing world. It does this by calling forth the intellectual potential of its students, nurturing each one's spiritual and moral growth, and deepening in them a sense of social responsibility. The university is committed to combining education for life with preparation for professional excellence.

Sacred Heart University is Catholic in tradition and spirit. As a Catholic university, it seeks to play its appropriate role in the modern world. It exemplifies in its life the Judeo-Christian values of the God-given freedom and dignity of every human person. Inspired by the ecumenical spirit of the Second Vatican Council, Sacred Heart University welcomes men and women of all religious traditions and beliefs who share its concerns for truth, scholarship, the dignity of the human person, freedom, and the betterment of human society. It values religious diversity as enhancing the university community and creating opportunities for dialogue in the common search for truth. Through its curricular and cocurricular activities and campus ministry programs, the university provides the context in which students have the opportunity to appropriate in a critical fashion their own religious traditions.

EXAMPLE: THE OHIO STATE UNIVERSITY

The Ohio State University has as its mission the attainment of international distinction in education, scholarship, and public service. As the state's leading comprehensive teaching and research university, Ohio State combines a responsibility for the advancement and dissemination of knowledge with a land-grant heritage of public service. It offers an extensive range of academic programs in the liberal arts, the sciences, and the professions.

Ohio State provides accessible, high-quality undergraduate and graduate education for qualified students who are able to benefit from a scholarly environment in which research inspires and informs teaching. "At Ohio State, we celebrate and learn from our diversity, and we value individual differences. Academic freedom is defended within an environment of civility, tolerance, and mutual respect."

In its 16-page document introducing and discussing its mission, the university provides the reader with an in-depth review of its goals and a list of specific objectives for each. Representative elements from the conclusion of this report follow:

The Ohio State University is an extraordinarily complex, varied, and resourceful institution that exists to serve the people of this state and this nation in the pursuit of knowledge and the resolution of problems. Each section of this document, each paragraph—indeed, each sentence—contains only a hint of the outstanding programs and activities that exist and take place here. In scope and depth of excellence, it stands alone among Ohio's other fine institutions of higher education. Already a leading national research university, Ohio State is poised to assume a position of national preeminence.

Summary of University Objectives
Part One

- Ohio State must invest well—in faculty, student, and staff quality—the most important single issue in supporting Ohio State's education, scholarship, and public service. This is essential to strengthen the university's identify and assure its achievement as a premier comprehensive public teaching and research university.

- Ohio State must continue to enhance its graduate programs. This is essential in order to provide the highest quality of expertise to meet public needs, to continue to recruit and retain the finest faculty, and to assure that Ohio possesses one of the front-rank public research universities in the country to support the interests of its citizens.

- Aggressive efforts to secure increased levels of private support are central to Ohio State's excellence and to its continued and enhanced reputation. This is essential to enhance areas of both disciplinary and interdisciplinary teaching and research.

- Ohio State will move to a position of preeminence in higher education and will increasingly be seen as a national leader among major research universities. This is essential to give high-ability students a distinctive and necessary educational option within their own state; to secure increasing levels of research investments from outside the state; and to contribute to the college/university work force and knowledge base necessary for the state of Ohio to secure the level of economic productivity and wealth and quality of life possible in the next century.

Part Two

- Ohio State must continue to expand its base of extramural research support with the objective of becoming well-placed among the top half of the big ten universities within the decade. This is essential in order to attract the best students and give them the most up-to-date training in a distinctive format where teaching and research are inextricably intertwined, to provide employment in the state, and to invigorate discovery in critical areas of basic science and technology.

- Ohio State will continue to provide skilled and educated graduates from across the state who are well prepared to become leaders in both the public and private sectors. This is an essential statewide role of the university and an essential element in furthering economic betterment and quality of life.

- Ohio State will play an even stronger role in the state's economic development and continue to nurture scientific and technological advancements in Ohio through application of research. This is essential in order to enable the state to compete successfully in the expanding global economy.

Part Three

- Ohio State will continue to strengthen the quality of its academic programs in the liberal arts, the sciences, and the professions. This is essential to assure that outstanding programs are sustained and those poised for excellence are enhanced. It is also essential that uncompetitive programs be invigorated, downsized, or eliminated.

- Ohio State will rigorously analyze its academic priorities and structure, make changes appropriate to a changing world reality, and support selected areas of excellence. This is essential in the increasingly competitive world of higher education, especially that of research universities, during an era of severe resource constraint.

- Ohio State will make its academic support structure as efficient and effective as possible, while directing all available moneys to academic areas of excellence. This is essential as an element of continuing quality improvement in institutional performance and in academic achievement.

Part Four

- Ohio State will continue to improve the quality of its student body with the goal of placing the university in the top half of the big ten universities within the decade. This is essential to create an outstanding educational experience for all students and to provide the state with the future private sector, civic, governmental, and political leadership it needs.

- Ohio State will continue efforts to assist state economic development by keeping Ohio's finest students in Ohio. This is essential to sustaining the long-term welfare and quality of life for the people of Ohio.

- Ohio State will continue to strengthen its curriculum and enhance the quality of the academic experience and will continue to recognize that the learning exists in real and important ways outside of the classroom. The out-of-classroom experience must be enhanced. This is essential in attracting and preparing the finest students.

- Ohio State will meet its challenges with creativity and determination, aggressively pursuing funding from all available sources. This is essential if we are to remain competitive with the front-rank comprehensive public teaching and research universities in this country.

Part Five

- Ohio State will continue an aggressive pursuit of diversity among faculty, staff, and students. Essential to this effort is retention as well as recruitment.

- Ohio State will continue to view selective admissions as an important aid in enhancing the diversity of its student body. This is essential in attracting and supporting more of the finest students who would want to pursue their studies at our university.

- Ohio State will remain a leader in graduate education of minority students. This is essential in providing opportunity and expertise in our most highly educated work force.

- Ohio State will continue efforts to make the campus environment one in which we celebrate and learn from diversity, and in which respect and civility are promoted. This is essential to the quality and future well-being of our society.

DISSEMINATION AND IMPACT

Each of these statements provides institutional leaders, faculty, and governmental leaders with a clear picture of what is important to the institution and a base in which schools, colleges, and departments can build as they develop their own mission and priority statements. These statements can also play a major role in communicating what that institution is to the outside community, parents, and prospective students. One of the issues that presidents and chief academic officers must address is how to communicate the mission and vision for the institution to its faculty, staff, and students. Surveys on a number of campuses have shown that the vast majority of faculty and students are actually unaware of the mission statement of their institution or if one even exists.

EXAMPLE: SYRACUSE UNIVERSITY

In 1992, when Syracuse University revised both its missions and vision to become more student-centered, documents were developed to set the stage for the future.

Mission
To promote learning through teaching, research, scholarship, creative accomplishment, and service.

Vision
To be the leading student-centered research university with faculty, students, and staff sharing responsibility and working together for academic, professional, and personal growth.

In addition, a university-wide task force of administrators, faculty, staff, and students was established to develop a statement that addressed the issue of relating these statements to how individuals acted. After many months of work and over 25 draft statements, the task force produced a compact that was adopted by the university senate. It was then further expanded to describe the behavior expected in each of the four areas cited in the compact.

The Syracuse University Compact
We the students, faculty, staff, and administrators of Syracuse University will:

- Support scholarly learning as the central mission of the university

- Promote a culturally and socially diverse climate that supports the development of each member of our community

- Uphold the highest ideals of personal and academic honesty

- Maintain a safe and healthy environment for each member of our community

In all aspects of university life, we will work together to reach these goals.

In addition to the wide dissemination of these documents during their development, there was a concerted effort to bring all three documents to the attention of the community on an ongoing basis. Several strategies were used:

1) In presentations, the chancellor and other key administrators made continual references to the documents.

2) They were used as the basis for discussions on priorities and re-source allocations.

3) They were included in the all university handbooks for faculty, students, and staff and in the materials disseminated to prospective faculty and students.

4) They were referred to during interviews, the all-university convo-cation for new students, and in the new faculty orientation.

5) The priorities that were established in these documents serve as a base for faculty rewards and resource allocation.

6) Press releases and other university publications made frequent men-tion of the vision and mission of the institution.

As a direct result of these and a number of associated efforts, a 1996 report (Diamond & Adam, 1996) showed a significant shift in how faculty, chairs, and deans perceived the university as to its priorities and the importance placed on teaching.

SUMMARY

Developing a quality mission and vision statement is never enough. However, it is the crucial first element in the change process. The process of developing a sound statement is as important as the statements themselves: It is an opportunity to include various constituents as the institution formulates its unique characteristics and future goals.

REFERENCES

Diamond, R. M., & Adam, B. E. (1996). *Syracuse University revisited, 1991-1996.* Syracuse, NY: The Center for Instructional Development, Syracuse University.

Kotter, J. P. (1996). *Leading change.* Cambridge, MA: Harvard Business School Press.

Kouzes, J. M., & Posner, B. Z. (1995). *The leadership challenge.* San Francisco, CA: Jossey-Bass.

4

Developing Institutional, School, and College Guidelines for Promotion and Tenure

The number of documents that are developed to describe the guidelines for the faculty reward and recognition system tend to be directly related to the size and structure of the institution. At smaller institutions where departments are often combined or consist of only a few faculty, there are often two major documents: the institutional document and a document that includes a statement for each of the major academic areas, divisions, or units. At large institutions, there is commonly an additional document with discipline-specific statements for individual departments (see Figure 4.1).

The priorities and procedures of the different levels must be completely compatible. The criteria used and the materials requested from the candidate must also be consistent. Since the institution-wide statement sets the guidelines for the school-/college-level statements, it must be developed first. The same sequence holds true between the school/college and the departmental statements. Following this sequence can cut down on the number of necessary revisions and can reduce stress among faculty and administrators.

While both the process of developing these statements and the topics being addressed will be similar in many ways, there will be differences in several areas:

FIGURE 4.1

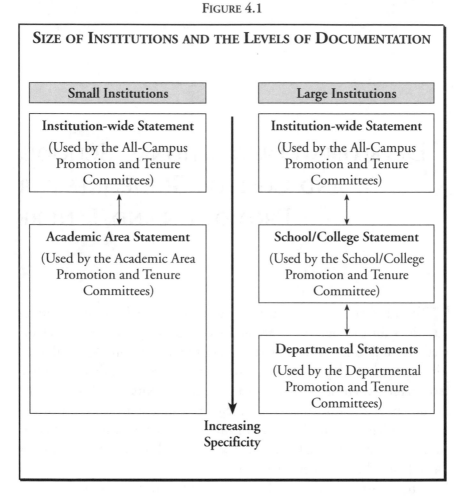

SIZE OF INSTITUTIONS AND THE LEVELS OF DOCUMENTATION

Small Institutions	Large Institutions
Institution-wide Statement (Used by the All-Campus Promotion and Tenure Committees)	**Institution-wide Statement** (Used by the All-Campus Promotion and Tenure Committees)
Academic Area Statement (Used by the Academic Area Promotion and Tenure Committees)	**School/College Statement** (Used by the School/College Promotion and Tenure Committee)
	Departmental Statements (Used by the Departmental Promotion and Tenure Committees)

Increasing Specificity

1) The closer the document is to the operational unit/department, the more specific it must become. Details and timelines are spelled out, and operational concerns (mentoring/recruiting/membership or committees) are addressed.

2) The closer the document is to the operational unit/department, the more closely the descriptions of scholarly, professional, and creative work are tied to the discipline and the unique strengths and priorities of the unit.

3) While the all-institution statement will focus primarily on major policies and common guidelines, the other documents (school, college, and department) will address how time policies and guidelines will be functionally applied.

For our purpose, we will focus first on institution-wide statements and the school/college document. Using examples from a number of institutions, we will focus on the developmental process and what might be included. (The departmental statement is the focus of the next chapter.)

ESTABLISHING THE TASK FORCE

The committee or task force that is charged with developing an all-campus document should be established by the chief academic officer. While there have been some instances where an existing committee has been given this assignment, such an approach can create problems (e.g., the committee may already be overloaded with work or its membership may be inappropriate). In selecting members for the committee, it is important to include highly respected faculty members for all academic areas and representative deans and chairs. In addition, appropriate standing committees, such as promotion and tenure appeals and budget, should be represented since the work of the task force will probably have a direct impact on the work of those other committees. While the task force may as a result be larger than most, representation and ownership in the process is a must.

Particular care should be taken for the selection of the chair of the task force. Ideally a faculty member, this individual should have excellent process skills and be respected as a teacher and researcher. He or she should also recognize the importance of the activity, write well, and be efficient. To facilitate the process, a high quality support staff member should be assigned to assist the chair as needed. A budget for supplies, refreshments, working luncheons, and some travel to national meetings should also be made available.

CHARGING THE TASK FORCE

The more specific the charge that is given to the task force, the better. The charge should include a clear statement of what is expected, the issues that the group should address, and a general timeline. The chief academic officer should attend the task force's first meeting to answer questions and provide a frame of reference for its activities (i.e., the importance of the work). The chief academic office should also be readily available to meet with the task force when needed. (A fine example of the letter of invitation and a potential list of quotations that was given to the task force at the University of Memphis is found in Chapter Two.)

EXAMPLE: MICHIGAN STATE UNIVERSITY

The charge to the committee on improvement, evaluation, and reward for teaching at Michigan State University (MSU) focused both on what they were to consider and on the specific elements of the process itself:

- Investigating and recommending methods and structures for improving, evaluating, and rewarding teaching in academic units

- Ascertaining ways in which teaching is now evaluated and rewarded

- Establishing strategies and methods to improve teaching

- Collecting, reviewing, and disseminating information on programs and policies for improving and rewarding teaching already in existence at Michigan State University

- Analyzing in greater detail the data collected in the UCAP teaching survey and similar surveys conducted at MSU in order to identify specific issues which shaped faculty's choices about teaching

- Contacting and visiting other institutions of higher learning to collect information and data on similar initiatives dedicated to improving, evaluating, and rewarding teaching

- Seeking assurances of faculty and administrative organizational structures, funding support, and adequate staffing to achieve the long-range goals of this report

As was done at the University of Memphis, it is also helpful to provide each committee member with a basic set of readings and a number of additional resources. (The annotated bibliography at the back of this book has been prepared to assist you in this selection.)

THE PROCESS

Each task force will have its own style and will follow its own procedures. What is common to all successful task forces is that the process be open. As noted earlier, some have used faculty—and, in some cases, academic administrator—questionnaires or surveys to gain insight into the existing attitudes toward the present system. When this approach is used, data should be reported out to the academic community for comment and discussion as rapidly as possible. In cases where the data and/or report have been keep private, there has been little discussion and even less improvement in the faculty rewards system. Trust does not develop when openness does not exist. Committee members should look for input as the document evolves, and should regularly report progress to their own departments, with individual faculty, and administrators. In addition, prior to completion of the report, open meetings should be held to discuss and debate all or parts of the documents.

EXAMPLE: PORTLAND STATE UNIVERSITY

In the cover letter accompanying the final report of the task force at Portland State University, the provost reviewed for the faculty the charge to the task force and the process that was followed.

During the 1995 fall term, a university-wide committee was charged by the provost with the task of suggesting revisions to Portland State University's existing promotion and tenure guidelines. This review was prompted by a national reexamination of the issues of faculty responsibilities and rewards. Following is a brief listing of some of the national articles and publications on faculty roles and rewards that were circulated to the committee in this process (available in the reserve library).

* Boyer, E. (1990). *Scholarship reconsidered: Priorities of the professoriate.* Princeton, NJ: Carnegie Foundation for the Advancement of Teaching.

- Boyer, E. (1994, January). *Scholarship assessed.* Presentation at the AAHE Faculty Roles and Rewards Forum. New Orleans, LA.

- Diamond, R. (1994). *Serving on promotion and tenure committees: A faculty guide.* Bolton, MA: Anker.

- Edgerton, R. (1993, July/August). The reexamination of faculty priorities. *Change.* pp. 10–25.

- Rice, E. (1991). The new American scholar. *Metropolitan Universities Journal.*

- Pister, C. (1991, June). *The Pister report: The report of a university-wide task force on faculty rewards.* Santa Cruz, CA: The University of California.

- Reports of a number of disciplinary associations on the issue of defining scholarly work including:

  > American Academy of Religion
  > American Assembly of Collegiate Schools of Business
  > American Chemical Society
  > American Historical Association
  > Association of American Geographers
  > Association for Education in Journalism
  >   and Mass Communication
  > Geological Society of America
  > National Council of Administrators of Home Economics

The committee also had the benefit of a report, "Redefining Scholarship for the College of Liberal Arts and Sciences" (Portland State University, January 1995) which addressed a number of key questions and identified issues that needed to be considered at the departmental level. This report provided a foundation for the all-university committee.

Questions This Committee Attempted to Answer

1) Why redefine scholarship?

2) What are the core expressions of scholarship? Are they discovery, integration, application, and interpretation?

3) How are these expressions related to the traditional activities of academics?

4) Can there be a scholarship of teaching? Does it need to go beyond local excellence?

5) Is there a scholarly activity in service? Is there some activity beyond good citizenship? Is it outreach? Does it need to go beyond local excellence?

6) What are the criteria that can be used to define scholarship? What is meant by quality? By impact?

7) What are the core of fundamental expectations of all faculty?

Questions for the Department to Consider

1) What is the department mission?

2) What are the right kinds of faculty profiles for our department?

> What are possible concentrations?
>
> Do any of them include a reduced teaching load?
>
> Are they voluntarily chosen or assigned?
>
> Do they differ for tenured and nontenured faculty?
>
> Is a research profile the only one that leads to tenure?
>
> How do people change profiles?

3) What are the procedures for establishing profiles? The goal setting procedure?

4) How can quality and impact be documented, especially for scholarship of teaching or outreach?

5) How can we support the development of an individual faculty member's scholarly agenda?

6) How can these procedures be used for faculty development?

7) What can the dean's office do to help us in this process?

The Charge to the Committee

In this context, the provost asked the committee to review PSU's existing promotion and tenure criteria to ensure that they rewarded activities that were aligned with the PSU mission. The committee was specifically charged with proposing revisions to the section of the criteria titled, "Portland State University Policies and Procedures for the Evaluation of Faculty Members for Tenure, Promotion, and Merit Increases, October 1990."

COMMUNICATING CHANGES

One of the challenges every committee will face is how best to communicate the changes they are proposing to the faculty and other interested parties.

EXAMPLE: PROPOSED CRITERIA REVISIONS, ST. NORBERT COLLEGE

At St. Norbert College, an approach was used to highlight the changes in a way that facilitated comparison for each change that was proposed (see Figure 4.2).

FIGURE 4.2

CRITERIA REVISIONS

Current Version	Proposed Revision
The applicant shall submit evidence of sustained scholarly achievement in his or her field as recognized by peers both within and without the College. Expected indicators include such contributions as juried publications, presentations, performances, or exhibitions of work appropriate to the field.	The applicant shall submit evidence of sustained scholarly achievement related to his or her field as recognized by peers both within and without the College. Expected indicators include such contributions that have been favorably evaluated by a jury of one's peers, such as publications, presentations, performances, or other scholarly works.

WHAT SHOULD BE INCLUDED IN THE GUIDELINES

While the policy documents that have been produced vary considerably in their structure, content, and specificity, they do have much in common. Sensitive to the needs and the style of the institution, these policies have been designed to bring coherence and fairness to the faculty reward system, to mesh it more carefully with the priorities of the institution, and to reduce conflicts.

In general, the guidelines include:

- An introduction or preamble that provides a context for the document (i.e., What was the need? How it was produced?)

- The mission statement of the institution

- A description of the roles of the faculty (Some institutions have retained the traditional triad of teaching, research, and service. Others have adapted the four forms of scholarship introduced by Boyer: discovery of knowledge, integration of knowledge, application of knowledge, and scholarship of teaching. Still others have combined the two.)

- A review of the characteristics of scholarly, professional, and creative work that will meet the standards of the institution and the documentation that will be expected. An important suggestion: As noted in Chapter 1, there are substantial differences among the disciplines in how scholarly, professional, and creative work is defined and described. It will substantially reduce the work and the strain of all-university or all-college committees if they focus on the common characteristics of scholarly work and then charge the departments with defining the terms that they use. Experience has shown, for example, that while some disciplines are comfortable with the four forms of scholarship as defined by Boyer and Rice, others are not, and trying to develop a single set of definitions for a number of disciplines can be counterproductive.

- The faculty review process:

    Will there be annual and post-tenure reviews, mid-semester, and external reviews?

Who will be responsible for what, and when?

- What will be the steps in the promotion and tenure process: How many committees will be involved, how will they be established, and how will members selected?

- What will be the relationship between promotion and tenure decisions?

- What documentation will be basic across the institution, and will a "selected" professional portfolio be used? If so what should be included?

- Under what conditions can the tenure clock be stopped? (i.e., is there flexibility in the timeline?)

- The approval process

In addition, a number of the policy statements include a description of other rewards beyond promotion, tenure, and merit pay that the institution will provide: leaves, travel, summer fellowships, grants for teaching innovation, and so on. In most cases, these statements are designed to provide the basis on which school/college and departmental guidelines are developed, recognizing as they do the differences in priorities and in the roles of the faculty that exist among various units.

AREAS OF PARTICULAR FOCUS

While many of these guidelines represent modest changes from the documents that preceded them, several demonstrate a definite shift in focus.

FOCUS ONE: GREATER EMPHASIS ON THE RELATIONSHIP OF THE PROMOTION AND TENURE SYSTEM TO THE MISSION OF THE INSTITUTION

EXAMPLE: PORTLAND STATE UNIVERSITY

Departments, schools, and the college have the primary responsibility for establishing respective missions and programmatic goals consistent with the university's vision of the future and its strategic plan. Together, departments/schools and individual faculty members are expected to engage throughout each faculty member's career in joint career development activities to ensure that faculty academic activities advance both the individual's scholarly agenda and the department's/school's mission.

Focus Two: Expansion in the Range of Activities that Qualify as Scholarly (Professional and Creative)

EXAMPLE: ROWAN COLLEGE

Recognizing the different ways that faculty may engage in the scholarship of discovery and the scholarship of integration, at Rowan College, we view the work of research and creative activity as including any of the following: research, creative works, applied research, and evaluation of funded research and creative projects.

Research

Research may be interpreted in may different ways. We have elected to define research as the pursuit of an active or continuing agenda of reading, writing, speaking, or other forms of scientific inquiry whose purpose is to create new knowledge or integrate existing knowledge. Products of research may include a) books or chapters in books or textbooks; b) edited works in books or textbooks; c) monographs; d) papers in refereed journals or conference proceedings; e) papers, roundtables, or demonstrations presented at academic or professional meetings; f) other papers and reports (e.g., trade, in-house, or technical); g) translations, abstracts, reviews, or criticisms; and h) computer software.

Creative Activity

Creative activity may also be interpreted in many different ways. In our model, we define creative activity as an expression of the scholarship of discovery and integration for those faculty engaged in disciplines for which research, as it may traditionally be defined, may not apply. Such faculty may sometimes, but not always, focus on disciplines in the fine, performing, or communicative arts. For our model, the expressions or products of creative activity include: a) novels and books; b) poems, essays, plays, and musical scores;

c) radio and television products, films, and videos; d) competitions, commissions, and other artistic exhibitions; e) direction or choreography of creative or artistic works; f) performances as vocalists, instrumentalists, dancers, actors, or other forms of performing arts; and g) design or arrangement of creative or artistic works. Within this category, editing of artistic or creative journals or other learned publications and managing or consulting on exhibitions, performances, and displays are also included.

Applied Research and Evaluation

Applied research and evaluation includes, but is not limited to: a) applied study or research; b) sponsored or contracted study or research; and c) program, policy, or personnel evaluation study of research for the local campus or other institutions or agencies.

Funded Research and Creative Projects

This category includes, but is not limited to: a) leadership in multidisciplinary centers and task forces; b) grant-seeking and proposal development to public and private sponsoring agencies; and c) supervision and management of sponsored creative and artistic projects.

Focus Three: Clarification in the Criteria that Will Be Used and in the Range of Documentation that Is Acceptable

EXAMPLE: The Medical College of Pennsylvania and Hahnemann University

By definition, scholarship must be public so that it contributes to the discipline. An activity is scholarly if it:

- Requires a high level of expertise
- Breaks new ground or is innovative
- Can be replicated or elaborated upon
- Can be documented
- Can be peer reviewed
- Has an impact on the discipline or some community of people

EXAMPLE: PORTLAND STATE UNIVERSITY

The term scholar implies a high degree of intellectual vitality. Scholarship is a demanding and rigorous concept that applies equally to faculty research and other creative activities, teaching and curricular activities, and community outreach; and it is expressed in a variety of forms from discipline to discipline or interdisciplinary field.

A scholar is a person who is engaged at the highest levels of lifelong learning and inquiry. The character of a scholar is demonstrated by academic attainment and rigorous academic practice. An active learner, over time, develops competencies in all four expressions of scholarship: discovery, integration, interpretation, and application (Boyer, 1991; Rice, 1991). However, it is also quite common and appropriate for scholars to vary in the relative preference they hold for one expression over another. In expressing scholarship, an individual usually moves fluidly among all four forms of expression, which are presented as follows in no particular order of importance.

1) **Discovery**

   Discovery is the rigorous testing of researchable questions suggested by theory or models of how phenomena may operate. It is active experimentation or exploration, with the primary goal of adding to the cumulative knowledge in a substantive way and of enhancing future prediction of the phenomena. Discovery may also involve original creation in writing, as well as creation, performance, or production in the performing arts, fine arts, architecture, graphic design, cinema, and broadcast media or related technologies.

2) **Integration**

   Integration places isolated knowledge or observations in perspective. Integrating activities make connections across disciplines, theories, or models. Integration illuminates information, artistic creations, or original work in a revealing way. It brings divergent knowledge together, or creates and/or extends new theory.

3) Interpretation

Interpretation is the process of revealing, explaining, and making knowledge clear to others. In essence, this is communicating knowledge and instilling skills and understanding that others may build upon and apply.

4) Application

Application is a process by which the scholar asks how state-of-the art knowledge can be responsibly applied to significant problems. Application is primarily concerned with assessing the efficacy of knowledge within a particular context, refining its implications, and assessing its generalizability.

EXAMPLE: THE MEDICAL COLLEGE OF PENNSYLVANIA AND HAHNEMANN UNIVERSITY

Testing Skills

The ability to deliver instruction to the student using techniques which will present and reinforce information, stimulate thinking, trigger discussion and synthesis, as well as the ability to improvise in order to take advantage of unplanned "teachable moments." Evidence of teaching competency should be provided using the following data sources:

1) *Systematic peer reviews:* colleagues, departmental curriculum, evaluation committee, and chair evaluation

2) *Systematic undergraduate and/or graduate student reviews:* rating of instruction, index of popularity of electives, and content analysis of unsolicited student comments/letters

3) *Educational consultant reports:* ratings of performance via workshops, direct observations, etc.

4) *Videotapes of exemplary teaching* with external/internal analysis of teaching by recognized experts in effective teaching

5) *Student, graduate, or faculty outcomes*

6) *Preceptor or employer evaluations*

Curriculum Development and Instructional Design
Curriculum/program development involves setting up an educational program or curriculum. Instructional design is the process of systematically transforming curriculum/program goals into educational objectives, teaching methods, and instructional materials. Summaries of curricula or programs submitted for review can be appended to the vitae as described in the Components of the Dossier section. Include (i) instructional units for the objectives; (ii) selection of teaching method(s) for the objectives and learners (e.g., lectures, small groups, problem-based learning, clinical rounds); (iii) preparation of educational materials (e.g., handouts, computer-assisted instructional materials); and (iv) evaluation of program/curriculum. Evidence should be included which supports the value, merit, and/or worth of the curriculum/program. Examples of such evidence include:

- Peer review evidence

- Review by external education specialists

- Student, graduate, or faculty outcomes

- Preceptor, student, or employer evaluations

- Documented use of the educational materials outside the institution

- Invitations to serve as a consultant or invited professor at other teaching institutions that are seeking assistance with a similar curriculum/program

EXAMPLE: THE UNIVERSITY OF DELAWARE

Scholarship, Solicited Peer Evaluation
Solicited peer evaluations serve as a major indicator of an individual's impact on the profession.

These peer evaluations are always required for promotion. Although the number may vary by rank and department or division, every dossier must include outside peer reviews, solicited by the departmental committee and written by individuals with established reputations in the candidate's field. These statements should analyze and evaluate critically the candidate's work and accomplishments, and they should also comment on the candidate's potential for future development.

FOCUS FOUR: INCREASED EMPHASIS ON THE GUIDELINES PROVIDED TO FACULTY

EXAMPLE: FLORIDA INTERNATIONAL UNIVERSITY

Responsibilities of the Departmental Chairperson

One of the chairperson's most important roles is guiding a faculty member's efforts to achieve promotion and tenure. The chairperson is a colleague and an administrator, providing ongoing advice, counsel, direction, evaluation appraisal, and resources which assist the candidate's efforts.

The promotion/tenure process begins when the faculty member joins the university. The chairperson should advise the faculty member of the advantages and disadvantages inherent in receiving tenure credit for prior service. To effectively guide the new faculty member, the chairperson should do the following things:

- Advise new faculty members of 1) the university's promotion/tenure process; 2) their promotion/tenure responsibilities; 3) the impact of their assignments on the promotion/tenure process; 4) the promotion/tenure policies and procedures of the department, school/college, and the university, and the impact of the expectations of each of these academic units on the promotion/tenure process.

- Make clear to the candidate that evaluation is a continuing process based on performance related to expectations. She or he is responsible for creating a positive environment to help the candidate meet department, school/college, and university expectations.

- To help assure these expectations are met, meet regularly with each faculty member to discuss his or her progress in the areas of teaching, research, and service.

- Consult informally with faculty members each semester on their progress toward their goals and objectives and their congruence with the goals and objectives of the academic units.

- Provide nontenured faculty members with written annual appraisals which must be discussed prior to insertion in personnel files.

- Encourage senior faculty members to serve as mentors and may advise candidates to seek mentors who can provide valuable experiences to all parties of the promotion/tenure process.

- Be conscious of his/her responsibilities to faculty members, especially when assigning duties to nontenured faculty, since overburdensome or unrelated activities detract from the faculty member's professional development.

- Ensure that the department's promotion/tenure policies and procedures are on file in the dean's office, that faculty members are aware of them, and that these policies and procedures are followed.

- Supervise the preparation of a candidate's application file. This role is especially important in ensuring that the file is well-organized and complete and that departmental procedures for obtaining external letters of evaluation are followed.

The department chairperson's participation in the departmental decision on promotion/tenure will vary according to the policies of the individual department (see section on responsibilities of departmental faculty). Where chairpersons provide an independent review, they have an obligation to render their best professional judgment of the candidate's credentials, contributions, and potential using the standards appropriate to the scholarly or professional field. They should consider the candidate's accomplishments, contributions, assigned tasks, and potential to make significant professional contributions, and the university's criteria. When the chairperson has reached a decision on a candidate, a detailed written statement giving her or his reasons should be placed in the promotion/tenure file, and a copy should be sent to the candidate.

SPECIAL ISSUE TASK FORCES OR COMMITTEES

There are instances when institution-wide task forces will be established to focus on a specific issue that will have a specific bearing on the promotion and tenure process and criteria. For example, they may be charged with exploring the way that teaching can be evaluated on improving and assessing advising—both of which occurred at Syracuse University.

EXAMPLE: ELECTRONIC PUBLICATIONS, RUTGERS UNIVERSITY
Another such committee was established at Rutgers University to address issues related to publishing in an electronic environment as they affect promotion and tenure. Such issues, along with computer software development, are rising problems for both candidates and committee members as the focus of the review process moves away from the quality and significance of what was done to the media that was used. In its 1997 report, the Committee on Electronic Publishing and Tenure made the following general recommendations:

1) Electronic publication should be considered to be an appropriate means of scholarly, artistic, and professional communication, as are other means of presentation such as print and performance.

2) The content of electronic publication should be evaluated within the traditions and habits of each discipline as publication traditionally has been in other media.

3) For purposes of appointment and promotion, the annual Academic Reappointment/Promotion Instructions should be modified to reflect recommendations 1) and 2), and the forms and instructions describing candidates' work should allow the electronic categories to be included.

4) In due course, the permanent availability of a scholarly work in substantively unchanged content should be a consideration in its evaluation, but this cannot yet be insisted on.

5) The use of electronic technologies and publication for teaching and service is also appropriate.

6) These recommendations should be periodically reviewed to assess their usefulness and the changed technological environment.

STOPPING THE TENURE CLOCK

Any statement related to the timing of the tenure system must be at the institutional level, and yet it is one element that tends, unfortunately, to be missing from many documents. There will be occasions when stopping the tenure clock is fair to both the candidate and the institution, so procedures for applying such an option must be established. In some instances, the need for such an adjustment to be made may be health or maternity related; in other cases, the need may result from an administrative assignment (department chair or curriculum project) or a grant that will take the individual away from his or her research focus. While it may be an option that is not used often (except in the case of maternity leave), it is an option that should be available. All too often, faculty are caught in the impossible position of being unable to complete an institutional assignment without jeopardizing their career as a faculty member.

DEVELOPING GUIDELINES

In an effective system, the various documents must be designed to support a system that is consistent and appropriate. It must be fair to both the candidates, to the committees that make recommendations, and to the administrator who must make the final decision as to the action that will be taken. Different criteria and priorities at different levels can lead to unfair action, confusion, poor decisions, and frustration.

INSTITUTIONAL PROMOTION AND TENURE GUIDELINES, MINNOWBROOK CONFERENCE ON INSTITUTIONAL PRIORITIES AND FACULTY REWARDS

Recognizing the importance of these documents, a task force of academic deans, provosts, chairs, and faculty met at the 1997 Minnowbrook

Conference on Institutional Priorities and Faculty Rewards (part of a national project coordinated by the Center for Instructional Development, Syracuse University) to develop guidelines for those engaged in improving institutional promotion and tenure policies and practices and for developing the promotion and tenure guidelines for the units that report to them. Recognizing the context-specific nature of policies and procedures, the task force chose to identify key issues and questions for the task force or committee to consider as they provide academic leadership in the area of faculty recognition and rewards. This is their report, which includes a list of key questions to ask when developing promotion and tenure guidelines that can be used as the committee works to develop the overall promotion and tenure guidelines at the school or college level.

Background

Tenure is probably the most important decision we make in a college or university. By tenuring faculty, we determine the future of where we go as an institution, what its strengths will be, and whether or not its priorities will be met. Therefore, the attention we give to tenure is critically important.

Unfortunately, academics have done a poor job of explaining the need for tenure to the general public who see it simply as a long-term employment policy; however, it is critically important because of the ideas of academic freedom and the freedom to make any sort of statement without fear of recourse. This degree of freedom is critical for a democracy, for a free society, and in order to advance any kind of science.

In developing the overall promotion and tenure statement for your institution, school, or college, there are a number of key factors that must be considered:

1) What is your institution's mission, and how does it play out in the work of an institution and the tenure promotion process? Is the mission consistent throughout the structure of the university, from the provost's office to the faculty and the departments? It is essential that the criteria used in your statement supports the priorities of your institution as expressed in the

mission statement of your institution and the individual school and colleges within it. On many campuses, this has required a campus/school/college review of the mission, making sure that it not only clearly identifies the unique characteristics of the institution and/or program it can build, but also that this process actively involves the entire academic community. An effective mission cannot be produced by administrative fiat.

2) Within the institution, what does tenure mean, and where does it reside? Does it reside in the department, does it reside in the university, does it reside with the faculty, or is it a shared responsibility of the whole tenure issue? A quality process cannot be developed until these questions are answered. On many campuses, the answer is determined by the size of the institution, the scope of its programs, history, and the autonomy given to its individual units.

3) Who should participate in the development of the promotion and tenure policy and process? Institutions are made up of numerous units, often with totally different priorities and strengths; therefore, a sensitivity to diversity needs to be a critical part of the mission policy and tenure process. We also need to remember that whatever process we put in place must work in a dynamic and ever-changing environment. Finally, the statement must clearly define tenure for eligible positions, which positions are tenure track and which are not, and under what conditions a person can move from one track to another.

4) When, and for what reasons, is faculty work evaluated? Is the evaluation formative, summative, or both? Subtopics under this section are the following: What is the relationship of probationary reviews, annual reviews, and third-year reviews to the promotion and tenure review, and how important is consistency among these reviews? Is faculty development to be a formal part of the process of preparing someone for tenure? If faculty are to be prepared for and supported during the full tenure process, procedures must be established and clearly articulated in the document. New faculty must not only know

what to expect but also what support they can expect during the process.

5) How will quality be determined? What are the standards and criteria? What documentation is required? What are the criteria considered in the promotion and tenure decision? While some institutions are using the four categories of scholarship developed by Ernest Boyer and Eugene Rice, others are modifying them or retaining faculty work under the traditional categories of research, teaching, and service. A more recent focus has been on those elements (criteria) that must exist if any work is to be considered scholarly, professional, or creative for promotion and tenure decisions. Two approaches, with many common elements, can prove helpful here. In *Scholarship Reassessed* (Glassick, Huber, & Maeroff, 1996), six standards must be present in any activity in order for it to be considered scholarly:

- Has clear goals

- Indicates adequate preparation

- Uses appropriate materials

- Produces significant results

- Is effectively presented

- Includes a reflective critique

The six features of scholarly and professional work developed by Diamond and Adam (1993) are:

- Requires a high level of discipline-related expertise

- Breaks new ground, is innovative

- Can be replicated or elaborated

- Has a process and results that can be documented

- Produces results that can be reviewed by peers

- Has significance and impact

Campuses that are including statements such as these in their documents (modified as they feel appropriate) are finding that the existence of these criteria significantly reduces the problem of faculty from one field trying to review the work of faculty from another.

The policy document must describe the dimensions of evaluation that will be acceptable. They must permit candidates to go beyond standard formats and recognize creativity.

6) The statement must address the difficulty and importance of recognizing teaching, service, and outreach. It must also recognize the ever-growing presence of technology. In all these areas, the questions of impact outcomes and so on must be addressed.

7) What are the standards for early promotion and tenure, the criteria for promotion to associate professor and to professor? What are the differences between what we expect of someone at an associate professor level to demonstrate versus someone at the professor level? Should promotion and tenure be combined or considered separately? Should collegiality be a criterion in promotion and tenure and, if so, how? How should external reviews be done? Are they needed? Can the tenure clock be stopped, and if so, under what conditions?

8) The policy must recognize diversity of departments and disciplines. Not only are departments different in their priorities, but in what faculty in these units do and how they define research and scholarship. A quality statement must support these differences.

9) The policy must also recognize that different faculty have different, but often equally important, strengths.

10) The policy needs to consider the impact of change in a dynamic environment. How should work be done out of one's official discipline or how can interdisciplinary work be evaluated? How can assignments outside of the departments on behalf of the university or vice chancellor be evaluated?

11) The policy must also address a number of administrative and procedural issues. What are the roles and responsibilities of faculty and administrators in the evaluation process? How participatory is the process? How are issues of openness and confidentiality addressed? Who, in reality, makes the decision and who participates?

Keep in mind that the provost and/or dean needs to rely on professional judgment of those in the discipline. At what level are faculty involved? In committees? As a department? How do rank and tenure status play a role in faculty involvement? Should students be involved? Does the process of faculty involvement have to be modified for very small departments? All of these are key questions.

It must also describe the process. What are the steps in the evaluation process? How is a decision reached? Along the way? At the last step? What appeals process is there? How is the outcome communicated to the faculty member? Is there a consistency throughout the process and between the institution's policies and the actual process?

12) And finally, there are external forces that must be addressed. What are the legal issues and documentation required? What is the impact of accreditation issues? What is the impact of budgetary issues? For example, are there quotas regarding the proportion of faculty who are tenured? On a unionized campus, it is essential that those on the negotiating teams from both sides see the potential of the two documents, the internal policies, and the various contracts working together rather than in opposition.

As provost and dean, you need to be sensitive to the role and the policies of your board of governors, trustees, regents, or other externally responsible groups who establish guidelines that will impact many elements in the promotion and tenure system. As you develop your document, the key to success is not only in what it includes but also in how it was put together.

FIGURE 4.3

KEY QUESTIONS TO ASK WHEN DEVELOPING PROMOTION AND TENURE GUIDELINES
(Minnowbrook Report)

Mission and priority statement
- What is the rationale for the statements?
- How does the school/college mission relate to the institutional mission?

Procedures/timelines
- What is the review process (i.e., third year, etc.)?
- Who is responsible for what?
- Are there procedures for early tenure decisions?
- Are promotion and tenure decisions separate, or are they combined?
- Can the tenure clock be stopped and under what conditions?
- Are external reviews to be done and under what conditions? Is funding available to pay reviewers?
- How will disciplinary differences be protected?
- How will differences in individual assignments be considered?
- How will individual strengths and interests be considered?
- Is collegiality a factor? If so, how is it defined and documented?

Candidate's work
- What are the committee's criteria for evaluating scholarly, professional, and creative work?
- What is the range of activities that, if documented, would meet these criteria?
- Documenting scholarship: What will show evidence that the candidate's work is scholarly, professional, and creative?
- Documenting teaching: How will teaching be assessed? What types of methods will be employed (i.e., review of course documents, class observations, student ratings, student performance assessment)?

Differences of opinion
- When there are different recommendations at different levels, how will they be resolved?
- What is the appeal process?

Faculty development
- How do the recruitment, interviewing, and appointment processes for new faculty communicate the priorities of the school and college?
- Is there a formal or informal mentoring plan for new faculty? If yes, how are assignments made?
- Is there a formal orientation program for new faculty?
- Is there a formal orientation plan for faculty serving on promotion and tenure committees?

Recognizing that faculty may want to bring about change, you must find ways to ensure fairness and equity and to allow participation in a continuously changing environment.

CONCLUSION

Institutional statements are foundational elements in a promotion, tenure, and faculty reward system. They also serve a pivotal role between the mission statement of the institution and the more focused documents that are produced at the school/college and departmental level. The more comprehensive they are, the more sensitive they are to the differences among academic units and to the range of faculty work on the campus; and the more detail they provide as to what criteria will be used to determine scholarly professional and creative work, the more effective they will be. A quality faculty reward system across all academic units requires quality institutional, school, and college documents.

To assist you in developing your institution, school, or college guidelines, a task force at the Minnowbrook Conference developed a list of key questions that you should consider (see Figure 4.3).

REFERENCES

Boyer, E. (1991). *Scholarship reconsidered.* Princeton, NJ: Carnegie Foundation for the Advancement of Teaching.

Boyer, E. (1994, January). *Scholarship assessed.* Delivered at the AAHE Faculty Roles and Rewards Forum. New Orleans, LA.

Diamond, R. (1994). *Serving on promotion and tenure committees: A faculty guide.* Bolton, MA: Anker.

Diamond, R. M., & Adam, B. E. (1993). *Recognizing faculty work: Reward system for the year 2000.* San Francisco, CA: Jossey-Bass.

Edgerton, R. (1993, July/August). The reexamination of faculty priorities. *Change.* 10–25.

Glassick, C., Huber, M. T., & Maeroff, G. (1997). *Scholarship assessed: Evaluation of the professoriate.* San Francisco, CA: Jossey-Bass.

Pister, C. (1991, June). *The Pister report: The report of a university-wide task force on faculty rewards.* Santa Cruz, CA: The University of California.

Portland State University. (1995, January 25). *Redefining scholarship for the college of liberal arts and sciences.* Portland, OR: Portland State University.

Rice, E. R. (1991, January). The new American scholar: Scholarship and the purposes of the university. *Metropolitan Universities Journal, I* (4), 7-18.

5

Developing Departmental Guidelines

Specific, clear departmental statements about promotion and tenure procedures and criteria are essential to a successful faculty rewards system. The departmental document should identify departmental priorities and demonstrate how they are aligned with the faculty reward system, spell out procedures in detail, articulate the unique characteristics of each discipline, and describe how scholarship is defined in the field. It can provide new faculty with an understanding of what is important and how the priorities of the department support the mission of the institution. It is also this document that should provide clear and essential guidelines to those who serve on the departmental promotion and tenure committee and to faculty who are preparing for promotion and tenure review. In addition, it is this statement that is the basis upon which other committees, deans, provosts, and administrators must rely as they review the recommendations that are being made. Unfortunately, the departmental documents are often too general, too hastily wrought, or downright nonexistent.

EXAMPLE: UNIVERSITY OF MEMPHIS
A report issued by the Task Force on Faculty Roles and Rewards at the University of Memphis (1995) stresses the centrality of the department's role in the promotion and tenure process.

> Accountability begins at the departmental level with clearly defined standards for evaluation of faculty for tenure and promotion. Specific guidelines should be developed at the departmental level,

95

reviewed by a college-level faculty advisory committee to the dean, and approved by the dean and the provost. These guidelines are critical to an effective tenure and promotion process. The guidelines should be distributed to each faculty member at the time he/she joins the faculty, at the time of midterm review, and at the time he/she applies for tenure or promotion. The guidelines should be discipline-specific, although in harmony with general university guidelines. Written guidelines containing the specific criteria and procedures for faculty evaluations should be updated as needed. Departmental standards should be included in the tenure and promotion materials sent forward from the department to the college and university levels on the behalf of the candidate.

At the heart of this process is the need for all departments to 1) spell out specific requirements for tenure and promotion; 2) inform faculty yearly as to their progress; and 3) communicate these criteria to the college committees, deans, and the provost.

In addition to the development and distribution of specific standards, departments are also urged to assist new, nontenured faculty through the use of a mentor system. The use of mentors to aid in faculty development is of crucial importance.

While a growing number of quality departmental documents are being developed, many existing statements do not support or facilitate a quality decision-making process. Joan North, dean of the College of Professional Studies at the University of Wisconsin, Stevens Point, spoke for many of her colleagues at the 1998 National Forum on Faculty Roles and Rewards when she reported circumstances that exist in far too many instances:

- The information forwarded with a recommendation is neither clear nor concise. There is often a reluctance by the department to identify poor performance—often from a genuine compassion for less stellar colleagues. In addition, some departments fear legal ramifications from negative decisions or find genuinely and irreconcilably differing views on what defines quality.

- The candidate has no voice, letting the evidence speak for itself or relying on the department to interpret the evidence. Essential information is thus missing.

- The dean must spend considerable time probing through extensive materials to identify where problems exist—problems in either quality of the candidate or in the process itself.

When a department ignores evidence of poor performance, waiting to see if the dean catches it, the department in fact relinquishes its power, its ability to define its own quality and be in charge of its own future, three roles that most faculty in that department would rather maintain. When guidelines are poor, when candidates, committees, deans, and the provost are left to struggle as best they can through the process, everyone—and the institution itself—suffers. The clearer the document; the more closely it meshes with the priorities of the institution; the more sensitive it is to the departmental context, the discipline it represents, and the range of faculty work that is required for a department to reach its full potential; the fairer the system will be.

STARTING THE PROCESS

Work does not usually begin on the development of a new or revised departmental promotion and tenure document without a formal request from the dean or chief academic officer. As with every other instance, the clearer and more detailed this charge is, the more efficient the process will be, and the greater the likelihood that the document itself will be substantially better as well as more compatible with those developed by other departments.

EXAMPLE: SYRACUSE UNIVERSITY

The following are sections from the charge given to the departments within the Maxwell School at Syracuse University by its dean, John Palmer.

The general goal of improving the quality of our undergraduate education and teaching has been an explicit priority of the Maxwell School since 1988-89. To this end, the goals outlined below have been agreed upon by the dean and department chairs.

Unless otherwise noted, the specific initiatives either have been implemented school-wide or have been adopted by some departments and are in process in others. They also will be a continuing focus of biweekly meetings of the dean and department chairs throughout this year.

1) **Improve Faculty Teaching Effectiveness**

   a) Develop departmental policy statements on what is expected/required and the role that teaching will play in various reward systems.

   b) Undertake student evaluations of all courses.

   c) Have complete, informative syllabi for all courses on record in department files before the beginning of semester and passed out in the first class.

   d) Institute annual peer review and feedback for all non-tenured faculty, along with the assignment of senior faculty as teaching mentors, and the development of teaching portfolios for the tenure review process.

   e) Institute systematic (but less frequent) peer review for all tenured faculty, and develop teaching portfolios for the promotion review process.

2) **Deploy Faculty Teaching Resources More Effectively**

   a) Implement a policy of greater teaching and advising responsibilities (and recognition of same in the various reward systems) for less active scholars.

Approximately one month after this charge was given, James Follain, then chair of the economics department, was asked what factors were considered as his unit began to address the issue of the importance of teaching and the faculty reward system. These were his observations at that time:

1) **Why We Moved Aggressively**

- Leadership of the university and the Maxwell School made it clear this was a high priority.

- We believe we do a good job in the classroom; a formal system that documents this can only help.

- We believe those departments that exhibit responsiveness to important university objectives are likely to be successful in requests for support.

- We believe in accountability and incentives, as long as they are approved by the department.

- We believe we know something about incentives and were anxious to do something constructive.

2) **Stylized Facts We Faced**

- The market emphasizes scholarly output.

- Successful teaching benefits from an ongoing and active research agenda.

- A tuition-driven university such as this cannot and should not ignore its primary "client": the student.

- The correlation between good teaching and research is high, though not perfect.

- We have a tradition of playing hard ball at the time of salary review.

- Our department has a long and successful tradition of requiring student evaluations of teaching.

This implies that good teaching is an essential part of our jobs; however, teaching performance alone cannot be the sole nor even the dominant determinant of salary or merit raises. It also suggests that our department would be receptive to a plan that would evaluate teaching.

3) **Development of a Plan to Evaluate Teaching**

- Develop a teaching evaluation document similar to our research evaluation report.

- Work with a teaching evaluation committee which consists of three experienced and good teachers.

- Read education literature on the subject, which tended to confirm our own views. This is probably similar to the opinions of noneconomists who study the works of economists on the economy!

- Developing a good process or document is very hard.

4) **Process to Evaluate Teaching: Key Points**

- Devote attention to outliers (the exceptional in the group).

- Those deemed as excellent should be rewarded.

- Those deemed as below the norm required will be dealt with on a case-by-case basis.

- Consider quantity versus quality.

- Student evaluations are important.

- Portfolios and peer reviews also matter.

5) **Costs and Benefits of the Process and Exercises to Develop One**

Costs

- Time-consuming, especially up front.

- Nontenured people will take teaching more seriously. Time will tell whether this matters at tenure time.

Benefits

- Destroys the myth that teaching does not matter.

- Excellence is rewarded.

- Poor performers are to be held accountable.

- Discussions of teaching performances are common.

- Improves the image of our department.

As these comments so clearly indicate, the development of these policy statements must take place within the context of the mission of the institution, the priorities of the school or college in which the department exists, and the discipline.

EXAMPLE: UNIVERSITY OF NORTH TEXAS

At the University of North Texas, the dean of the college of arts and sciences, Nora Bell (now president of Wesleyan College in Georgia), took a somewhat different approach by asking her chairs to respond to a series of carefully constructed questions. Notice how carefully the promotion and tenure issues have been placed in the context of the mission of the institution and the priorities and strengths of the unit.

It will be the responsibility of the chair to oversee the development of the departmental statement to inform all new appointees of its existence and what is called for and to insure that the guidelines that are developed are followed. Those that play an active role in the drafting of the document must keep in mind that there are four distinct areas in which these policy statements are used.

In developing the faculty reward system statement, the department is, in effect, establishing its major policy document. Since the system cannot be in place without addressing the issues of priorities, mission, and resources, the very process of developing this statement can often go a long way toward establishing a common vision and a community within your unit. The process, therefore, requires extensive faculty input, and it must include a review of all relevant institutional, school, college, and departmental statements. While some departments already have clear missions and priority statements, most do not. In many instances, it is the process of articulating their faculty reward systems that places the need for a clear goal statement on the agenda of the unit. The departmental statement when complete must support the priorities of the institution, it must be as specific as possible, and as part of the process, the writers must build on the statements and guidelines developed by the related disciplinary and accrediting association. Those involved must also remember that developing such a document is a political process and that everyone in the unit as well as those to whom the department reports must feel that they have had an opportunity to provide input and feedback. This documents the primary vehicle for communicating the priorities of your discipline to others at your institution.

PROMOTING DISCUSSION

Dialogue and debate are key elements in the process of developing promotion and tenure policies and guidelines. It is here where the unique issues of the institution will be addressed in the context of its history and culture. Active involvement not only helps ensure that the final recommendations will be accepted by the academic community, but also that key issues and concerns of faculty and administration are openly addressed. The following are examples of concerns raised and questions asked by faculty and chairs at several institutions as they participated in the process.

> *Quality teaching is given lip service by the administration. The reward system is so biased that any time put into teaching is wasted. Quite frankly, if a baboon could publish two or three papers a year, it would be given tenure and a large salary, while a top-notch instructor with limited research would be denied tenure.*

> *I have never heard anyone at . . . define teaching. For people here—faculty and students—the task is learning, not teaching, because we question every opinion and inference. Nobody measures learning.*

> *There are serious problems in evaluating individual contributions in collaborative research projects. Yet the most significant teaching and research projects tend to be collaborative in many disciplines. Our annual review and tenure/promotion system is not well designed to deal with collaborative work. Solving this requires better and different documentation methods than we now use (although there were no specific suggestions on how to improve current documentation).*

How can we make it easier for persons to work across discipline boundaries or on "unusual" activities valued by the institution? Disciplines tend to be very narrow in what they value, perhaps even xenophobic. This makes it difficult for faculty to contribute to the university mission through work that is unusual or crosses discipline boundaries unless the discipline itself values activity.

Who is the "jury" for evaluating unusual contributions? If not the department, which tends to take a narrow view in most cases, then who? How can conflicting views be reconciled?

The six-year time frame for tenure is arbitrary. Why not have a longer period?

In some disciplines, very long-term research projects tend to have the most significant impacts. For example, significant publications may not occur until the end of long-term projects. Yet the annual review and even the tenure systems are biased against participation in such long projects.

How are various activities going to be weighted?

How much credibility will department guidelines be given at the dean's level and at the provost's level?

It would be helpful to have examples of a faculty portfolio under the new guidelines. What would be included in the portfolio?

What do we mean by community outreach? What is uniquely community outreach that does not overlap with research or teaching?

The examples in the document are vague and abstract. Need something real like an open-ended listing of possible service options.

When the draft suggests that involvement in governance is not a valued activity, then why would faculty get involved?

Faculty have some concerns that a portfolio will not be accepted at other institutions and will limit job opportunities at other institutions.

While some concerns will be more fundamental than others, it is essential that the faculty have ample opportunity to raise them during the developmental process and that each is addressed. Without open discussion during the writing process, there will be a better than even chance that any statement, no matter how good it is, will be voted down at the departmental level.

WHAT TO INCLUDE
IN THE DEPARTMENTAL STATEMENT

EXAMPLE: MINNOWBROOK CONFERENCE, 1997

During the summer 1997 meeting at the Minnowbrook Conference Center of Syracuse University, a second group of participants addressed the department statement on promotion and tenure. Focusing on the process, the role of the document, and its contents, the participants made a number of observations and recommendations. The following material is based on their report (a list of task force members is found at the end of this chapter).

Developing the Departmental Statement

To ensure the development of a fair and appropriate reward system, a number of recommendations are made:

1) First and foremost, each department needs to develop a statement of faculty performance expectations for promotion, tenure, and salary increases (or other forms of reward and recognition, if they exist). This departmental statement needs to be compatible with institution-wide expectations and must reflect the mission of the institution, but in addition, it should contain such department-specific information as:

   a) Normative statements about faculty work emanating from the major disciplinary associations to which department faculty belong

   b) The uniqueness of any aspect of the department's mission or priorities for action which may explain nontraditional faculty career patterns in that unit

   c) The weight given to faculty performance for personnel decisions for faculty at different stages of their careers

d) The kinds of evidence or documentation which faculty are required (or allowed) to submit for evaluation

e) The criteria for "early" promotion or tenure, where these are possible

2) The development of departmental performance expectations documents must involve the unit faculty as a whole so that consensus can be built and faculty feel ownership of the document. This is especially important in large departments where faculty careers may take different shapes. There needs to be consensus about:

a) The kinds of work which are appropriate for faculty in this discipline

b) The kinds of acceptable evidence to document that work

c) The differences in performance expectations (if any) for faculty at different academic ranks

d) The kinds of professional, community, or institutional service which are rewarded in this department.

3) The departmental document must be acceptable to the dean and chief academic officer of the institution, as well as to any oversight committee that makes recommendations regarding priorities and rewards to the dean or chief academic officer. Until the document has been approved—in writing—by senior administrators, it cannot be used to assess the performance of department faculty. The chair's role in this process is to explain and justify any controversial or unusual facets of the department document so as to make them acceptable to superiors.

4) As noted, the departmental (as well as institutional) expectations for faculty performance should be shared with candidates for positions, should be thoroughly discussed with any new (or newly hired) faculty, and should be reviewed by the entire department on a regular basis.

5) The documents required of candidates must be clearly specified and should include a personal narrative or reflective essay describing what is included, why it is included, and the scholarly, professional, and creative priorities of the candidate.

6) This statement should also include sections that address annual peer review, midterm evaluation, and feedback. Included in the guidelines should be statements regarding departmental policies on workload, probation, timing, and the criteria that will be used annually and at other key times in a faculty member's career—both three-year and post-tenure reviews—and so on. The statement will also describe what a faculty member is responsible for in the tenure and review process and when and if a mentoring system is available. The departmental statement should also address the issue of how teaching effectiveness will be determined and in many instances may identify helpful resources available to faculty who are up for review or who are serving on promotion and tenure committees.

7) The document should describe the criteria that will be used to determine scholarly, professional, and creative work.

8) The document should also describe how special assignments (requiring extensive time away from traditional scholarly, professional, and creative work) will be taken into account and documented and should address issues of collegiality.

9) The statement should suggest and elaborate on a menu of options for peer review of teaching, including user surveys, naturally occurring groups, pedagogical colloquia, course portfolios, oral portfolios, teaching portfolios, classroom visitations, external and internal reviewers of teaching materials, reflective essays, and videotaping.

10) It is suggested that the focus be on a selected professional portfolio where the number of items are limited, allowing for an indepth review of what is included.

11) Finally, it is extremely important that the chair and the department promotion and tenure committee render all personnel judgments based on these written documents. Only in this way can claims of favoritism, partiality, subjectivity, etc. be obviated.

Each department's statement will be based on the discipline(s) involved, the size of the institution, the size of the department, and the structure of the unit. While each department's statement will be different, they all will need to address a number of common issues. It will be up to the unit to determine how scholarship, professional, and creative work can be described and documented; to determine what the specific mission of the unit and its priorities are; and how the entire process of review will take place at the department level. The document that is produced, if it is done well, will also guide the candidate in the preparation of his or her documentation and establish for all those involved in the review process the criteria that they should use. It will be one goal of those who write the document to ensure that the guidelines of the school, college, and the institution are followed and supported. A list of those factors that the writer(s) of this departmental statement should consider can be found in Figure 5.1.

FACULTY HIRING PRACTICES

Dissemination of the statement should also be an integral part of the interview process. All prospective faculty should be given copies of the policy, and since it includes a statement of departmental priorities and practices, it should be discussed with each candidate with respect to his or her individual strengths and the assignment they would be given. In some instances, this would involve a formal commitment, in the form of an appointment letter as to which of their activities would be viewed as scholarly/professional for promotion and tenure considerations. These conversations during the hiring process can also lead to commitments of resources and to individual assignments. As Tierney and Bensimon (1996) have pointed out, the focusing on the promotion and tenure policies during the interview process can be a major early stage in introducing future faculty into the culture and priorities of the department.

FIGURE 5.1

DEPARTMENTAL STATEMENT ON PROMOTION AND TENURE

Checklist of Elements to Include*

1) Departmental mission and priority statement with rationale

2) Research priorities of the department

3) Procedures, timelines, and eligibility for promotions and tenure

4) Range of activities that quality as scholarly, professional, or creative, and under what conditions

5) Articulation with institutional and school/college statements

6) Promotion and tenure criteria. Differential weights for different activities (i.e., teaching, community service, etc.)

7) Guidelines and policies for documentation (scholarly, professional, and creative work, teaching, and service). How much should be included?

8) Description of the appeals process

9) How committees are structured and selected

10) Recruiting: How are positions advertised, interviews conducted, and appointments made to support the mission and priorities of the unit?

11) Mentoring: What system is in place to support new faculty?

12) Faculty support: What recourses are available to support faculty?

13) Merit salary guidelines and criteria: What is the relative importance given to teaching, community, and institutional service?

14) Special assignments: How special assignments that involve extensive time will be taken into account—under what conditions can the tenure clock be stopped?

15) Issues of collegiality and how they will be determined

* Some topics may be school/college guidelines or union contracts to be referenced.

RESOURCES

As you develop your departmental statement, there are a number of resources that you should review as part of the process.

STATEMENTS FROM YOUR DISCIPLINE

One of the most common problems facing faculty coming up for promotion and tenure review is that their materials will be reviewed by faculty from other fields who may have a different definition of scholarly work. A quality departmental statement that specifically defines scholarly, professional, and creative work in your field will help to avoid this problem. As part of a major national project at Syracuse University, more than 20 national associations have been actively involved in developing statements that describe the work of faculty in their fields and discuss the conditions under which the discipline believes this work should be appropriate for their promotion decisions.

These statements have been designed to assist departments and individual faculty by being descriptive rather than prescriptive, allowing each unit to determine, based on its own priorities, which specific faculty activities are appropriate for its use.

Statements have been completed or are nearing completion by the following associations and disciplines:

- American Academy of Religion
- American Association of Colleges of Nursing
- American Association of Colleges for Teacher Education
- American Chemical Society
- American Historical Association
- American Library Association/American Council of Research Libraries
- American Physical Society
- American Psychological Association/The Society for the Teaching of Psychology
- American Society of Civil Engineers

- Association for Education in Journalism and Mass Communication
- Association of American Geographers
- Association of American Medical Colleges
- Association of College and Research Libraries
- Council of Administrators of Family and Consumer Sciences
- Council of Social Work Education
- Geological Society of America
- International Association for Management Education
- Joint Policy Board for Mathematics
- Modern Language Association
- National Association on Black Studies
- National Council of Administrators of Home Economics
- National Office for Arts Accreditation in Higher Education
    - Landscape Architectural Accreditation Board
    - National Architectural Accrediting Board
    - National Association of Schools of Art and Design
    - National Association of Schools of Dance
    - National Association of Schools of Music
    - National Association of Schools of Theater
- National Women's Study Association
- Society for College Science Teachers

According to the associations, each field has significant areas of discipline-related faculty work that should be, but have not been, recognized in the faculty reward system. Consulting and building on these statements can add strength to your department statement.

PROCEDURE GUIDES

Two publications have been developed specifically to assist in the implementation of a quality promotion and tenure process. In both cases, there is an emphasis on using the various documents and guidelines that have been produced, with particular emphasis on the department guidelines: Having the statement is one thing; making sure it is being used and followed is another.

- Diamond, R. M. (1994). *Serving on promotion and tenure committees: A faculty guide.* Bolton, MA: Anker.

- Diamond, R. M. (1995). *Preparing for promotion and tenure review: A faculty guide.* Bolton, MA: Anker.

Another small book that you might find useful is

- Tierney, W. G., & Bensimon, E. M. (1996). *Promotion and tenure: Community and socialization in the academe.* Albany, NY: State University of New York Press. In it you will find a number of excellent suggestions on how to build community through the recruitment, hiring, and mentoring processes, with special attention given to the promotion and tenure system.

SAMPLE DEPARTMENTAL GUIDELINES

Departmental guidelines tend to range from short, six- to eight-page documents to more comprehensive documents of 20 pages or more. The key to length tends to be less a factor of who is writing it than what is being asked for by the dean and what is contained in the school, college, and institutional documents. For example, if the other statements describe in detail what is to be included in an evaluation of teaching effectiveness or what criteria will be used for promotion from one grade to another, this information can be referred to but not necessarily included in the departmental statement. However, in most instances, the information provided tends to be very carefully worded with an attempt to provide as much detail as possible and to leave as little as possible open to different interpretation.

The following excerpts have been selected to show how different departments have addressed three of the key issues.

1) RELATIONSHIPS OF THE PROMOTION AND TENURE SYSTEM TO THE VISION AND MISSION STATEMENTS

EXAMPLE: IOWA STATE UNIVERSITY, COLLEGE OF ENGINEERING
The College of Engineering aspires to prepare engineers of the 21st century by using innovative teaching methods and modern education technology to provide students with the following traits and abilities:

- Broad-based and fundamentally sound technical education

- Responsiveness to social, economic, political, and environmental issues

  - Capability for career-long learning

  - Appreciation of good teamwork for problem solving

  - Command of effective communication skills

- High standards for professional behavior through adherence to principles of ethical conduct

The college strives to enhance its research with emphases on curiosity-driven basic research, task-oriented applied research, and both disciplinary and multidisciplinary activities. Multidisciplinary research areas where the college already has considerable strengths include:

- Computational methods

- Controls and instrumentation

- Energy engineering

- Engineered quality and reliability

- Engineering materials

- Environmental quality

- Manufacturing systems

Based on faculty interest, resource availability, and the outlook for future engineering and technology development, the college intends to focus its multidisciplinary research and graduate program development on and to achieve national prominence in four of these areas: materials, quality and reliability, environment, and energy.

As a land grant university's engineering college, we have an important service mission through outreach and extension efforts. The college envisions delivering this service to the following groups:

- Professional groups and industry through continuing education and technology transfer activities

- Nontraditional students by offering credit courses at suitable hours on campus and off campus using modern communication technologies

- K-12 students to nurture their interest in science and technology and citizens of the state to enhance their awareness of modern engineering technology

The college strives to build upon its existing strengths, achieve excellence in fulfilling the land-grant university missions, and arrive at national distinction through appropriate investment and resource development in selected disciplinary and multidisciplinary programs.

EXAMPLE: HOPE COLLEGE, ARTS DIVISION
In the context of Hope College's educational mission, the departments of art, dance, music, and theater have three goals. First, they are committed to offering academic programs of recognized excellence. Second, they are committed to offering courses strongly imbedded in the philosophy of the liberal arts. Third, they are committed to encouraging student reflection on how the arts inform and are informed by human values and faith.

EXAMPLE: UNIVERSITY OF NEW HAMPSHIRE, DEPARTMENT OF HEALTH MANAGEMENT AND POLICY
The Master's in Health Administration Program has the following goals and objectives in response to its stated mission:

Teaching Goal and Objectives

Goal. To provide health management generalist education primarily for individuals with health service experience currently working in the field that will enable them to enhance their concepts, knowledge, and skills.

Objectives. With this goal as the guiding concept, the program will have as its main objectives the development of the following student competencies:

- Demonstration of an understanding of the distinctive characteristics of health service organizations

- Demonstration of an understanding of a systems approach to health management

- Demonstration of an ability to apply analytical tools

Research and Scholarship Goal, Objectives, and Approach to Measurement

Goal. To contribute to the knowledge base in the field of health management and policy by refining existing knowledge or developing new knowledge.

Objectives. With the above goal as a guiding concept, the program has the following objectives:

- To encourage each faculty member to be engaged in one or more scholarly projects associated with health management and policy

- As a program, to contribute to the literature in the field of health management and policy

Measurement. Identification, classification, and assessment of faculty scholarly contributions to the field via information contained in their annual reports.

Service Goal, Objectives, and Approach to Measurement

Goal. To provide technical assistance and professional service to representatives of the health care system and to the university.

Objectives. With the above goal as the guiding concept, the program has the following related service objectives:

- Through faculty leadership, participation, and contributions, assist professional health service associations and organizations, including state agencies, in their operations

- Through faculty leadership, participation, and contributions, provide health management and policy practitioners with information and knowledge

- Through faculty leadership, participation, and contributions, assist the university, school, and department in their operations

Measurement. Identification, classification, and assessment of faculty service activities via information contained in their annual reports.

EXAMPLE: MONMOUTH COLLEGE, DEPARTMENT OF SOCIAL WORK

Social Work Program Objectives

1) The primary objective of the social work program is the preparation of students for entry-level social work practice

2) To prepare students for graduate-level social work education

3) To contribute to the education of students from all parts of the college

4) To prepare social work majors to understand and appreciate human diversity as it exists in society

5) To prepare students for the internalization of the values and ethics of the social work profession

Relationship of Program Objectives to Institutional Mission

The objectives of the social work program are consistent with the mission of the college and its academic and operational goals. The social work objectives relate directly in the following areas:

1) We will offer a broad range of degree programs of high quality.

2) We will strengthen degree offerings by maintaining accreditation.

3) We will seek to build a more diverse student body by enrolling larger numbers from various ethnic minorities.

4) We will ensure that each professional program addresses human and social values, so that professionals will be prepared to understand the human dimensions of current and future problems.

5) We will provide an effective program which fosters student initiative, self-government, and citizenship in a multicultural community.

6) We will enlarge the spirit of cooperation and involvement between Monmouth College and our surrounding communities.

7) We will maintain the excellence of the faculty who teach in professional programs by requiring appropriate credentials, providing for professional development, and supporting interaction with professionals in the field.

2) SCHOLARSHIP IN THE DISCIPLINE

EXAMPLE: OTTERBEIN COLLEGE, ENGLISH DEPARTMENT
The English department recognizes the importance and existence of scholarship in the many contributions made by faculty to their fields of expertise and interest, to their students and fellow teachers, and to their college. We take scholarship to be a fundament of a thriving liberal arts college faculty. By scholarship, we mean the kind of intellectual work whose primary, intended outcome can be found in any of three categories. We thus understand scholarship to

designate an inclusive term involving a broad range of intellectual activity with multiple outcomes, rather than confining it merely to a single outcome (as has historically been the case). In articulating the variety of enterprises that comprise the three outcome categories, we have used Ernest Boyer's *Scholarship Reconsidered*, as well as other readings, such as the recent statement on scholarship by the Modern Language Association (MLA). The categories pertaining to outcome are as follows:

1) **The presentation of one's scholarly or creative ideas in a traditional public form which involves peer review. This includes:**

Scholarship of creative enterprise:

- Creative work in the arts: poetry, fiction, drama, nonfiction

- Interdisciplinary creative work that collaborates with the performing and visual arts

Scholarship of critical enterprise:

- Articles in academic journals; presentations at conferences; academic books; book reviews; keynote speeches at conferences; scholarly bibliographies

- Editing collections of articles or primary works; translating works of literature or academic works

- Interdisciplinary research and presentations, projects, or publications to academic audiences

- Grant writing that is peer judged outside of one's institution, related to disciplinary or interdisciplinary projects

- Academic reports (e.g., on archival projects or electronic projects)

- Presenting a field in its interconnectedness with other fields or in its connections with social, moral, etc. issues (possibly an outgrowth of integrative studies work)

- Consulting work based on one's disciplinary expertise

2) **The development and effective teaching of courses**

Scholarship of pedagogical enterprise:

- Creating workshops on teaching for teachers (on- or off-campus)

- Developing, teaching, and presenting a new course to a professional audience (including the research needed to increase one's understanding of a particular subject, author, topic, etc.—also including research into teaching methods, etc.)

- Developing, teaching, assessing, and presenting an interdisciplinary course to an audience of peers

- Developing, assessing, and presenting an interdisciplinary program to an audience of peers

- Articles or books on pedagogy

- Textbooks or manuals for teachers

- Grant writing that is peer judged outside of one's institution and related to research and teaching

3) **The contribution of service to the college and external communities**

Scholarship of engagement:

- Connecting humanities' scholarship to public needs, locally, nationally, or globally, in team projects, oral presentations, or publications

- Writing or presenting research for a nonacademic audience about areas within one's academic expertise

- Working as a consultant in the community (involving research and production of documents); e.g., dramaturgy

- Creating and assessing a new academic program (to the extent that this involves professional expertise and research;

e.g., into similar programs, studies done about relevant issues, etc.)

We take these outcomes—presentation of ideas, teaching, and service—not to represent a hierarchy; instead, we recognize the value, importance, and vital necessity of all three. Thus, over the course of a career at Otterbein, faculty in this department are expected to engage in scholarly activity within the outcomes articulated in the aforementioned categories, both inside and outside the college. Faculty are expected to conduct scholarship in one or more of the areas of expertise for which they were hired. Because our department bears significant responsibility for the integrative studies program, we would also expect to see faculty research emerging in relationship to that program.

3) PROCEDURES

EXAMPLE: SYRACUSE UNIVERSITY, DEPARTMENT OF PUBLIC ADMINISTRATION

Procedure for Annual Performance Review of Nontenured Faculty

- Each nontenured faculty is reviewed annually by a four- or five-person committee of tenured members of the department. This committee is designated the "mentor committee."

- The department chair appoints the mentor committee during the first semester of a nontenured faculty member's service. Whenever possible, the mentor committee includes both faculty whose teaching and research interests are similar to those of the nontenured faculty member and others whose teaching and research interest are in other areas. To the extent possible, continuity of membership on the mentor committee is maintained until tenure review is completed.

- The mentor committee provides counsel to the nontenured faculty member with regard to teaching and advising, research, and other job-related matters.

- The mentor committee prepares each spring a written evaluation of the nontenured faculty member's performance. The annual evaluations are based on evidence about teaching and advising, research, and (where applicable) service. Such evidence may include, in addition to that submitted by the nontenured faculty member, information collected by the mentor committee from interviews with students about a faculty member's teaching and advising, assessment of scholarship submitted by outside evaluators, etc. The written evaluation includes, where appropriate, suggestions for improvements in teaching, research, or service, as well as the committee's overall assessment of the faculty member's progress toward tenure.

- The mentor committee discusses its written evaluation with the nontenured faculty member (who receives a copy of the evaluation) in a meeting also attended by the department chair. Since university procedures require that a department chair submit evaluative comments as part of the annual review of a nontenured faculty member, the department chair will either associate him/herself fully with the mentor committee's report or submit a separate statement of evaluation.

- If the nontenured faculty member objects to any aspect of the evaluation prepared by the mentor committee and/or the department chair, he or she may submit a written statement that describes the basis for those objections.

- The mentor committee's report, the department chair's report, and any statement furnished by the nontenured faculty member, are submitted by the department chair to the dean and the vice chancellor according to standard university procedures.

Procedure for Reappointment of Nontenured Faculty

- During the semester in which a contract renewal decision is required, the nontenured faculty member's mentor committee will conduct a "mini-tenure review" and prepare a written report that includes a recommendation regarding the contract renewal decision.

- In evaluating the teaching record of a candidate for contract renewal, the mentor committee will examine course evaluations as well as information made available by the candidate. The mentor committee may also meet with the candidate's current or former students, observe his or her classes, and solicit written evaluations from former students.

- In evaluating the research and scholarship record of a candidate for contract renewal, the mentor committee will read and evaluate all manuscripts and publications produced by the faculty member. The mentor committee may also seek evaluations of the candidate's research from external specialists.

- After reviewing the faculty member's teaching and research record, the mentor committee prepares the report.

- The mentor committee discusses its written evaluation and recommendation with the candidate for contract renewal (who receives a copy of the evaluation and recommendation) in a meeting also attended by the department chair.

- If the candidate for contract renewal objects to any aspect of the evaluation and recommendation, he or she may submit a written statement that describes the basis for those objections.

- The mentor committee's report and recommendation, along with any statement of objection furnished by the candidate for renewal, are furnished to all tenure-track members of the faculty in advance of a meeting of the faculty.

- At the meeting, tenure-track faculty will discuss the report and recommendation (and any statement submitted by the candidate). The department's tenured faculty will vote on both.

- The results of the faculty vote, along with the mentor committee's report and any statement furnished by the candidate, will be submitted by the department chair to the dean and the vice chancellor according to standard university procedures.

EXAMPLE: UNIVERSITY OF NORTH TEXAS,
DEPARTMENT OF COMMUNICATION STUDIES

Research/Scholarship

As a part of its mission, the department of communication studies supports research, including scholarly creative activities, that advance knowledge, bolster classroom instruction, and promote the application of knowledge for the benefit of society. Consequently, faculty members in the department are expected to engage actively in a program of communication research and scholarship. The department recognizes that for a faculty member to be recommended for tenure and to reflect his or her continuing growth, he/she must be engaged in a significant program of communication research and scholarship of sufficient quality and quantity to ensure that the faculty member is committed to the scholarly development of the discipline. The faculty member's program of research and scholarship should be ongoing throughout the probationary period.

Generally speaking, scholars in the department of communication studies engage in scholarship that leads to publication either in traditional publication outlets of the discipline or in presentation before professionals within the discipline. The department places the highest premium on peer-reviewed published research. The department also understands that creative presentation constitutes scholarship. To help assess the scholarly quality of the work, creative presentations require critical assessment by fellow professionals which addresses the level and quality of this scholarship. A faculty member cannot rely entirely on creative presentations and/or scholarly paper presentations for the awarding of tenure.

It is expected that a substantial portion of the faculty member's program of research and scholarship will be published and presented at a national or international level to scholars in the field of communication. A greater value will be assigned to single and first-authored research and scholarship. Significant collaborative research also is valued. Generally, the value assigned to items of research and scholarship will be determined by dissemination:

- Greatest weight will be given to national and international levels.

- Moderate weight will be given to regional and specialized levels.

- Least weight will be given to the state level.

A faculty member is expected to provide documentation that he/she is engaged in a significant program of research and scholarship. The faculty member should be prepared to document the significance of each entry, such as rejection rate, editorial policy statement, editorial board, and evidence of peer review. Appropriate forms of documentation include:

- Scholarly books

- Peer-reviewed yearbook articles

- Peer-reviewed journal articles

- Peer-reviewed monographs

- Research-based textbooks

- Peer-reviewed and invited performances and exhibitions

- Critical assessments of peer-reviewed and invited performances and exhibitions

- Book reviews in communication journals

- Performance reviews in communication and performance journals

- Editorships of scholarly materials

- Memberships on editorial boards

- Ad hoc reviewer for journals

- Peer-reviewed and invited presentations of scholarly papers at professional conventions and conferences

- Refereeing/reviewing competitive convention papers and programs

- Critiquing creative presentations

- Critiquing scholarly/research presentations

- Panelist on special convention programs

- Grant proposals

- Abstracts

- Translations

- Bibliographies

- Works in professional and consumer publications which demonstrate high standards of professional practice

- Citations by other scholars

EXAMPLE: NORTHERN ILLINOIS UNIVERSITY, DEPARTMENT OF MATHEMATICAL SCIENCE

General Criteria for Promotion and Tenure

All faculty members being considered for promotion and/or tenure will be evaluated in the areas of 1) scholarship, 2) teaching, 3) service to the department and university and, in the case of faculty in mathematics education, 4) activities in professional education. An accumulation of achievements in all of these areas will be considered, but a candidate whose performance in either areas 1) or 2) is unsatisfactory will not be recommended for promotion or tenure. Promotion will not normally be recommended until an individual has successfully served a minimum of six years in rank, at NIU and other institutions of higher education.

In greater detail, the criteria used in making these evaluations are as follows:

For promotion from assistant professor to associate professor and/or tenure.

1) Superior scholarship in the past and definite promise of continued excellence. Evidence that the faculty member is in the process of achieving professional recognition among leaders in

the individual's discipline. Scholarship should emphasize the acquisition of new knowledge, but in the case of faculty in mathematics education, weight may be given to the published dissemination of knowledge. Evidence of scholarly achievement and promise may include:

a) Publication of scholarly papers in recognized journals appropriate to the individual's discipline

b) Publication of monographs and books reflecting an advanced level of scholarship

c) Postdoctoral fellowships and memberships in various institutes, during the academic year and the summer

d) Invitations to address colloquia or seminars at other universities

e) Active participation in discussions and seminars, both formal and informal

f) Recommendations of established scholars in the field

g) Participation in professional meetings and contributions of papers and abstracts; NSF and other postdoctoral research grants

h) Service as a referee for recognized journals

i) Service as a reviewer for papers in the mathematical sciences

2) Contributions to the propagation of the mathematical sciences. These may include:

a) Good teaching as recognized by students and colleagues

b) Development of new course materials

c) Design and/or implementation of new courses or curricula

d) Authorship of textbooks or lecture notes

e) Direction of dissertations or theses

f) Active participation in discussions, both formal and informal, concerning the teaching and development of course offerings in the mathematical sciences

g) Academic responsibilities undertaken as coordinator of a multisection course

h) Activities in other areas of education

3) Service to the department, university, and profession. These may include:

a) Service on department and university committees; service as an advisor to students

b) Sponsorship of student organizations

c) Service as a coordinator of a multisection course

d) Service to professional societies

e) Activities in professional education. Such service may include professional education of teachers of mathematics (and prospective teachers of mathematics) in the elementary and secondary schools.

f) Service to a local, district, regional, state, or national pre-college or college educational administrative unit or professional organization as a teacher, consultant, director, or coordinator of a mathematical science continuing education activity

g) Service as a member or chair of a program or organizing committee for, or participation at, a local, state, or national conference, institute, or workshop designed to contribute directly or indirectly to the mathematical science continuing education activity

h) Service as a member or chair of a program or organizing committee for, or participation at, a local, state, or national conference, institute, or workshop designed to contribute directly or indirectly, to the mathematical science continuing education of professional personnel in administrative units

i) Service as a specialized consultant to an educational unit

j) Service to the professional community through membership on a local, state, or national educational study or advisory board, panel, or commission

k) Authorship of a paper, chapter, or book, or editorship of a collected work, intended for clientele of the administrative units

For early promotion or tenure. In order for a candidate to qualify for early promotion or tenure, the candidate's record of achievement must show clear evidence of a quality of scholarship that is extraordinary as compared to normal departmental standards. This extraordinary level of achievement should be reflected in letters of evaluation from prominent experts outside of the department.

1) **Service.** Faculty members in the department of mathematics must demonstrate a commitment to quality service to the department, the college, and the university. The department recognizes the merit of service to local, state, regional, national, and international constituencies. While service is expected of probationary faculty, it should not interfere with faculty members' fulfilling research and teaching obligations.

Professional service activities (paid or unpaid) may include, but are not limited to, the areas that follow. Although this list is not exhaustive, additional service activities should be evaluated in light of whether the candidate serves by virtue of professional education and expertise in communication.

To the department, college, and university:

- Committees
- Task forces
- Councils
- Faculty senate
- Development programs

- Recruitment
- Special presentations

To the profession:

- Office in association
- Program planner
- Committee work
- Chairing programs
- Directing intercollegiate and secondary debate tournaments and performance festivals
- Judging/critiquing in intercollegiate and secondary debate tournaments and performance festivals

To other constituencies:

- Conducting workshops
- Delivering lectures
- Consulting in problem solving
- Consulting in training programs
- Producing applied trade/corporate publications
- Providing expert opinions

CONCLUSION

Each of these statements attempts to relate the nature of the discipline to the mission statements of the school, college, and institution. In most instances, the mission statements are placed at the beginning of the document. It will be up to the candidate to relate the contents of his or her professional portfolio directly to these priorities.

As noted earlier, departmental reviews of faculty are often viewed with skepticism by institutional committees, deans, and other senior administrators. This skepticism may be well founded; there are countless examples of promotion or tenure documents sent up from the department which, for academics or administrators from other disciplines, lack credibility. The documents may read like a whitewash of the faculty member's record of performance, glossing over gaps or shortcomings in an effort to be "collegial." Or the documents may extol a performance which, to outside eyes, seems ordinary. There also have been cases in which the departmental documents seem overly critical or condemnatory of a faculty member's performance, leaving outsiders to wonder whether these reviews constitute some kind of personal attack rather than a supposedly objective assessment of performance.

It is the responsibility of the chair and department committee to enhance the credibility of the department's promotion and tenure documents. It is only at the department level that the disciplinary expertise exists to assess a faculty member's performance as a teacher or scholar. Smaller departments and some fields of study may need to go outside of the institution to get the level of specialization that some reviews would require. It is important that the policy of the unit and institution include procedures for this process.

The credibility of departmental documents will be enhanced if:

- The documents evaluate the faculty member's performance in terms of the departmental and institutional expectations for faculty performance, or in light of other written statements which approve (or fail to approve) of a faculty member's performance in nontraditional areas.

- The documents bolster their conclusions by citing expectations for faculty performance disseminated by the major disciplinary associations to which department faculty belong.

- The documents "bite the bullet" when it comes to making hard decisions about a colleague's performance: They make it clear to readers that the department has taken the responsibility for monitoring and assessing the quality of its own members. When departments fail to exercise this responsibility, they invite outsiders, often with no expertise in the discipline, to usurp that role.

- The documents assess a faculty member's contribution fairly and consistently; they are neither whitewashes of shoddy performance nor ad hominem attacks on an unpopular colleague. They make the case for their conclusions by dealing with and evaluating the quantitative and qualitative evidence.

The need to align, or realign, faculty roles and rewards at the department level, points to new, exciting, and essential roles for the department chair. The chair is the person who achieves alignment within the department for faculty roles and rewards, and the chair is the mediating agent between each individual faculty member's personal goals and the needs of the department: These are different conceptions of the role of the department chair from those traditionally cited. At a time when higher education is being forced to rethink what we do and why and how we do it, it is fitting that department chairs rethink how they can be most effective as leaders whose actions, at least as much as those of anyone else in the institution, affect the quality of faculty careers, student life, and academic programs.

A NOTE OF THANKS

Much of the material in this chapter on what should be included in a departmental statement was based on a task force report developed at the Syracuse University 1997 Minnowbrook Conference on Institutional Priorities and Faculty Rewards. Members of the task force on the departmental statement were:

John Ed Allen (University of North Texas)
Howard B. Altman (University of Louisville), *Chair*
Thomas Brownlee (American University)
Judith Grunert (Syracuse University)
Carla Howery (American Sociological Association)
Donlin M. Long (Johns Hopkins University)
W. Bede Mitchell (Appalachian State University)
Joan North (University of Wisconsin, Stevens Point)
Carol Parke (Syracuse University)
Kay Schallenkamp (Emporia State University)
Andy Schoolmaster (University of North Texas)
Dan Smothergill (Syracuse University)

REFERENCES

Boyer, E. (1990). *Scholarship reconsidered: Priorities of the professoriate.* Princeton, NJ: Carnegie Foundation for the Advancement of Teaching.

Diamond, R. M. (1994). *Serving on promotion and tenure committees: A faculty guide.* Bolton, MA: Anker.

Diamond, R. M. (1995). *Preparing for promotion and tenure review: A faculty guide.* Bolton, MA: Anker.

Tierney, W. G., & Bensimon, E. M. (1996). *Promotion and tenure: Community and socialization in academe.* Albany, NY: State University of New York Press.

University of Memphis, Task Force on Faculty Roles and Rewards. (1995, January 31). *Report of the task force on faculty roles and rewards.* Memphis, TN: The University of Memphis.

THE UNION CONTRACT

Far from encumbering the process of change in higher education, collective bargaining provides a means for implementing flexible procedures to accomplish desired reforms and to negotiate solutions as issues arise. Collective bargaining has a significant, positive role to play in the current efforts to broaden the definition of scholarship, to better recognize and reward effective teaching and service, and, in general, to promote the quality of faculty work.

The Collective Bargaining Task Force
Minnowbrook Conference on
Institutional Priorities and Faculty Rewards, 1997

Traditionally viewed as a document more focused on the grievance process, academic freedom, types of appointments, and retrenchment procedures than on facilitating change at an institution, the union contract can play a major role in helping colleges and universities prepare for the decades ahead by providing guidelines that can lay the groundwork for a faculty reward system that supports the mission of the institution.

While the working relationship between the negotiating teams will often determine the nature of the final document, the contract brings to the promotion and tenure and merit pay system the characteristics of fairness and appropriateness that all sides want. In addition, it can either encourage or discourage experimentation and innovation in the teaching and learning process. It is essential that the faculty leaders and administrators involved in the negotiations realize that the document they will produce has the potential to be a positive force for institutional improvement and personal growth.

The National Education Association's executive committee recognized this potential in 1994 when it approved a formal statement on faculty reward structures that provided the following guidelines to faculty serving on contract negotiation teams.

The NEA endorses the following and believes that its goals can be achieved only with fairness, equity, and professional dignity through strengthened shared governance and collective bargaining.

1) NEA's policy on Evaluation and Promotion in Higher Education is found in NEA Resolution D-18 which provides as follows:

   The National Education Association affirms the importance of teaching in institutions of higher education and believes, therefore, that research and publication ought not to be the only criteria on which higher education faculty are evaluated and/or promoted.

   The Association further believes that its higher education members must be allowed to determine through the collective bargaining process the methods by which they are evaluated and promoted.

2) Since teaching takes up the majority of faculty work time, it should be rewarded accordingly. Campuses need to recognize good teaching through appropriate evaluation systems that include student, faculty, and administrator input. Teaching, as a noble enterprise, should be justly rewarded.

3) The reward structures should reflect the mission of the institution. Institutions whose mission is community outreach should reward service. The proper balance between teaching, service, and research is contingent on faculty and administration agreement upon the institutional mission of the particular campus.

4) The faculty and the department should be party to the development of the mission statement for the campus and the revision of reward systems to reflect that mission. The balance of the workload should reflect the discipline and mission of the campus. Service is a major, but often misunderstood and underrated component of the triad of research, teaching, and service. Higher education faculty contribute significantly to the effective and efficient operations of their institutions. They also impact their communities, states, and the nation through their service activities.

5) Reward systems should be flexible and allow faculty to pursue and seek advancement in a variety of ways and should be flexible enough to allow faculty to pursue different interests at different times in their careers. Evaluation should be linked to performance of assigned responsibilities and career growth and development, as well as to tenure, promotion, and renewal. The evaluations should be formative to encourage risk-taking and growth.

6) Many institutions do not evaluate temporary or adjunct faculty. Temporary faculty should be evaluated and given assistance with teaching techniques. New faculty should be given a comprehensive orientation to the institution, its mission and goals, and the role of faculty.

7) Mentoring programs should be in place on all campuses to assist new faculty with the tenure and socialization process. Mentoring programs should further the affirmative action goals related to advancing the teaching and research opportunities for all faculty.

8) The development of better ways to document and evaluate good teaching should be a high priority. Higher education should do a better job of promoting the use of effective teaching techniques for graduate assistants, adjuncts, and permanent faculty, especially techniques related to reaching nontraditional students.

9) Campuses need to dedicate more resources to faculty development and to providing access to current instructional technology.

10) The academic or instructional department should be the linchpin for goal setting. The department is the place where the institutional goals directly intersect with faculty work and the students. There is a need to recognize that the disciplines will vary in their approach to the mix of teaching, research, and service. For example, chemistry has traditionally valued professional service and outreach along with research; geography has placed a heavy emphasis on teaching; creative products have been valued in the arts. Attention should be paid to the criteria being developed by the disciplines, and efforts should be made to work collaboratively with the discipline associations.

WHAT SHOULD BE INCLUDED

The topic of what might be added to the negotiated contract to help improve the quality of the initiatives and the promotion and tenure system was the focus of a working group at the 1997 summer conference that was one of a series on Institutional Priorities and Faculty Rewards, sponsored by the Center for Instructional Development at Syracuse University with support from a number of foundations and agencies. The working group included faculty members, administration, and staff of the American Association of University Professors (AAUP), the National Education Association (NEA), and the American Federation of Teachers (AFT).

The participants believed that the bargaining agreement should not only address a number of key procedural issues but that it could, if designed for the purpose, help in the development of a policy that recognized the differences among the disciplines and the various roles of faculty.

The task force report recommended that the formal contract should address:

• The critical role of departments in developing their own promotion and tenure standards

- The critical role of faculty in determining the means of salary distribution and criteria for the distribution of any selective increases so as to ensure that teaching and service as well as scholarly activities/research are recognized and rewarded

- Measures to ensure consistency and balance in the standards for workload, merit evaluation, and promotion and tenure criteria

- Assuring adequate instructional resources and the commitment to teaching effectiveness as reflected in hiring practices and instructional support

- Improving peer review procedures by preparing, training, and recognizing faculty peer evaluation

- Consideration of released time, peer assistance, and other resources for instructional improvement

- Protecting rights, responsibilities, and rewards for faculty participating in distance or distributed learning, as well as safeguarding their intellectual property

- Protecting academic freedom and due process rights throughout faculty evaluation and reward procedures

- A faculty role in academic governance and the evaluation of administrators and institutional effectiveness to ensure shared accountability for fulfilling the institutional mission

- Maintaining an adequate proportion of full-time, tenure-track faculty

EXAMPLE: CENTRAL MICHIGAN UNIVERSITY

1) THE IMPORTANCE OF THE ACADEMIC UNIT
AND THE DIFFERENCES AMONG THE DISCIPLINES

The 1996–1999 agreement between Central Michigan University (CMU) and the CMU Faculty Association (a NEA affiliate) is 90 pages long and covers everything from the university calendar and employee benefits to grievance procedures, salary stipulations, and the process for establishing and eliminating academic departments. In the document are statements and guidelines that support many of the elements of a quality faculty reward system that have been highlighted in previous chapters. In addition, the agreement includes many of the topics addressed in school, college, and departmental guidelines.

A major characteristic of the Central Michigan agreement is the detail it contains regarding the involvement of faculty in the development of guidelines and the way that it recognizes that departments are not all alike in their priorities or in the roles of their faculty. [N.B.: While only a selection of parts from the agreement are included here, the original numbering of those parts is retained.]

Reappointment, Promotion, and Tenure Policies

1) The pursuit of knowledge and learning manifests itself in different ways in various fields and disciplines, such as sciences, arts, humanities, and applied arts. Departmental colleagues are best informed and are in the best position to arrive at specific criteria and standards to evaluate a bargaining unit member's work. Criteria refer to the areas of evaluation (e.g., teaching, scholarly and creative activity, professional growth, and university service). Standards refer to the written performance requirements in each evaluation area developed in compliance with this Agreement. Departments develop and systematize these criteria and standards so that they may serve as guidelines for departmental recommendations regarding reappointment, promotion, and tenure. After approval by the provost, these written standards form the basis not only for departmental evaluations but also for subsequent evaluations at higher levels.

Bases of Judgment for Reappointment, Promotion, and Tenure

2) Reappointment, promotion, and tenure decisions result from deliberations and judgments occurring at various levels within the institution and begin with recommendations by departments to the college level where recommendations are made to the university level for decision. At each level, the criteria and standards applied shall be those developed in compliance with this Agreement. Both parties recognize that greater scrutiny

may be given to judgments as their relative importance increases.

a) The bases for judgment for reappointment and tenure, except for bargaining unit members in Intercollegiate Athletics, are:

- The competence of a bargaining unit member which includes demonstrated achievement in the following areas:

    - Teaching competence

    - Scholarly and creative activity

    - Professional growth of a significant nature

    - University service which may be supplemented by public service related to the bargaining unit member's discipline

- The promise of a bargaining unit member which includes:

    - An evaluation, based upon performance up to the present time, as to the bargaining unit member's potential for professional growth and development

    - A judgment as to whether the bargaining unit member will contribute to the goals and objectives established by the department

- The future needs of the university

Department Procedures, Criteria, Standards, and Bylaws

1) The bargaining unit members of each department shall, by majority vote

a) Establish procedures for participation in formulating the department's criteria and standards which, in turn, must be determined by a majority of the voting members of the department

    b) Establish procedures for participation in determining the department's recommendations in the areas of reappointment, promotion, and tenure

    c) Establish procedures for participation in determining the department's bylaws

2) The voting members of each department shall, by majority vote, establish bylaws for the internal governance of the department. The bylaws may address topics such as sabbatical leave recommendations, allocation of department funds over which the department has discretion, and department assignment of department professional responsibilities.

2) THE IMPORTANCE OF TEACHING AND THE RELATIONSHIP OF TEACHING AND RESEARCH

Throughout the Central Michigan University statement contract, the writers have related its contents to the mission and priorities of the institution.

1) Central Michigan University is an institution where there is a collective pursuit of knowledge and learning by its faculty and student body. The institution achieves highest stature when students not only are exposed to excellent teaching but are themselves stimulated to create or discover knowledge. Faculty should be motivated to see, as their main goal, teaching knowledge and teaching the creation of new knowledge or research. Ideally, faculty should be constantly involved in teaching and research, for they are, in fact, part of the same process of learning. Reappointment, promotion, and tenure policies should recognize the importance of both teaching and research. Recognition should also be given to faculty who devote time in working and consulting with students in activities related to learning.

2) Both parties recognize that teaching competence is one of the criteria utilized in recommendations and decisions pertaining to reappointment, promotion, and tenure. The choice of evidence demonstrating teaching competence shall reside primarily with the various departments as described in their procedures, crite-

ria, standards, and bylaws. Individual bargaining unit members also may forward evidence of their choice if that evidence is not prohibited by departmental procedures, criteria, standards, and bylaws. It is understood that the evidence of teaching competence used in departmental personnel recommendations is subject to the same process of review by the dean and provost as provided for in this Article. Nothing in this paragraph shall require any recommending or decision-making body at the university to ignore student comment with respect to such matters except as noted in Letter of Agreement #1 (student opinion survey). Conversely, nothing in this paragraph shall bind departments to require student evaluations. If student comments are utilized at any level where a recommendation or decision is made, such comments shall be shared with the individual bargaining unit member on a timely basis so as to provide an opportunity for the bargaining unit member to address such comments prior to a decision at each level at which the comments are raised. A failure to provide such comments to bargaining unit members on a timely basis shall be remedied by a review as set forth under paragraph 24 of this Article.

3) FLEXIBILITY IN ASSIGNMENTS

While a number of contracts have tended, often with the encouragement of trustees, board members, and other external constituents, to develop a rather rigid approach to workloads, the Central Michigan agreement recognizes the need for flexibility.

Faculty Workload

1) The workload of bargaining unit members encompasses many professional duties and responsibilities necessary to their varied roles. Faculty have considerable discretion in carrying out their professional duties and responsibilities and will operate within university policies and procedures. These duties and responsibilities normally include but are not limited to:

   a) Teaching, consistent with master syllabi, and/or providing instructional support in a variety of manners and settings

b) Advising and consulting with students

c) Engaging in scholarly and creative activity

d) Supporting the proper and efficient functioning of the department, college, and university as a whole (e.g., performing committee work)

e) Supporting the university and broader academic community through professional or public service related to the bargaining unit member's discipline

2) The department and dean share responsibility for appropriate faculty workloads.

3) With respect to the establishment of appropriate faculty workloads, departmental faculty may, in accordance with the provisions of their department procedures, criteria, standards, and bylaws, make recommendations concerning said workloads. These recommendations may include the definition of a full-time workload and a system of equivalencies for the nonteaching activities.

4) In the development of workload recommendations, the following guidelines apply to teaching faculty:

a) The instructional portion of a faculty member's full-time workload consists of nine (9) to twelve (12) credit hours per semester as determined by the department.

b) Adjustments to her/his instructional workload may be made for various academic purposes, such as curricular or professional development activities, advising responsibilities, and supervision of theses or dissertations, as long as these adjustments are not in violation of university policy or a university commitment to accreditation or professional standards.

5) Adjusted workloads shall be recommended by the department and approved by the dean.

4) FACULTY MENTORING AND GUIDANCE

One of the strengths of the Central Michigan document is the care that is taken to detail the faculty assessment process and the information that should be provided on a regular basis to each faculty member. In addition to supporting a formal mentoring system for new faculty, the contract describes a series of meetings between individual faculty, chairs, and deans to discuss the criteria that are being used for promotion and tenure decisions and the candidate's performance in this context.

Conferences for Assistance to Bargaining Unit Members

1) Once each year, the bargaining unit member's dean shall have an individual conference with the nontenured bargaining unit member (excluding bargaining unit members who have received notification of tenure or nonreappointment or who have resigned). The meeting shall be scheduled by the dean and shall also be attended by the chairperson.

2) The purpose of the meeting is for the dean to review with the bargaining unit member the criteria, standards, and procedures existing at the department, college, and university levels which apply to that bargaining unit member's consideration for reappointment, tenure, or promotion. At the meeting, the chairperson shall review the existing information in the department records and inform the bargaining unit member to what extent he/she is or is not meeting criteria and standards. In addition, the dean shall review the existing information in the office of the dean and inform the bargaining unit member to what extent he/she is or is not meeting the criteria and standards established in conformity with this Agreement.

3) The dean shall inquire at the conference whether the bargaining unit member has any questions regarding criteria and standards or application of criteria and standards pertaining to reappointment, tenure, or promotion consideration for that bargaining unit member. The dean shall furnish to the bargaining unit member a written statement of the extent to which

he/she is meeting the criteria and standards and a summary of questions asked by the bargaining unit member and responses to those questions furnished by the dean. The written statement also will summarize other matters discussed pertaining to the bargaining unit member's performance with regard to the criteria and standards. The bargaining unit member may furnish a statement reflecting an alternative understanding of the content of the meeting.

Conferences for Tenured Bargaining Unit Members

4) Once every three (3) years, the bargaining unit member's dean shall have an individual conference with the tenured bargaining unit member. The meeting shall be scheduled by the dean and shall also be attended by the chairperson.

5) At the meeting, the dean and chairperson shall:

   a) Review the performance and achievements of the tenured bargaining unit member and, if relevant, discuss any serious performance deficiencies which are perceived to exist.

   b) For those seeking promotion or professor salary adjustment, review with the tenured bargaining unit member the criteria, standards, and procedures existing at the department, college, and university levels which apply to the member's consideration for promotion or professor salary adjustment and inform the member to what extent he/she is or is not meeting the standards and criteria established in conformity with this Agreement.

   c) Offer assistance for the member's continuing professional development.

5) ANTICIPATING THE EXPECTED AND UNEXPECTED

Since the university had been developing revised promotion and tenure guidelines at both the institutional and departmental level, the agreement provides options to faculty who find themselves caught in a possible change of criteria and procedures.

Department Procedures, Criteria, Standards, and Bylaws

1) Changes, except in the areas of reappointment, promotion, and tenure, shall take effect upon the approval of the provost.

   Approved changes concerning reappointment, promotion, and tenure shall take effect the next July 1 and will apply as follows:

   a) *Reappointment and tenure.* Two (2) years after the effective date of the approved changes, except that a bargaining unit member may choose to be reviewed under new department standards sooner than the two-year time period. If the bargaining unit member does not expressly elect this option, he/she will be reviewed under department standards that were effective immediately prior to the approved revision. For example, changes in reappointment or tenure standards approved in 1996–97 take effect July 1, 1997 and shall be applied to reappointment or tenure applications in 1999–2000 (unless a bargaining unit member elects to be reviewed under the new standards in 1997–98 or 1998–99).

   b) *Promotion.* One (1) year after the effective date of the approved changes, except that a bargaining unit member may choose to be reviewed under new department standards sooner than the one-year time period. If the bargaining unit member does not expressly elect this option, he/she will be reviewed under department standards that were effective immediately prior to the approved revision. For example, changes in promotion standards approved in 1996–97 take effect July 1, 1997 and shall be applied to promotion application(s) in 1998–99 (unless a bargaining unit member elects to be reviewed under the new standards in 1997–98).

Reappointment, Promotion, and Tenure Policies

1) Under extraordinary circumstances, at the express request of the bargaining unit member who is applying for tenure, additional

nontenured appointments may be granted. Such extensions of the probationary period may not exceed two (2) years and are made only when consistent with the needs of the university and the professional development of the bargaining unit member. Such extraordinary appointments are made only upon the recommendation of the department and with the approval of the dean and the provost.

Central Michigan University is certainly not the only institution that has developed an approach to its negotiated contract that is sensitive to the differences among faculty and disciplines and to the needs of the institution. While a review of over 200 contracts shows that the majority appear to have changed little over the last decade or so, there are a growing number that are including sections that address many of the areas we have discussed. Interestingly, while the language and structure may vary considerably, the goals of the writers and the issues that are being addressed are often identical.

ROLES AND RESPONSIBILITIES

The following are excerpts from a number of contracts from NEA-, AFT-, and AAUP-affiliated institutions. Examples have been selected to address a variety of topics and are from large and small, private and public four-year institutions.

A number of contracts include sections that describe, often in some detail, the expected roles of faculty at the institution and set a context for assessment. Sometimes they are relatively brief, as in the Utica College excerpt, or more in-depth as seen in the University of Montana material. Note the section in the Montana statement dealing with the scholarship of the creative arts.

EXAMPLE: UTICA COLLEGE, AAUP

The evaluation of the professional activities of all employees in a public institution of higher education is essential to the maintenance of academic and professional standards of excellence. The purpose of professional evaluations shall be to encourage the improvement of individual professional performance and to provide a basis for decisions on reappointment, tenure, and promotions. An evaluation of professional activities shall be based on total professional performance. Written evaluation shall be on file for all employees.

Evaluation of a member of the teaching faculty shall be based on total academic performance, with especial attention to teaching effectiveness, including, but not limited to, such elements as:

1) Classroom instruction and related activities

2) Administrative assignments

3) Research

4) Scholarly writing

5) Departmental, college, and university assignments

6) Student guidance

7) Course and curricula development

8) Creative works in individual's discipline

9) Public and professional activities in field of specialty

Teaching observation, as described below, is one factor in total evaluation of academic performance of the teaching staff.

1) At least once during each academic semester, nontenured and noncertified members of the teaching staff shall be observed for a full classroom period. One observation shall take place during any scheduled class during the first ten weeks of a semester. The employee shall be given no less than 24 hours of prior notice of observation.

EXAMPLE: UNIVERSITY OF MONTANA, AFT

The faculty member should have both a depth and breadth of knowledge in his/her chosen field and be able to communicate this knowledge to the students. The faculty member should maintain an active interest in the advances and current thinking in his/her subject and be able to relate such information to his/her teaching in an organized manner through incorporation into course materials.

Moreover, the faculty member should maintain a critical attitude toward his/her teaching and should strive continuously to improve it. Obviously, the faculty member shall avoid persistent intrusion of totally unrelated material into classroom presentations.

The effective teacher feels and exhibits enthusiasm for his/her subject and creates an environment that stimulates imaginative thinking. The faculty member should have a deep interest in the students' progress and welfare, which includes counseling and advising assigned advisees as well as other students on their programs of study and other academic matters, and maintaining a responsible, professional relationship with the students. The faculty member will carefully ensure equal application of class standards and requirements. Faculty shall preserve the records necessary to compute final grades for one academic term.

Each faculty member has obligations and responsibilities to assist in the proper administration of university affairs. It is, therefore, to be expected that he/she will serve on committees, attend university functions, and render public service in the area of his/her professional competence. As a scholar, the person is responsible to the university and to society to keep informed about advances in knowledge and to engage in an active program of research or creative activities as judged by peers. This part of his/her activity, though in general not formally scheduled, is nevertheless essential. In large measure the welfare of society depends on it. Although the artist faculty member may be a scholar, he/she should have the unqualified option of being a productive artist. Creative work in any field, such as literature, music, art, and drama, through its contributions to our cultural life, ranks equally with research and scholarly publications. These functions and responsibilities should not be thought of as mutually exclusive, but as overlapping and complementary. Thus, active participation in the work of learned societies is related to a person's work as both scholar and member of the faculty. Similarly, preparation of papers for publication, which is an example of a person's function as a scholar, may well grow out of his/her work as a teacher.

TEACHING

The importance of teaching in relation to research is a topic that has received a great deal of national attention. As should be expected, the balance between the two varies significantly from one type of institution to another. Park College's contract makes it very clear where the college's priorities lie.

EXAMPLE: PARK COLLEGE, AFT

Faculty members are encouraged to engage in research and to publish the results of such research. However, a faculty member's right to research and to publish the results of such research is specifically conditioned upon the requirement that such activity shall not interfere with the performance of the faculty member's other duties. Research, writing, or publication during the academic year for substantial pecuniary return or involving a reduced work load shall be undertaken only with the prior written authorization by the vice president for academic affairs.

While some institutions still rely primarily on the student rating form to evaluate teaching effectiveness, a growing number are significantly expanding the range of data that are to be collected. In a number of institutions, the statement serves as an excellent method of educating faculty as to the variety of assessment methods that can be used and the range of material they are expected to submit.

EXAMPLE: EASTERN MICHIGAN UNIVERSITY, AAUP

The required and most important criterion is instructional effectiveness. The teaching faculty shall give evidence of ability and commitment to lead students of varying capabilities into a growing understanding of the subject matter, tools, and materials of their disciplines. The faculty member shall demonstrate his/her continuing concern for instructional effectiveness through methods of presentation and evaluation of students. In support of instructional effectiveness, a faculty member must maintain a high level of knowledge and expertise in his/her discipline or area of specialization. In the case of nonteaching and library faculty, satisfactory professional performance shall be the equivalent of instructional effectiveness.

Evaluation techniques for all faculty members include class-room visitation, student evaluations of teaching, department head evaluations, and, where appropriate, assessment of academic advising of students.

All full evaluations (including full professional performance evaluations of tenured faculty) must include classroom visitations by the department head and members of the appropriate departmental committee.

Very few policy statements, however, address the issues of student learning as an aspect of assessing effective teaching. One exception is the reference to helping students think critically and creatively in the following portion from the Shawnee State University document.

EXAMPLE: SHAWNEE STATE UNIVERSITY, NEA

For the purpose of evaluation, teaching effectiveness may be exemplified by the following:

1) Knowledge of the subject matter

2) Ability to clearly communicate course requirements and expectations of students

3) Effectiveness in communicating subject matter by several means or methods such as lecture, discussion, demonstration, laboratory exercise, and practical experience

4) Effectiveness in assisting students in course-related work outside of class

5) Effectiveness in advising students in degree-related matters

6) Ability to help students think critically and creatively

Notice the varying range of detail that is provided in the following segments from the contracts of Eastern Michigan University, Roger Williams University, the South Dakota Board of Regents, Pittsburg State University (Kansas), and Temple University.

EXAMPLE: ROGER WILLIAMS UNIVERSITY, NEA

Assessment of the general capabilities of individual faculty members shall be in relation to his or her specific discipline, program, or duties, and to the needs and interests of the university. This process may involve classroom visitation and is not limited to consultation with faculty members of the program, school, or college; with students in his or her courses; and with any other pertinent individual possessing knowledge of his or her performance. The faculty member, other faculty members in the academic unit, current and/or former students, the dean, and the vice president for academic affairs may generally be consulted for input during the evaluation process.

Excellence in Teaching

Excellence in teaching is the primary criterion for awarding reappointment, promotion, and tenure. Although the university is committed to effective teaching first and foremost, other factors also enter into the evaluation process. These may include, but are not limited to, program development and academic advisement, scholarly and/or creative activities, and institutional and/or community service.

The appropriate dean shall notify the faculty member of the date and time for classroom visitations. The faculty member may advise the dean of any reason the classroom visitation should not take place on such a date and time, which the appropriate dean shall consider. Since the purpose of the dean's classroom visitation is to observe and evaluate the faculty member's performance, the dean will position himself or herself as unobtrusively as possible and will not ordinarily participate in classroom activities unless invited to do so by the faculty member. Within ten (10) working days after the classroom visitation, the appropriate dean shall present a written summary of his or her evaluation of the class session, to which the faculty member may respond in writing within ten (10) working days of receipt and may arrange with the dean for a second classroom visitation. Normally, the dean's visits shall not exceed one (1) visit per course per semester unless by mutual agreement.

The following evaluation criteria will be used:

1) Effective assessment of classroom learning and clear academic standards

2) Ability to stimulate the interest of students, evoke their responses, and involve them in the learning process

3) Continuing development and updating of instructional materials and teaching methods

4) Effective teaching

Effectiveness in Program Development and Academic Advising
The following evaluation criteria will be used:

1) Contributions to curriculum planning and assessment, whether disciplinary or interdisciplinary, departmental, or institutional

2) Development and delivery of mini-courses, workshops, and conferences related to the discipline and other educational programs

3) Responsible and well-informed advisement of assigned advisees, particularly with respect to timely completion of graduation requirements and selection and achievement of educational goals

EXAMPLE: **SOUTH DAKOTA BOARD OF REGENTS, NEA**
A fundamental mission of a university is to provide opportunities for learning and academic achievement. Related to this mission is the professional evaluation of student achievement according to standards of the discipline and university. Thus, all faculty unit members with teaching assignments are expected to demonstrate competence in teaching and in evaluation of student performance; offer consistently challenging and current courses that afford students opportunities to learn the information, methods of inquiry, and professional skills identified in the course descriptions and relevant departmental or program mission statements; instruct and evaluate at levels meeting or exceeding university standards for the discipline; incorporate scholarly activities or findings into their teaching on a regular basis; make available opportunities for stu-

dents to learn of the primary sources of information associated with the area of study; provide students with performance expectations; be regularly available for out-of-class consultation with students; periodically review and revise course content, classroom activities, out-of-class assignments, and evaluation procedures; participate actively in university efforts to implement assessment policies and procedures; be conscientious in advising students assigned to them with respect to the requirements of academic programs and the selection of electives consistent with the student's goals (the student's responsibility for degree and program requirements are understood); and adhere to the university's standards and procedures for ensuring academic integrity.

Teaching includes the following or similar activities, the recognition and importance of which will vary depending upon the mission of the university, the role of a discipline within the university's functions, and the individual faculty unit member's assignment:

Teaching undergraduate courses; advising undergraduate students; teaching graduate courses; advising graduate students; developing and teaching new undergraduate courses; developing and teaching new graduate courses; developing, supervising, and evaluating internships; teaching courses in the honors program; teaching continuing education unit courses; conducting noncredit workshops, institutes, and seminars on campus; conducting noncredit workshops, institutes, and seminars off campus; individual studying; guiding and evaluating undergraduate project papers; guiding and evaluating graduate project papers; guiding and evaluating theses; guiding and evaluating dissertations; serving on graduate committees; experimenting with instructional methods and techniques; developing assessment policies and procedures; preparing proposals for curricular change; and sponsoring field trips that provide meaningful learning experiences for students.

EXAMPLE: PITTSBURG STATE UNIVERSITY, NEA

Teaching refers to the broad area of student/faculty interaction for educational purposes. Generally, a faculty member who excels in teaching is a person who guides and inspires students, maintains scholarship through sustaining breadth and depth of knowledge, contributes to understanding of subject matter, and facilitates the learning of students. A teacher should be able to demonstrate breadth of teaching competence in the content area; graduate committee memberships; theses and special investigations directed; honors courses taught; contributions to course and curriculum development; use and preparation of instructional media (textbooks, laboratory manuals, computer programs, class projects, cases, videotapes, films, slides, transparencies, individual instructional modules, models, mock-ups, etc.); experimental instructional methods and techniques; attendance at institutes and other programs relevant to instruction; and evidence of impact on students (student evaluations, pre- and post-testing results, state board results, certification examination results, job placement, graduate school admissions, GRE, and Miller Analogies results, etc.). Different categories of accomplishments are necessary to adequately reflect library and instructional media faculty activity.

EXAMPLE: TEMPLE UNIVERSITY, AFT

Effective teaching has many manifestations. It comprehends classroom instruction and a broad range of faculty-student relationships. The following are among the traits valued in the teacher: command of subject; familiarity with advances in the field; ability to organize material and to present it with force and logic; capacity to awaken in students an awareness of the relation of the subject to other fields of knowledge; grasp of general objectives; ability to vitalize learning; ability to arouse curiosity toward further and more independent learning; ability to stimulate advanced students to highly creative work; maintaining a sufficiently high standard of achievement; and fairness and judgment in grading. The teacher's personal attributes, such as social graciousness and sense of humor, are also important.

The extent and skill of the faculty member's participation in the general guidance and advising of students and his or her contribution to student welfare are of importance in the appraisal of the teacher's value to the university.

SCHOLARLY, PROFESSIONAL, AND CREATIVE WORK

While most institutions' contracts include sections that list the range of activities that are to be considered appropriate to meet the research/scholarship aspect of faculty work, a growing number are expanding both the range of activities that meet these criteria and the variety of materials that are appropriate for documentation. The following sections from Eastern Michigan University, the South Dakota Board of Regents, Pittsburg State University, and Temple University are examples of this type of expanded description.

Notice in all four statements that scholarship has been expanded to include selected work completed in the context of teaching, service, and the creative and performing arts, recognizing clearly the differences among the disciplines.

EXAMPLE: EASTERN MICHIGAN UNIVERSITY, AAUP

Scholarly and/or Creative Activity
The manner in which each of the scholarly and/or creative activities listed below is counted toward fulfilling the evaluation criteria of each department is governed by its Departmental Evaluation Document.

A faculty member shall give documented evidence of his/her contribution to his/her discipline or area of specialization within the discipline or in an interdisciplinary specialization by scholarly investigation (e.g., research) and/or creative activity, and of its publication or other dissemination in one of the following ways:

1) In the classroom

2) Among practitioners in his/her discipline

3) Among a wider community

It is intended that the faculty member shall utilize his/her expertise to address problems in his/her discipline or area of specialization through research and/or creative activity which clearly contributes to the discipline through:

1) Scholarly investigation, creative activity, and/or research of an original and/or previously unreported nature.

2) Applied research, investigation, or scholarly analysis of existing research, information, and creative endeavors resulting in the development of new data, information, applications, and/or interpretations.

3) In disciplines where practice and tradition include faculty involvement in student research, which is subsequently published or otherwise disseminated, such research shall not be barred from consideration as appropriate scholarly activity, insofar as said faculty involvement is shown to fulfill the expectations in 1) or 2) above.

EXAMPLE: SOUTH DAKOTA BOARD OF REGENTS, NEA

Scholarly, Professional, and Creative Activity
The mission of a university requires of each faculty unit member a serious commitment to scholarship. Scholarship, broadly defined, is a prerequisite for competent and current teaching, contributes to the expansion of knowledge and the development of the arts, and enhances the services provided to the public. Each faculty unit member is expected to continue learning in his or discipline through appropriate journals and books and to participate in the discipline's professional deliberation.

The product of scholarly activity may take a variety of forms, but it cannot be only for the classroom or take place only in the classroom; it also must involve the presentation of one's ideas and works to one's professional peers or the learned public for debate and judgment. Such presentations may occur in a variety of settings, but to be worthy of recognition, it is expected—at a minimum—that a faculty member initiates a proposal to present or be invited to present and that the proposal be accepted for outside presentation to a learned audience.

The recognition and importance of the different forms and presentation of scholarship will vary depending upon the mission of the university, the role of a discipline within the university's functions, and the individual faculty member's assignment. Thus, although scholarship and creative activity include the following and similar activities, not all of these need be recognized or judged to be important or sufficient for each faculty unit member: publication of the results of research, scholarship, and creative endeavor in scholarly journals and books or textbooks; chapters in professional books, abstracts, and book reviews; publication of poems, novels, plays, musical compositions, etc.; exhibition of works of art; musical performance; delivery of invited lectures, papers, speeches, or presentations at other conferences; creative application of existing technologies; patents on inventions; application for research or development grants; presentation of recognized original works to colleagues or the campus community; national recognition as an expert in a field related to the faculty unit member's professional responsibilities; contribution as a coauthor or copresenter of one's own research results to joint research projects involving other professionals.

EXAMPLE: PITTSBURG STATE UNIVERSITY, NEA

Excellence in Research, Scholarship, and/or Creative Endeavor
A member of the faculty who excels in the field of research, scholarship, and/or creative endeavor conducts creative work appropriate to the area of specialization and disseminates such creative work to other colleagues on the Pittsburg State University campus, as well as on other campuses. Persons whose primary strength is in the field of scholarly activity may find that such activity manifests itself as much in the work of students as through their own direct efforts. Criteria in this category will consist of demonstrable activity in such areas as publications (papers, monographs, textbooks, book reviews, abstracts, etc.); production, exhibition, or performances of creative works; lectures, papers, speeches presented at meetings or other educational institutions; attendance at institutes, short courses, or seminars related to the faculty member's discipline; grants and awards received; evidence of national or international recognition; and current research, scholarly activity, and/or creative endeavor projects in progress. The emphasis in this category

is in the presentation of data that will substantiate the continuing scholarship of the faculty member in a particular discipline.

Scholarship and Creative Work

1) ***Research and publication.*** In most of the fields represented in the program of the university, publications in media of quality are expected as evidence of scholarly interest. Quality of production is more important than quantity. Each of the following is valued according to its quality and significance: scholarly books, textbooks, reviews, reports, articles in scholarly and professional journals, and participation in projects of scholarly interest.

2) ***Works of art.*** In certain fields, such as art, music, and literature, distinguished creation receives consideration equivalent to distinction attained in research. Public recognition as reflected in professional awards; the assignment of unusual tasks and commissions; the acceptance of the faculty member's work in permanent collections or its publication in leading professional journals; invitations to participate in significant exhibits; and any other public honor on the local, national, or international science are valued.

3) ***Professional recognition.*** Demonstrated professional distinction is recognized as a criterion for promotion. In certain areas, such as drama and speech, distinguished performance is considered. The faculty member's record is scrutinized for evidence of achievement, leadership, and the development of new ideas.

SERVICE

Another area that has received increased attention over the last decade is service: the support that faculty provide to the institution, the community, and their profession. The two examples that follow vary considerably in length but clearly identify the importance of the faculty's service role. The statement from the South Dakota Board of Regents clearly reflects not only the scope of service activities that faculty can and should be involved in, but also the importance of these contributions in the context of being a faculty member at a public institution.

EXAMPLE: PITTSBURG STATE UNIVERSITY, NEA

A faculty member whose contribution to the university is in the field of service should be productive in any one or a combination of the following: institutional service or professional service. The service must be performed because of competencies relevant to the faculty member's role at the university. Service provided through an ad, vocational interest, or associated with special talents not related to the university appointment would not be considered. Excellence may be achieved by displaying leadership concerning academic and other university affairs through counseling and advising of students in academic matters and personal problems. Faculty members may participate broadly in continuing education programs by teaching in noncredit courses or planning and leading workshops, seminars, and discussion groups. Outstanding public service contributions may be made by helping to implement regional community service and other types of field services. A significant contribution may be as an officer of a professional, technical, or scholarly society at the state or national level. The faculty member may also be highly regarded as a consultant to government and industry on technical matters. In all service categories, evidence must be presented to substantiate the quality and quantity of the service provided.

EXAMPLE: SOUTH DAKOTA BOARD OF REGENTS, NEA

Scholars have special insights and abilities to contribute to the deliberative processes through which universities, professions, and society as a whole respond to their changing circumstances. The public support for the universities gives rise to significant service responsibilities to the state society. By tradition, the professoriate has contributed to meeting such expectations of public service and has assisted in the governance and operation of universities and of professional groups.

There are three aspects of service: service to the department, college, school, or institution; service to the profession or discipline;

and service to the community, state, region, nation, or international community.

A variety of activities are classified as service. The needs of the institution and the expertise of faculty members may require that faculty members concentrate efforts in certain service areas to the exclusion of activity in other service areas.

The recognition and importance of the different forms of service will vary depending upon the mission of the university, the role of a discipline within the university's functions, and the individual faculty member's assignment. Thus, although service includes the following, or similar, activities, not all of these need to be recognized or judged to be important or sufficient for each faculty member.

Service to the Institution

All faculty members are expected to be willing to participate in the academic governance of their universities, to contribute to the work of departmental committees or task forces, and to participate in searches for new members of the department.

Service to the institution also includes the following, or similar, activities: significant work for departmental, school, college, and university committees; service on the academic senate and its committees; significant responsibilities relating to the academic or support services of the university community; contributions to the development of library or other learning resources; institutional studies, library, or other learning resources; institutional studies or reports, such as those required by accrediting organizations; coordination, advisement, and supervision of student organizations or student activities; and participation in institutionally sponsored student support activities.

Service to the Discipline or Profession

Service to the discipline or profession includes the following, or similar, activities; significant contributions as an officer of local, regional, national, or international professional associations; participation in meetings, conferences, and conventions of professional associations; editing professional journals; evaluating manuscripts that have been submitted to a journal; reviewing proposals for textbooks in one's field of specialization for a publisher; serving as an organizer or session chairperson of a meeting of a local, regional, national, or international professional association; supporting special projects, including academic institutes or workshops.

Service to the Community, State, Region, Nation, and World
The mission statement adopted by the board of regents directs each university to perform public service. Significant faculty activity that contributes to the institution's performance of its service mission includes the following or similar activities: discipline-related service to the community, state, region, nation, or international community; institutes, short courses, seminars, and workshops related to the faculty member's discipline; consultation related to the faculty member's discipline; service as the designated representative of the university, or professional practice involving the exercise of independent professional judgment.

INSTITUTIONAL AUTONOMY

The South Dakota document also includes a policy statement that addresses the degree of freedom of priorities given to individual institutions working within a state system. Notice, however, that consistency is required between priorities and programs of each institution and its mission as defined at the state level.

EXAMPLE: **SOUTH DAKOTA BOARD OF REGENTS, NEA**

Institutional Selection of Activities
The universities have substantial autonomy to select and determine the relative importance of various activities in the areas of teaching, scholarship, and creative activity, and service.

Faculty unit members have a legitimate interest in knowing which professional activities are to be recognized and their university's determinations of the relative importance of the recognized activities. To that end:

1) Each university shall select the teaching, scholarship, and service activities, consistent with those activities and principles

identified herein, that are to be recognized in the evaluation and promotion processes.

2) Each university shall determine the relative importance of the three areas of professional activity and the relative importance of selected activities within each category.

3) The university's selections shall be consistent with the mission and programs of the university as approved by the board.

4) The selection of activities and the relative importance of the activities may vary within a university and across the system.

5) The university's selection shall be consistent with the guarantee of academic freedom as provided to faculty members.

NONTRADITIONAL APPOINTMENTS

There are occasions when faculty with nontraditional backgrounds are hired because they bring exceptional talents to the institution. Other faculty may be hired to serve a nontraditional role that will not provide opportunities to do scholarly work.

EXAMPLE: ROGER WILLIAMS UNIVERSITY, NEA

Exceptional Appointments and Promotions
Nothing in this agreement should be construed to prohibit the appointment or promotion by the president of an individual of exceptional talent or accomplishment who does not meet all the stated criteria. In considering candidates for exceptional appointment or promotions, the president of the university shall consider facts including, but not limited to: a) evidence of the ability of the candidate to render a unique academic contribution to the university; b) evidence of a candidate's extraordinary competence in the area of his or her discipline or specialty if the candidate's discipline or specialty does not customarily demand fulfillment of those academic degree requirements set forth as minimum criteria for appointment or promotion to each rank.

Written policies should also address how the individual will be judged for promotion and tenure.

EXAMPLE: SHAWNEE STATE UNIVERSITY, NEA

If a faculty search committee selects a finalist for a faculty position who does not meet all initial criteria for that position, the dean— in consultation with the search committee—may recommend that individuals be hired with specific conditions to be placed on his/her contract, such as completion of the terminal degrees by a specified date. Said conditions of employment shall remain continuous and binding unless officially removed by the provost and approved by the president and board of trustees. Any condition shall be in- cluded on the Worksheet Summary for the candidate. If that can- didate is recommended by the provost and the president and ap- proved by the board of trustees, only those conditions recom- mended by the committee shall become part of the conditional contracts issued to that faculty member.

FLEXIBILITY

In earlier chapters, we discussed the need to have in place a policy for providing some degree of flexibility when the situation requires it. One such area is the ability to stop or modify the clock in the tenure and promotion process. While the following statement from the University of Hawaii addresses this issue to a point, it does not cover what options exist when faculty members are given an assignment (a major project, a term as department chair, etc.) that would not allow them to complete their scholarly work within the traditional timeline.

EXAMPLE: THE UNIVERSITY OF HAWAII, NEA

The probationary period may be interrupted during periods when the faculty member does not hold a full-time contract or is on leave without pay. If the faculty member signs a contract for a po- sition in which less than 100% of the funds come from the general revenues of the state, or less than 100% from funds deemed by the employer to be assured for an indefinite period, the probationary period may also be interrupted. However, if the faculty member's probationary period has begun, and the faculty member is transferred by the administrative head to a position for which less than 100% come from state funds, the faculty member shall continue to accrue probationary credit for services. By specific written agreement, the faculty member and the employer may agree that periods when the faculty member is on leave without pay or is serving under contract for a position for which less than 100% of the funds come from state funds or from funds deemed by the employer to be assured for an indefinite period will count toward the probationary period.

It is also extremely useful if the contract encourages and provides guidelines for flexibility in the specific assignments given to faculty and strategies for dealing with their assessment based on changes that may occur.

EXAMPLE: SOUTH DAKOTA BOARD OF REGENTS, NEA

. . . the faculty unit member and department head will discuss what, consistent with institutional policies and subject to the concurrence of the dean and vice president, the department expects the faculty unit member to do with respect to teaching and academic advising; research, scholarship, or creative activity; and service. Such discussion will be repeated whenever a significant change in workload is anticipated. In the event of a disagreement in the percentages, either the faculty member or his/her department head may consult departmental peer groups established by Commission on Higher Education (COHE) in an attempt to resolve the differences. In the event that such differences are unresolved, the academic dean shall unilaterally assign responsibilities to the faculty member.

EXAMPLE: PITTSBURG STATE UNIVERSITY, NEA

The following segment from the Pittsburg State University document is an excellent example of placing the policies and procedures into an institutional context.

Pittsburg State University is committed to facilitating high levels of faculty achievement in teaching, scholarly activity, and service.

As in any institution, levels of achievement of faculty competencies vary within the diverse components that make up the university. It is a difficult but not impossible task to attain equal levels of high achievement in all areas simultaneously. It is more realistic to find high levels of achievement in some combination of teaching, scholarly activity, and service.

The particular combination varies from one individual to the next and is recognized as being a blend of personal choice and university needs. No matter what level of achievement is attained in any one area, satisfactory performance is the norm for all three.

The appraisal of teaching, scholarly activity, and/or service tasks can be placed on a continuum from unsatisfactory to highly satisfactory. Quite often, it is difficult to quantify such judgments. In order to provide faculty with some specific guidelines as to what would be considered an acceptable level of accomplishment for any one year, a number of variables must be taken into consideration: interests, expertise, and the desires of the faculty member; goals and objectives of the department; and needs of the department as perceived by the department chairperson after consultation with the department as a whole. Furthermore, departmental standards of performance should be consistent with other departments of the school/college. These variables are relevant to the criteria upon which an appraisal of the performance of the faculty member would be based. The degree to which accomplishments are achieved represents the qualitative aspect of the performance appraisal process. Since individual goals and objectives provide the primary basis of the faculty's evaluation, and since interdepartmental consistency provides the secondary basis of the faculty's evaluation, there should be a clear understanding on both the part of the faculty and the department chairperson and the school/college dean concerning the qualitative and quantitative aspects of expected accomplishments.

Achievement is relative to the objectives stated, the tasks performed, and the individual whose performance is being appraised. The degree of achievement is a matter of judgment based upon the statement of objectives, the annual report of accomplishments, and other information available to the department chairperson.

REVIEWS AND MENTORING

Union contracts can also be extremely helpful in describing the faculty review process and any follow-up procedure that may be in place. This section can address both pre- and post-tenure reviews and can be instrumental in establishing a formal mentoring system for the institution.

EXAMPLE: EASTERN MICHIGAN UNIVERSITY, AAUP

In a faculty member's first year of employment at EMU, no annual activity report is required. His/her interim evaluation during that year shall be conducted using information obtained through classroom visits, review of instructional materials, and discussion with the department head and the appropriate departmental committee, and it shall focus primarily on instructional effectiveness.

In other interim-evaluation years and following receipt of the faculty member's annual activity report, the department head and appropriate departmental committee shall meet with the faculty member to discuss his/her instructional and service activities and review the results of the required evaluation techniques of instructional effectiveness. They shall include in their discussions a review of the faculty member's performance where improvement might reasonably be expected by the time the faculty member undergoes a full evaluation. If the faculty member requests, the evaluators may give some indication as to whether or not his/her scholarly/creative activity is developing in a way that is appropriate for the department's standards.

EXAMPLE: SHAWNEE STATE UNIVERSITY, NEA

A full-service faculty member in the continuing contract process shall be assigned a departmental mentoring committee prior to or within his/her second year of service. The committee will be comprised of the candidate's dean and two faculty members in the person's respective area or related areas who have achieved continuing contract status. Faculty will be requested to serve as volunteer mentors. If there are no volunteers, the chair/dean of that department/college shall appoint the mentors. All existing faculty not holding continuing contracts with more than three years of service may elect to have a mentoring committee appointed.

This committee shall initially review the candidate's progress toward continuing contract status and shall inform the candidate and the continuing contract committee in writing of the results of the review. The dean shall have the option of making specific comments and/or recommendations.

POST-TENURE REVIEW

Post-tenure review has received increased attention over the last few years. Ideally, it should be perceived as one element in a continuum of faculty development, a process that includes review and career development and support.

EXAMPLE: PORTLAND STATE UNIVERSITY, AAUP

Institutional Career Support-Peer Review

Preamble. Recognizing the traditional and current importance of tenure as protection of the exercise of academic freedom, and recognizing the importance of competent teaching, research, and community service, the following Institutional Career Support-Peer Review plans have been agreed upon.

Objectives. The intent of the Institutional Career Support-Peer Review process is to promote and sustain high standards of performance and professional development for all unit members holding tenured positions at Portland State University, regardless of their particular function.

The following are specific purposes addressed by this plan.

1) To provide a positive and systematic process for career review and development planning, involving the member and a supportive group of peers.

2) To provide institutional support for the realization of a mutually agreed upon professional development plan. The career review and plan will center on the individual's particular past and desired future contributions to the member's academic unit.

3) To assure a balance between the personal commitment to specific goals on the part of the member, the institutional support necessary to help achieve these professional goals, and the goals of the relevant department as formulated by its faculty.

EXAMPLE: **EASTERN WASHINGTON UNIVERSITY, NEA**

Career Development Plans

After an individual receives tenure and throughout his/her career, the individual faculty member and the department will develop a mutually agreed upon career development plan. This plan will focus on the continued professional growth of the faculty member and the desired future contributions to the member's academic unit. The career development plan for tenured faculty is for goal-setting purposes and remains within the department, with the dean receiving a copy for informational purposes only.

Every five years, each faculty member will participate in a regular career support-peer review of their career development plans. The sole purpose of this review is to provide a positive and systematic procedure for faculty development in the context of the department plan. This review will consist of the faculty member and a group of peers from the department and may include faculty members from other departments in the university at the discretion of the faculty member and department.

Career support-peer review shall not be used in making promotion, disciplinary, or dismissal decisions.

WHAT TO INCLUDE IN THE PROFESSIONAL PORTFOLIO

A well-designed document can also help set institutional standards as to what should be included in the materials that a faculty member forwards to promotion and tenure committees (his or her professional portfolio). The following excerpt from the Eastern Michigan University contract does a fine job of describing the significant role the narrative statement can play in helping the candidate articulate what has been included and how—according to the candidate—these materials meet the criteria that have been established.

EXAMPLE: EASTERN MICHIGAN UNIVERSITY, AAUP

It is the responsibility of each faculty member to document in clear and explicit terms both the quantity and quality of his/her activities. An application for evaluation shall include a narrative statement for each evaluation criterion explaining how and to what extent the activities claimed have met the standards set forth in the departmental evaluation document and the term of this agreement, or where, if applicable, they have exceeded those requirements.

For example, a given departmental evaluation document may specify that a faculty member's participation in meetings of professional societies, or regional or local subgroups of which societies, will serve as a valid category/type of activity which may be cited in support of the faculty member's application for promotion. Such participation alone, however, does not relieve the faculty member of the burden of providing documented evidence detailing in clear and explicit terms in what specific respects his/her participation in such activity contributed to his/her discipline or area of specialization, or satisfies such other criteria for which it is offered. EMU and the association intend to stress particularly the requirement that each evaluation candidate must, in his/her claims of scholarly and/or creative activity, explain in clear and explicit terms precisely how, why, and to what extent each of the cited activities has contributed to the discipline or area of specialization and otherwise fulfills the scholarly/creative activity criterion of his/her evaluation document and the terms of this agreement, or where, if applicable, they have exceeded those requirements.

In those instances where a faculty member has cited activities which appear in refereed journals, are published by reputable sources, or are presented in a clearly refereed format, reference to these activities and inclusion of copies of these materials (where feasible) shall be deemed to satisfy the documentation requirement.

If dissemination of scholarly/creative activity is via the classroom, the faculty member shall provide a narrative statement which establishes specifically how the scholarly/creative activity and/or its results have changed/improved the course content, the instructional methodology, and/or the overall teaching-learning process.

EXAMPLE: THE UNIVERSITY OF MONTANA SYSTEM, AFT

The following excerpt from the Montana University System agreement addresses the contents of the document within the area of teaching and the role of the faculty member in defining what specific matters should be included.

> In each case, it shall be the responsibility of the individual to identify his/her positive contributions to the college. Individuals will be evaluated only within the scope of their assignment and in light of resources and opportunities available to them. Since the primary mission of the college is instruction, effective teaching must be positively evaluated in every case, and each evaluation must include contributions in at least one other area. Each evaluation must include indications of professional growth and development since the previous evaluation.
>
> Effective classroom teaching must be a criterion in every personnel evaluation. Effective teaching encompasses both mastery of appropriate bodies of knowledge and communication of that knowledge to students. Demonstration of effective classroom teaching may include, but is not limited to, such means as peer observations and student evaluations. It is the responsibility of the persons evaluated to determine the most appropriate means of documenting effective classroom teaching.
>
> It is recognized that quality teaching and ongoing professional development are interdependent. Indications of professional growth and development since the previous evaluation must be included in each evaluation. Professional growth and development includes, but is not limited to, active involvement in professional organizations, involvement with industry, attendance at professional conferences or seminars, continued formal education, independent reading, etc.

CONCLUSION

If written with care, the union contract can play a major role in the development of a fair and appropriate faculty reward system. It cannot only help an institution reach its goals, but it can also—in its sensitivity to individuals and the disciplines—help improve the quality of faculty lives and the quality of the institution and its programs.

A quality contract of this nature does not happen by chance. It requires a talented and committed negotiation team that works to develop a statement that supports both the institution and the individuals it covers, a document that facilitates positive change, a statement that promotes cooperation and community.

It also requires that the writers of the document be composed of the widest possible group of constituents and that the development of the document be fair and open. It requires that the negotiators take the time to be sensitive to the climate that the contract will produce and to review the range of issues that should be addressed. Figure 6.1 is a checklist listing the topics that should be considered if a quality promotion, tenure, and merit pay system is to exist.

FIGURE 6.1

UNION CONTRACT CHECKLIST
Promotion and Tenure: Elements to Consider Including

(Note: Some elements may be covered by other policy statements)

Relationship of the faculty reward system to the mission of the institution

Recognition of the differences among departments and disciplines

Recognition of individual strengths of faculty

The active involvement of faculty in the development of institutional, school/college, and departmental guidelines

The establishment of a faculty mentoring program

The ability to stop or modify the tenure clock based on individual assignments and needs

The preparation of faculty serving on promotion and tenure committees

The education of faculty preparing for promotion and tenure

Guidelines for documentation

> The range of materials that can be included to document effective teaching and advising

> The range of materials that can be included to document service

Criteria that will be used to determine scholarly, creative, and professional work

> Examples of the range of activities that can meet these criteria

The use of a narrative statement to provide structure, sequence, and retrieval to the documentation.

Options for nontraditional appointments.

ANNOTATED BIBLIOGRAPHY: PROMOTION AND TENURE RESOURCES

Arreola, R. A. (1995). *Developing a comprehensive faculty evaluation system: A handbook for college faculty and administrators on designing and operating a comprehensive faculty evaluation system.* Bolton, MA: Anker.

A practical handbook of protocols, worksheets, and assessment instruments that can be used in developing a faculty evaluation system. Also includes a number of case studies and a formula for determining merit pay.

Boyer, E. L. (1990). *Scholarship reconsidered: Priorities for the professoriate.* Princeton, NJ: Carnegie Foundation for the Advancement of Teaching.

An ideal introduction to rethinking the definition of scholarly or professional work. This work has provided a basis for much of the change in thinking about scholarship at colleges and universities. An excellent volume for launching campus discussion.

Braskamp, L. A., & Ory, J. C. (1994). *Assessing faculty work.* San Francisco, CA: Jossey-Bass.

Describes the expanding role of faculty assessment and limitations of present practices and discusses how assessment can be used to improve the quality of teaching and learning. A discussion of the scholarly nature of faculty work is followed by useful sections on relating institutional expectations to assessment and on collecting and organizing evidence of teaching effectiveness.

Centra, J. A. (1994). *Reflective faculty evaluation.* San Francisco, CA: Jossey-Bass.

An extension of his 1979 publication on determining faculty effectiveness, with a significant addition in the area of teaching portfolios, self-reporting, and the role of colleagues and department chairs in teaching evaluation. Includes an in-depth review of specific techniques and sources of information.

Centra, J. A, Froh, R. C., Gray, P., & Lambert, L. M. (1987). *A guide to evaluating teaching for promotion and tenure.* Syracuse, NY: Center for Instructional Development, Syracuse University.

A practical guide that discusses what should be evaluated to assess teaching effectiveness. Sources of information are discussed, and various data collection techniques are described. Examples are provided, along with the advantages and limitations of the various approaches.

Chait, R., & Trower, C. A. (1997). *Where tenure does not reign: Colleges with contract systems.* Washington, DC: American Association for Higher Education.

Provides an overview of institutions that are using alternate forms of faculty contracts with a discussion of policy implications and impact.

Diamond, R. M. (1999). *Aligning faculty rewards with institutional mission: Statements, policies, and guidelines.* Bolton, MA: Anker.

A practical guide to what should be included in institutional, school/college, and departmental promotion and tenure guidelines and union contracts. Addresses the issues of institutional mission and vision statements. Examples from numerous institutions throughout.

Diamond, R. M. (1994). *Serving on promotion and tenure committees: A faculty guide*. Bolton, MA: Anker.

A handbook for faculty serving on promotion and tenure committees. This guide outlines problem cases and provides committees with procedural recommendations designed to make the process fair to the candidate and easier on the committee.

Diamond, R. M. (1995). *Preparing for promotion and tenure review: A faculty guide*. Bolton, MA: Anker.

Designed to help faculty prepare for promotion and tenure review. Makes recommendations about questions to ask and the materials to provide. Includes a number of illustrative examples on preparing and documentation.

Diamond, R. M., & Adam, B. E. (Eds.). (1995). *The disciplines speak: Rewarding the scholarly, professional and creative work of faculty.* Washington, DC: American Association for Higher Education.

Includes statements from 14 scholarly and disciplinary associations describing the range of faculty work in their fields. A second volume will be published in 1999.

Diamond, R. M., & Adam, B. E. (1993). *Recognizing faculty work: Reward systems for the year 2000.* New Directions in Higher Education, 81. San Francisco, CA: Jossey-Bass.

Provides a model for relating the faculty reward system to institutional priorities as they are enacted at the level of the academic unit. Includes a number of campus case studies and discusses intrinsic rewards and the professional portfolio.

Edgerton, R., Hutchings, P., & Quinlan, K. (1991). *The teaching portfolio: Capturing the scholarship in teaching.* Washington, DC: American Association for Higher Education.

Provides a rationale for the teaching portfolio and discusses documents that might be presented. Includes examples of teaching-related materials and reflective statements and discusses the process of getting started in the use of this approach to documenting teaching.

Elman, S. E., & Smock S. M. (1985). *Professional service and faculty rewards: Toward an integrated structure.* Washington, DC: National Association of State Universities and Land-Grant Colleges.

Addresses issues related to recognizing professional service in the faculty reward system. Provides a rationale for including this work in the recognition system and describes the range of faculty activities that fall in this area.

Glassick, C. E., Huber, M. T., & Maeroff, G. I. (1997). *Scholarship assessed: Evaluating the professoriate.* San Francisco, CA: Jossey-Bass.

This follow up to Ernest Boyer's *Scholarship Reconsidered* focuses on definitions and documentation of scholarship. Includes results from the 1994 survey on institutional changes in the faculty reward system.

Hutchings, P. (1993). *Campus use of the teaching portfolio: Twenty-five profiles.* Washington, DC: American Association for Higher Education.

Detailed accounts of what 25 campuses are doing with teaching portfolios. Each profile answers a common set of questions, including what the portfolio consists of, how it is evaluated, and the impact the process has had on teaching and learning. Includes public and private institutions of various sizes and missions.

Licata, C. M., & Morreale, J. C. (1997). *Post-tenure review: Policies, practices, precautions.* Washington, DC: American Association for Higher Education.

An excellent introduction to the topic. Includes a number of specific case studies and a set of useful recommendations.

Lynton, E. A. (1995). *Making the case for professional service.* Washington, DC: American Association for Higher Education.

Discusses the importance of professional service and describes how and under what conditions this work should be considered scholarly. Five case studies are included.

Morreale, J. C., & Licata, C. M. (1997). *Post-tenure review: A guidebook for academic administrators of colleges and schools of business.* St. Louis, MO: AACSB.

While this work focuses on schools of business and management, much of its contents would be useful to any institution developing a post-tenure review system.

National Education Association. *Entering the profession: Advice for the untenured.* (1994). Washington, DC: National Education Association.

Designed for faculty on unionized campuses, this guidebook pays particular attention to the formal appeal process. (Single copies available at no cost from the NEA.)

Seldin, P. (1997). *The teaching portfolio: A practical guide to improved performance and promotion/tenure decisions* (2nd ed.). Bolton, MA: Anker.

This faculty guide describes a rationale for the use of a teaching portfolio and provides detailed recommendations for assembling such a dossier. Includes a number of representative samples.

Seldin, P., & Associates. (1990). *How administrators can improve teaching.* San Francisco, CA: Jossey-Bass.

Thirteen nationally prominent educators talk about improving teaching by developing institutional policies and practices that support and reward good teaching.

Tierney, W. G., & Rhodes, R. A. (1993). *Enhancing promotion, tenure, and beyond: Faculty socialization as a cultural process.* ASHE-ERIC Higher Education Report Volume 22, No. 6. Washington, DC: The George Washington University.

Discusses how faculty values are shaped and how these values are reflected in faculty roles. Discusses promotion and tenure as part of a socialization process.

Wergin, J. F. (1994). *The collaborative department: How five campuses are inching toward cultures of collective responsibility.* Washington, DC: American Association for Higher Education.

Includes five detailed cases illustrating different approaches to shifting the focus of incentives and rewards from the individual faculty member to the department. Pulls together central issues that the five institutions (Kent State, Rochester Institute of Technology, Syracuse University, University of California, Berkeley, University of Wisconsin, Madison) confront about collective responsibility.

Whicker, M. L., Kronenfeld, J. J., & Strickland, R. A. (1993). *Getting tenure.* Newbury Park, CA: Sage Publications.

Traces the steps in the traditional promotion and tenure process. The authors emphasize the politics of promotion and tenure.

REFERENCES

American Historical Association Task Force to Redefine Scholarly Work. (1992, November). *Redefining scholarly work*, draft report. Washington, DC: American Historical Association.

Arizona Board of Regents. (1997). *Governance in action*. Phoenix, AZ: Arizona Board of Regents.

Arizona Board of Regents. (1997, May 30). *Charters, missions, and mandates: Historical context for discussion of faculty workload at Arizona's public universities*. Board meeting.

Boyer, E. (1987). *College: The undergraduate experience in America*. New York, NY: HarperCollins.

Boyer, E. (1990). *Scholarship reconsidered: Priorities of the professoriate*. Princeton, NJ: Carnegie Foundation for the Advancement of Teaching.

Boyer, E. (1994, January). *Scholarship assessed*. Delivered at the AAHE Faculty Roles and Rewards Forum. New Orleans, LA.

Caret, R. L. (1993, September). *The role of the faculty at Towson State University*. Address to the senate. Towson, MD: Towson State University.

Diamond, R. M. (1994). *Serving on promotion and tenure committees: A faculty guide*. Bolton, MA: Anker.

Diamond, R. M. (1995). *Preparing for promotion and tenure review: A faculty guide.* Bolton, MA: Anker.

Diamond, R. M., & Adam, B. E. (1993). *Recognizing faculty work: Reward system for the year 2000.* San Francisco, CA: Jossey-Bass.

Diamond, R. M., & Adam, B. E. (1996). *Syracuse University revisited, 1991-1996.* Syracuse, NY: The Center for Instructional Development, Syracuse University.

Diamond, R. M., & Adam B. E. (1997). *Changing priorities at research universities (1991-1996).* Syracuse, NY: The Center for Instructional Development, Syracuse University.

Edgerton, R. (1992, September). AAHE's new Forum on Faculty Roles and Rewards launches its first conference. *AAHE Bulletin, 45* (1), 14-15.

Edgerton, R. (1993, July/August). The reexamination of faculty priorities. *Change.* 10–25.

Florida Board of Regents. (1995, May 16). *Tenure recommendations.* Tallahassee, FL: Florida Board of Regents.

Glassick, C., Huber, M. T., & Maeroff, G. (1997). *Scholarship assessed: Evaluation of the professoriate.* San Francisco, CA: Jossey-Bass.

Gray, P., Diamond R. M., & Adam, B. E. (1996). *A national study on the relative importance of research and undergraduate teaching at colleges and universities.* Syracuse, NY: Center for Instructional Development, Syracuse University.

Gray, P., Froh, B., & Diamond, R. M. (1992). *A national study of research universities on the balance between research and undergraduate teaching.* Syracuse, NY: The Center for Instructional Development, Syracuse University.

Hope, S. (1992). *Assessing faculty work: Administrative issues.* Conference paper. Syracuse, NY.

Howery, C. (1997, Summer). Presentation at the Minnowbrook Conference on Institutional Priorities and Faculty Rewards. Blue Mountain Lake, NY.

Kotter, J. P. (1996). *Leading change.* Cambridge, MA: Harvard Business School Press.

Kouzes, J. M., & Posner, B. Z. (1995). *The leadership challenge.* San Francisco, CA: Jossey-Bass.

Laidlaw, W. (1992). *Defining scholarly work in management education,* draft report. St. Louis, MO: American Assembly of Collegiate Schools of Business.

Oregon State Board of Higher Education Committee on Academic Productivity. (1993, October). *Academic responsibilities and productivity.* Salem, OR: Oregon State Board of Higher Education.

Pister, C. (1991, June). *The Pister report: The report of a university-wide task force on faculty rewards.* Santa Cruz, CA: The University of California.

Portland State University. (1995, January 25). *Redefining scholarship for the college of liberal arts and sciences.* Portland, OR: Portland State University.

Rice, E. R. (1991, January). The new American scholar: Scholarship and the purposes of the university. *Metropolitan Universities Journal, 1* (4), 7-18.

Shaw, K. (1992, February 17). *Restructuring Syracuse University.* Report to the university. Syracuse, NY: Syracuse University.

Tierney, W. G., & Bensimon, E. M. (1996). *Promotion and tenure: Community and socialization in academe.* Albany, NY: State University of New York Press.

University of Guelph. (1995). *The final report of the strategic planning commission.* Guelph, Ontario: University of Guelph.

University of Memphis, Task Force on Faculty Roles and Rewards. (1995, January 31). *Report of the task force on faculty roles and rewards.* Memphis, TN: The University of Memphis.

Weiser, C. J. (1998, October). *The value system of a university: Rethinking scholarship.* Handout, Scholarship Unbound workshop.

INDEX

MCSD
Self-Paced Training Kit

ANALYZING REQUIREMENTS AND DEFINING
MICROSOFT® .NET
SOLUTION ARCHITECTURES

Exam 70-300

PUBLISHED BY
Microsoft Press
A Division of Microsoft Corporation
One Microsoft Way
Redmond, Washington 98052-6399

Library of Congress Cataloging-in-Publication Data pending.

Printed and bound in the United States of America.

1 2 3 4 5 6 7 8 9   QWT   8 7 6 5 4 3

Distributed in Canada by H.B. Fenn and Company Ltd.

A CIP catalogue record for this book is available from the British Library.

Microsoft Press books are available through booksellers and distributors worldwide. For further information about international editions, contact your local Microsoft Corporation office or contact Microsoft Press International directly at fax (425) 936-7329. Visit our Web site at www.microsoft.com/mspress. Send comments to *tkinput@microsoft.com*.

Acquisitions Editor: Kathy Harding
Project Editor: Karen Szall

Body Part No. X09-35331

Contents

About This Book

Welcome to *MCSD Self-Paced Training Kit: Analyzing Requirements and Defining Microsoft .NET Solution Architectures*, Exam 70-300. By completing the chapters and the associated activities in this course, you will acquire the knowledge and skills necessary to prepare for the Microsoft Certified Solution Developer (MCSD) Exam 70-300. This self-paced course provides content that supports the skills measured by this exam. Answer the questions at the end of each chapter to review what you have learned and help you prepare more thoroughly. The course also includes solution documents that provide you with examples of the outputs of each phase in the Microsoft Solutions Framework (MSF) development process.

Note   For more information about becoming a Microsoft Certified Professional, see the section titled "The Microsoft Certified Professional Program" later in this introduction.

Each chapter in this book is divided into lessons. Most lessons include hands-on procedures that allow you to practice or demonstrate a particular concept or skill. Each chapter ends with a short summary of all chapter lessons and a set of review questions to test your knowledge of the chapter material.

The "Getting Started" section of this introduction provides important setup instructions that describe the hardware and software requirements to complete the procedures in this course. It also provides information about the networking configuration necessary to complete some of the hands-on procedures. Read through this section thoroughly before you start the lessons.

Intended Audience

This book was developed for information technology (IT) professionals who plan to take the related Microsoft Certified Professional exam 70-300, Analyzing Requirements and Defining Microsoft .NET Solution Architectures, as well as IT professionals who design, develop, and implement software solutions for Microsoft Windows–based environments using Microsoft tools and technologies.

Prerequisites

This training kit requires that students meet the following prerequisites:

- A general understanding of the software development life cycle.
- Practical working knowledge of Microsoft .NET development technologies.
- Familiarity with the MSF Process Model.
- Basic familiarity with object modeling and data modeling methodologies.
- Experience working with Microsoft Visio Professional 2000.
- One year experience as part of a software development team.

Reference Materials

You might find the following reference materials useful:

- MSF Process Model white paper on the Microsoft Solutions Framework Web site at *http://www.microsoft.com/msf/*
- Unified Modeling Language (UML) modeling techniques from the following resources:
  - Booch, Grady, Ivar Jacobson, and James Rumbaugh. *The Unified Modeling Language User Guide* (Addison-Wesley, 1999)
  - Rosenberg, Doug, with Kendall Scott. *Use Case Driven Object Modeling with UML: A Practical Approach* (Addison-Wesley, 1999)

About the CD-ROM

For your use, this book includes a Supplemental Course Materials CD-ROM. This CD-ROM contains a variety of informational aids to complement the book content:

- An electronic version of this book (eBook). For information about using the eBook, see the section "Setup Instructions" later in this introduction.
- Files you will need to perform the hands-on procedures. Also included are sample solution documents.
- A practice test that contains 100 questions. Use the questions to practice taking a certification exam and to help you assess your understanding of the concepts presented in this book.

For additional support information regarding this book and the CD-ROM (including answers to commonly asked questions about installation and use), visit the Microsoft Press Technical Support Web site at *http://www.microsoft.com/mspress /support/*. Note that product support is not offered through this Web site. For information about Microsoft software support options connect to *http://www.microsoft.com /support/*. You can also e-mail tkinput@microsoft.com or send a letter to Microsoft Press, Attention: Microsoft Press Technical Support, One Microsoft Way, Redmond, WA 98052-6399.

Features of This Book

Each chapter opens with a "Before You Begin" section, which prepares you for completing the chapter. The chapters are then broken into lessons. At the end of each chapter is an activity made up of one or more exercises. These activities give you an opportunity to use the skills being presented or explore the concepts being described.

The "Review" section at the end of the chapter allows you to test what you have learned in the chapter's lessons. Appendix A, "Questions and Answers," contains all of the book's questions and corresponding answers.

Notes

Several types of notes appear throughout the lessons.

Tip   These boxes contain explanations of possible results or alternative methods.

Important   These boxes contain information that is essential to completing a task.

Note   Notes generally contain supplemental information.

Caution   These warnings contain critical information about the possible loss of data.

More Info   References to other sources of information are offered throughout the book.

Planning   Hints and useful information will help you plan implementation in your environment.

Conventions

The following conventions are used throughout this book.

Notational Conventions

- Characters or commands that you type appear in **bold** type.
- *Italic* in syntax statements indicates placeholders for variable information. *Italic* is also used for book titles.
- Names of files and folders appear in Title caps, except when you are to type them directly. Unless otherwise indicated, you can use all lowercase letters when you type a file name in a dialog box or at a command prompt.
- File name extensions appear in all lowercase.
- Acronyms and abbreviations appear in all uppercase.
- Monospace type represents code samples, examples of screen text, or entries that you might type at a command prompt or in initialization files.
- Square brackets [ ] are used in syntax statements to enclose optional items. For example, [*filename*] in command syntax indicates that you can choose to type a file name with the command. Type only the information within the brackets, not the brackets themselves.
- Braces { } are used in syntax statements to enclose required items. Type only the information within the braces, not the braces themselves.

Keyboard Conventions

- A plus sign (+) between two key names means that you must press those keys at the same time. For example, "Press ALT+TAB" means that you hold down ALT while you press TAB.
- A comma (,) between two or more key names means that you must press each of the keys consecutively, not together. For example, "Press ALT, F, X" means that you press and release each key in sequence. "Press ALT+W, L" means that you first press ALT and W at the same time, and then release them and press L.
- You can choose menu commands with the keyboard. Press the ALT key to activate the menu bar, and then sequentially press the keys that correspond to the highlighted or underlined letter of the menu name and the command name. For some commands, you can also press a key combination listed in the menu.
- You can select or clear check boxes or option buttons in dialog boxes with the keyboard. Press the ALT key, and then press the key that corresponds to the underlined letter of the option name. Or you can press TAB until the option is highlighted, and then press the spacebar to select or clear the check box or option button.
- You can cancel the display of a dialog box by pressing the ESC key.

Chapter and Appendix Overview

This self-paced training kit combines notes, hands-on procedures, and review questions to teach you about designing solutions architecture in a Microsoft .NET environment. It is designed to be completed from beginning to end, but you can choose a customized track and complete only the sections that interest you.

The book is divided into the following sections:

- "About This Book" contains a self-paced training overview and introduces the components of this training. Read this section thoroughly to get the greatest educational value from this self-paced training and to plan which lessons you will complete.

- Chapter 1, "Introduction to Designing Business Solutions," describes the Microsoft Solutions Framework (MSF). It begins with an overview of the MSF Process Model and its various phases. The chapter also describes the key activities performed in designing an application and the deliverables associated with those activities. In addition, the chapter describes the case study that is used in the course. All the practices and solution documents are created for the case study.

- Chapter 2, "Gathering and Analyzing Information," describes the process of gathering and analyzing information for designing a business solution. The chapter begins by describing the types of information that you need to gather, sources of information, and some techniques, such as interviews, shadowing, and prototyping that can be used for gathering information. The chapter then describes how to analyze all the information that is gathered from interviews and other gathering techniques. The chapter discusses use cases, usage scenarios, and other techniques that can be used for analyzing information.

- Chapter 3, "Envisioning the Solution," discusses the envisioning phase of the MSF development process. The chapter begins by describing the purpose of the envisioning phase in application design. It then describes the roles and responsibilities of team members during this phase. It also discusses the major tasks of the envisioning phases. Finally, the chapter describes how to define the vision of the project and analyze risks associated with the project.

- Chapter 4, "Creating the Conceptual Design," describes the conceptual design process of the planning phase in the MSF development process. The chapter first discusses the purpose of the planning phase and provides an overview of the three design processes that occur during the planning phase: conceptual, logical, and physical design. The chapter also explains the purpose and benefits of functional specification. The chapter then describes the conceptual design process in detail, and discusses the three steps of conceptual design: research, analysis, and optimization.

- Chapter 5, "Creating the Logical Design," explains the logical design process of the planning phase. The chapter begins with an overview of the purpose and benefits of logical design, and then describes the team composition and the roles of each member during this process. The chapter then describes in detail how to create the logical design for a business solution. It also discusses the various tools and techniques that can be used for documenting the outputs of logical design. Finally, the chapter describes how to optimize the logical design. Validating against requirements is recommended as the best strategy for optimizing the logical design in this chapter.

- Chapter 6, "Creating the Physical Design," describes the physical design process of the planning phase. The chapter first discusses the purpose of physical design. The chapter also discusses the deliverables of physical design. The chapter then describes in detail the tasks involved in completing the physical design process: research, analysis, rationalization, and implementation.

- Chapter 7, "Designing the Presentation Layer," discusses how to design the presentation layer of an application. The chapter begins with an overview of the presentation layer and its two components: user interface and user process. The chapter then describes how to design the user interface and user process components of an application and also recommends some guidelines for the design process.

- Chapter 8, "Designing the Data Layer," describes how to design the data layer for an application. The chapter also discusses how to optimize data access and implement data validation in an application.

- Chapter 9, "Designing Security Specifications," describes the design guidelines for creating security specifications for an application. The chapter recommends some tools and methods for assessing the threats to an application and the mitigation techniques that can be used for resolving the threats. The chapter also describes some security features of Microsoft .NET technologies. Finally, the chapter discusses the steps and the guidelines that can be followed for designing authentication, authorization, and auditing for an application.

- Chapter 10, "Completing the Planning Phase," describes the tasks and plans on which the project team works to complete the planning phase of the project. This chapter describes the guidelines and recommended practices for designing for scalability, availability, reliability, performance, interoperability, and globalization and localization. The chapter discusses how to plan for administrative features such as monitoring, data migration, and licensing specifications. In addition, the chapter discusses the development plan, the test plan, the pilot plan, the deployment plan, and the migration plan. The chapter also discusses the purpose and contents of a technical specification document.

- Chapter 11, "Stabilizing and Deploying the Solution," describes the tasks involved in stabilizing and deploying a solution. The chapter first discusses the stabilizing phase and explains in detail the various types of testing that can be performed to stabilize a solution. The chapter also describes the tasks involved in conducting a pilot. Next, the chapter describes the process of deployment. The chapter discusses how to plan for deployment, and the various strategies that can be used for deploying a solution.

- Appendix A, "Questions and Answers," lists all of the review questions from the book showing the page number where the question appears and the suggested answer.

- The glossary provides definitions for many of the terms and concepts presented in this training kit.

Where to Find Specific Skills in This Book

The following tables provide a list of the skills measured by certification exam 70-300, Analyzing Requirements and Defining Microsoft .NET Solution Architectures. The table specifies the skill and the location in this book where you can find the lesson relating to that skill.

Note   Exam skills are subject to change without prior notice and at the sole discretion of Microsoft.

Envisioning the Solution

Skill Being Measured	Location in Book
Develop a solution concept.	Chapter 3, Lesson 2
Analyze the feasibility of the solution.	Chapter 3, Lesson 2
• Analyze the business feasibility of the solution.	
• Analyze the technical feasibility of the solution.	
• Analyze available organizational skills and resources.	
Analyze and refine the scope of the solution project.	Chapter 3, Lesson 2
Identify key project risks.	Chapter 3, Lesson 4

Gathering and Analyzing Business Requirements

Skill Being Measured	Location in Book
Gather and analyze business requirements. • Analyze the current business state. • Analyze business requirements for the solution.	Chapter 2, Lessons 1 and 2, and Chapter 4, Lesson 4
Gather and analyze user requirements. • Identify use cases. • Identify globalization requirements. • Identify localization requirements. • Identify accessibility requirements.	Chapter 2, Lessons 1 and 2, and Chapter 4, Lesson 4
Gather and analyze operational requirements. • Identify maintainability requirements. • Identify scalability requirements. • Identify availability requirements. • Identify reliability requirements. • Identify deployment requirements. • Identify security requirements.	Chapter 2, Lessons 1 and 2, and Chapter 4, Lesson 4
Gather and analyze requirements for hardware, software, and network infrastructure. • Identify integration requirements. • Analyze the IT environment, including current and projected applications and current projected hardware, software, and network infrastructure. • Analyze the impact of the solution on the IT environment.	Chapter 2, Lessons 1 and 2, and Chapter 4, Lesson 4

Developing Specifications

Skill Being Measured	Location in Book
Transform requirements into functional specifications. Considerations include performance, maintainability, extensibility, scalability, availability, deployability, security, and accessibility.	Chapter 4, all lessons; Chapter 6, Lesson 3; and Chapter 10, Lesson 1
Transform functional specifications into technical specifications. Considerations include performance, maintainability, extensibility, scalability, availability, deployability, security, and accessibility.	Chapter 10, Lesson 4

- Select a development strategy.
- Select a deployment strategy.
- Select a security strategy.
- Select an operations strategy.
- Create a test plan.
- Create a user education plan.

Creating the Conceptual Design

Skill Being Measured	Location in Book
Create a conceptual model of business requirements or data requirements. Methods include Object Role Modeling (ORM).	Chapter 4, all lessons and Chapter 2, Lesson 3

- Transform external information into elementary facts.
- Apply a population check to fact types.
- Identify primitive entity types in the conceptual model.
- Apply uniqueness constraints to the conceptual model.
- Apply mandatory role constraints to the conceptual model.
- Add value constraints, set-comparison constraints, and subtype constraints to the conceptual model.
- Add ring constraints to the conceptual model.

Creating the Logical Design

Skill Being Measured	Location in Book
Create the logical design for the solution.	Chapter 5, all lessons
• Create the logical design for auditing and logging.	
• Create the logical design for error handling.	
• Create the logical design for integration.	
• Create the logical design for globalization.	
• Create the logical design for localization.	
• Create the logical design for security.	
• Include constraints in the logical design to support business rules.	
• Create the logical design for the presentation layer, including the user interface (UI).	
• Create the logical design for services and components.	
• Create the logical design for state management.	
• Create the logical design for synchronous or asynchronous architecture.	
Create the logical data model.	Chapter 5, Lesson 3
• Define tables and columns.	
• Normalize tables.	
• Define relationships.	
• Define primary and foreign keys.	
• Define the XML schema.	
Validate the proposed logical design.	Chapter 5, Lesson 4
• Review the effectiveness of the proposed logical design in meeting business requirements. Business requirements include performance, maintainability, extensibility, scalability, availability, deployability, security, and accessibility.	
• Validate the proposed logical design against usage scenarios.	
• Create a proof of concept for the proposed logical design.	

Creating the Physical Design

Skill Being Measured	Location in Book
Select the appropriate technologies for the physical design of the solution.	Chapter 5, Lesson 2
Create the physical design for the solution.	Chapter 6, all lessons; Chapter 7 all lessons; Chapter 9, Lesson 3

- Create specifications for auditing and logging.
- Create specifications for error handling.
- Create specifications for physical integration.
- Create specifications for security.
- Include constraints in the physical design to support business rules.
- Design the presentation layer, including the UI and online user assistance.
- Design services and components.
- Design state management.

Create the physical design for deployment.	Chapter 10, Lesson 2

- Create deployment specifications, which can include coexistence and distribution.
- Create licensing specifications.
- Create data migration specifications.
- Design the upgrade path.

Create the physical design for maintenance.	Chapter 10, Lesson 2

- Design application monitoring.

Create the physical design for the data model.	Chapter 8, Lesson 2

- Create an indexing specification.
- Partition data.
- Denormalize tables.

Validate the physical design.	Chapter 6, Lessons 3 and 4

- Review the effectiveness of the proposed physical design in meeting the business requirements. Business requirements include performance, maintainability, extensibility, scalability, availability, deployability, security, and accessibility.
- Validate use cases, scenario walk-throughs, and sequence diagrams.
- Create a proof of concept for the proposed physical design.

Creating Standards and Processes

Skill Being Measured	Location in Book
Establish standards. Standards can apply to development documentation, coding, code review, UI, and testing.	Chapter 11, Lesson 2
Establish processes. Processes include reviewing development documentation, reviewing code, creating builds, tracking issues, managing source code, managing change, managing release, and establishing maintenance tasks. Methods include Microsoft Visual Studio .NET Enterprise Templates.	Chapter 11, Lesson 2
Establish quality and performance metrics to evaluate project control, organizational performance, and return on investment.	Chapter 11, Lessons 1 and 2

Getting Started

This self-paced training course contains hands-on procedures to help you learn about building solution architecture in a Microsoft .NET environment.

Hardware Requirements

Each computer must have the following minimum configuration. All hardware should be on the Microsoft Windows 2000 Professional Hardware Compatibility List.

- Pentium II, 266 MHz or faster
- 128 MB RAM
- 4-GB hard drive
- CD-ROM drive
- Microsoft Mouse or compatible pointing device

Software Requirements

The following minimum software is required to complete the procedures in this course.

- Microsoft Windows 2000 Professional with Service Pack 3, or Microsoft Windows XP Professional
- Microsoft Office 2000 Professional with Service Pack 3 or later
- Microsoft Visio 2000 Professional or later

Setup Instructions

Set up your computer according to the manufacturer's instructions.

The Solution Documents

The Supplemental Course Materials CD-ROM contains a set of files that you will need to copy to your hard disk to complete many of the exercises in this book. To access the Solution Documents folder:

1. Insert the Supplemental Course Materials CD-ROM into your CD-ROM drive.

   Note   If Autorun is disabled on your machine, run StartCD.exe in the root directory of the CD-ROM or refer to the Readme.txt file.

2. Select Solution Documents on the user interface menu, and then browse to the chapter folder you want to view.

The eBook

The CD-ROM also includes a fully searchable electronic version of the book. To view the eBook, you must have Microsoft Internet Explorer 5.01 or later and the corresponding HTML Help components on your system. If your system does not meet these requirements, you can install Internet Explorer 6 SP1 from the CD-ROM prior to installing the eBook.

To use the eBook

1. Insert the Supplemental Course Materials CD-ROM into your CD-ROM drive.

   Note   If AutoRun is disabled on your machine, refer to the Readme.txt file on the CD-ROM.

2. Click eBook on the user interface menu and follow the prompts.

   Note   You must have the Supplemental Course Materials CD-ROM inserted in your CD-ROM drive to run the eBook.

The Microsoft Certified Professional Program

The Microsoft Certified Professional (MCP) program provides the best method to prove your command of current Microsoft products and technologies. Microsoft, an industry leader in certification, is on the forefront of testing methodology. The exams and corresponding certifications are intended to validate your mastery of critical competencies as you design and develop, or implement and support, solutions with Microsoft products and technologies. Computer professionals who become Microsoft certified are recognized as experts and are sought industry-wide.

The Microsoft Certified Professional program offers multiple certifications, based on specific areas of technical expertise:

- *Microsoft Certified Professional (MCP)*. Demonstrated in-depth knowledge of at least one Microsoft Windows operating system or architecturally significant platform. An MCP is qualified to implement a Microsoft product or technology as part of a business solution for an organization.
- *Microsoft Certified Solution Developer (MCSD)*. Professional developers qualified to analyze, design, and develop enterprise business solutions with Microsoft development tools and technologies including the Microsoft .NET Framework.
- *Microsoft Certified Application Developer (MCAD)*. Professional developers qualified to develop, test, deploy, and maintain powerful applications using Microsoft tools and technologies including Microsoft Visual Studio .NET and XML Web services.
- *Microsoft Certified Systems Engineer (MCSE)*. Qualified to effectively analyze the business requirements, and design and implement the infrastructure for business solutions based on the Microsoft Windows and Microsoft Server 2003 operating system.
- *Microsoft Certified Systems Administrator (MCSA)*. Individuals with the skills to manage and troubleshoot existing network and system environments based on the Microsoft Windows and Microsoft Server 2003 operating systems.
- *Microsoft Certified Database Administrator (MCDBA)*. Individuals who design, implement, and administer Microsoft SQL Server databases.
- *Microsoft Certified Trainer (MCT)*. Instructionally and technically qualified to deliver Microsoft Official Curriculum through a Microsoft Certified Technical Education Center (CTEC).

Microsoft Certification Benefits

Microsoft certification, one of the most comprehensive certification programs available for assessing and maintaining software-related skills, is a valuable measure of an individual's knowledge and expertise. Microsoft certification is awarded to individuals who have successfully demonstrated their ability to perform specific tasks and implement solutions with Microsoft products. Certification brings a variety of benefits to the individual and to employers and organizations.

Microsoft Certification Benefits for Individuals

As a Microsoft Certified Professional, you receive many benefits:

- Industry recognition of your knowledge and proficiency with Microsoft products and technologies.
- A Microsoft Developer Network subscription. MCPs receive rebates or discounts on a one-year subscription to the Microsoft Developer Network (*http://msdn.microsoft.com/subscriptions/*) during the first year of certification. (Fulfillment details will vary, depending on your location; please see your Welcome Kit.)
- Access to technical and product information direct from Microsoft through a secured area of the MCP Web site (go to *http://www.microsoft.com/traincert /mcp/mcpsecure.asp*).
- Access to exclusive discounts on products and services from selected companies. Individuals who are currently certified can learn more about exclusive discounts by visiting the MCP secured Web site (go to *http://www.microsoft.com /traincert/mcp/mcpsecure.asp*, log in, and select the "Other Benefits" link).
- MCP logo, certificate, transcript, wallet card, and lapel pin to identify you as a Microsoft Certified Professional (MCP) to colleagues and clients. Electronic files of logos and transcript can be downloaded from the MCP secured Web site (go to *http://www.microsoft.com/traincert/mcp/mcpsecure.asp*) upon certification.
- Invitations to Microsoft conferences, technical training sessions, and special events.
- Free access to *Microsoft Certified Professional Magazine Online*, a career and professional development magazine. Secured content on the *Microsoft Certified Professional Magazine Online* Web site includes the current issue (available only to MCPs), additional online-only content and columns, an MCP-only database, and regular chats with Microsoft and other technical experts.
- Discount on membership to PASS (for MCPs only), the Professional Association for SQL Server. In addition to playing a key role in the only worldwide, user-run SQL Server user group endorsed by Microsoft, members enjoy unique access to a world of educational opportunities (go to *http://www.microsoft.com /traincert/mcp/mcpsecure.asp*).

An additional benefit is received by Microsoft Certified System Engineers (MCSEs):

- A 50 percent rebate or discount on a one-year subscription to *TechNet* or *TechNet Plus* during the first year of certification. (Fulfillment details will vary, depending on your location. Please see your Welcome Kit.) A *TechNet* subscription provides MCSEs with a portable IT survival kit that is updated monthly. It includes the complete Microsoft Knowledge Base as well as service packs and kits.

An additional benefit is received by Microsoft Certified System Database Administrators (MCDBAs):

- A 50 percent rebate or discount on a one-year subscription to TechNet or TechNet Plus during the first year of certification. (Fulfillment details will vary, depending on your location. Please see your Welcome Kit.) A *TechNet* subscription provides MCSEs with a portable IT survival kit that is updated monthly. It includes the complete Microsoft Knowledge Base as well as service packs and kits.
- A one-year subscription to *SQL Server Magazine*. Written by industry experts, the magazine contains technical and how-to tips and advice—a must for anyone working with SQL Server.

A list of benefits for Microsoft Certified Trainers (MCTs) can be found at *http://www.microsoft.com/traincert/mcp/mct/benefits.asp*.

Microsoft Certification Benefits for Employers and Organizations

Through certification, computer professionals can maximize the return on investment in Microsoft technology. Research shows that Microsoft certification provides organizations with:

- Excellent return on training and certification investments by providing a standard method of determining training needs and measuring results.
- Increased customer satisfaction and decreased support costs through improved service, increased productivity and greater technical self-sufficiency.
- Reliable benchmark for hiring, promoting, and career planning.
- Recognition and rewards for productive employees by validating their expertise.
- Retraining options for existing employees so they can work effectively with new technologies.
- Assurance of quality when outsourcing computer services.

Requirements for Becoming a Microsoft Certified Professional

The certification requirements differ for each certification and are specific to the products and job functions addressed by the certification.

To become a Microsoft Certified Professional, you must pass rigorous certification exams that provide a valid and reliable measure of technical proficiency and expertise. These exams are designed to test your expertise and ability to perform a role or task with a product, and are developed with the input of professionals in the industry. Questions in the exams reflect how Microsoft products are used in actual organizations, giving them "real-world" relevance.

- Microsoft Certified Product (MCP) candidates are required to pass one current Microsoft certification exam. Candidates can pass additional Microsoft certification exams to further qualify their skills with other Microsoft products, development tools, or desktop applications.

- Microsoft Certified Solution Developers (MCSDs) are required to pass three core exams and one elective exam. (MCSD for Microsoft .NET candidates are required to pass four core exams and one elective.)

- Microsoft Certified Application Developers (MCADs) are required to pass two core exams and one elective exam in an area of specialization.

- Microsoft Certified Systems Engineers (MCSEs) are required to pass five core exams and two elective exams.

- Microsoft Certified Systems Administrators (MCSAs) are required to pass three core exams and one elective exam that provide a valid and reliable measure of technical proficiency and expertise.

- Microsoft Certified Database Administrators (MCDBAs) are required to pass three core exams and one elective exam that provide a valid and reliable measure of technical proficiency and expertise.

- Microsoft Certified Trainers (MCTs) are required to meet instructional and technical requirements specific to each Microsoft Official Curriculum course they are certified to deliver. The MCT program requires ongoing training to meet the requirements for the annual renewal of certification. For more information about becoming a Microsoft Certified Trainer, visit *http://www.microsoft.com/ traincert/mcp/mct/* or contact a regional service center near you.

Technical Training for Computer Professionals

Technical training is available in a variety of ways, with instructor-led classes, online instruction, or self-paced training available at thousands of locations worldwide.

Self-Paced Training

For motivated learners who are ready for the challenge, self-paced instruction is the most flexible, cost-effective way to increase your knowledge and skills.

A full line of self-paced print and computer-based training materials is available direct from the source—Microsoft Press. Microsoft Official Curriculum courseware kits from Microsoft Press are designed for advanced computer system professionals and are available from Microsoft Press and the Microsoft Developer Division. Self-paced training kits from Microsoft Press feature print-based instructional materials, along with CD-ROM–based product software, multimedia presentations, lab exercises, and practice files.

Microsoft Certified Technical Education Centers

Microsoft Certified Technical Education Centers (CTECs) are the best source for instructor-led training that can help you prepare to become a Microsoft Certified Professional. The Microsoft CTEC program is a worldwide network of qualified technical training organizations that provide authorized delivery of Microsoft Official Curriculum courses by Microsoft Certified Trainers to computer professionals.

For a listing of CTEC locations in the United States and Canada, visit the Web site at *http://www.microsoft.com/traincert/ctec/*.

Technical Support

Every effort has been made to ensure the accuracy of this book and the contents of the companion disc. If you have comments, questions, or ideas regarding this book or the companion disc, please send them to Microsoft Press using either of the following methods:

E-mail:

tkinput@microsoft.com

Postal Mail:

Microsoft Press
Attn: MCSD Self-Paced Training Kit: Analyzing Requirements and Defining Microsoft .NET Solution Architectures, Editor
One Microsoft Way
Redmond, WA 98052-6399

For additional support information regarding this book and the CD-ROM (including answers to commonly asked questions about installation and use), visit the Microsoft Press Technical Support Web site at *http://www.microsoft.com /mspress/support/*. To connect directly to the Microsoft Press Knowledge Base and enter a query, visit *http://www.microsoft.com/mspress/support/search.asp*. For support information regarding Microsoft software, please connect to *http://www.microsoft.com/support*.

C H A P T E R   1

Introduction to Designing Business Solutions

About This Chapter

In this introduction to designing business solutions, you will learn about
Microsoft® Solutions Framework (MSF), a set of models, principles, and guidelines for designing applications. You will learn about the MSF Process Model and
its various phases. You will also learn about the key activities that you perform in
designing an application, and about the deliverables associated with those activities. In addition, you will be introduced to the case study that illustrates the concepts and practices that you will learn.

Before You Begin

To complete the lessons in this chapter, you must have

- A general understanding of the software development life cycle.
- General knowledge of Microsoft technologies.

Lesson 1: Overview of Microsoft Solutions Framework

MSF provides a set of models, principles, and guidelines for designing and developing enterprise solutions in a way that ensures that all elements of a project, such as people, processes, and tools, can be successfully managed. MSF also provides proven practices for planning, designing, developing, and deploying successful enterprise solutions. In this lesson, you will learn about the process model and team model that MSF provides.

After this lesson, you will be able to

- Describe the phases in the MSF Process Model.
- Describe the roles in the MSF Team Model.
- Describe the MSF disciplines: risk management, readiness management, and project management.
- Describe how managing tradeoffs helps to ensure the success of an enterprise project.
- Describe the purpose of iteration in an enterprise project.
- Describe the waterfall model and the spiral model.

Estimated lesson time: 15 minutes

What Are Process Models?

To maximize the success of enterprise projects, Microsoft has made available packaged guidance for effectively designing, developing, deploying, operating, and supporting solutions, including those created with Microsoft technologies. This knowledge is derived from the experience gained within Microsoft and from customers and vendors about large-scale software development and service operation projects, the experience of Microsoft's consultants in conducting projects for enterprise customers, and the best knowledge from the worldwide Information Technology (IT) industry.

A process model guides the order of project activities and represents the life cycle of a project. Historically, some process models are static and others do not allow checkpoints. Two such process models are the waterfall model and the spiral model.

Waterfall and spiral models

Figure 1.1 shows the waterfall model's cascading checkpoints and the spiral model's circular approach to process.

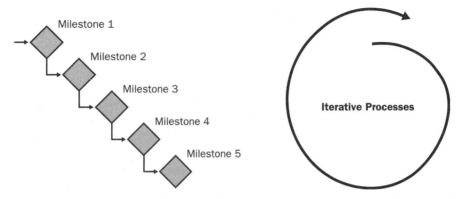

Figure 1.1.   The waterfall model and the spiral model

These models provide two different approaches to the project life cycle. The preceding illustration shows the waterfall model's cascading checkpoints and the spiral model's circular approach to process.

- *Waterfall model.* This model uses milestones as transition and assessment points. When using the waterfall model, you need to complete each set of tasks in one phase before moving on to the next phase. The waterfall model works best for projects in which the project requirements can be clearly defined and are not liable to modifications in the future. Because this model has fixed transition points between phases, you can easily monitor schedules and assign clear responsibilities and accountability.

- *Spiral model.* This model is based on the continual need to refine the requirements and estimates for a project. The spiral model is effective when used for rapid application development of very small projects. This approach can generate great synergy between the development team and the customer because the customer is involved in all stages by providing feedback and approval. However, the spiral model does not incorporate clear checkpoints. Consequently, the development process might become chaotic.

How the MSF Process Model Works

The MSF Process Model describes a generalized sequence of activities for building and deploying enterprise solutions. This process is flexible and can accommodate the design and development of a broad range of enterprise projects. The MSF Process Model is a phase-based, milestone-driven, and iterative model that can be applied to developing and deploying traditional applications, enterprise solutions for e-commerce, and Web-distributed applications.

MSF Process Model

The MSF Process Model combines the best principles of the waterfall and spiral models. It combines the waterfall model's milestone-based planning and resulting predictability with the spiral model's benefits of feedback and creativity.

Figure 1.2 shows the MSF Process Model.

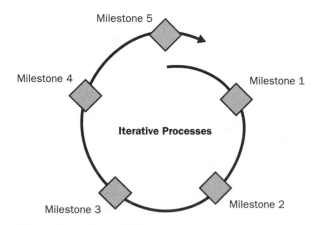

Figure 1.2.   The MSF Process Model

Phases of the MSF Process Model

The MSF Process Model consists of five distinct phases:

- Envisioning
- Planning
- Developing
- Stabilizing
- Deploying

Each phase culminates in a milestone. Figure 1.3 illustrates the phases and milestones of the MSF Process Model. You will learn about these phases in detail in Lesson 2.

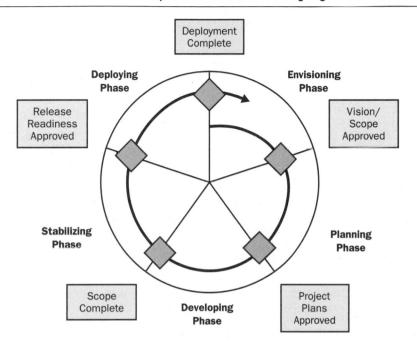

Figure 1.3.   Phases and milestones of the MSF Process Model

How to Organize Project Teams

Along with the MSF Process Model, MSF provides the MSF Team Model for organizing project teams. The MSF Team Model emphasizes the importance of clear
roles, responsibilities, and goals of individual members to the success of the
project. This model also increases the accountability of each team member. The
flexibility of the MSF Team Model helps you to adapt it to the scope of the project,
the size of the team, and the skills of the team members. This model forms the
basis of creating effective, resilient, and successful project teams.

Roles in the MSF Team Model

In an enterprise solution project, a large number of activities must be performed,
and the project must be viewed from several perspectives. To accommodate these
needs, the MSF Team Model specifies six distinct roles, and each role has clearly
defined responsibilities and goals.

Important   The team works toward a single vision, and team members operate as
peers. Within the team, each role contributes to and is equally responsible for the
success of the project.

The roles in the MSF Team Model are as follows:

- *Product management.* Responsible for managing customer communications and expectations. During the design phase, product management gathers customer requirements and ensures that business needs are met. Product management also works on project communication plans such as briefings to the customers, marketing to users, demonstrations, and product launches.

- *Program management.* Responsible for the development process and for delivering the solution to the customer within the project constraints.

- *Development.* Responsible for developing the technology solution according to the specifications provided by the program management role.

- *Testing.* Responsible for identifying and addressing all product quality issues and approving the solution for release. This role evaluates and validates design functionality and consistency with project vision and scope.

- *Release management.* Responsible for smooth deployment and operations of the solution. Release management validates the infrastructure implications of the solution to ensure that it can be deployed and supported.

- *User experience.* Analyzes performance needs and support issues of the users and considers the product implications of meeting those needs.

In a small project, individuals on the project team can take on more than one role. Note that combining roles on a project introduces risk to the project. Therefore, it is important to assign appropriate roles to the members. For example, it is not recommended that an individual be assigned to both the program management role and the development role.

To help minimize risks, use Table 1.1 as a guide in determining which roles can be combined and which ones should not be combined.

Table 1.1. Combining Roles Within a Team

Role	Product management	Program management	Development	Testing	User experience	Release management
Product management		N	N	P	P	U
Program management	N		N	U	U	P
Development	N	N		N	N	N
Test	P	U	N		P	P
User experience	P	U	N	P		U

Table 1.1.   Combining Roles Within a Team   *(continued)*

Role	Product management	Program management	Development	Testing	User experience	Release management
Release management	U	P	N	P	U	

Legend:

P: Possible

U: Unlikely

N: Not recommended

Additional team members

In addition to the roles defined previously, the project team also includes the project stakeholders, though they are not part of the MSF Team Model. These stakeholders include the following roles:

- *Project sponsor.* One or more individuals initiating and approving the project and its result.
- *Customer (or business sponsor).* One or more individuals who expect to gain business value from the solution.
- *End user.* One or more individuals or systems that interact directly with the solution.
- *Operations.* The organization responsible for the ongoing operation of the solution after delivery.

MSF Disciplines

MSF guidance includes disciplines for managing the people, processes, and technology elements that most projects encounter. The three key MSF disciplines are risk management, readiness management, and project management.

MSF risk management process

The MSF risk management discipline advocates proactive risk management, continuous risk assessment, and decision making throughout the project life cycle. The team continuously assesses, monitors, and actively manages risks until they are either resolved or turn into problems to be handled as such.

The MSF risk management process defines six logical steps through which the team manages current risks, plans and executes risk management strategies, and documents knowledge for the enterprise.

1. *Risk identification* allows individuals to identify risks so that the team becomes aware of any potential problems.

2. *Risk analysis* transforms the estimates or data about specific project risks that emerges during risk identification into a form the team can use to make decisions about prioritization.

3. *Risk planning* uses the information obtained from risk analysis to formulate strategies, plans, and actions.

4. *Risk tracking* monitors the status of specific risks and documents the progress in their respective action plans.

5. *Risk control* is the process of executing risk action plans and their associated status reporting.

6. *Risk learning* formalizes the lessons learned and relevant project documents and tools, and records that knowledge in reusable form for use within the team and by the enterprise.

More Info   You will learn more about MSF risk management in Chapter 3, "Envisioning the Solution."

MSF readiness management process

The MSF readiness management discipline includes a process to help you develop the knowledge, skills, and abilities (KSAs) needed to create and manage projects and solutions. Figure 1.4 illustrates the four steps of the readiness management process: define, assess, change, and evaluate.

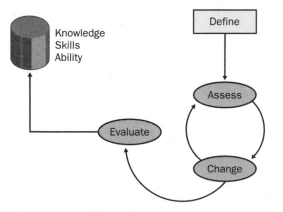

Figure 1.4.   MSF readiness management

Each step of the process includes a series of tasks to help reach the next milestone.

- *Define.* During this step, the team identifies the scenarios, competencies, and proficiency levels needed to successfully plan, create, and manage the solution. This is also the time to determine which competencies and corresponding proficiency levels are required for each role in the organization. The assigned role determines whether an individual needs to be proficient in one or many of the defined competencies.

- *Assess.* It is during this step that the team begins analysis of the current competencies as they relate to the various job roles. The purpose of this analysis is to determine the skills of individuals within each of these roles. The team then compares the competencies identified in the previous step to the current competencies. Comparing current skill levels to required skill levels is necessary to develop a learning plan, so that team members can reach the necessary competency levels.

- *Change.* During this step, team members begin to improve their skills by means of structured learning to raise current proficiency levels to the desired levels. This step consists of:

  - *Training.* The learning and mentoring that occurs according to what was outlined in the learning plan.

  - *Tracking progress.* The tracking of progress that enables individual or overall readiness to be determined at any time during the life cycle. This tracking enables the team members to make necessary adjustments to the learning plan.

- *Evaluate.* During this step, the team determines whether the learning plans were effective and whether the lessons learned are being successfully implemented on the job.

The MSF readiness management process is an ongoing, iterative approach to readiness. The process is adaptable for both large and small projects. Following the steps in the process helps manage the various tasks required to align individual, project team, and organizational KSAs.

MSF project management process

To deliver a solution within project constraints, strong project management skills are essential. Project management is a process that combines a set of skills and techniques to address the following tasks:

- Integrate planning and conduct change control
- Define and manage the scope of the project
- Prepare a budget and manage costs
- Prepare and track schedules
- Ensure that the right resources are allocated to the project
- Manage contracts and vendors and procure project resources
- Facilitate team and external communications
- Facilitate the risk management process
- Document and monitor the team's quality management process

The MSF Team Model does not contain a project manager role; however, most project management functions are conducted by the MSF program management role.

The differentiating factor of the MSF approach to project management is that the project management job function and activities do not form a hierarchical structure in the decision-making process. MSF advocates *against* a rigid, dictatorial style of project management. This rigid style hinders the development of an effective team of peers, which is a key success factor of MSF.

In MSF, all team roles fulfill a specific goal, all of which are considered equally important. Major decisions are made by consensus of the core team. If that consensus cannot be achieved, the program management role makes the final decision on the issue by transitioning into the role of decision leader to enable the project to continue. Program management makes the decision with the goal of meeting the customer's requirements and delivering the solution within the constraints. After the decision is made, the team returns to operating as a team of peers.

How to Manage Tradeoffs

Projects frequently fail, are completed late, or exceed the planned budget. Ambiguous project scope can contribute to or be the cause of each of these problems. The *scope* of a project specifies what the solution will and will not do. To effectively define and manage the scope, you need to:

- Identify project constraints
- Manage tradeoffs
- Establish change control
- Monitor project progress

In the process of identifying and managing tradeoffs, you are not necessarily reducing the features of a solution, but identifying tradeoffs might result in a reduction of features. Managing tradeoffs provides a structured way to balance all parts of the project while realizing that you cannot attain all of your goals at the same time. Both the team and the customer must review the tradeoffs and be prepared to make difficult choices.

The tradeoff triangle and the project tradeoff matrix are two of the tools that MSF uses for managing tradeoffs.

Tradeoff triangle

In projects, there is a clear relationship between such project variables as resources, schedule, and features of the project. The relationship between these variables is illustrated in Figure 1.5.

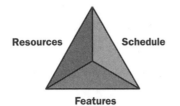

Figure 1.5.   The tradeoff triangle

As illustrated by the triangle, any change to any one of the components implies that a corresponding change might need to be made to the other components. The key to developing a solution that meets the customer requirements is to determine and maintain the correct balance between resources, deployment date, and features.

Often, project teams are reluctant to reduce the number of features in the solution. The tradeoff triangle helps to explain the constraints and present the options for tradeoffs.

Note   If you add quality as a fourth dimension to the tradeoff triangle, the triangle transforms into a tetrahedron. By reducing the quality requirements, you could simultaneously reduce resources, shorten the schedule, and increase the number of features, but this strategy is the worst approach for developing a solution.

Project tradeoff matrix

The *project tradeoff matrix* is a tool that the team and the customer can use when making tradeoff decisions. These decisions are made early in the project.

Figure 1.6 is an example of a project tradeoff matrix.

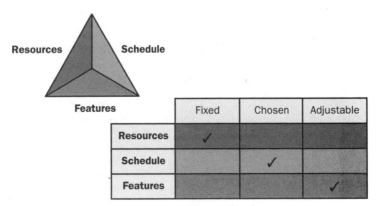

Figure 1.6.   A project tradeoff matrix

The tradeoff matrix helps identify the project features that are considered essential, the features that are not essential but that would be good to include, and the features that can be eliminated or added to the next version to accommodate the other two variables. To understand how the tradeoff matrix works, the variables of resources, schedule, and features can be inserted into the blanks of the following sentence:

Given fixed _____, we will choose a _____ and adjust _____ if necessary.

The following are the various logical possibilities:

- Given fixed resources, we will choose a schedule and adjust the feature set if necessary.
- Given fixed resources, we will choose a feature set and adjust the schedule if necessary.
- Given a fixed feature set, we will choose appropriate resources and adjust the schedule if necessary.
- Given a fixed feature set, we will choose a schedule and adjust resources if necessary.
- Given a fixed schedule, we will choose appropriate resources and adjust features if necessary.
- Given a fixed schedule, we will choose a feature set and adjust resources if necessary.

Important   For the tradeoff process to work effectively, both the team and the customer must agree to and formally approve the tradeoff matrix for the project. This approval process is also referred to as *signing off*.

How to Use Iteration in Projects

While development of the solution continues through its phases, each iteration of the process brings the solution closer to its final release. Iterations are continued within a specific phase until the goal for the phase has been reached. In addition, an iteration allows the project to be developed in smaller steps, with future iterations being based on the success or failure of an earlier step. Deliverables such as the vision/scope document and other documents, code, designs, and plans are developed in an iterative manner. Instances of iteration in a project life cycle include:

- Creating versioned releases
- Creating living documents
- Creating periodic builds (weekly or daily)

Versioned releases

When using MSF, a team develops solutions by building, testing, and deploying a core of functionality, and then adding sets of features to the solution in every release. This is known as a *version release strategy*.

Figure 1.7 illustrates how functionality develops during the creation of many versions of a solution. The time between versions depends on the size and scope of the project.

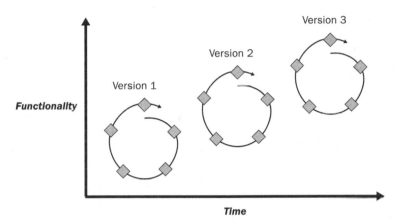

Figure 1.7.   Functionality of versioned releases

Versioned releases improve the team's relationship with the customer and ensure that the best ideas are reflected in the solution. Customers will be more receptive to deferring features until a later release if they trust the team to deliver the initial and subsequent solution releases on time. Several guidelines facilitate the adoption of versioned releases:

- *Create a multiple version release plan.* Thinking beyond the current version enhances a team's ability to make good decisions about what to create now and what to defer. This allows the team to make the best use of the available resources and schedule. In addition, you can prevent unwanted expansion of scope by providing a timetable for future feature development.
- *Work through iterations rapidly.* A significant benefit of versioning is that it delivers usable solutions to the customer quickly and improves them incrementally over time. Maintain a manageable scope so that iterations are achievable within acceptable time frames.
- *Deliver core functionality first.* Delivering a basic solution that is solid and usable is more effective than developing a solution that the customer cannot use for weeks or months. Delivering core functionality first enables developers to incorporate customer feedback that will motivate feature development in subsequent iterations.

- *Create high-risk features first.* During risk assessment, the team identifies the riskiest features. Schedule these features for proof-of-concept testing first. If you encounter any problems that require major changes to the architecture, you can implement the changes earlier in the project and minimize the impact to schedule and budget.

Living documents

To ensure that you do not spend too much time refining the early phases of the project, you need to create *living documents*—that is, documentation that changes as the project changes. Living documents allow teams to make modifications to any aspect of the project design and development when there is a change in requirements. This process ensures that the completed solution meets the final requirements and not just the initial set of requirements. MSF project documents are developed iteratively.

For example, the MSF Process Model recommends that planning documents start out as generalized documents without extensive details. They are submitted for review by the team and stakeholders during the initial stages of the project. As the solution progresses through different phases, the documents are developed into detailed plans. These plans are once again reviewed and modified iteratively. The type and number of these plans depends on the size of the project.

Daily builds

MSF recommends the preparation of frequent builds of the components of a solution for testing and review. This approach applies to developing code in addition to builds of hardware and software components. By creating daily builds, you can ensure that you understand the stability of the total solution and have accumulated ample test data before releasing the solution.

Using the daily build approach is particularly effective for larger, complex projects that are divided into smaller subsystems. Separate teams develop and test these subsystems and then consolidate them into a single solution. Developers complete core functionality of the solution or product first, and add additional features later. Development and testing occur continuously and simultaneously. Creating daily builds ensures that all code is compatible and allows the various subteams to continue their development and testing iterations.

Lesson 2: Phases in the MSF Process Model

As stated in Lesson 1, the MSF Process Model is milestone based and consists of five phases: envisioning, planning, developing, stabilizing, and deploying. During each phase, the project team performs a distinct set of activities. In this lesson, you will learn about the various phases in detail. You will also learn about the milestones and deliverables of each phase.

After this lesson, you will be able to

- Describe the tasks, milestones, and deliverables of the envisioning, planning, developing, stabilizing, and deploying phases of the MSF Process Model.

Estimated lesson time: 30 minutes

What Is the Envisioning Phase?

The MSF process begins with the envisioning phase. *Envisioning* can be defined as creating a broad description of the goals and constraints of the project. In this phase, you identify the team and what the team must accomplish for the customer. The purpose of the envisioning phase is to build a shared vision of the project among all the key stakeholders of the project.

During the envisioning phase, the program management team identifies the tasks and deliverables that address the requirements and goals of the project. This phase culminates in a *vision/scope approved* milestone. This milestone indicates that the customer and the team agree about the purpose and direction of the project.

Envisioning process

The team performs the following key tasks during the envisioning phase:

- *Setting up the team.* Creation of a project team that represents all roles of the MSF Team Model. (The person who creates this team is usually identified by senior management.) When setting up a team, it is important to consider the skills, experience, and performance level of the team members. In addition, there are practical considerations such as availability of resources and project budget.
- *Defining the project structure.* Identification of an administrative structure for the project team and the standards for managing the project.
- *Defining the business goals.* Analysis of the business problem and opportunities in order to identify the objectives for the solution.
- *Assessing the current situation.* Evaluation of the current situation and analysis of the difference between the current and expected situation. The purpose of this evaluation is to create the problem statement and identify the direction of the project.

- *Creating a vision statement and defining the scope of the project.* Creation of a vision statement that communicates the long-term direction for guiding the team toward its business goals. Identification of the scope of the project defines what will and will not be included in the solution.

Note   A shared and clearly articulated vision is fundamental to the success of the project.

- *Defining requirements and user profiles.* Identification of the stakeholders, end users, and sponsors for the project and documentation of their requirements for the solution. This information helps to evaluate the vision/scope of the project and to create a solution concept.
- *Developing a solution concept.* Creation of a baseline solution concept, that is, the outlining of the approach that the team will take to create the solution. This concept is created by using the requirements that have been identified.
- *Assessing risk.* Identification and assessment of the risks to the project, and creation of a risk mitigation plan. This is an iterative step that is conducted during all stages of the product life cycle.
- *Closing the envisioning phase.* End of the envisioning phase. Accomplished when the vision/scope document is formally approved by all stakeholders and the project team.

Milestones of the envisioning phase

Each phase in the MSF Process Model has interim milestones and a major milestone. *Interim milestones* are associated with the various activities that are performed in a phase, such as creating a team and creating a vision/scope document. The *major milestone* indicates that the team can progress to the next phase in the MSF Process Model. For example, the major milestone of the envisioning phase is the vision/scope approved milestone. When the team reaches this milestone, the team can progress to the planning phase of the MSF Process Model.

The interim milestones of the envisioning phase are as follows:

- *Core team organized.* The key members of the team have been identified. The team might not be completely assembled at this time. A project structure document specifies the roles and responsibilities of each member of the team. This document also outlines the hierarchy of accountability in the team, the points of contact with the customer, and the structure of the team.
- *Vision/scope created.* The first version of the vision/scope document is completed and is distributed among the team, customers, and stakeholders for review. During the review cycle, the document undergoes iterations of feedback, discussions, and corresponding modifications.

The envisioning phase culminates with the *vision/scope approved* milestone. At this stage, the project team and the customer have agreed on the direction for the project, the scope of the solution, and a general timetable for delivering the solution.

Deliverables of the envisioning phase

The team creates deliverables for each task in the envisioning phase. Together, these deliverables provide context and direction for the team for the remainder of the project, and communicate the project vision and scope to the customer. The deliverables that the team creates during the envisioning phase include:

- Vision/scope
    - Problem statements and business objectives
    - A review of the existing processes
    - A broad definition of user requirements
    - User profiles identifying who will benefit from the solution
    - A vision statement and scope definition
    - The solution concept outlining the approach the team will take to plan the project
    - Solution design strategies
- Project structure
    - A description of all MSF team roles and a list of corresponding team members
    - A project structure and process standards for the team to follow
- Risk assessment
    - A preliminary risk assessment
    - A list of the primary identified risks
    - Plans for mitigating or eliminating the identified risks

What Is the Planning Phase?

During the planning phase, the team determines what to develop and plans how to create the solution. The team prepares the functional specification, creates a design of the solution, and prepares work plans, cost estimates, and schedules for the various deliverables.

The planning phase involves the analysis of requirements. These requirements can be categorized as business requirements, user requirements, operational requirements, and system requirements. These requirements are used to design the solution and its features and to validate the correctness of the design.

After gathering and analyzing the requirements, the team creates the design of the solution. The team creates *user profiles* that specify the various users of the solution and their roles and responsibilities. The team then creates a series of usage scenarios. A *usage scenario* specifies the activity performed by a particular type of user. Therefore, the team needs to create usage scenarios for all user profiles. After creating usage scenarios, the team creates use cases for the usage scenarios. A *use case* specifies the sequence of steps that a user will perform in a usage scenario.

Design stages

The three design stages are:

- *Conceptual design,* in which you view the problem from the perspective of the users and business requirements and define the problem and solution in terms of usage scenarios.
- *Logical design,* in which you view the solution from the perspective of the project team and define the solution as a set of services.
- *Physical design,* in which you view the solution from the perspective of the developers and define the technologies, component interfaces, and services of the solution.

You document the solution design in the functional specification. The functional specification describes the behavior and appearance of each feature of the solution. It also describes the architecture and the design for all features.

Design process

The team performs the following key tasks during the planning phase:

- *Developing the solution design and architecture.* Identification of business requirements, user requirements, and technologies and the use of this information to design a proposed application model.
- *Creating the functional specification.* Creation of a functional specification that describes the requirements that must be met by the solution.
- *Developing project plans.* Identification of and planning for the tasks that will be performed by the project team, and the consolidation of these plans into a master project plan. The master project plan also includes items such as the approach, dependencies, and assumptions for the solution.
- *Creating project schedules.* Creation of the master project schedule. This schedule consists of milestone-based schedules for each of the team roles in the project team.
- *Creating the development, testing, and staging environments.* Creation of a separate environment in which to develop and test the solution. This environment is independent of the environment in which the solution will finally be deployed.
- *Closing the planning phase.* Completion of the milestone approval process. Documentation of the results of completing the tasks performed during the planning phase.

Milestones of the planning phase

During the planning phase, the team performs multiple tasks. The interim milestones of the planning phase are as follows:

- *Technology validation complete.* During technology validation, the team evaluates the products and technologies that will be used to create or deploy the solution. The team also audits the customer's current production environment. This includes server configurations, network, desktop software, and all relevant hardware.

- *Functional specification complete.* At this milestone, the functional specification is completed and submitted for review to the customers and stakeholders. Remember that the design document is different from the functional specification. The design document is written for the project team and describes the internal workings of the solution.

- *Master plan complete.* The master plan is a combination of the plans of various roles on the team. Its length and complexity depends on the size of the project.

- *Master project schedule complete.* The master project schedule includes all detailed project schedules and the solution release date. Like the master project plan, the master project schedule combines and integrates information from each of the roles on the team, in this case scheduling information.

- *Development and test environments set up.* A working environment allows proper development and testing of the solution and avoids any negative impact on systems to which the solution will eventually be deployed. This is also the environment in which the infrastructure components, such as server configurations, deployment automation tools, and hardware, are identified and configured.

The major milestone of the planning phase is the *project plan approved* milestone. At this milestone, the project team and key project stakeholders agree that interim milestones have been met, that due dates are realistic, that project roles and responsibilities are well defined, that everyone agrees to the deliverables for the project, and that mechanisms are in place for addressing areas of project risk.

Deliverables of the planning phase

The planning phase deliverables provide the basis for making future tradeoff decisions. The following deliverables are produced during the planning phase:

- Functional specification
- Risk management plan
- Master project plan and master project schedule

What Is the Developing Phase?

During the developing phase, the project team creates the solution. This process includes creating the code that implements the solution and documenting the code. In addition to developing code, the team also develops the infrastructure for the solution.

Development process

The team performs the following key tasks during the developing phase:

- *Starting the development cycle.* Verification that all tasks identified during the envisioning and planning phases have been completed so that the team can begin developing the solution.

- *Creating a prototype application.* Verification of the concepts of the solution design in an environment that resembles the environment to which the solution will be eventually deployed. This environment is as similar as possible to the production environment. This task is completed before development begins.

- *Developing the solution components.* Development of the solution's core components and the extension of these components to the specific needs of the solution.

- *Building the solution.* A series of daily or frequent builds that culminate with major internal builds that signify points when the development team is delivering key features of the solution.

- *Closing the developing phase.* Completion of all features, and delivery of code and documentation. The solution is considered complete, and the team enters a milestone approval process.

Milestones of the developing phase

During the developing phase, the team creates a proof-of-concept application and then creates the solution. The interim milestones of the developing phase are as follows:

- *Proof-of-concept application complete.* The proof-of-concept application tests key elements of the solution in a test environment. The team leads the operations team and users through the solution to validate their requirements.

- *Internal builds complete.* Because a solution is developed in segments, it is a good practice to synchronize the solution segments at product level. You do this with the help of internal builds. The number and frequency of internal builds depends on the size and complexity of the project.

The developing phase culminates in the *scope complete* milestone. At this milestone, all features are complete and have gone through unit testing. The product is now ready for external testing and stabilization. Additionally, customers, users, operations and support personnel, and key project stakeholders can evaluate the product and identify any issues that must be addressed before the solution is shipped.

Deliverables of the developing phase

The deliverables of the developing phase include:

- Source code and executable files
- Installation scripts and configuration settings for deployment
- Finalized functional specification
- Performance support elements
- Test specifications and test cases

What Is the Stabilizing Phase?

During the stabilizing phase, the team performs integration, load, and beta testing on the solution. In addition, the team tests the deployment scenarios for the solution. The team focuses on identifying, prioritizing, and resolving issues so that the solution can be prepared for release. During this phase, the solution progresses from the state of all features being complete as defined in the functional specification for this version to the state of meeting the defined quality levels. In addition, the solution is ready for deployment to the business.

Stabilization process

The team performs the following key tasks during the stabilizing phase:

- *Testing the solution.* Implementation of test plans to validate the solution. Once the solution is considered stable, a pilot is conducted in a test environment. A rigorous test includes:
  - Component testing
  - Database testing
  - Infrastructure testing
  - Security testing
  - Integration testing
  - User acceptance and usability testing
  - Stress, capacity, and performance testing
  - Regression testing
  - Recording the number of bugs
- *Conducting the pilot.* Deployment of the solution in a staging area and testing of the solution with actual users and real usage scenarios.

Test tracking and reporting

Test tracking and reporting occurs at frequent intervals during the developing, testing, and stabilizing phases. During the stabilizing phase, reporting is dependent upon the issue and bug count. Regular communication of test status to the team and other key stakeholders ensures a well-informed team.

Milestones of the stabilizing phase

The interim milestones of the stabilizing phase are as follows:

- *Bug convergence.* A milestone of the stabilizing phase that marks the point at which the team makes measurable progress against the active issue and bug count. At bug convergence, the rate of bugs resolved exceeds the rate of bugs found. Because the bug rate will still rise and fall—even after it starts its overall decline—bug convergence usually manifests itself as a trend rather than a fixed point in time.

  After bug convergence, the number of bugs should continue to decrease until zero-bug release. Bug convergence informs the team that the end of the project is near.

- *Zero-bug release.* A milestone of the stabilizing phase that marks the point at which the issue and bug count has met the zero-defect metric for this point in the project.

- *Release candidates.* A series of milestones of the stabilizing phase that reflect incremental improvements in the reduction of the issue and bug count as compared to that of the zero-bug release milestone.

- *Golden release.* A milestone of the stabilizing phase that is identified by the combination of zero-defect and success criteria metrics.

The stabilizing phase culminates in the *release readiness* milestone. After the solution has been reviewed and approved, it is ready for full deployment in the production environment. The release readiness milestone occurs when the team has addressed all issues and has shipped the product. At the release readiness milestone, the responsibility for managing and supporting the solution is officially transferred from the project team to the operations and support teams.

Deliverables of the stabilizing phase

The deliverables of the stabilizing phase are as follows:

- Final release
- Release notes
- Performance support elements
- Test results and testing tools
- Source code and executable files
- Project documents
- Milestone review

What Is the Deploying Phase?

During this phase, the team deploys the solution technology and site components, stabilizes the deployment, transfers the project to operations and support, and obtains final customer approval of the project. After deployment, the team conducts a project review and a customer satisfaction survey. The deploying phase culminates in the *deployment complete* milestone.

Deployment process

The team performs the following key tasks during the deploying phase:

- *Completion of deployment and operations procedures.* Formal documentation of deployment and operational procedures to outline how the project team intends to perform deployment and transition tasks.
- *Deployment and stabilization.* Completion of the actual component and site deployments.
- *Project review.* Completion of post-project reviews with the customer and project team.

Note   Stabilizing activities might continue during this phase because the project components are transferred from a test environment to a production environment.

Milestones of the deploying phase

The interim milestones of the deploying phase are as follows:

- *Core components deployed.* Most infrastructure solutions include a number of components that provide the underlying structure for the entire solution. Though these components do not represent the solution from the perspective of the customer, successful deployment of sites depends on these components. Depending on the solution, the core technology might need to be deployed before or simultaneously with site deployments. To avoid delays, core components must be reviewed and approved for deployment while other parts of the solution are still being stabilized.
- *Site deployments complete.* At the completion of this milestone, all intended users must be able to access the solution. Lead developers for each site must confirm that their sites are operating. This milestone might not be applicable for projects that do not include client-side deployments.
- *Deployment stable.* At this milestone, the customer and team agree that the sites are operating satisfactorily. Some issues might arise with the various site deployments. These issues can be tracked and resolved.

Note The customer might agree that the team has met its objectives before it can declare the solution to be in production and close the project. Making this agreement requires a stable solution and clearly stated success criteria. For the solution to be considered stable, appropriate operations and support systems must be implemented.

The period between the deployment stable milestone and the deployment complete milestone is sometimes referred to as a *quiet period*. Although the team is no longer active, team resources will respond to issues that are presented to them. Typical quiet periods last between 15 and 30 days. During this period, the team measures the effectiveness and performance of the solution and can estimate the maintenance effort required for continuing operations. The team can also work on the next release of the solution during this time.

- *Deployment complete*. This milestone is the culmination of the deploying phase. By this time, the deployed solution should be providing the expected business value to the customer.

It can be difficult to determine when a deployment is complete. Newly deployed systems often go through a continuous process of identifying and managing production support issues. The team can have a difficult time closing the project because of the ongoing issues that arise after deployment. Therefore, the team needs to clearly define a completion milestone for the deployment rather than attempting to reach a point of absolute finality.

Deliverables of the deploying phase

The deliverables of the deploying phase are as follows:

- Operation and support information systems
  - Procedures and processes
  - Knowledge base, reports, and logbooks
- Documentation repository for all versions of documents and code developed during the project
- A training plan
- Project completion report
  - Final versions of all project documents
  - Customer satisfaction data
  - Definition of next steps

Lesson 3: Introducing the Case Study— Adventure Works Cycles Application

This lesson introduces the scenario that is used to illustrate the concepts and procedures for designing applications that are based on the Microsoft .NET Framework. This scenario will be used in many of the forthcoming lessons.

After this lesson, you will be able to
- Recognize the basic business requirements of the case study application.

Estimated lesson time: 10 minutes

The Adventure Works Cycles Case Scenario

The purpose of this case study is to enable you, the application architect, to understand the nature of business problems that you will need to solve. Adventure Works Cycles, a large, multinational manufacturing company, produces and distributes metal and composite bicycles to North American, European, and Asian commercial markets. While its base operation is located in Bothell, Washington, and employs 500 people, several regional sales teams are located throughout the company's market region.

In 2000, Adventure Works Cycles bought a small manufacturing plant, Wide World Importers, which is located in Mexico City, Mexico. Wide World Importers manufactures several critical subcomponents for the Adventure Works Cycles product line. These subcomponents are shipped to the Bothell location for final product assembly. In 2001, Wide World Importers became the sole manufacturer and distributor of the touring bicycle product group.

After a successful fiscal year, Adventure Works Cycles is looking to broaden its market share by focusing its sales efforts on the company's best customers, extending product availability through an external Web site, and reducing the cost of sales by reducing production costs.

What Are the Business Problems?

The business problems can be categorized according to the various departments— Sales, Human Resources (HR), Wide World Importers Acquisition, Purchasing, Information Systems, Production, System Administration, and Engineering.

Business problems in the Sales department

Sales representatives from regional sales offices have assigned sales territories in the United States, Canada, England, Australia, Germany, and France. Each regional office consists of several sales representatives and a team manager. In their daily sales activities, sales representatives use both laptops and Handheld PCs that run Microsoft® Windows CE.

A typical work day for a sales representative starts with the representative dialing in to the regional office and downloading current data such as inventory, product, and promotional information. During customer visits, the sales representative takes orders on the laptop or Handheld PC. At the end of each day, the sales representative sets up appointments for the following day or week, checks the appointments of other representatives in the area for possible collaboration, and updates the contact list. The sales representative dials back in to the regional office, sends updated information, and receives any new internal communications from the base office or regional office. The company currently uses Microsoft Outlook® for e-mail.

The sales teams have identified the following requirements that will enable them to perform their jobs better:

- *Customer segmentation and profiling.* The sales team needs to be able to extract valuable information from raw data available in the databases to answer questions such as the following:
  - What are the early warning signs of problems?
  - Who are the best customers across all product lines? With whom should the sales team focus its efforts for building long-term relationships?
  - What are customers' issues, categorized according to demographic groups (geographic location, revenue history, and so on)?
  - What products are the customers buying and at what rate?
- *Sales activity.*
  - The current discount policy allows sales representatives the discretion to discount a particular order up to 15 percent. Sales managers can increase their own discounts or customer discounts up to 20 percent. The product should allow employees to provide appropriate discounts to customers, depending on the employee's role.
  - To support sales activity throughout the world, the sales team needs international support, including the ability to have product information, especially dates and pricing, available in multiple languages and currency types.
- *Internal communication.* Each sales representative must receive customer and sales data pertinent only to that representative. Each team manager must receive relevant customer and appointment data along with detailed information for each sales representative on that manager's team. A manager must be able to assign customers to sales representatives based on their relationships with the customers, though usually customers are assigned by region.

- *Opportunity management.* Sales representatives need a method to store and access sales opportunity data and, when a sale is generated, to convert some or all of the information into a sales order without reentering information.

- *Decision support system.* The decision support system should provide the following features:

  - Allow marketing/sales staff to query and use customer data to generate standard reports; execute custom queries; obtain information related to promotion tracking, sales forecasting, and customer segmentation; and access third-party data sources and financial evaluation tools.

  - Present all customer activity in a unified way, including multiple contacts, conversations, and transactions.

  - Allow marketing personnel to initiate new promotions and programs on a multinational basis. Currently, sales representatives do not know how to associate these programs with specific areas for the best impact.

  - Identify, analyze, and share all aspects of customer relationships with individuals throughout multiple departments.

Business problems in the HR department

The current retention rate of Adventure Works Cycles employees is 90 percent for hourly employees and 75 percent for salaried employees. Management predicts that they will need to hire 35 percent more workers during the next fiscal year to replace departing employees and meet the projected increase in production. In addition, the acquisition of Wide World Importers has significantly increased the department's hiring and employee retention tasks because of the increase in employees and job candidates.

Management has determined that they need a solution to track both employee reviews and the resumes of prospective employees. In addition, they want to improve their ability to forecast the number of employees needed and to plan for changes in work compensation and benefits. The HR department requires the following features from the solution:

- *Resume and review management.* All resumes and reviews are stored in documents of different formats. A system is needed to provide:

  - Unified storage for all file types

  - Access to existing employee data (relational database tables) with links to reviews or resumes

  - Tools for converting all files types to documents that can be shared internally across departments

  - Ability to secure some areas of documents, such as salary information, from designated users

  - Ability to search resumes or reviews for keywords or phrases

- *Analysis and planning.* The HR department needs support for performing the following types of analysis:
  - Compensation and benefits analysis, including impact of international currency exchange rates
  - Planning to assess the required workforce
  - Payroll cost simulations and forecasting

Business problems in the Wide World Importers Acquisition department

Wide World Importers is located in Mexico City, Mexico. They manufacture several critical components used in the Adventure Works Cycles product line. Adventure Works Cycles recently purchased Wide World Importers in an effort to expand its infrastructure to support the expected growth of the company. Wide World Importers is considered a separate business unit from Adventure Works Cycles; however, it is imperative that some applications and data be shared between the two companies. The business problems associated with this department are as follows:

- *Data transfer.* Adventure Works Cycles cannot migrate and transfer data regularly because:
  - Wide World Importers does not have a high-speed data transfer utility for moving data from their local database to the three Microsoft SQL Server™ databases in Bothell.
  - Adventure Works Cycles has a centralized environment; it needs to enhance the scalability of its production database by transitioning to a distributed environment.
  - The data is currently not being transferred by means of a secure network connection.
- *Administration and support.* Wide World Importers has limited Information Systems (IS) support. Departments maintain their own workstations and the servers that support the Oracle database are monitored and maintained by two administrators and the IS manager. The company lacks many of the standardized processes used by Adventure Works Cycles in its daily operations management.

Business problems in the Purchasing department

Adventure Works Cycles currently uses several vendors to supply various components and raw materials for its product line. The Purchasing department has identified a major supplier who is interested in establishing an Electronic Data Interchange (EDI) with Adventure Works Cycles to transmit critical data and documents such as purchase orders, invoices, payments, and product specifications. Purchasing agents and accounting employees spend more than 50 percent of their time handling these major vendors. After the EDI solution is fully implemented, the Purchasing department manager anticipates a 30 percent increase in employee efficiency in these departments.

The Adventure Works Cycles application must provide the following features:

- The ability for Adventure Works Cycles and the vendors to transmit and receive a variety of data and file types, including structured and semi-structured data
- The ability for vendors to submit their data directly to the Microsoft SQL Server™ purchasing tables
- A Web-based system that provides secure information specific to each vendor
- The ability to automatically detect when the vendors have incoming files or other data ready for Adventure Works Cycles to receive

Business problems in the Information Systems department

The Adventure Works Cycles Internet site is being developed. Currently, customers can access basic product information, find the closest sales office, and request printed information. They cannot order products online or view the status of an existing order. The ability to search the current Web site for product information is limited to viewing products by category. To increase its customer base and provide additional functionality for existing customers, Adventure Works Cycles is expanding its Internet site to include the following features:

- Online product ordering for customers
- Online order-status checking
- Better search capabilities for product information
- Ability to access explicit sections of engineering product specifications
- Ability to view product information and pricing in international currency and character sets

In addition to the Internet site, Adventure Works Cycles has a small intranet Web site consisting of a home page and links to all department sites. Each department is responsible for maintaining its own site and notifying the IS department of any changes that need to be made to its links on the home page. The focus for the intranet site is to improve internal communication. Jose Lugo, Adventure Works Cycles' finance manager, says that it is difficult to get information from one department and supply it to other departments. The department managers want to route more file transactions and data access through the internal Web site. This intranet site must support the following features:

- The ability to search for information across departmental sites.
- The ability to change or update to internal information (pricing changes, customer complaints, and so on).
- The availability of product data to all departments. It must be visible and adaptable to multiple needs (sales, marketing, and engineering).

Business problems in the Production department

The Adventure Works Cycles product line consists of nine bicycle product groups. Each product contains one or more subcomponents, depending on the customer order. Currently, production receives a specification from the Engineering department and uses it to assemble the product. A product clerk enters all the specification information used by production. Certain basic product information is available to customers on the external Web site. However, customers do not have access to the entire product specification. The entire product specification is available to the sales staff from the internal site.

As products move through each assembly area, subcomponents and other value-added materials are added to the product until it reaches the final assembly area. Some of the problems associated with production workflow are as follows:

- *Scheduling and production.* To avoid delays in production, the team needs:
  - Easier access to manufacturing data, such as work orders and inventory levels, that is applicable to a specific assembly area.
  - The ability to analyze workflow data.
- *Inventory auditing.* Instead of manually auditing and updating the inventory system, the company wants to use barcode scanning by using a Handheld PC with the existing inventory audit application.

Business problems in the System Administration department

Full availability of Adventure Works Cycles' key systems has become a focus for the System Administration department. Complaints about the amount of system downtime have been increasing steadily.

The System Administration department does not have central control of database management functions. As a result, each database group is developing its own practices and procedures. This decentralized approach might not be an optimal use of resources. In addition, the IS staff has requested a better method of monitoring system resources across all operating systems.

The System Administration department at Adventure Works Cycles must provide the following functionality to address these business problems:

- Availability of services at all times to support Adventure Works Cycles' key systems
- Backup and recovery systems for all databases being used at Adventure Works Cycles, including data stored at World Wide Importers
- Monitoring of all resources across all operating systems

Business problems in the Engineering department

The Engineering department is responsible for designing the major components for all Adventure Works Cycles products. The team needs a system to manage the documentation needs of the department. Some of the requirements of this system are as follows:

- *Collaborative content management.* The department needs an automated system that allows them to control how drawings and specifications are reviewed, approved, and released to manufacturing for use.
- *Accessing and storage of multiple file types.* The department needs a consistent method for storing, retrieving, and archiving various files, such as computer-aided design (CAD) drawings and XML product specifications. This system must be linked to the tabular data used to track drawing and specification versions.

What Are the Requirements of the Adventure Works Cycles Application?

The Adventure Works Cycles application is a Web-based retail application. It is intended for both customers and other businesses, such as retail stores reselling Adventure Works Cycles products. In addition, the application needs to host one or more pages to allow potential job applicants to submit resumes to Adventure Works Cycles and retrieve and edit the resumes.

Business tasks

The Adventure Works Cycles application must support the following tasks:

- Customers must be able to place orders.
- Customers must be able to delete orders.
- Application system must be able to reject orders.
- Customers must be able to modify existing orders that are being processed.
- Customers and resellers must be able to review existing orders.
- Customers must be able to create new customer records.
- Customers must be able to edit customer information.
- Customers must be able to submit resumes for employment consideration.
- Customers must be able to retrieve and edit previously submitted resumes.

Note   Customers and resellers can access only their own information.

Web site requirements

The Internet Web site for Adventure Works Cycles must support the following features:

- Every page on the Web site must display a search option with appropriate search controls and a navigation bar on the left side.

- The customer must be able to search for products by using a part of a product description and a price range.

- The home page must display products that are on sale and special offers, and it must include a picture and description of each product.

- A Groups page must display a hierarchical list of links to groups of bicycle models or bicycle parts in a tree structure.

- A Product Details page must display information about a single product model. It must contain the product name and description, a large picture, and a price range. If the model is available in multiple sizes, multiple colors, or both, appropriate drop-down lists must be provided. When the customer selects a size or color, the other list is repopulated, and the price range narrows to the price of the specific product.

- A Current Order page must display the products a customer has ordered and the quantity of each product, and it must include unit and total prices. A customer must be able to change quantities or remove items from this page. A Continue Shopping button must take the customer back to the last instance of the Products page visited.

- A Customer Sign-in page must allow registered customers to sign in with their e-mail addresses and passwords. New customers must be able to register from this page. (Resellers will not use this page.)

- A Sign-in Information page must allow customers to input or change their e-mail addresses, passwords, and other personal information.

- An Address Maintenance page must allow customers to create, view, update, and delete billing and shipping addresses in their profiles.

- An Addresses Selection page must allow customers to select or remove billing and shipping addresses for an order.

- An Order Summary page must display an order, and it must include sales tax, shipping cost, and the details of reseller discounts. The customer must be able to change the quantities and remove items.

- An Arrange Payment page must allow customers to use credit cards that are on file in the database or to input new credit card information. Resellers must be able to select payment types and input purchase order numbers.

- An Order Confirmation page must display a summary of the submitted order, and it must include an order date, a confirmation number, and order status.

- An Order Status Lookup page must display a list of all orders entered by the signed-in customer. The customer must be able to select one of the orders so that it can be displayed in the Order Confirmation page.

- An Available Jobs page must allow customers to submit their resumes.

In the remaining chapters, you will learn how to design a solution that meets the requirements of the Adventure Works Cycles application.

Summary

- The MSF Process Model is a combination of the waterfall and spiral process models.
- The MSF Process Model is a milestone-based, iterative approach to developing solutions.
- The MSF Team Model specifies six roles for project teams that are involved in developing solutions: product management, program management, development, testing, release management, and user experience.
- You need to define the scope of a project by managing tradeoffs.
- MSF recommends an iterative approach to designing solutions.
- You implement iterations in a development life cycle by creating versioned releases and maintaining living documents.
- You create the vision/scope document during the envisioning phase of the MSF Process Model.
- You create functional specifications during the planning phase of the MSF Process Model.
- You create the solution during the developing phase of the MSF Process Model.
- You test the solution and conduct pilots during the stabilizing phase of the MSF Process Model.
- You deploy the solution in the production environment and submit the solution to the operations and support team during the deploying phase of the MSF Process Model.

Review

The following questions are intended to reinforce key information presented in this chapter. If you are unable to answer a question, review the lesson materials and try the question again. You can find answers to the questions in the appendix.

1. Describe the differences between the waterfall model and the spiral model, and describe how MSF uses both in the MSF Process Model.

2. In the MSF Team Model, who is responsible for the design process?

3. The tradeoff triangle describes the three types of tradeoffs that a project team and the customer can make. What is a fourth tradeoff that could be considered but that should never be compromised?

4. Using the following statement, complete the tradeoff matrix below.

   "Given a fixed feature set, we will choose resources and adjust the schedule as necessary."

	Fixed	Chosen	Adjustable
Resources			
Schedule			
Features			

5. Describe the purpose of performing daily builds in the MSF Process Model.

6. When you reach the release readiness milestone, what phase have you completed?

7. During which phase of the MSF Process Model is the initial risk assessment document created?

8. When are test cases established in the MSF Process Model?

9. List several types of tests that are performed during the stabilizing phase.

10. Why is it important to create a vision statement for the project during the envisioning phase?

11. What are some of the key tasks that are performed during the planning phase?

12. Describe the *quiet period* and the activities that occur during this period.

C H A P T E R   2

Gathering and Analyzing Information

About This Chapter

Gathering and analyzing information are steps that you perform throughout the Microsoft® Solutions Framework (MSF) Process Model. These lessons provide you with an overview of how to gather and analyze information. You will learn about the types of information that you need to gather, sources of information, and some techniques for gathering information. In addition, you will learn how to analyze all the gathered information and become familiar with some techniques for analyzing information.

Note   This chapter presents information that is not specific to a particular phase in the MSF process but that is relevant to all phases. It is important to learn information gathering and analysis techniques before you start the process of envisioning and designing a solution.

Before You Begin

To complete the lessons in this chapter, you must

- Be familiar with the MSF Process Model.
- Have Microsoft Visio® 2000 Professional, for creating diagrams.

Lesson 1: Gathering Information

When gathering information, you need to be aware from the outset of the various types and characteristics of information to ensure that you gather the appropriate information. The purpose of this lesson is to introduce you to the various ways you can think about the information you need to gather about a business challenge. By taking a broad view of information, you can increase your chances of gathering all of the input you need to make an effective analysis.

After this lesson, you will be able to

- Identify the types of information that you should gather.
- Identify the techniques for gathering information.
- Identify various sources of information for gathering requirements.
- Create an information gathering strategy.

Estimated lesson time: 20 minutes

Categories of Information

An enterprise architecture is a representation of a business—a dynamic system—at a single point in time. The enterprise architecture for a business aligns information technology groups and processes with the goals of a business. To gather information about an enterprise architecture, use four descriptive categories from an enterprise architecture model to guide and classify the information you gather. The four categories are business, applications, operation, and technology.

Business

The *business* category describes how the business works. It describes the functions and the cross-functional activities that an organization performs. Information from this category also describes the business's high-level goals and objectives, products and services, financial structures, integrated business functions and processes, major organizational structures, and the interaction of these elements. It includes broad business strategies and plans for transforming the organization from its current state to its future state.

Application

The *application* category includes the services and functionality that can cross organizational boundaries and link users of different skills and functions to achieve common business objectives. Information in the application category describes the automated and non-automated services that support the business processes. It provides information on the interaction and interdependencies of the business's application systems.

Automated business services can include complete applications, utilities, productivity tools, components, and code modules that allow for the analysis of information or task functionality.

In an organization, identical tasks are often repeated multiple times by using different tools. As you gather information about processes in the organization, investigate the different applications used to conduct company activities. These existing applications or portions of these applications can provide core services for any new solution. It is more cost effective to reuse than to re-create these services. The information you gather will help to refine the business processes by indicating potential inefficiencies or redundancies.

The application category provides information about the current use of systems and services. You will also obtain indicators about future directions when you gather information from resources such as users and business documents.

Operations

The *operations* category describes what the organization needs to know to run its business processes and operations. This category includes standard data models, data management policies, and descriptions of the patterns of information consumption and production in the business.

You should identify the information's origin, ownership, and consumption. Tracking and analyzing its access and use patterns provides the basis for making data distribution, replication, and partitioning decisions, in addition to identifying what is needed to establish standards and guidelines for replication, repositories, and data warehousing. Often, the consumers of information are not adequately questioned to determine not only what information they need, but also what they do with the information when they have it.

The relationship between key business processes and the information required to perform these processes helps to set standards and guidelines for creating, retrieving, updating, and deleting information and data; for sharing critical documents and data; and for defining security levels and standards for access. Realize that not all information is centralized or easy to access by each person or system that needs the information. Often, the information most critical to a business resides on database servers, on the workstations that make up the active working environment of the business, and possibly in the heads of the employees (meaning that the information is not recorded anywhere).

Technology

The *technology* category defines the technical services needed to perform and support the business mission, including the topologies, development environments, application programming interfaces (APIs), security, network services, database management system (DBMS) services, technical specifications, hardware tiers, operating systems, and more.

This category also provides information about the standards and guidelines that a business uses for acquiring and deploying workstation and server tools, base applications, infrastructure services, network connectivity components, and platforms.

Technology provides the link between applications and information. Applications are created and based on different technologies. They use technology to access information, which is stored by using various storage technologies.

You can use information from the technology category to determine the standard interfaces, services, and application models to be used in development. This information can translate into development resources for the project teams, including component and code libraries, standards documents, and design guidelines. This information can also provide a basis for an application's design goals and constraints.

What Are the Techniques for Gathering Information?

There are six main techniques that you can use for gathering information:

- Shadowing
- Interviewing
- Focus groups
- Surveys
- User instruction
- Prototyping

Note   You might not use all of these techniques. You need to identify which techniques will work best for the specific source you are going to extract information from. In addition, you need not be an expert on all of the techniques. For implementing these techniques, you might need training or the help of an expert.

Shadowing

Shadowing is a technique in which you observe a user performing the tasks in the actual work environment and ask the user any questions related to the task. You typically follow the user as the user performs daily tasks. The information you obtain by using this technique is firsthand and in context. In addition, you understand the purpose of performing a specific task. To gather as much information as possible, you need to encourage the user to explain the reasons for performing a task in as much detail as possible.

Shadowing can be both passive and active. When performing *passive shadowing*, you observe the user and listen to any explanations that the user might provide. When performing *active shadowing*, you ask questions as the user explains events and activities. You might also be given the opportunity to perform some of the tasks, at the user's discretion.

Tip   Shadowing works well for tasks that are performed frequently. However, if a task is performed only occasionally, finding an opportunity to shadow someone for that specific task might be difficult.

Shadowing is a good way to get an idea of what a person does on a day-to-day basis. However, you might not be able to observe all the tasks during shadowing because more than likely the person will not, during that session, perform all the tasks he or she is assigned. For example, accounting people might create reports at the end of the month, developers might create status reports on a weekly basis, and management might schedule status meetings only biweekly.

In addition to the information that you would collect from the individual, you might collect relevant work artifacts, such as documents and screen shots of the current solution.

Note   In information gathering, an *artifact* is any item that is physically available in the business environment that describes an element or core business process. Artifacts are discussed in detail later in this lesson.

Examples of questions for shadowing

While gathering information by using the shadowing technique, you encourage the user to answer the following questions:

- How do users structure their work?
- What decisions do users make when starting or completing a task?
- How does the current implementation define the way users perform their jobs?
- How often does the system interfere with their jobs?
- How do interruptions affect users? Can users resume where they left off after being interrupted?
- With how many people does a specific user interact during a given activity?
- What modifications has the user made over time to make it easier to complete the task?
- Are there any variations in the steps that the user performs to complete the task? What are these variations, and under what conditions are the variations used?

In addition to learning how users perform their tasks, you can learn about the parts of the current solution and process that cause users to feel dissatisfied or frustrated.

During the shadowing process, look for answers to the following questions:

- How do users currently perform these tasks?
- How can the processes be made more efficient? Should any tasks that are performed manually be performed by an automated solution?
- Which related tasks might affect the design of the solution?
- What system features are needed to support the tasks?
- What are the performance criteria?
- How should the features of the solution be structured?
- How can the current system be improved?
- Which features of the current system are being used frequently, and which features are being used rarely?
- What do users like and dislike about the current system?
- How can training and support costs be reduced?
- What information about the users is not documented?
- What are the users' working environments?
- What are the characteristics and preferences of users?
- What are the concepts and terminology used by the users?
- What training has been provided to users?
- What training do users need?
- Have users been through training, or are they self-taught? How does the training or lack of training affect their ability to use the system and perform their tasks?

Note   Ensure that you observe and question both the management and users. If there are external customers, include them in your observations.

Interviewing

While shadowing provides an effective means to discover what is currently being done in a business, it might not provide all the necessary information. Shadowing is not the best option for gathering information about tasks such as management-level activities; long-term activities that span weeks, months, or years; or processes that require little or no human intervention. An example of a process that requires no human intervention is the automatic bill-paying service provided by financial institutions. For gathering information about such activities and processes, you need to conduct interviews.

An *interview* is a one-on-one meeting between a member of the project team and a user or a stakeholder. The quality of the information a team gathers depends on the skills of both the interviewer and the interviewee. An interviewer who becomes an ally can learn a great deal about the difficulties and limitations of the current solution. Interviews provide the opportunity to ask a wide range of questions about topics that you cannot observe by means of shadowing.

Some important points to remember before conducting interviews include:

- Start with non-specific set of questions and encourage interviewees to think about all the tasks they perform and any information they can provide.
- Using the answers to the questions, ask interviewees to put the larger tasks they perform in order, and to break the larger tasks into smaller tasks.
- Specifically ask interviewees to identify information that is usually missing and alternative paths that can occur.
- Reiterate through the preceding steps several times and continue to ask interviewees what else might be involved.
- Ask interviewees for ideas that they have to improve the situation, but avoid assuming that those ideas are the correct solution.

Examples of questions for interviewing

While conducting an interview, structure questions carefully so that you do not ask misleading questions or questions that ask for more than one type of information. Some of the questions that you might ask during an interview are:

- What problems do you encounter while performing your tasks?
- What kind of help do you need when you work remotely?
- Do you have special needs that are not documented?
- What business policies help you or hinder you in performing your job?
- What individuals or documents provide essential information that you need to do your job?
- What other users or systems, such as third-party suppliers or support specialists, affect your work?

Focus groups

A *focus group* is a session in which individuals discuss a topic and provide feedback to a facilitator. Focus groups concentrate on group interviewing techniques. Use this method in cases in which there are more users than you can involve directly in the information gathering process. For the information gathered during a focus group to be useful, ensure that the participants of the focus group represent the users or stakeholders associated with the business. You should also ensure that you have appropriately defined the topic of the focus group and that you keep the group focused on this topic.

Focus groups allow you to gather detailed information about how an activity fits into the business as a whole. Individuals in a focus group can fill knowledge gaps for one another and provide a complete description of a business process.

Focus groups might not be successful if the participants are located in different geographical locations. Focus groups also might not work if the users that were identified to participate do not perform the same activity or do not have enough knowledge about the activity. Finally, focus groups are not successful if the facilitator is unable to direct the meeting and keep the discussion focused.

Surveys

Surveys consist of sets of questions that are created to gather information. Examples of surveys include user registration forms and customer feedback or satisfaction forms.

Creating survey questions can be a labor-intensive process. You need a trained professional for creating the survey questions and analyzing the results of the survey. You can use surveys to gather information and to identify further information gathering activities that you need.

One of the benefits of using surveys is that they enable users to respond anonymously. You can collect information that might be impossible to collect with any other technique. However, you might need to treat the responses to the survey with confidentiality to protect the respondents. You might want to modify or neutralize the language so that the identity of the person remains confidential. Surveys provide results that can be tabulated and easily interpreted.

Note   The results of a survey can be affected by user attitudes. Surveys are therefore very subjective.

Examples of information that can be collected by using surveys include:

- Organizational structures, policies, or practices that facilitate or interfere with tasks
- Frustrations with technical support structures or policies
- Special needs related to hardware or software
- Training issues, such as the effectiveness of current training programs, types of training programs that users like, and training programs that work best in the users' work environment

User instruction

When you use the *user instruction* technique, users actually train you on the tasks that they perform. This allows you to participate in the activity and view each step of the process from the user's perspective. You might also gain knowledge that an individual has learned over time and that is unavailable from artifacts or systems.

User instruction can be time consuming if the process you are investigating is long. This method could also be frustrating for the researcher if the user is not accustomed to teaching others. In addition, different users might perform the same task differently. Consequently, you should collect information from multiple users.

Planning   Identify the experts in different activities within the business. They might know shortcuts that overcome problems in a process. Experts can act as models for developing new processes or improving existing processes.

You can also use *help desks* at a business to gather information about the user experience. A help desk is a useful source because it provides a direct perspective on the problems experienced by users. Gathering information from help desk is one way of benefiting from user instructions.

By allowing users to teach you the tasks they perform, you can gather information to determine:

- User interface design
- Training needs for both current and future processes
- System performance criteria
- The impact of the physical environment on a task

Prototyping

Prototyping allows you to gather information by simulating the production environment. You can use several tools to collect information, such as a camera to monitor visual activity or a computer program to monitor keystrokes and mouse clicks. The tool that you select for prototyping depends on the type of information you want to collect.

Use prototypes when it is impossible to shadow a person in the normal work environment. The data that you collect by prototyping is typically empirical rather than responses from users. Therefore, you can easily validate this data. However, the cost of prototyping might be high.

Prototypes can help you to verify or document information from the user and business perspectives, including:

- Customer quality requirements
- Response-time requirements and goals
- Ease of use
- Integration of current technologies and applications
- User interface issues, such as the features that users want to see added to an application
- Verification of workflow processes

What Are the Sources of Information?

You have learned about the different types of information that you can gather in a business. This information can be found in various forms. The number and diversity of information sources depends on the size of the business. Some of the information sources are:

- Artifacts
- Systems
- People

Artifacts

An *artifact* in information gathering is an item that is physically available in the business environment and that describes an element or core business process. As in archeology, artifacts help us understand the current environment. They provide information about tasks, processes, business needs, and constraints. Examples of artifacts include training manuals, video recordings, regulatory requirements, earlier program files or tapes, help desk documentation, and financial reports.

You can easily identify some artifacts that are used in a business. For example, employees keep frequently used artifacts around their work areas. Other artifacts might be stored in file cabinets or on computer media and are therefore less visible. You might require access to proprietary artifacts to review all information thoroughly. Use discretion in handling artifacts that are directly or indirectly part of the intellectual property that allows a business to compete in the marketplace.

Individuals in a business typically develop their own artifacts. For example, a user might create an instruction sheet for an application or process, or outline how to accomplish a task in e-mail messages. These unofficial artifacts provide valuable information. They indicate not only what people do in their daily work, but also the type of support information that is lacking in the current solution and possibly why they need to perform these tasks. Sometimes these artifacts will be the only documentation you will find related to certain processes.

During a project, the project team creates artifacts such as project meeting notes, summaries of the information gathered within the business, and the vision document. Some artifacts, such as meeting notes, are used exclusively by the project team. However, the vision document is shared by both the project team and stakeholders.

Systems

Systems describe an element of the business that is performing an action. A specific system is a set of discrete processes that accomplish an action. A system might be composed of subsystems. A system can be a tangible process, such as an inventory tracking system, or an intangible process, such as the methods that a manager uses to identify and resolve problems within a department.

Systems can be complex because they can contain multiple subsystems and many categories of information. In addition, all the subsystems might not be readily apparent. For these reasons, you might need to budget additional time to understand a system completely. Systems indicate how a business conducts day-to-day activities.

Tip   It is a good practice to enlist the help of someone who is an expert on the system and have the expert lead you through the different processes that the system performs.

People

The people who are stakeholders in the business can be the source of valuable insights into the business, often providing information that is not documented anywhere. These stakeholders include executives, developers, managers, customers, and users. In cases where documentation is incomplete (or non-existent), people might be the only source for the information you need to learn about the business.

Before approaching people to gather information, take the time to identify the different roles that the people perform in the business. For example, the group of people who provide support and information to users to help them perform their tasks might provide insight into which areas cause the most difficulties for users. Long-term employees with experiences in multiple operations within the business can provide insight as to how different activities relate to each other. Also, if the business uses a third-party vendor for any of its processes, the vendor might have a unique perspective on the efficiency of the business and its processes.

Planning   Before talking to users, you should gain some experience with the systems that they use. Gaining this experience helps you avoid broad questions like "How do you use the system?" "What do you do throughout the day?" or "What is a workday like for you?"

How to Define the Information Gathering Strategy

When gathering information, you should define an information gathering strategy. Defining an information gathering strategy includes identifying the users, defining questions, and choosing an appropriate technique for gathering information.

When defining an information strategy, you need to keep in mind the following questions:

- What sources do you want to poll for information?
- What information do you need to collect?
- What techniques will you use to collect the information and to what sources will each technique be applied?
- How will you record the information you collect?
- What time frame will you use to collect the information?

The following are some of the guidelines that you can use to define an information strategy:

- *Use multiple information gathering techniques.* If you rely on only one information gathering technique, you might have an incomplete view of the business. By combining various techniques, you overcome any shortcomings associated with any one technique. For example, assume that a process occurs once per month in the accounting department of a business. If you shadow a user in the accounting department for a few days, you might miss important information about the process because the user might not perform the tasks for this process while you are shadowing. By complementing shadowing with a focus group or a follow-up interview, you can gather information about all the processes that occur in the accounting department.

- *Identify the most effective technique.* Weigh the advantages and disadvantages of each technique when you are developing your information gathering strategy. For example, you might need to collect information as quickly as possible to respond to an immediate business challenge. Surveys take time to plan, administer, and analyze. Instead, shadowing, interviews, or user instruction can help you gather information quickly.

- *Remember all perspectives, types of information, and information sources.* Regardless of the information gathering technique, remember that you need to gather information from both user and business perspectives. Explore as many sources of information as possible within the time you have to gather information.

- *Gather information from groups that use similar business processes.* Different groups in a business might be following similar processes and might have responded to similar business challenges. Information gathered from those groups might help the project team to look at the business challenge from a new perspective.

Lesson 2: Analyzing Information

In this lesson, you transition from the process of gathering information to the process of analyzing information. The processes of gathering and analyzing information are iterative. You gather some information and analyze it. As you review that information, you will undoubtedly discover that you have more questions. You will then formulate your questions and take them back to the appropriate sources for clarification. Having this new information will help you to continue analyzing the business. This form of collaboration will continue throughout the life cycle of the project, although most of the information gathering and analysis will occur at the beginning of the life cycle.

After this lesson, you will be able to

- Analyze enterprise architecture information.
- Describe use cases and usage scenarios.
- Create internal project documentation.

Estimated lesson time: 20 minutes

Enterprise Architecture Information

When you think you have gathered enough information from the customer, you will have a large amount of information that you need to review to determine what information is most relevant to the business challenge. You need to synthesize the information to create a detailed description of the current state of the business.

As you analyze the information you have gathered, verify that you have enough information to indicate the current state of the business and product requirements, including:

- Security needs.
- Support structures for the solution and their characteristics.
- Planned changes in the business that could affect the product design.
- Performance that users expect or that the business needs to remain competitive.
- Existing applications that will need to interact with the new product.
- How the existing business processes affect the solution.

As you synthesize and analyze the information, you can identify any gaps that exist in the information you collected, and, if necessary, gather additional information.

When the development team actually develops the final product, it will need to verify that the final product meets all the requirements that were established during the gathering and analyzing processes. The team will also need to document the effects that the new product might have on the existing environment in terms of new requirements for the business, such as support, maintenance, and extensibility issues. The new requirements must also adhere to the constraints that you documented during analysis.

High-Level Use Cases and Usage Scenarios

After you have synthesized the information, you can develop use cases and usage scenarios to document the business processes and business and user requirements in more detail. The use cases and usage scenarios that you develop will provide structure for the development team when it designs the solution. In addition, each use case and usage scenario will correspond to one or more requirements. This correspondence allows you to ensure that the requirements are being met.

Use cases

Use cases show the functionality of a system and how an individual interacts with the system to obtain value.

The purposes of use cases are to:

- Identify the business process and all activities from start to finish.
- Document the context and environmental issues.
- Establish a connection between business needs and user requirements.
- Describe needs and requirements in the context of use.
- Focus users and the development team.

Use cases provide the following benefits:

- Provide context for requirements
- Facilitate common understanding
- Provide the basis for usage scenarios
- Facilitate objectivity and consistency in evaluating user suggestions

Usage scenarios

Use cases describe the high-level interactions between an individual and a system. *Usage scenarios* provide additional information about the activities and task sequences that constitute a process. Together, use cases and usage scenarios provide a description of a workflow process.

You will learn how to create use cases and usage scenarios in Lesson 4.

Draft Requirements Document

After the team has gathered information from the customers, one of the steps in analysis is to create a draft requirements document. This document includes a preliminary list of requirements from the information that is gathered by the team. The main purpose of this document is to record any possible requirements and, in doing that, to ensure that no valuable information is lost. The information that you gather from different sources will include requirements and wants from the business and user perspectives. The requirements indicate what the product or solution needs to do to solve the business challenge as derived from the business and user perspectives. The wants indicate what stakeholders and users would like to see in the final product or solution.

The requirements listed in the draft requirements document are not refined and therefore can be a combination of requirements and wants. These requirements are refined further in later stages of envisioning and planning, when the team gathers more information from the customers.

You will learn more about identifying requirements, wants, and constraints in Chapter 4, "Creating the Conceptual Design."

Example of an interview

Following is an example of an interview from the Adventure Works Cycles scenario that was introduced in Chapter 1, "Introduction to Designing Business Solutions."

Summary of an interview with the territory sales manager

We had a great year in sales this year. Our jobs have been a lot easier since the company equipped us with laptop computers and PDAs. We have been doing some forecasting for the next year, and we are starting to see a slow decline in sales, particularly if we continue to operate like we have in the past. The sales department has established a number of goals for the new fiscal year. The top three goals are (a) focus on our best customers, (b) use sales staff time more effectively, and (c) manage sales opportunities better.

We don't have an easy way to analyze our customer base. Currently, customer data is stored in our systems, but there's no easy way to retrieve the data and allow us to view the data in different ways. To better identify our best customers and why they are our best customers, we need a way to access our data and to be able to analyze it in a meaningful way.

Another problem we've experienced in recent months is in presenting our products and achieving sales in our foreign markets. Currently, all the information on our computers is written in English only. We need to store multilingual and multiregional information in the database rather than depending on the sales force to translate the information.

Example of an interview   *(continued)*

Our team needs to obtain the latest pricing information on a daily basis, and we should be doing this every day. Currently, the sales representative connects to the corporate network and downloads the new pricing list each day in the morning. However, the download process does not identify which prices have been modified for that individual sales representative. So the sales representative must download the entire list every morning. You can imagine how customers feel when they have negotiated a deal with us only to find out that the price was incorrect.

Another area that needs definite improvement is in our sales opportunities management. Employees are supposed to use our customer management system to plan, execute, and track sales and marketing strategy. In addition to that, sales representatives need to install a large application on their laptop computers and connect to the corporate network to use it. We want to be more mobile than that; we want to be able to access this information from a Web site. The information must be easy to access and meaningful for the sales representatives and the company; otherwise it doesn't help anyone. We want to achieve the following goals with the new system: Minimize the amount of technical knowledge that sales and marketing needs to access the data, and allow the staff to obtain standard reports, generate custom queries, track promotions, and view customer segmentation information. In addition, we want this system to be flexible enough so that we can add third-party data sources and financial evaluation tools. No matter who views a particular customer's information, that individual must get a clear, unified view of the customer and the customer's relationship with us.

Example of a use case diagram

Figure 2.1 shows a preliminary use case, which is based on the interview shown in the previous section.

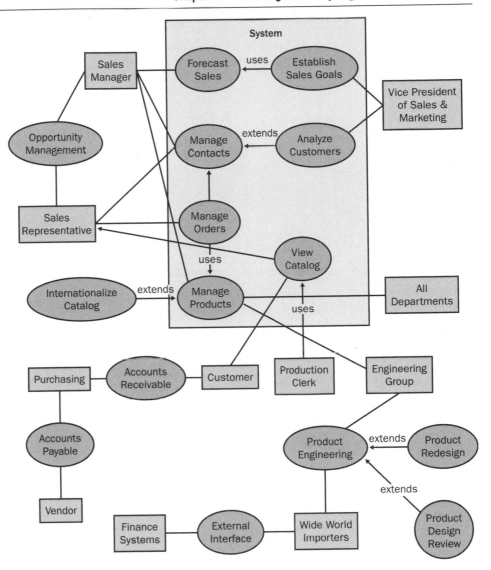

Figure 2.1. Use case diagram

Example of a draft requirements document

Figure 2.2 contains a list of draft requirements that you might have identified from the interview and use case.

	A	B	C	D	E	F	G	H
1								
2		Req ID	Req desc	Priority	Source	UC ID	Current func	V-Next
3		1	can sync up with our online applications to record all the information collected throughout the day		Territory sales manager		x	
4		2	retrieve the customer data and allow us to view the data in different ways		Territory sales manager		x	
5		3	determine who our best customers are		Territory sales manager			

Figure 2.2. Draft requirements document

As you analyze information, you will most likely find that you need to gather additional information. The number of iterations that you conduct depends on the business challenge, the complexity of the problem, and other factors, such as time limits imposed by stakeholders.

Figure 2.3 is an example of the draft requirements document with additional questions that you might ask your customers for clarification about specific requirements.

	A	B	C	D	E	F
1						
2		Req ID	Req desc	Priority	Source	Questions from this item:
3		1	can sync up with our online applications to record all the information collected throughout the day		Territory sales manager	What specific information is collected? What does "sync up" mean, with what? What specifically is done differently after "synching up"? What specific information is really necessary and on what timing during the day? Week?
4		2	retrieve the customer data and allow us to view the data in different ways		Territory sales manager	What specific ways do you view this customer data? What does "customer data" mean?
5		3	determine who our best customers are		Territory sales manager	How do you define best? Revenue, percentage of revenue, frequency, certain collections of products?

Figure 2.3. Additional questions for requirements

Internal Project Team Documentation

After gathering information, as a part of analysis, the team creates several internal documents that are not typically provided to the customers. These documents—the actors catalog, business rules catalog, and glossary—are living documents and are refined during the course of project life cycle.

Actors catalog

The *actors catalog* contains information about all the actors that will be used in use cases. (An *actor* is an entity that interacts with the system.) The actors catalog contains the following information:

- Actor name
- Responsibility of the actor
- Source for this information

For example, in the Adventure Works Cycles scenario, a sales representative is an actor whose responsibilities include establishing contacts with customers within a geographic region, and acquiring knowledge about products and their specifications and information about all the customers. The source of this information is tracked in case you need to go back to the source for additional information or clarification.

Figure 2.4 is an example of an actors catalog.

	A	B	C	D	E
1					
2		Actor	Responsibilities	Source	Business Title
3		Sales Representative	Establish contact with customers	Sales Manager	
			Needs to know about the products and their		

Figure 2.4.   Actors catalog

Business rules catalog

The *business rules catalog* is a living document that lists the business rules for a solution. The business rules catalog is a predecessor for the requirements document. This document is created early in the design process, when the team gathers information. This document, like the actors catalog, is meant only for the team and is typically not provided to the customer.

The business rules catalog includes the following fields to document information about a business rule:

- Identification number for the business rule, for tracking and traceability
- Short title for the business rule
- Description of the business rule
- Authority (the source of the business rule)
- UC/BR (use case or business rule), which specifies either the use case to which the business rule might refer or another business rule to which the business rule relates
- Current functionality, which indicates the functionality related to the business rule in the current system

For example, a business rule identified during interviews and conversations with the sales manager in the Adventure Works Cycles scenario is that sales representatives can provide a discount of up to 10 percent to their customers. However, sales managers can approve and provide a discount of up to 20 percent to their customers.

Figure 2.5 is an example of a business rules catalog.

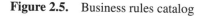

	B	C	D	E	F	G
1						
2	BR ID	Business Rule Title	Business Rule	Authority	UC/BR	Current func.
3	100	Discount	The Sales Representative can provide a discount of up to 10% only	Sales Manager	UC5.01	
4						
5						

Figure 2.5.   Business rules catalog

Glossary

When designing a business solution, the team will identify terms that need to be defined. The *glossary* contains a list of these terms and their meanings. The purpose of the glossary is to ensure that everyone is using the same terms and that everyone understands what those terms mean.

Lesson 3: Using Modeling Notations

You use models to describe business processes, to understand the current state of the business, and to model new processes that do not exist but that you plan to create in the future. Models help you depict business processes and their relationship with other processes. You also depict the tasks that comprise the process. In this lesson, you will learn about the benefits of models and the different types of modeling notations that you can use.

Note   This lesson assumes that you use Microsoft Visio® for Enterprise Architects for creating diagrams.

After this lesson, you will be able to

- List the benefits of modeling.
- Describe the role of Unified Modeling Language (UML) in conceptual design.
- Describe the purpose of various UML views.
- Describe the purpose of the various UML diagrams.
- Describe the role of Object Role Modeling (ORM) in conceptual design.
- Describe the relationship between UML views and the different phases of the MSF Process Model.

Estimated lesson time: 20 minutes

Benefits of Modeling

You use models to describe both the current and proposed solution to a business challenge. Some of the benefits of using models are:

- Models provide you with a common terminology that can describe both the current and proposed solutions.
- Models help to describe complex problems in a simpler structure and enable easy communication.
- Models enable consensus by helping the project team understand the business challenge, the business and user requirements, and the information that must be gathered.

As the business processes are modeled and adapted to reflect the requirements, you can build a model of the architecture that describes the final business solution. Two commonly used modeling notations are:

- Unified Modeling Language (UML)
- Object Role Modeling (ORM)

What Is UML?

UML is a standard modeling language that you use to model software systems of varying complexities. These systems can range from large corporate information systems to distributed Web-based systems.

UML was developed to provide users with a standard visual modeling language so that they can develop and exchange meaningful models. UML is independent of particular programming languages and development processes. You use UML to:

- Visualize a software system with well-defined symbols. A developer or application can unambiguously interpret a model written in UML by another developer.
- Specify the software system and help build precise, unambiguous, and complete models.
- Construct models of the software system that can correspond directly with a variety of programming languages.
- Document the models of the software system by expressing the requirements of the system during its development and deployment stages.

More Info   For additional information about UML, you might find the following references useful: *The Unified Modeling Language User Guide* by Grady Booch, Ivar Jacobson, and James Rumbaugh (Addison-Wesley, 1999) and *Use Case Driven Object Modeling with UML: A Practical Approach* by Doug Rosenberg with Kendall Scott (Addison-Wesley, 1999).

- It is a simple, extensible, and expressive visual modeling language.
- It consists of a set of notations and rules for modeling software systems of varying complexities.
- It provides the ability to create simple, well-documented, and easy to understand software models.
- UML is both language independent and platform independent.

What Are UML Views?

UML enables system engineers to create a standard blueprint of any system. UML provides a number of graphical tools that you can use to visualize and understand the system from different viewpoints. You can use diagrams to present multiple views of a system. Together, the multiple views of the system represent the model of the system.

You use models or views to depict the complexity of a software system. The various UML views depict several aspects of the software system. The views that are typically used are:

- *The user view.* The user view represents the goals and objectives of the system from the viewpoint of the users and their requirements for the system. This view represents the part of the system with which the user interacts. The user view is also referred to as the *use-case view.*

- *The structural view.* The structural view represents the static or idle state of the system. The structural view is also referred to as the *design view.*

- *The behavioral view.* The behavioral view represents the dynamic or changing state of the system. The behavioral view is also referred to as the *process view.*

- *The implementation view.* The implementation view represents the structure of the logical elements of the system.

- *The environment view.* The environment view represents the distribution of the physical elements of the system. The environment of a system specifies the functionality of the system from the user's point of view. The environment view is also referred to as the *deployment view.*

What Are UML Diagrams?

The various UML views include diagrams that provide multiple perspectives of the solution being developed. You might not develop diagrams for every system you create, but you must understand the system views and the corresponding UML diagrams. Similarly, you might not use every diagram to model your system. You need to identify which models will best suit the needs of modeling the system successfully.

Use the following UML diagrams to depict various views of a system:

- *Class diagrams.* A class diagram depicts various classes and their associations. Associations are depicted as bidirectional connections between classes.

- *Object diagrams.* An object diagram depicts various objects in a system and their relationships with each other.

- *Use case diagrams.* A use case diagram represents the functionality that is provided to external entities by the system.

- *Component diagrams.* A component diagram represents the implementation view of a system. It represents various components of the system and their relationships, such as source code, object code, and execution code.

- *Deployment diagram.* A deployment diagram represents the mapping of software components to the nodes of the physical implementation of a system.

- *Collaboration diagrams.* A collaboration diagram represents a set of classes and the messages sent and received by those classes.

- *Sequence diagrams.* A sequence diagram describes the interaction between classes. The interaction represents the order of messages that are exchanged between classes.

- *State diagrams.* A state diagram describes the behavior of a class when the external processes or entities access the class. It depicts the states and responses of a class while performing an action.

Note   You can use Visio to generate UML diagrams. Visio enables you to design and document your solution from the initial analysis and design stages to the final deployment of your system.

Relationship Between UML Views and the MSF Process Model Phases

You create different UML diagrams in different phases of the MSF Process Model. The software development life cycle is typically composed of the UML notations to depict various views of a system. For example, during the planning phase, you might use a set of diagrams to depict the proposed design for the solution. During the developing phase, you can use a different type of diagram to depict software components.

Figure 2.6 depicts the UML views and the diagrams associated with the views.

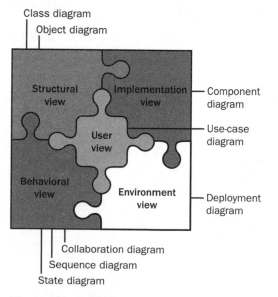

Figure 2.6.   MSF Process Model and UML views

Table 2.1 lists the UML views and the corresponding phases of the MSF Process Model.

Table 2.1.   UML Views and the MSF Process Model Phases

UML views	UML diagrams	Purpose	Create the diagram	Use the diagram
User view	Use case diagrams	To understand user requirements	Envisioning and planning phases	All phases
Structural view	Class diagrams, Object diagrams	To identify the basic components of the system	Planning phase	Developing and stabilizing phases
Behavioral view	Collaboration diagrams, Sequence diagrams, State diagrams	To identify the behavior of the system in various circumstances and conditions	Planning phase	Developing and stabilizing phases
Implementation view	Component diagrams	To know how the various structural blocks identified in structural view can be grouped and packaged	Planning phase	Developing and stabilizing phases
Environment view	Deployment diagrams	To know the physical and deployment aspects of the system	Planning phase	Developing and stabilizing phases

What Is ORM?

The *Object Role Modeling* (*ORM*) method is a fact-oriented method for analyzing information, in terms of objects and the roles they play, at the conceptual level. By using this methodology, you can document business rules and design databases to model complex, data-related business requirements.

You use ORM to model business requirements during the conceptual design stage of the planning phase. A benefit of the ORM method is in its conceptual approach to modeling. This approach helps to ensure the correctness, clarity, adaptability, and productivity of a solution by allowing you to describe the solution by using concepts and language that people can understand easily.

The quality of a solution depends on its design. To design a solution, you build a formal model of the application area. The application area is called the *universe of discourse* (UoD) in ORM. ORM uses a natural language and intuitive diagrams. You present information as elementary facts. An *elementary fact* asserts that an object has a property, or that one or more objects participate in a relationship.

Note   The associated language, FORML (Formal Object-Role Modeling Language), is supported in Visio for Enterprise Architects.

> **More Info**   For more information about modeling languages, see *Information Modeling and Relational Databases: From Conceptual Analysis to Logical Design* by Terry Halpin (Morgan Kaufmann Publishers, 2001).

ORM conceptual schema design procedure

The ORM *conceptual schema design procedure* (CSDP) focuses on the analysis and design of data. The conceptual schema specifies the information structure of the application: the *types of fact* that are of interest; *constraints* on these facts; and the *derivation rules* for deriving some facts from others. The CSDP consists of the following tasks:

- Analyzing external information and transforming it into elementary facts.
- Applying a population check to fact types. (All combined instances of an item in the UoD are known as that item's *population*.)
- Identifying primitive entity types in the conceptual model.
- Applying uniqueness constraints to the conceptual model.
- Applying mandatory role constraints to the conceptual model.
- Adding value constraints, set-comparison constraints, and subtype constraints to the conceptual model.
- Adding ring constraints to the conceptual model.

Analyze and transform external information into elementary facts

This is the most important stage of the CSDP. In this stage, the information required from the system is presented in natural language. Examples of such information include output reports and input forms of the required system. ORM models represent the set of all valid data use cases in the UoD.

Some of the important terms used in modeling are:

- *Instance.* An item of interest in the UoD.
- *Population.* The group of all combined instances of a given type of item of interest in the UoD is known as that item's *population*. In database terms, all rows in a table make up that table's population.
- *Set.* Any group of instances, but a set is not necessarily the same as a population. A set could be part of a population, or a combination of instances from more than one population. All populations are sets, but not all sets are populations.
- *Fact instance.* An individual observation of the relationship between two or more data values.
- *Fact type.* The set of fact instances that share the same object types and predicate relationships.

- *Object type.* The set of all possible instances of a given object.
- *Predicate.* A verb phrase that the domain expert uses to relate object types.

Consider the following example of a fact instance:

The author known as Hemingway wrote the book known by the title "A Farewell to Arms."

In this example, the author, Hemingway, and the book, *A Farewell to Arms,* are both data values, related by the action verb "write."

Table 2.2 contains another example. This table displays data used by a university to maintain details about its academic staff and academic departments.

Table 2.2.   Example of a table used to store data

Employee Number	Employee Name	Department	Room	Telephone Extension	Telephone Access
715	Adams, J	Computer Science	69-301	2345	Local
720	Bassli, S	Biochemistry	62-406	9642	Local
139	Canuto, S	Mathematics	67-301	1221	International
430	Culp, S	Computer Science	69-507	2911	International
503	D'Hers, T	Computer Science	69-507	2988	Local
651	Jones, B	Biochemistry	69-803	5003	Local

Each fact defines a relationship between two objects. Some of the elementary facts that can be stated from the above table are:

- The Instructor with Employee Number 715 has Employee Name "Adams, J."
- The Instructor with Employee Number 715 works for the Department named "Computer Science."
- The Instructor with Employee Number 715 occupies the Room 69-301.
- The Instructor with Employee Number 715 uses the Telephone Extension 2345.

The name of the Object Role Modeling method reflects the way it uses objects and roles. Objects are either values or entities. *Values* are character strings or numbers and are identified by constants such as "Adams, J" and 715. *Entities* are real-world objects that have descriptions, such as the Instructor with Employee Number 715.

You can combine facts. For example, two facts stated earlier can be combined as follows:

The Instructor with Employee Number 715 and Employee Name "Adams, J" works for the Department named "Computer Science."

Apply a population check to fact types

To apply a population check, you must enter a meaningful sample population into the model. *A meaningful sample population* represents instances of information in the UoD, and the real-world problem that the project team is trying to solve. The sample population can be from sources such as reports, charts, graphs, input screens, and forms. In the data maintained by the university about its academic staff and academic departments displayed earlier, each row in the table represents one fact instance. Each column in the table represents instances of an object type's role in the fact type.

Identify primitive entity types

To model business requirements, you must identify object types in the UoD. Object types can be classified as entity types and value types. Primitive entity types represent the most basic entity types in a UoD, and they are mutually exclusive and exhaustive. They are the lowest common denominator of a group of entity types. All primitive entity types are atomic and mutually exclusive:

- *Atomicity.* Primitive entity types are atomic because they cannot be broken down into other entity types or structures.
- *Mutual exclusivity.* The populations of two or more primitive entity types never overlap. A union of the members of two or more primitive entity types will never produce redundant instances.

 An example of a primitive entity type would be the combination of the Start-Time and StopTime object types into a new Time primitive entity type.

Consider the following fact types:

- Professor obtained Degree from University
- Senior Lecturer obtained Degree from University
- Lecturer obtained Degree from University

The common predicate in these fact types suggests that the entity types—Professor, Senior Lecturer, and Lecturer—can be combined to the single primitive entity type: Academic.

Apply uniqueness constraints

You should explicitly test and enforce uniqueness to ensure the strict use of elementary facts and to eliminate redundancy. A *uniqueness constraint* prevents duplication of role instances spanned by the constraint. A uniqueness constraint placed across all roles in a predicate effectively prevents the duplication of instances of the fact type. Uniqueness constraints are used to assert that entries in one or more roles occur *at most once*.

Some of the benefits of uniqueness constraints are that they:

- *Prevent fact redundancy.* Uniqueness constraints ensure that no fact instances are repeated.

- *Enforce internal uniqueness.* A uniqueness constraint on roles within a single predicate is an internal uniqueness constraint. An internal uniqueness constraint ensures that fact table entries for a role, or combination of roles within a single predicate, occur only once. All instances of a fact type must be unique for the fact type to be elementary. For example, the university academic staff is classified as professors, senior lecturers, or lecturers, and each instructor specializes in a research area. The internal uniqueness constraints on the fact types assert that each instructor has at most one rank, holds at most one specialization, works for at most one department, and has at most one employee name.

- *Enforce external uniqueness.* An external uniqueness constraint spans roles from two or more predicates and ensures that instances of the role combination occur only once. For example, the external uniqueness constraint stipulates that each department and employee name combination applies to, at most, one academic.

Apply mandatory role constraints

In a relationship, you might have to enforce the fact that every instance of an object type has information recorded. You accomplish this by placing constraints on the object type's population. A *mandatory role constraint* forces all instances of an object type to participate in a role.

Mandatory role constraints have the following characteristics:

- *Global nature.* Mandatory role constraints are global in nature, to the extent that they force the enumeration of the entire population of an object type. This constraint is important because it forces you to consider all instances for inclusion in all other roles in which an object type participates. For example, if you model a mandatory constraint on an employee's name and birth date, you must know both items for all employees.

- *Implied with functional dependency.* A role is functionally dependent on another if there is a many-to-one or a one-to-one relationship between the roles, and if the first role in the relationship always has a uniqueness constraint. For example, if it is mandatory that each father have a child, and that children are functionally dependent on their fathers, it is mandatory that all children have fathers.

Mandatory role constraints are expressed in FORML notation by the inclusion of the word "Each" in front of an object type. Consider the following example:

```
Each Person has Name.
```

In the FORML expression, the word "Each" indicates that the Person role in this fact type has a mandatory role constraint on it and that the name of each instance of the object type Person is known.

Add value constraints, set-comparison constraints, and subtype constraints

Constraints are used to limit populations. ORM provides several methods of limiting the domain of an object type. The domain of a population represents all of the possible values that exist in the population. It is not necessary to use each member of the domain.

For example, an object could be constrained to allow only a number between 1 and 5, or to allow only the names of the days of the week.

Value constraints

Limit the population of an object type to a specific domain of allowable values. The FORML expression of a value constraint follows the pattern of specifying the object type and then the phrase "The possible values of," followed by the object type and the word "are," followed by an enumerated list of values. The following FORML expression represents a value constraint on the Person object type that restricts the domain of the object type to Jeff, Maria, and Pierre.

```
Person(Name) is an entity object type.
Every Person is identified by one distinct Name.
The possible values of "Name" are: "Jeff", "Maria","Pierre".
```

Set constraints

Often, a relationship exists between the populations of two different fact types. ORM uses set constraints to capture these relationships. *Set constraints* limit the instances that can participate in a fact type. A set constraint is external and spans roles in two different fact types. By constraining the roles in two different fact types, you constrain the fact instances in each of the fact types. Set constraints restrict two populations in relation to each other. Some of the different types of set constraints are:

- *Set exclusion constraint.* Prevents instances in one set from appearing in another.

  ```
  No Employee that is paid some HourlyWage is paid some Salary.
  ```

- *Set equality constraint.* Forces all instances in one set to appear in another.

  ```
  Employee e is paid some Salary if and only if Employee e works as som
  e SalesManager.
  ```

- *Set subset constraint.* Limits instances in one set to those that are also in another.

  ```
  If Employee e works as some SalesManager then Employee e works as som
  e Salesperson.
  ```

Entity subtypes

You might need to control a subset of an object type's population differently from the entire population. This subset of the population might participate in different fact types. In addition, you must classify a subset of a group of objects into more specific groups to understand them or gather more useful information from them.

For example, the specialization of the population of the Vehicle object type might result in the object types GasVehicle and DieselVehicle. You could further specialize each of those as ConsumerVehicle and CommercialVehicle object types.

An *entity subtype* is an object type that is contained in another object type. Entity subtypes must be well defined in terms of relationships played by their supertypes. Entity subtypes with the same supertype might overlap. You must be able to identify entity subtypes and supertypes.

An object type's FORML expression is annotated to represent every entity subtype in which the object type participates, either as a parent or as a child. The following FORML expression represents the subtype relating to the Salesperson object type:

```
Salesperson is an entity object type.
Salesperson is primarily identified by the identification scheme of Empl
oyee.
Salesperson is a subtype of Employee /
  Employee is a supertype of Salesperson.
Employee is the primary supertype of Salesperson.
Subtype definition: The subset of Employee who is Salesperson.
Each Manager is a Salesperson but not every Salesperson is necessarily a
 Manager.
```

Add ring constraints to the conceptual model

An *object type* plays just one role in a fact type. When two roles in a fact type are played by the same object type, the path from the object type through the role pair and back to the object type forms a ring. For example, consider the following fact type: *Person voted for Person.* This has two roles—voting and being voted for. However, both roles can be played by the same object, such as PersonA voting for PersonA.

Ring constraints control the population of an object type's roles when the object type has two roles in a single fact type. Different types of ring constraints are:

- *Irreflexive.* An irreflexive (ir) ring constraint prevents an instance from being related to itself. The FORML expression for an irreflexive ring constraint is:

  ```
  No Object is related to itself.
  ```

- *Symmetric.* The symmetric (sym) ring constraint ensures that a mirror image of every tuple exists in the fact type's population. In functional programming languages, a *tuple* is a data object containing two or more components. The FORML expression for a symmetric ring constraint is:

```
If Object o1 is related to Object o2
then Object o2 is related to Object o1.
```

- *Asymmetric.* An asymmetric (as) ring constraint ensures that no mirror images of any tuple exist in the fact type's population. The FORML expression for an asymmetric ring constraint is:

```
If Object o1 is related to Object o2
then it cannot be that
Object o2 is related to Object o1.
```

- *Antisymmetric.* An antisymmetric (ans) ring constraint ensures that no mirror images of any tuple exist in the fact type's population, and that no instance is related to itself. The FORML expression for an antisymmetric ring constraint is:

```
If Object o1 is related to Object o2
and o1 is not the same Object as o2, then it cannot be that
Object o2 is related to Object o1.
```

- *Intransitive.* An intransitive (it) ring constraint enforces hierarchical relationships between instances in a population. The FORML expression for an intransitive ring constraint is:

```
If Object o1 is related to Object o2
and Object o2 is related to Object o3
then it cannot be that
Object o1 is related to Object o3.
```

- *Acyclic.* An acyclic (ac) ring constraint prevents a path from looping back on itself through a chain of relationships. The FORML expression for an acyclic ring constraint is:

```
An Object cannot cycle back to itself through one or more application
s of the relationship:
Object is related to Object.
```

Lesson 4: Creating Use Cases and Usage Scenarios

Use cases and usage scenarios capture the functional requirements of a system. In this lesson, you will learn more about use cases and usage scenarios and how to create them.

After this lesson, you will be able to

- Create use cases.
- Describe usage scenarios.
- Create usage scenarios.
- Refine requirements from use cases and usage scenarios.

Estimated lesson time: 10 minutes

How to Create Use Cases

Use cases are functional descriptions of the transactions that are performed by the system when a user initiates an event or action. The use cases that you develop should represent the system processes, including all events that can occur in all possible situations.

Use cases consist of elements that are inside the system and are responsible for the functionality and behavior of the system. They are the actions that the system performs to generate the results that the users request. This model allows the project stakeholders to agree on the capabilities of the system and system boundary.

A use case diagram documents the following design activities:

- Identifying the system
- Identifying actors
- Defining the interactions between the actor and the system
- Determining the system boundary

Identifying the system

A *system* is a collection of subsystems that have a real-world purpose. For example, in a sales and marketing scenario, the order system might have a subsystem that determines applicable discounts for a customer invoice. When you develop use cases, you identify a single system or subsystem. A collection of use cases indicates the relationships among the subsystems that make up the system, in addition to the relationships between systems that interact with each other.

Identifying actors

The actor is an integral part of the use case. The use case represents the interactions between an actor and the system. An *actor* is an entity that interacts with the system to be built for the purpose of completing an event. An actor can be:

- A user of the system.
- An entity, such as another system or a database, that resides outside the system.

For example, in the Adventure Works Cycles scenario, some of the actors are sales representatives, sales managers, customers, and production clerks.

The roles played by actors explain the need and outcome of a use case. By focusing on the actors, the design team can concentrate on how the system will be used instead of how it will be developed or implemented. Focusing on the actors helps the team to refine and further define the boundaries of the system. Defining the actors also helps to identify potential business users that need to be involved in the use case modeling effort.

When looking for actors, ask the following questions:

- Who uses the system?
- Who starts the system?
- Who maintains the system?
- What other systems use this system?
- Who gets information from this system?
- Who provides information to the system?
- Does anything happen automatically at a preset time?
- Who or what initiates events with the system?
- Who or what interacts with the system to help the system respond to an event?
- Are there any reporting interfaces?
- Are there any system administrative interfaces?
- Will the system need to interact with any existing systems?
- Are any actors already defined for the system?
- Are there any other hardware or software devices that interact with the system and that should be modeled during analysis?
- If an event occurs in the system, does an external entity need to be informed of this event? Does the system need to query an external entity to help it perform a task?

Defining the interactions between the actor and the system

After you have identified the system and the actor, you need to describe the interaction between them. You need to create one use case for each interaction. Describe only those interactions that are important to the business challenge and the vision statement.

Determining the system boundary

One of the more difficult aspects of use case modeling is determining the exact boundary of the system to be built. People who are new to use case modeling might find it difficult to determine whether certain actors should be part of the system.

To define the boundary of the system, the team should try to answer the following questions:

- What happens to the use cases associated with that actor?
- Who or what interacts with those use cases now?
- What if you find new requirements? Will these requirements be a part of the system?
- Are these requirements necessary for this system?
- Are these requirements something this system would logically do?
- Can these requirements be handled by one of the current actors?
- Are these requirements something the customer/user would expect the system to do?

Figure 2.7 depicts an example of a diagram of a set of use cases.

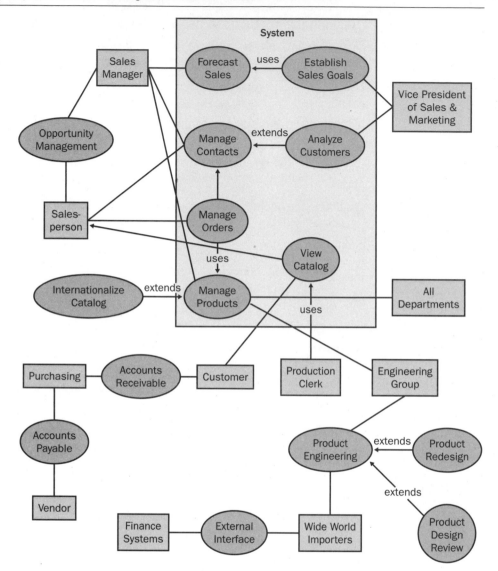

Figure 2.7. Example of a diagram of a set of use cases

Typically, an actor is shown as a stick figure, a single use case is shown as an ellipse, and a set of cases are enclosed in a box, which represents a system.

What Are Usage Scenarios?

Use cases describe the high-level interactions between an actor and a system. The use cases grouped together describe a workflow process in detail. Usage scenarios provide additional information about the activities and task sequences that constitute a process. Usage scenarios document the sequence of tasks.

Usage scenarios describe in detail a particular instance of a use case. It takes many usage scenarios to document a use case completely. Whereas use cases are diagrams, usage scenarios are narratives.

Usage scenarios depict objects in a workflow process. Objects are something that are affected by the system, something that affects the system, or something that a system needs to be aware of to function properly. For example, objects in a training center include the customer, the training course, and the sales representative. Objects provide a view of the characteristics and behavior of elements in the problem domain that is addressed by the business challenge. In the conceptual design phase, you create usage scenarios that depict the objects in the problem domain.

In addition to objects, usage scenarios depict exceptions. *Exceptions* are atypical events or alternate task sequences to meet the use case. An example of an exception condition for entering information for a new customer into the training center contact system is when the system is down and the sales representative must use other means to take customer information.

Tips for handling exceptions in a system include:

- Ask "what if" to capture exceptions to the work task or step.
- Determine the relative probability of each exception.
- Discuss how the exception is currently handled and any alternative methods.
- Incorporate handling of high-probability exceptions into the design of the solution.

When you develop usage scenarios, you might identify a task that must be treated as a use case. For example, in the "Register customer for course" use case, you might determine that the task sequence "Process customer payment" is a high-level use case that is part of the workflow process and has several usage scenarios.

Consequently, each usage scenario for "Register customer for course" ends with "Entering course number." Then you create all relevant usage scenarios for the new "Process customer payment" use case.

You identify the use cases that correspond to the workflow process and then develop usage scenarios that describe the task sequences for each use case. From the usage scenarios, you can determine the current state requirements.

Why Create Current State Usage Scenarios?

After you identify a use case, you can determine the different usage scenarios that can occur for the use case. You then use the information that you gathered from users to describe the different usage scenarios possible for the use case. Creating a usage scenario helps you determine if you gathered the appropriate level of information. Gathering the required amount of information for describing the current state is part of the iterative aspect of gathering and analyzing information.

You can create scenarios for both the current and the future states of the business environment. The *current state scenario* depicts how business activities are currently conducted; the *future state scenario* presents the activities as the business wants them to be. For both states, the scenario emphasizes business processes, information, users, and tasks.

In some situations, full scenarios need be developed only for use cases that are known to have many exceptions or dependencies. This allows the project team to balance costs against the potential benefits. Use cases and scenarios should be developed iteratively, and can be discovered or continued during development work on the initial set of use cases.

Benefits

Although there are various ways to analyze current work processes, use cases and usage scenarios are especially effective in modeling the process. Creating use cases and scenarios provides the following benefits:

- By measuring productivity levels of the current system, the team can determine whether the new system has achieved usability goals.
- The team can identify the problems in the system and what works in the system.
- The team might discover that the problems perceived by users are different from the actual problems and their causes. The team can then concentrate on the real problems.

Creating a usage scenario

To create a usage scenario, you need to perform the following tasks:

- Determine the preconditions for the usage scenario, specifying information or conditions that must exist before a scenario can be executed.
- Identify the postconditions for the usage scenario, which identify the work or goal completed during the task sequence.
- Break the activity into discrete steps.
- Identify exceptions that might occur for any step. You might need to develop usage scenarios for these exceptions.
- Identify the requirement that this particular usage scenario addresses, for tracking and traceability.
- Identify the source for this usage scenario, for further discussion and clarification.

Following is an example of how you can derive a usage scenario from the Adventure Works Cycles use case:

Use case title: Customer requests product literature

Abbreviated title: Customer requests product literature

Use case ID: UC05.1

Requirements ID: 14.1

Description: Customer wants to obtain information for a product. The customer is able to view a copy online, print a copy, or request a hard copy to be delivered by mail.

Actors: Customer

Preconditions:

Customer has Internet access.

Customer has browsed to the Adventure Works Cycles Web site.

Customer has clicked **Browse Product Descriptions**.

Product information exists in the database, and the site is working properly.

Task sequence	Exceptions
Customer scrolls to desired product.	Product is not in current view.
Customer selects product by clicking on product graphic or details.	
Customer views basic product information (name, description, image, in-stock status, price, item number).	Any piece of data is not available.
Customer clicks **Need Complete Specification?**	
Customer views full product specification online (UC05.1.3).	Customer chooses printable version (UC05.1.2).
Customer clicks **Mail Me Full Brochure** (UC05.1.1).	Customer is not in database. Customer completes and saves profile.
	Customer is in database. Customer confirms address.
Customer clicks **Submit**.	Submit process fails.
Customer browses away from product specification.	

Postconditions: The request to receive the full specification by mail is complete and saved in the database.

Unresolved issues: How should saved requests best be queued for fulfillment?
If submit process fails three times, what process should be invoked?

Authority: Mike Danseglio

Modification history:

Date: November 6, 2002

Author: Heidi Steen

Description: Initial version

Note   Although this chapter teaches you how to create a detailed usage scenario, you would not create such a detailed usage scenario until the conceptual design phase. This example is used to teach you the technique of how to create a usage scenario.

How to Refine Requirements

As mentioned earlier, when you analyze information with use cases and usage scenarios or by using any other tool, you also refine the list of requirements. When you create more detailed use cases, you can differentiate between requirements, wants, and constraints, and also identify any hidden requirements from the gathered information. The requirements and wants will eventually define the features of the completed solution. At this stage, the team only describes, organizes, and prioritizes the requirements and wants. Later, in the process of developing the product, the development team will determine the features of the product.

Note   Refining requirements typically happens during the envisioning phase and the conceptual and logical design processes of a project life cycle. You create a first level of requirements during envisioning, and then further refine them to eventually derive the feature set and determine which requirements are in scope for this version of the product. Once you progress to physical design, any change in requirements will cause the project to re-iterate. Therefore, you should get an agreement from the customer about the requirements during the conceptual and logical design.

Requirements and wants

Requirements indicate the characteristics of the process that are essential for meeting the goals of the business. Wants are important but not essential to achieving the business goals or resolving the business challenge. Wants are based on the actual day-to-day experiences of people. However, they represent an ideal state of how people would like things to be in the business. As you discuss the requirements and wants with the customer, some wants might become requirements, and some requirements might become wants.

Constraints and assumptions

Constraints indicate the parameters to which the final business solution must adhere. They are aspects of the business environment that cannot or will not be changed. Often, these constraints become design goals for the application. If constraints are not identified properly, the project team might design a product that cannot be deployed within the business.

Examples of possible constraints that you should document include:

- Budget limitations
- Characteristics of existing or supporting systems
- Network system architecture
- Security requirements
- Operating systems
- Planned upgrades in technologies
- Network bandwidth limitations
- Maintenance and support agreements and structures
- Knowledge level of development or support staff
- Learning limitations of users

Assumptions are identified as you talk to the customer and analyze the data you have gathered. Assumptions and constraints are very similar. An example of an assumption is "We will use Microsoft .NET as the basis of the new solution." In this case, the team is assuming that it will build the solution by using .NET.

A constraint prevents you from accomplishing something; an assumption is a piece of knowledge that you possess when beginning the project—it might be good or bad.

Hidden requirements

It is especially important to identify hidden requirements. Imagine completing the design and then learning about a merger your client will go through in the near future, meaning that you need to consider interacting with the systems of the acquired company. Your customers might feel the need to withhold this information, not realizing the impact to the project. Some examples of hidden requirements are:

- Interoperability with peer networks and the Internet
- No firewall to enable barrier-free connectivity
- Mergers, acquisitions, and other changes in the business constituency
- Meeting regulatory requirements that come into being after the project is in process
- Maintenance of the deployed system after the expiration of the stipulated period
- Personnel changes that might affect the project or the team

Activity: Gathering and Analyzing Information

In this activity, you use what you learned in the lessons to work through information gathering exercises.

Exercise 1: Preparing for an Interview

You will be interviewing the human resources manager at Adventure Works Cycles to gather information about their current system. To prepare, you want to develop a series of questions to ask during the interview. What questions would you formulate for the interview?

After you have completed your list, view the document named "Interview with the Human Resources Manager" in the \SolutionDocuments\Chapter02 folder on the CD to determine whether there are any other questions you would ask during the interview or in a subsequent interview with the human resources manager.

Some possible questions are:

- How many employees does human resources have to account for currently?
- How are the employees classified (full time versus part time versus contractors)?
- How many new employees does the company anticipate it will hire in the next fiscal year?
- What are the shortcomings of the current solution that you would like to see addressed in the new solution?
- Describe how the hiring process works today.
- Describe how the review process works today.
- Describe how the usage of benefits is analyzed today, and how the results of the analysis are used to make future decisions about benefits.
- How many different documents do you store for each employee? For each employment candidate?
- What categories do you use to manage employees and candidates (such as skills, levels, industry keywords, or specialities)?
- Are all documents currently in Microsoft Word format? If not, what other formats are they in?
- What are the various storage areas for your documents? (List all network drives and databases, including server names.)
- Who has the authority and ability to view, change, or enter employee and candidate records?

Exercise 2: Deriving Use Case Statements for the Sales Automation Project and for the Web Enhancement Project

Your team has completed most of the information gathering for the Adventure Works Cycles project. Using the interviews for the territory sales manager, the information services manager, the vice president of production, and the Web customer, and the shadowing report for the sales associate, derive as many use case statements as you can. Derive only the use case statements here. You will complete the full usage scenario in a later exercise. Develop use cases that follow the Actor-Action-Object format: An example of a use case statement would be "Sales Representative views product information."

Use Visio to create a UML use case diagram.

To see one possible solution for this exercise, see the Visio document named C02Ex2_Answer.vsd in the \SolutionDocuments\Chapter02 folder on the CD.

Exercise 3: Developing Draft Requirements from Initial Information Gathering

You have started the initial gathering of information by talking to people in the Sales department, the network adminstrator, and the project sponsor. You also have a beginning collection of use cases. Identify phrases in the interviews or use cases that might eventually be requirements.

Use the Microsoft Excel document named C02Ex3.xls in the \SolutionDocuments\Chapter02 folder on the CD to record your work. Use the Original Tab to write down the actual phrases from the interview. To guide your work, three examples have been given in the Revised tab. To see one possible solution, see the document named C02Ex3_Answer.xls in the \SolutionDocuments\Chapter02 folder on the CD. The Original Tab contains the phrases from the interviews that are potential requirements. The Revised Tab shows revised phrases starting with the Sales Manager comments. The phrases have also been reorganized into related groups. This document also shows questions that could be derived from the first three potential requirement statements from the Sales Manager.

Exercise 4: Developing a Usage Scenario

You need to document the usage scenario for the use case "Customer requests product literature." You will first need to define the actor, the objects, and the system. You will then need to complete the precondition and postcondition. Next, complete the task sequence and note any exceptions. Use the information in the interview and shadowing documentation, in addition to your own experience with developing software and completing online purchases.

Use the Excel document named C02Ex4 in the \SolutionDocuments\Chapter02 folder on the CD to record your work. To see one possible solution for this exercise, see the document named C02Ex4_Answer in the same folder on the CD.

Summary

- Gathering and analyzing information are steps that you perform throughout the Microsoft Solutions Framework (MSF) Process Model.
- Gathering and analyzing are iterative collaboration processes between you and your customer.
- Some techniques for gathering are interviewing, shadowing, user instructions, and prototyping.
- Analysis involves creating use cases and usage scenarios, draft lists of requirements, actors catalogs, and business rules catalogs.
- Modeling represents another method of describing business processes. Models indicate relationships and behavior among business processes, in addition to the tasks that make up the processes.
- ORM is a fact-oriented method for analyzing information at the conceptual level.
- UML is a standard modeling language that you use to model software systems of varying complexity.
- UML views depict several aspects of a software system by using UML diagrams.
- UML diagrams depict various views of a system.
- Creating use cases involves:
    - Identifying the system
    - Identifying actors
    - Defining interactions between the system and the actors
    - Determining the system boundary
- Use cases describe the interactions between an actor and a system and are used to describe a workflow process.
- Usage scenarios provide information about the activities and task sequences that constitute a process.
- After you begin analysis, you need to eliminate redundancies to determine the information that is most important to the business and the business challenge.
- You need to distinguish between requirements and wants when you synthesize the information from both the business and user perspectives.
- Constraints indicate the parameters to which the final business solution must adhere and indicate the aspects of the business environment that cannot be changed.

Review

The following questions are intended to reinforce key information presented in this chapter. If you are unable to answer a question, review the lesson materials and try the question again. You can find answers to the questions in the appendix.

1. What is the difference between the interviewing and focus-group techniques of gathering information?

2. When should you use prototyping instead of shadowing to gather information?

3. How do you identify the most effective information gathering technique for a project?

4. What is the purpose of creating use cases?

5. What is an actors catalog?

6. What is ORM?

7. What is UML?

8. What are the purposes of the various UML views?

9. What is an actor in a use case?

10. What is the purpose of a usage scenario?

11. What are the steps in creating a usage scenario?

C H A P T E R 3

Envisioning the Solution

About This Chapter

The success of a project depends on the ability of the project team members and the customers to share a clear vision of the goals and objectives of the project. You define the vision of the project during the envisioning phase of the Microsoft® Solutions Framework (MSF) Process Model. In the following four lessons, you will learn about the envisioning phase and the roles and responsibilities of team members during this phase. You will also learn how to define the vision of the project and analyze risks associated with the project.

Before You Begin

To complete the lessons in this chapter, you must

- Understand the MSF Process Model.
- Understand techniques for gathering and analyzing information.

Lesson 1: The Envisioning Phase

The envisioning phase is the period during which the team, the customer, and the sponsors define the high-level business requirements and overall goals of a project. The main purpose is to ensure a common vision and reach consensus among the team members that the project is both valuable to the organization and likely to succeed. During envisioning, you should focus on creating clear definitions of the problem. The envisioning phase culminates in the vision/scope approved milestone.

After this lesson, you will be able to

- Describe the purpose of the envisioning phase.
- Describe the roles and responsibilities of team members during the envisioning phase.
- List the guidelines for setting up the project team.
- Describe the deliverables of the envisioning phase.

Estimated lesson time: 5 minutes

Purpose of Envisioning

The first phase of the MSF Process Model is envisioning. During this phase, the team creates an overview of the business problem to be solved and how that problem relates to the business, the customers, and the environment. This helps the team get a clear vision of what the team must accomplish for its customers. For a successful project, you need to know what the customer wants to achieve with the solution.

Figure 3.1 indicates how the envisioning phase fits into the overall MSF Process Model.

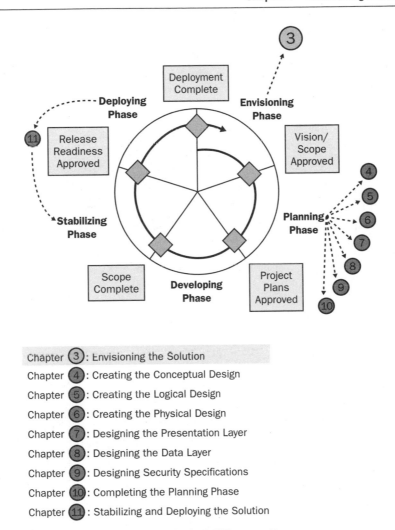

Figure 3.1.   Where are you in the MSF process?

For example, consider an organization that wants you to develop its Web site. "We need a Web site" is a good reason but not a good vision for the Web site project. To create the most effective solution, the team should identify the goals that the organization wants to achieve by building and deploying this Web site. In addition, the team needs to determine whether the Web site has any unique characteristics that the organization can take advantage of for maximum benefit. Does the organization want a complex site, or a site that supports a growing number of users? Perhaps the organization needs to plan for both complexity and scalability? The team should consider the intended market and expected volume of site visits. Another consideration for the team is the organization's brand and projection of image in the marketplace.

Envisioning serves many purposes. The team uses the envisioning phase to:

- Identify the goals and constraints of the project.
- Answer feasibility questions, gain approval from key stakeholders, and acquire a common set of expectations from everyone involved.
- Form the basis upon which team members build the solution later in the project.
- Define the scope of the project, which helps in the detailed planning effort of the next phase.
- Estimate the resources that are required to develop the solution.
- Identify and schedule the major milestones for the project.

Roles and Responsibilities of the Team Members

Although the project team works as a single unit to achieve the vision/scope approved milestone of the envisioning phase, each role has a specific focus during each phase of the project life cycle.

Figure 3.2 shows the roles for the project team during the envisioning phase.

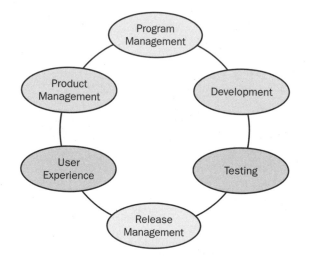

Figure 3.2.   The MSF Team Model

The MSF Team Model specifies six roles for a project in the envisioning phase:

- *Product management.* The responsibility of product management includes ensuring that the team addresses the customer requirements. The product management role collaborates with the program management role and drives the effort to establish a shared project vision. To accomplish this goal, product management studies and analyzes the business problem, business requirements, project vision, business goals, and user profiles.

- *Program management.* Program management establishes project design goals, defines success factors and metrics, articulates the solution concept, and sets up the project infrastructure.

- *Development.* The development team provides feedback to the team on the technical implications of developing the product and on the feasibility of the solution concept.

- *User experience.* The user experience team analyzes the performance needs and support issues of users and considers the product implications of meeting those needs.

- *Testing.* The testing team provides feedback to the team on the quality goal for the solution and specifies the actions that will be needed to achieve that level of quality. The testing team then applies decisions about the quality goal to testing strategies and acceptance criteria that will be used to measure quality.

- *Release management.* The release management team identifies what will be required to deploy the product, how the product will be deployed, when it will be deployed, and whether deployment will require additional infrastructure.

How to Form a Project Team

One of the tasks that you perform during the envisioning phase is setting up the team. It is important that the project team members are competent and can perform the tasks necessary for creating the solution. The task of forming a team brings together the skills that are essential for completing the project successfully. When identifying appropriate team members for a project, you need to consider the following for each member:

- *Knowledge.* Represents the information that an individual must possess to perform the job competently, such as knowledge of computer science fundamentals.

- *Skills.* Represent the behavior or abilities making up the competency and correspond to the skills of the team member, such as mathematical logic or artistic ability.

- *Performance level.* Represents the ability and the expected results from capable execution. For example, you might choose a person who meets deadlines consistently while meeting the quality requirements for the assigned task.

In addition to considering each individual's capabilities, there are some practical considerations to selecting team members. These include:

- Availability of the team members.
- Cost or project budget.
- Security clearance of the team members.

How to Prepare the Deliverables of the Envisioning Phase

Although there are interim milestones during the envisioning phase, such as formation of the core team, creation of the draft version of the vision/scope document, and creation of the draft version of the risk assessment document, there are three major deliverables of the envisioning phase. These are as follows:

- *Vision/scope document.* The vision/scope document describes the project goals and constraints. It outlines the product being developed, the needs it will meet, its features, and an initial schedule.

- *Project structure document.* The project structure document outlines the project organization structure and describes the project management process. It outlines who is responsible for each role in the MSF Team Model and identifies the team lead for each role.

- *Risk assessment document.* The risk assessment document provides an initial identification and analysis of risks associated with the project, along with mitigation and contingency plans to help the team in managing risks.

Depending on the extent of the project, additional deliverables for the envisioning phase can include:

- An initial list of testable features
- Preliminary requirements and use cases
- Preliminary architecture
- A graphical user interface (GUI) storyboard

In addition to the documents that are shared with the customers, the project team also develops the following documents for its internal use:

- An actors catalog
- A business rules catalog
- A glossary of terms

Note   You learned about these documents in Chapter 2, "Gathering and Analyzing Information."

Lesson 2: Creating a Vision/Scope Document

The final milestone of the envisioning phase is an approved vision/scope document. In this lesson, you learn how to create a vision/scope document for a project.

After this lesson, you will be able to

- Describe the contents of the vision/scope document.
- Create a problem statement.
- Create a vision statement.
- Create user profiles.
- Define the project scope.
- Create a solution concept.
- Identify project goals.
- Validate the vision/scope document.

Estimated lesson time: 20 minutes

What Is the Vision/Scope Document?

The vision/scope document is one of the final deliverables of the envisioning phase. This document contains the goals and constraints of a business solution. The vision/scope document represents the first agreement among everyone involved in the project. It guides the team to the high-level achievement of specific business goals. Initially, the team relies heavily on the vision/scope document to decide whether to go ahead with the project. After the project is approved, the team uses the vision/scope document to structure its planning efforts throughout the rest of the project.

To create the vision/scope document, the team conducts more interviews with customers and stakeholders, analyzes the high-level use case of the business to a lower level of detail, and identifies assumptions and constraints in the organization. Remember that you continue to gather and analyze information during all phases of the MSF process.

The vision/scope document must focus on understanding and defining the problem. The contents of the vision/scope document include the following:

- Problem statement
- Vision statement
- User profiles
- Scope of the project
- Solution concept
- Project goals
  - Business goals
  - Design goals
- Critical success factors
- Initial schedule

How to Create the Problem Statement

A *problem statement* is usually a short narrative describing the issues the business hopes to address with the project. It relates primarily to the current state of business activities. The more accurately the problem statement is defined, the more you are able to gauge its impact on the business needs of the organization.

Because the aim of any project is to solve a problem, the understanding of the problem determines the design of the solution. A problem statement outlines the business problem that the team is trying to solve. This statement must provide sufficient information about the business problem. A new team member can use the problem statement and the rest of the documentation to put the project into context.

Following are some examples of problem statements:

- Telephone operators cannot deal with the high number of calls because of the time it takes them to navigate through and interact with the current application.
- The organization needs to eliminate the ongoing costs associated with earlier versions of hardware and software.
- Users need clear directions from the system to resolve errors when they occur.
- We need to increase the number of online registrations by making our Web site easier to browse.

How to Create the Vision Statement

The purpose of the vision statement is to establish a common vision and reach consensus among the team members that the project is valuable to the organization and is likely to succeed. The vision statement also ensures agreement about the future of the project among the entire team.

Characteristics of a vision statement

A vision statement must be short enough to be remembered, clear enough to be understood, and strong enough to be motivational. A good vision statement has the following five characteristics:

- *Specific.* A vision statement should be specific and include the ideal state of the business problem so that the end result is meaningful.

- *Measurable.* By creating a vision statement that is measurable, the project team can determine the success of the project and whether it met the business goals.

- *Achievable.* Given the resources, the time frames, and the skills of the team members, the vision statement should be achievable. An achievable vision statement motivates the team to complete the project.

- *Relevant.* The vision statement should relate to the business problem being addressed. If the vision statement is not relevant, the project team might discover that they are trying to solve a business problem that does not exist, and the project might lose sponsorship.

- *Time-based.* The vision statement should clearly indicate the estimated time frame for the delivery of the solution.

Note   The above qualities of the vision statement are also referred to as *SMART characteristics*, each letter of the acronym standing for one of the five characteristics.

Examples of vision statements

Consider an organization whose e-commerce Web site is experiencing much lower online sales than the Web sites of its competitors. In the envisioning phase of solving this business problem, you might use the following vision statement:

Before the end of the year, we will become the top revenue-producing company in the industry by increasing our online sales.

Consider another example. An online library has a huge catalog of books, magazines, articles, white papers, and journals. The library wants its subscribers to be able to track all items in the catalog that they want to be able to find again, regardless of which computer they used to access the Web site. A vision statement for such a project might be as follows:

During the current fiscal year, we will enable all our subscribers to create bookmarks to selected pages from our Web site for access from any computer or device the end user might use.

Note that both vision statements have all five SMART characteristics. Both vision statements are specific, measurable, achievable, relevant to the business problem, and have an estimated time of availability.

How to Create User Profiles

A business solution is used by a set of customers. Before getting much further into the design of the solution, it is important to understand the users for whom you are developing the solution. To capture a clear description of each user, the team creates user profiles. *User profiles* identify the users so that the team can assess the expectations, risks, goals, and constraints of the project.

When creating user profiles, take into account the following considerations:

- *Goals.* An end-user's goal would include a list of the things that the user expects to accomplish by interacting with the product.

- *Constraints.* It is important to understand factors that might affect a user's ability to use the solution, such as hardware and software. For example, for certain solutions, you might need to consider the operating systems that are in use by all kinds of users. There is no reason to design a solution for one specific operating system if the users are using several different operating systems in the organization.

- *Support issues.* User profiles also contain information about the problems that users might have had with similar products. This information will help you plan for support features that users might require while using the new product.

- *Global users.* Determine whether the solution will support various cultures and localization needs.

- *Geographical boundaries.* Describe user locations, including geographical and physical locations, the number of users at each site, and the bandwidth and usage of the network links between sites.

- *Information flow between users.* Describe the communication that occurs between users, including the types of communication, their importance, and the volume of data that flows between the various user communities.

- *User functions.* Describe the tasks that the user performs, such as "completes customer profile," and "edits customer order and details." This information will be developed into the use cases.

- *Organizational communication.* Some organizations have rigid hierarchical divisions that restrict how, why, and when individuals can communicate across the lines of hierarchy. In such a situation, you need to accommodate these restrictions. Document the composition and boundaries of the organizational hierarchy.

- *Decision-making policies.* Describe decision-making policies that directly influence the effective implementation of the proposed solution.

- *Additional factors.* You should also document the availability and usage of resources at each user location, and identify any additional factors, such as incompatible protocols, network operating systems, and applications that might affect the success of a geographically based solution.

How to Define the Scope

One of the critical factors in the success of a project is clearly defining the scope of the project. *Scope* defines what will and will not be included in a project. The scope uses the project vision as defined in the vision statement and incorporates the constraints imposed on the project by resources, time, and other limiting factors. The scope is defined by the features that the customer considers mandatory in the solution. The team must address these features in the first release of the solution. While defining the scope, the team might decide to wait until future releases of the project to incorporate functionality that is not directly related to the core features of the solution. The features that are considered out-of-scope should be documented in a next-version or future-project document.

To begin defining the scope of the project, you continue to develop the high-level use cases that you created for analyzing the business and recording high-level business requirements. For the purpose of defining the scope, you identify the areas in the use case that directly impact the business challenge and address the business. You might need to prioritize the business challenges and identify those that will be dealt with in future versions of the solution. You can typically draw a box around the relevant parts of the high-level use case and derive a new use case diagram that you will subsequently use in the project.

Figure 3.3 shows the use case diagram that represents a part of the business. The scope of the project is enclosed in a box.

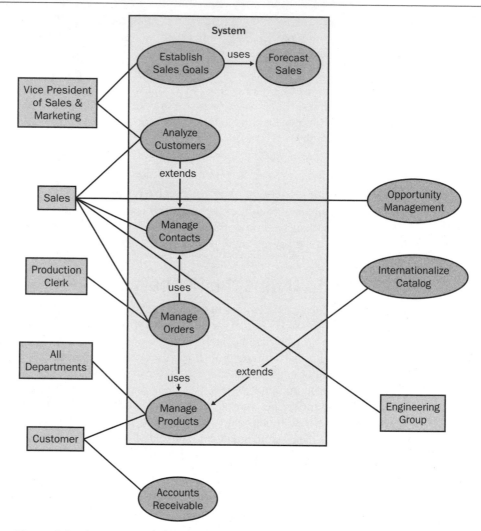

Figure 3.3.   Use case diagram showing the scope of the project

Figure 3.3 shows only the use cases that are now within the scope of the project. To understand what is not within the scope of the project, refer to the Microsoft Visio® document named AWC Use Cases in the \SolutionDocuments\Chapter03 folder on the companion CD.

Refining requirements

An important activity in defining the scope of a project is refining the requirements. Remember that you continue to analyze and refine requirements during both the envisioning and planning phases. During the envisioning phase, you analyze the gathered information and identify specific phrases that will lead to a requirement statement. You then work through those phrases to express the requirements in the language of "what the business needs and wants." You can also begin by collecting customer language directly from interviews and other sources. Consider the following high-level requirement:

The system must support localization to correspond to the end user's culture.

After refining this requirement during the envisioning phase, you have the following requirement:

The system must have procedures for globalization, localization, and accessibility.

The tradeoff triangle and priorities

Defining the scope means balancing the needs of a diverse set of end users and considering other priorities prescribed by the customer. Several variables might affect the potential success of the project, including costs, resources, schedule, functionality, and reliability. The key is to find the right balance between these variables.

The tradeoff triangle in Figure 3.4 shows the three most critical elements in setting the scope of a project. The tradeoff triangle dictates that resources, schedule, and features are three interconnected elements of any project, and that constraining or enhancing one or more of these elements requires tradeoffs.

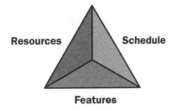

Figure 3.4.   The tradeoff triangle

Role of versioning

While defining the scope of the project, you identify the requirements that will be addressed by the various versions of the solution. During envisioning, you define which use cases and then which related candidate requirements will be handled by the solution.

The features of the solution correspond to requirements. The decision to include a feature of the solution depends on how the feature relates to the business problem selected in the first version of the use case and on how many users are affected by the feature. You should give highest priority to features that will affect the greatest number of users.

After identifying and prioritizing business problems, you can focus on the use cases related to the highest priority problem. With each version, focus on the set of features that addresses the most urgent problem and affects the maximum number of users. Eliminate the features that are required by smaller numbers of users and those that address other problems. This enables you to define the scope of the solution for each version and for the entire project.

More Info   Remember, the requirement statements develop into feature lists during the planning phase, near the end of logical design. Chapter 5, "Creating the Logical Design," describes the logical design stage.

Role of assumptions and constraints

The scope of the project is also affected by the assumptions and constraints made by the business and the customers. Typically, assumptions add to the constraints of the project. Examples of assumptions include:

- *We will use the Microsoft .NET Framework for development.*
- *We will use two development teams.*
- *We will have both OLAP and OLTP systems.*

Constraints indicate the parameters to which the final business solution must adhere. They are aspects of the business environment that cannot or will not be changed. Often, these constraints become design goals for the application. If constraints are not identified properly, the project team might design a product that cannot be deployed within the business.

Examples of possible constraints that you should document include:

- Budget limitations
- Characteristics of earlier supporting systems
- Network system architecture
- Security requirements
- Operating systems
- Planned upgrades to technologies
- Network bandwidth limitations
- Maintenance and support agreements and structures
- Knowledge level of development or support staff
- Learning limitations of users

List the constraints that affect the business challenge and the potential solution. The project team uses these constraints to design a solution that optimizes the requirements and conforms to the parameters established by the constraints.

Role of estimates

Depending on the assumptions and constraints of the project, you can provide estimates for developing the solution. Estimates include time, effort, and cost. You estimate the time it will take to build the solution, the resources required to build the solution, the cost of resources, and their effort.

In addition, you might want to add disclaimers and contractual details in the estimates section. This helps you clarify the extent of your responsibilities in the project.

Benefits of defining the scope

Some of the benefits of defining the scope of a project are as follows:

- The scope enables the team to focus on identifying the work that must be done.
- The scope enables the team to divide large and vague tasks into smaller and more specific tasks.
- The scope helps you specify the features that will be in each release of the solution.
- The scope includes defined feature sets and functions, which helps you to divide work among subcontractors or partners on the team.
- The scope clarifies what the team is and is not responsible for in the current deliverable.

Revising the scope

During the envisioning phase, the project variables start to become apparent. However, the team can more thoroughly understand the project variables with the help of a more detailed planning process. At this stage of the envisioning phase, the team is likely to know project variables only at a basic level. Defining and balancing the project variables is an iterative process. As analyzing, prototyping, and planning activities proceed, the team might need to revise the scope to:

- Incorporate a better understanding of user requirements.
- Incorporate a change in business requirements.
- Adjust the solution according to technical issues or risks.
- Make tradeoffs among the project variables, such as resources, schedule, and features, because project variables have changed.

How to Create the Solution Concept

The *solution concept* outlines the approach the team will take to meet the goals of the project and provides the basis for proceeding to the planning phase. After identifying the business problem and defining the vision and scope, the team creates the solution concept that explains in general terms how the team intends to meet the requirements of the project.

Figure 3.5 shows a sample solution concept for the scope identified for Adventure Works Cycles.

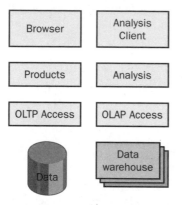

Figure 3.5.   Solution concept

Creating a business-oriented draft

The solution concept can serve as a business case. Because it focuses only on the concepts and not the details of the solution, it is not very technical. For the team to get approval and funding, the team should establish an executive sponsor who will use the vision/scope document to establish funding.

The solution concept includes a conceptual model of the system's software and hardware architectures. The solution concept is the proposed method of addressing the issues identified as being in scope. The team must evaluate the various options and select the one that is the best for its particular situation. A team can then narrow the range of solution concept options to a few alternatives.

For example, in the case of an e-commerce Web site, the choices might include building an e-commerce site internally from the very beginning, employing an outside company to build one, or purchasing a commercially available solution. Similar issues exist for hosting the e-commerce Web site: Should the site be hosted on local servers or should the company use a service provider?

Elements of the solution concept

After the team has evaluated its options, it chooses a solution concept that best meets its needs, resources, and the time frame available for implementation. The solution concept includes the following elements:

- Project success factors and acceptance criteria. These criteria include a checklist of requirements that must be satisfied before the solution goes into production.

- Initial approaches to developing and delivering the solution. These approaches include sample scenarios for the site and methods for implementing the solution, the number of users who will use the new solution, and a complete list of project deliverables that will make the new product operational.
- Initial description of functionality of the solution that will address the business problem.

Note   Creating user profiles and the solution concept need not be a linear process in solution design. These steps can be done in parallel.

How to Identify Project Goals

For a project to be successful, it is essential that you correctly identify the goals of the project. Project goals can be categorized as follows:

- Business goals
- Design goals

Business goals

Business goals represent what the customer wants to achieve with the solution. Business goals form the basis for determining the success criteria of the solution. The purpose of defining business goals is to clearly articulate the objectives for the project and to ensure that your solution supports those business requirements. The team needs to determine the best method for identifying the goals and agreeing on them.

Throughout the life of the project, the team makes tradeoffs among resources, schedule, and features. It is important that business goals are prioritized in a way that will allow the team to have a clear understanding about which ones the customer believes are most important, in case some of the goals cannot be achieved.

For an e-commerce project, business goals might include the following:

- Expand the company's geographic market beyond the current range of physical stores.
- Expand the company's demographic market to include younger consumers who have higher disposable incomes and who shop online with greater frequency than the current customer base.
- Shorten the time to sell products by using more efficient online sites.
- Integrate all suppliers worldwide by using a workflow process, and shorten the order placement and delivery cycle time.

Design goals

Design goals are similar to business goals in many ways. The difference is that *design goals* focus more on the attributes of the solution and less on what the solution will accomplish for the business. Design goals address not only what the team wants to accomplish but also what the team is *not* trying to accomplish with the solution. As with business goals, you need to prioritize design goals so that the team knows which goals must be accomplished, in case the project cannot achieve all of them.

Consider the case of an e-commerce Web site. Some of the design goals for the online shopping cart might include:

- Improve the user experience by reducing page-download wait times to 5 seconds or less.
- Limit dependency on connectivity with the server.
- Reduce the time and level of effort required for a user to complete the online registration.

For the server-side online library's server-side bookmark project, the design goals might include:

- The service and all supporting applications must be localized for users worldwide.
- The service must have an availability of 99.99 percent.
- The service cannot lose data.
- The service must permit access only by authorized users.

For designing the interface of a mobile application, some of the design goals might include:

- Users must be able to easily input and retrieve information.
- The application must be customized for the intended mobile device.

How to Validate the Vision/Scope Document

After creating an early version of the vision/scope document, the team reviews and modifies the document. The envisioning phase culminates in the *vision/scope approved* milestone. This milestone represents the point at which the project team and customer agree on the overall direction for the project, including the scope of the solution. This baseline version of the document is a project deliverable that is used in the subsequent phases of the project.

The vision/scope document is formally approved in a vision/scope meeting. The team validates the work done in the use cases, usage scenarios, and usage profiles with the appropriate stakeholders. (This validation is a process that will occur throughout the project.) By having the customer validate the completed work, the team prepares the customer to understand the tradeoffs that are made in defining the scope. The customer is also educated about the project and the team's approach, creating a feeling of involvement that can greatly reduce difficulties in consensus and in future feature discussions.

The vision/scope meeting ensures that the team and the customer arrive at a shared understanding regarding how the proposed solution will address the business challenge and how it is applicable to the current business scenario, given the scope that has been defined.

This meeting is a mechanism for the team to share ideas and achieve a shared vision with the customer. This meeting also enables the customers to understand that the team is listening to them and actively involved in the project. The team uses this meeting to decide whether the project should proceed. The available resources and the potential gains may not be worth the total cost of the project. This validation step allows the team to redefine either the project solution or the resources and constraints.

By approving the vision/scope document, the members of the project team, the customer, and the key stakeholders agree on the following:

- A broad understanding of the business needs that will be met by the solution
- The vision of the solution
- The design goals for the solution
- The risks that might be incurred by undertaking the project
- Project management's initial concept of the business solution
- The members of the project team
- The mechanism for managing the project

The complete vision/scope document for the Adventure Works Cycles case study is available in the \SolutionDocuments\Chapter03 folder on the companion CD. The Adventure Works Cycles team has defined the scope of version 1 of this project to include the sales order and analysis, contact management, and Web ordering processes. This leaves solutions for product tracking, human relations documentation, and vendor data for future versions or projects.

If any issues are discovered by the team that will cause significant changes in the scope or deliverables of the project, you might need to follow up with discussions or another vision/scope meeting.

Lesson 3: Creating the Project Structure Document

The project structure document is a key deliverable of the envisioning phase. This lesson describes the purpose of the project structure document and itemizes the major sections within the document.

After this lesson, you will be able to

- Describe the purpose of the project structure document.
- Describe the components of the project structure document.

Estimated lesson time: 5 minutes

What Is the Project Structure Document?

The project structure document defines the approach the team will take to organize and manage the project. It describes the team's administrative structure, standards and processes, and project resources and constraints. It serves as an essential reference for the project team members on how they will work together successfully.

The project structure document can be the formal documentation of the approach followed by each of the MSF team roles in the project. In addition, it documents the change management and configuration management approaches that will be implemented for the project. The level of detail in the project structure document depends on the project. If you expect a lot of changes during the later stages of the project, the project structure document should describe in detail how the team will handle the changes.

The change management section of the project structure document for a project named Scout is shown below. The two companies involved in the project used in this example are Adventure Works Cycles and Contoso, Ltd.

Change Management

The highest priority in Scout is the delivery of the first feature sets by the project completion date. (To be determined upon completion of the Project Master Plan. Estimated completion dates are September 1, 2003, for the Web site and November 15, 2003, for the sales automation project.) Therefore, change control procedures will be implemented as follows.

Change Control Process and Documentation Owners:

The program manager will be responsible for the change control process and documents. The application project manager for Adventure Works Cycles will be the primary decision maker in the change control process to manage changes requested by the customer.

___

Change Management   *(continued)*

Features by Version:

During planning, requirements gathering, and feature specification development, each feature will be identified as Critical V1.0, Want V1.0, Critical V2.0, Want V2.0, Critical V3.0, or Want V3.0.

Change Advisory Board:

The Scout Change Advisory Board is made up of members from Contoso, Ltd. (the development team and the program manager), and the Adventure Works Cycles team (project manager and developers), all of whom can make feature-set change requests. Other team members can take their feature set suggestions to any one of these individuals, who can then add the suggestions to the list for discussion at the next status meeting. If the individual deems the items critical, the individual can bring them up as critical issues and start the evaluation prior to the next status meeting.

Feature Evaluations:

The feature definition and its effect on the design, its effect on the solution, its value to version 1.0 (or any other version), and its risk will be evaluated by the team.

Feature Tradeoffs:

Features will be compared to other features, and any possible tradeoffs will be determined.

Resource Tradeoffs:

The tradeoff triangle will be reviewed and the appropriate element (resource or feature) will be added or deleted. (The schedule is fixed.)

Resolved Feature to Design:

After a feature is resolved as Critical V1.0, V2.0, or V3.0 or Want V1.0, V2.0, or V3.0 and resources are added or other features are deleted or reduced, the features enter the appropriate point in the design process. The budget and contract will be adjusted. (If Adventure Works Cycles decides that the schedule is worth adjusting for a feature, they can request the schedule change, and appropriate changes to the contract, design, budget, and schedule can be made.)

Change Cutoff:

Both companies agree that once the scope complete milestone is 70 percent complete, any new features will be introduced only on the V2.0 or V3.0 lists.

___

Team role and responsibility

Program management is responsible for facilitating the creation of the project structure document. The key inputs are supplied by the team members.

Components of the project structure

There are three primary components of the project structure document:

- Team and structure
- Project estimates
- Project schedules (early versions)

A project structure document is a tool for documenting the decisions made regarding the execution and management of the project, including:

- Team and customer roles and responsibilities
- Communication decisions
- Logistical decisions
- Change management decisions
- Progress assessment decisions

What Are Team and Customer Roles and Responsibilities?

The roles and responsibilities section of the project structure document lists the names of the people involved in the project and their contact information, such as telephone numbers and e-mail addresses. In addition, this section describes the decisions regarding responsibilities of various roles in the subsequent phases of the project.

Decisions during the planning phase

During the planning phase, the team needs to make decisions to answer the following questions:

- How will the project plans be developed?
- In creating the project plan, how will the team use the knowledge and experience gained from the reviews of other projects?
- Will the team have scheduled status meetings throughout the project?
- How often will customer reviews occur?
- How will the features be distributed among the various releases of the solution?
- Who will identify the risks associated with the project and define contingencies?
- What tools will be used to develop and track project plans?
- Will the team have review meetings during the planning phase? Who will attend the review meetings?

Decisions during the developing phase

During the developing phase, the team needs to make decisions to answer the following questions:

- With what groups, organizations, and third-party vendors will the team interact during the project? Who is responsible for creating and managing contracts with third-party vendors?

- What is the role and responsibility of each team lead in the development work?
- If different components in the solution are being developed by different teams, what are the roles and responsibilities of each of the component team leads in the project?
- Will each component team be assigned a help desk, a user experience team, and a testing team?
- What is the role of the executive staff in the project?
- What is the role of subcontractors, if required, in the project? Who will select subcontractors and monitor their work?

What Are Communication Decisions?

The communication decisions section of the project structure document specifies the communication processes that the team will follow during the project. These processes apply to communication within the team and with customers. The team makes decisions to answer the following questions:

- Who needs to be informed of the planning decisions?
- How will the customers, stakeholders, and team be informed of the planning decisions?
- What type of meetings will be held, where will they be held, and who will attend each type of meeting?
- Who will produce the agenda of the meetings?
- Who will facilitate the meetings?
- Who will prepare and distribute the minutes of meetings?
- Who must be informed of the project's progress, and how will they be informed?

Decisions regarding project files

Typically, a file is maintained for every project in an organization. This file contains information such as contracts, schedules, and plans. In the project structure document, the team decides what information will be maintained in the project files. Some of the decisions that must be made regarding the project file include:

- What information will be included in the project files, such as project specifications, schedules, plans, outstanding issues, contracts, and so on?
- Who will create and maintain the project files?
- Who can access the project files?
- Who will keep the project files after the project is complete, and for how long will they be kept?

Decisions regarding post-implementation reviews

Post-implementation reviews are an important part of a project. They help you evaluate whether the project was a success and identify the support you need to provide. Some of the decisions that must be made regarding post-implementation reviews include:

- When will the post-implementation review be conducted, and who will attend it?
- What subjects will be addressed during the post-implementation review?
- What information will be collected during the life cycle of the project to facilitate the post-implementation review? Who will collect this information?

What Are Logistical Decisions?

The logistical decisions section of the project structure document lists decisions made regarding the development of the solution. The team makes decisions to answer the following questions:

- What development practices will be used for the project? Some possibilities include:
  - Development methods such as product specification checks and a zero-defect checklist
  - Testing methods
  - Documentation methods
  - Marketing methods
- Who will define the content for the product specifications? Who will use the product specifications during the project, and how will they use the specifications?
- What are the tools that will be used to define the solution features?
- How will completion criteria for the product specifications be determined?
- Who will provide the team with any updates to the product specifications?
- What specifications will be provided to each of the third-party vendors working on the project? Who will create these specifications?
- How will zero-defect methods be defined and implemented for the project?
- Who will estimate the effort and time required for the project? What is the basis for this estimation (personal experience, post-implementation reviews, and so forth)?
- Who needs training in the technologies and skills supported by the solution, such as project management training? Who needs training on the solution during the planning phase?

What Are Change Management Decisions?

The change management decisions section of the project structure document covers the processes the team will follow to handle any changes in the project. Some of the decisions that are made regarding change management include:

- How will you define change on the project (for example, a change in schedule or an increase in project cost)?
- What is the release date? Who will determine the release date, and how will it be determined? What will the basis be for determining the release date?
- Who will define the change management process that will be used?
- How will proposed changes be identified and tracked? Who will track this information?
- How will you assess the impact of a change? How much deviation are you willing to accept before major rescheduling?

What Are Progress Assessment Decisions?

The progress assessment decisions section of the project structure document covers the processes the team will follow to track and evaluate the progress of the project. Some of the decisions that are made regarding progress assessment of the project include:

- How will the progress of the project be assessed? What information will be collected to measure progress?
- How will progress information for each task be obtained from team members? How often will this information be collected?
- How often will group schedules be updated? How often will the master project schedule be updated?
- Who will identify and assess the effect of each variance?
- Who will be involved in developing adaptive actions? Who will recommend and approve adaptive actions? How will you track the effectiveness of these actions?
- How will any outstanding issues be documented, tracked, and monitored?
- What criteria will be used to define exceptions for exception reporting? Who will be involved in assessing and resolving the exceptions?
- How will problems and issues be resolved between different teams? If a problem or issue cannot be resolved between teams, will the issue be escalated? If so, who will escalate it?

Lesson 4: Analyzing Risks

Risk is the possibility of a loss. The loss could be anything from the diminished quality of a solution to increased cost, missed deadlines, or project failure. MSF recommends that project risk be assessed continuously throughout a project. In this lesson, you will learn about analyzing risks and creating a risk document for the project.

After this lesson, you will be able to

- Describe the MSF risk management process.
- Identify the contents of a risk assessment document.
- Identify the risks for a project.

Estimated lesson time: 10 minutes

What Is the Risk Management Process?

Risks arise from uncertainty surrounding project decisions and outcomes. An essential aspect of developing a successful solution is controlling and mitigating the risks that are inherent in a project. Most individuals associate the concept of risk with the potential for loss in value, control, functionality, quality, or timeliness of completion of a project. However, project risks also include the failure to maximize gain in an opportunity and uncertainties in decision making that can lead to a missed business opportunity.

The MSF risk management process, as shown in Figure 3.6, is a proactive approach that the team practices continuously throughout the project. The team continually assesses what can go wrong and how to prevent or minimize any loss. MSF advocates tracking risk by using a formal risk assessment document and prioritizing risks.

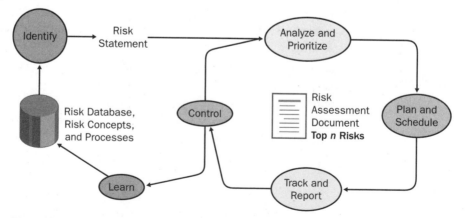

Figure 3.6.   MSF risk management process

The MSF risk management process defines six steps through which the team manages current risks, plans and executes risk management strategies, and documents knowledge for future projects. The six steps in the MSF risk management process are as follows:

1. *Risk identification* Identify the risks and make the team aware of potential problems.
2. *Risk analysis and prioritization* Convert the information and data about potential risks to information that the team can use to make decisions and prioritize resources for mitigating the risk.
3. *Risk planning and scheduling* Use the information developed in the risk analysis stage to formulate risk mitigation strategies, plans, and actions. Allocate time for risk planning in the project plan.
4. *Risk tracking and reporting* Monitor the status of specific risks and the progress of their specific mitigation plans. Report this progress to the team, customers, and key stakeholders.
5. *Risk control* Execute the risk mitigation plan and report the status of the risks to the team and customer.
6. *Risk learning* Document the lessons learned from the project so that the team and the organization can reuse this information.

Note The steps in risk management are logical steps; they do not need to be followed in chronological order. Teams often iterate through the identification, analysis, and planning steps as they develop experience on the project for a set of risks, and only periodically return to the learning step.

Contents of the Risk Assessment Document

During the envisioning phase, the team practices risk management by creating a risk assessment document, identifying and documenting all the known risks, and assessing them for probability of occurrence and impact.

The risk assessment document must contain the following items:

- *Risk statements*, which capture the nature of each risk
- *Risk probability*, which describes the likelihood of the occurrence of the risk
- *Risk severity*, which specifies the impact of the risk
- *Risk exposure*, which specifies the overall threat of the risk
- *Mitigation plans*, which describe the efforts for preventing or minimizing the risk
- *Contingency plans and triggers*, which specify the steps that you need to take when a risk occurs and when to take those steps
- *Risk ownership*, which specifies the name of the team member who is responsible for monitoring the risk on a regular basis

How to Create the Risk Assessment Document

The program manager creates the risk assessment document. The team might compare the risks associated with different solution concepts before documenting the solution concept.

For example, imagine that you are creating an e-commerce Web site. One option would be to create the site from the very beginning. However, this would require assembling and managing extensive development resources. You would also need a lot of time to complete the project. Another option would be to quickly move to the development process by using Microsoft Solution Accelerator for the Internet Storefront. The preconfigured source code, MSF project planning principles, and resource kit with reference documents and tools could help the team achieve its business goals. In addition, this would help mitigate the risks associated with building an e-commerce site from the beginning.

Calculating risks

When you create a risk assessment document, assign a numeric value to risk probability and impact. *Probability* measures the likelihood that a loss will occur; *impact* measures the severity of that loss, should it occur. Then calculate the exposure of each risk by multiplying the two numbers. This process allows you to compare risks and determine their relative severity and priority. For example, use a number between 1 and 4 to designate probability and impact for each risk, with 4 being the highest and 1 being the lowest. By multiplying the numbers representing probability and impact for a risk, you obtain an *exposure factor* between 1 and 16. This process allows you to identify and address the most severe risks first.

Important   You do not need to use the same numeric scale to assess both probability and impact. However, you must use a consistent scale to calculate the probability for every risk and its impact. If you can accurately calculate the financial loss that can be caused by each risk, you can express impact in financial terms. However, if you express the impact of some risks by using a number and others by using financial terms, you cannot compare the exposure of the different risks.

Creating a top 10 list

After creating the risk assessment document and ranking each risk according to its exposure, you can create a list of the top risks so that the team can focus on them. Often called a top 10 list, this list need not contain exactly 10 risks. The program manager should review the list frequently and update it according to the importance of the risks.

Risk exposure in an e-commerce project presents areas that are unique to the situation and that might be new to the team. Some possible risks to an e-commerce project include:

- Inexperience with Web site creation, deployment, and ongoing support
- Potential liabilities, such as image and brand damage for the company, if the site does not function correctly or suffers from availability issues
- Security risks, which include intrusion into the system by malicious users and theft of confidential customer data such as credit card numbers

Activity: Developing a Vision/Scope Document

In this activity, you will use what you learned in the lessons to work through the envisioning phase of a project. Each of the exercises is based on the following scenario.

Scenario

Adventure Works Cycles, a large, multinational manufacturing company, produces and distributes metal and composite bicycles to North American, European, and Asian commercial markets. Its base operation is located in Bothell, Washington, and employs 500 people; several regional sales teams are located throughout the company's market region.

Sales representatives from regional sales offices are responsible for assigned sales territories. Each regional office consists of several sales representatives and a team manager. In their daily sales activities, sales representatives use both laptops and Handheld PCs that run Microsoft Windows® CE.

A typical work day for a sales representative starts with the representative dialing in to the regional office and downloading current data such as inventory, product, and promotional information. During customer visits, the sales representative takes orders on the laptop or Handheld PC. At the end of the day, the sales representative sets up appointments for the following day or week, checks the appointments of other representatives in the area for possible collaboration, and updates the contact list. Finally, the sales representative dials back in to the regional office, sends updated information, and receives any new internal communications from the base office or regional office.

Currently, the sales teams at regional sales offices do not have an easy way to analyze the customer data. The customer data is stored in the systems, but there is no easy way to retrieve the data and allow the sales teams to request specific information. For example, the system does not provide a way to identify the best customers overall or the best customers of specific models. To better identify the best customers and to determine why they are the best customers, the company needs a way to access and analyze customer data in a meaningful way.

In recent months, the sales teams have been trying to present their products and achieve sales in the company's European and Asian markets. Currently, all the information they have in their systems is written in English. A sales representative working in the Hanover office has said that she actually translates the product information into German before she goes on her sales calls. She knows the language quite well, but there might be some technical terms that she might not translate correctly. Because of this translation process, inaccuracies might appear in the translated materials. The company therefore needs to store multilingual and multiregional information in the database rather than relying on the sales force to translate the information.

The sales team needs to obtain the latest pricing information on a daily basis. Currently, the sales representative connects to the corporate network and downloads the new pricing list each day in the morning. However, the download process does not identify which prices have been modified for that individual sales representative. So the sales representative is required to download the entire list every morning. Typically, sales representatives will find out that nothing pertaining to their area or product has changed, and the 20 minutes that it took to download the latest information were wasted.

This difficulty in downloading information to find out whether there are changes has had some unfortunate results. Most sales representatives have stopped downloading the pricing information on a daily basis. Because they have stopped downloading this information, sales representatives frequently miss changes that affect them. When sales representatives miss changes that affect them, they need to redo orders, recalculate pricing, and notify customers of the price changes. As a result, customers are unhappy when they find out that the prices offered to them were incorrect. Currently, the sales teams can override the system and sell products to customers at the prices that were initially negotiated. But this process has received criticism from the corporate base office because the company has lost money in recent months because of this approach.

Currently, the sales opportunities are managed by individual sales representatives and are not entered into the system. Each sales representative creates a Microsoft Word document and stores information such as contact name, address, telephone number, products the contact is interested in, date first contact was made, date last contact was made, and so on. In addition, the sales associate tracks "rules," which are statements that help the associate convert a sales opportunity into a sale. For example, a rule might be "Customer C will buy product P if (a) the price of product P is reduced by 5 percent or (b) product P comes with components X, Y, and Z as options."

The regional sales office employees are supposed to use the customer-management system to plan, execute, and track sales and marketing strategy. The problem with the system is that the customer management system is an older fourth-generation-language model, and getting anything even remotely meaningful out of it is very difficult. In addition, the sales associates are required to install a large application on their laptops and connect to the corporate network to use it.

The sales teams have identified the following requirements that will help them perform their jobs better:

- *Customer segmentation and profiling.* The sales team needs to be able to extract information from raw data available in the databases to answer questions such as the following:
    - What are the early warning signs of problems?
    - Who are the best customers across all product lines? On whom should the sales team focus its efforts for building long-term relationships?
    - What are customers' issues, categorized according to demographic groups?
    - Where are the best customers of Adventure Works Cycles?
    - What products are the customers buying and at what rate?
- *Sales activity.* To support sales activity throughout the world, the sales team needs international support, including Unicode characters, multiple languages, date and time data types, and multiple currency formats.
- *Internal communication.* Each sales representative must receive customer and sales data pertinent only to that representative. In addition, each team manager must receive relevant customer and appointment data along with detailed information for each sales representative on the team.
- *Opportunity management.* Sales representatives need a method to store and access sales opportunity data, and, when a sale is generated, to convert some or all of the information into a sales order without re-entering information.
- *Decision support system.* The decision support system should support the following tasks:
    - Allow marketing and sales staff with little technical knowledge to query and use customer data to generate standard reports; execute custom queries; obtain information related to promotion tracking, sales forecast, and customer segmentation; and access third-party data sources and financial evaluation tools.
    - Present a single unified view of the customer and the customer relationship.
    - Allow sales representatives to initiate new promotions and programs on a multinational basis. Currently, sales representatives do not know how to associate these programs with specific areas for the best impact.
    - Allow sales representatives to identify, analyze, and share all aspects of customer relationships with individuals in multiple departments.

Exercise 1: Writing Problem Statements

Read the sample scenario describing the Adventure Works Cycles Sales department, and write problem statements for the project described. Ensure that the problem statements you write outline the business problems and provide direction to the project team in the scenario.

Sample possible problem statements include the following:

Sales are lost because we cannot identify the best customer opportunities.

Product information can be incorrect because of manual translation of the product information by the sales representatives.

Sales representatives often work with incorrect price and product data, because of difficulty in downloading that information.

Sales representatives have to guess which customers to focus on and can end up spending their time less productively than possible.

Exercise 2: Writing a Vision Statement

Write a vision statement for the application described in the sample scenario.

Get the right information to each specific person when and where that person needs it, and increase sales totals for each representative over the next year.

Exercise 3: Developing Project Goals

From the scenario given, identify the project goals, including the business goals and the design goals.

Business goals include the following:

Increase sales over the next year by making the sales force more productive.

Focus on the best sales opportunities.

Improve sales tracking and marketing strategies.

Design goals include the following:

Improve sales activity throughout the world by providing international support.

Provide specific data pertinent only to a specific employee.

Summary

- Envisioning provides the team with a clear vision of what the team wants to accomplish for its customers.
- The members of a team must have the competencies and proficiencies required to perform the task for developing the solution.
- The scope of the project specifies what will and will not be included in the project.
- The deliverables of the envisioning phase include the vision/scope document, the risk assessment document, and the project structure document.
- The project team also develops documents such as the actors catalog, the business rule catalog, and a glossary of terms for its internal documentation.
- The vision/scope document includes information about the team and project structure, the problem statement, the vision statement, the scope of the project, the solution concept, user profiles, and project goals.
- The vision statement states the long-term solution that addresses the business problem.
- The problem statement specifies the problem that will be addressed by the solution.
- The scope of the project specifies what will and will not be included in the project.
- The scope of the project is affected by the assumptions, constraints, and estimates of the project.
- The solution concept specifies how the team intends to meet the goals of the project.
- User profiles identify all probable users of the solution and their expectations, goals, risks, and constraints.
- Business goals represent what the customer wants to accomplish with the solution.
- Design goals represent the attributes of the solution that the project team is going to develop.
- The project structure document includes information such the team's administrative structure, standards and processes, and project resources and constraints.
- The key components of the project structure document are:
  - Team and structure
  - Project estimates
  - Project schedules (early versions)

- A project structure document is a tool for documenting the decisions made regarding the execution and management of the project, including:
  - Team and customer roles and responsibilities
  - Communication decisions
  - Logistical decisions
  - Change management decisions
  - Progress assessment decisions
- The envisioning phase culminates with an approved vision/scope document.
- The team, key stakeholders, and customers indicate the completion of the envisioning phase by approving the vision/scope document.
- MSF advocates constant risk management throughout the life of the project.
- The MSF risk management process defines six steps through which the team manages current risks, plans and executes risk management strategies, and documents knowledge for the enterprise. The six steps are as follows:
  - Risk identification
  - Risk analysis and prioritization
  - Risk planning and scheduling
  - Risk tracking and reporting
  - Risk controlling
  - Risk learning
- During the envisioning phase, the team practices risk management by creating a risk assessment document. Contents of the risk assessment document include:
  - Risk statements
  - Risk probability
  - Risk severity
  - Risk exposure
  - Mitigation plans
  - Contingency plans and triggers
  - Risk ownership

Review

The following questions are intended to reinforce key information presented in this chapter. If you are unable to answer a question, review the lesson materials and try the question again. You can find answers to the questions in the appendix.

1. What is the purpose of envisioning?

2. What are the responsibilities of the various roles during the envisioning phase?

3. What are the outputs of the envisioning phase?

4. What is the purpose of specifying the project scope?

5. How does the envisioning phase end?

6. What kinds of change management decisions are recorded in the project structure document?

7. What is the difference between business goals and design goals?

8. What are the guidelines for creating user profiles?

9. What are the essential components of a risk assessment document?

10. What are the guidelines for assessing risks for a project?

C H A P T E R   4

Creating the Conceptual Design

About This Chapter

During the envisioning phase, the project team gathers enough information to start the project, which allows them to create the baseline vision/scope document. Near the end of the envisioning phase, the team moves on to the planning phase of the Microsoft® Solutions Framework (MSF) Process Model. During this phase, you ensure that the business problem to be addressed is fully understood so that you can design the solution that addresses the business problem. In addition, you plan how the solution will be developed and determine whether you have the resources to develop the solution.

During the planning phase, you create a collection of models and requirements documents. This collection of models and documents makes up the functional specification, or blueprint, of the solution. You begin working on the functional specification of the solution during the planning phase.

In this chapter, you will learn about the purpose of the planning phase and the three design processes that occur during the planning phase: conceptual, logical, and physical design. You will also learn about the purpose and benefits of functional specification. In addition, you will learn about the conceptual design process in detail.

Note   There are many modeling techniques that you can use to model business processes and key activities in a business. This training kit primarily uses use cases and usage scenarios for modeling business processes.

Before You Begin

To complete the lessons in this chapter, you must

- Understand the MSF Process Model.
- Be able to create use cases, usage scenarios, and use case diagrams.
- Be familiar with the outputs of the envisioning phase, such as vision/scope, project structure, and risk analysis documents.
- Be able to distinguish between the different kinds of information: business, user, system, and operations.

Lesson 1: An Introduction to the Planning Phase

During the planning phase, the team defines the solution: what to build, how to build it, and who will build it. During this phase the team prepares the functional specification, works through the design process, and prepares work plans, cost estimates, and schedules for the various deliverables.

In this lesson, you will learn about the purpose of the planning phase and the responsibilities of the various MSF roles during the planning phase. In addition, you will learn about the key deliverables of this phase.

After this lesson, you will be able to

- Describe the purpose of the planning phase.
- Describe the three steps and interim roles of the planning phase.
- Describe the responsibilities of the various MSF roles during the planning phase.
- Identify the common deliverables of the planning phase.

Estimated lesson time: 5 minutes

What Is the Planning Phase?

Before you start learning more about the planning phase and its deliverables, it is important to understand where the planning phase fits in the overall MSF process.

Figure 4.1 illustrates how the planning phase fits into the MSF Process Model.

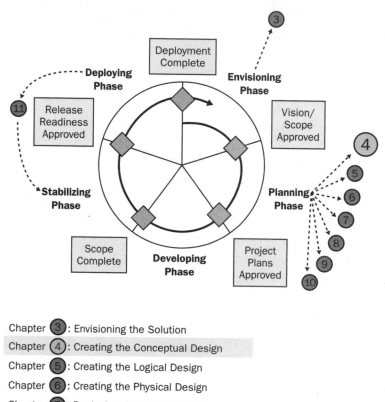

Figure 4.1.   Where are you in the MSF process?

Moving to the planning phase

During the envisioning phase, the team gathers enough information to determine the scope of the project. The planning phase can begin during the envisioning phase, whenever enough information has been gathered for the team to begin organizing and analyzing that information. During the planning phase, the team takes the work it has done during the envisioning phase and continues to elaborate on it and further organize and analyze it.

Figure 4.2 illustrates how the project team moves from the envisioning phase to the planning phase.

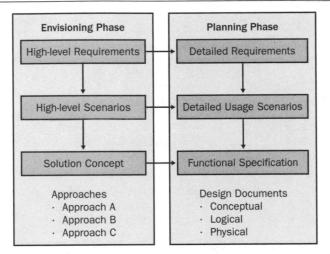

Figure 4.2.   Moving from the envisioning phase to the planning phase

Purpose of the planning phase

During the planning phase, the team continues with the work done during the envisioning phase, specifically the draft requirements, tasks and task sequences, and user profiles. The planning phase results in the architecture and design of the solution, the plans to accomplish developing and deploying the solution, and the schedules associated with tasks and resources. During the planning phase, the team works to articulate a clearer image of the solution. Although the planning process is intended to move the project forward, many teams get stuck in planning—in essence, they do too much planning. The key for the team is to know when it has enough information to move forward. Too little information is a risk, and too much information can cause a project team to stagnate.

The Three Design Processes: Conceptual, Logical, and Physical

There are three design processes in the planning phase: conceptual, logical, and physical design. These three processes are not parallel. Their starting and ending points are staggered. These processes are dependent on each other. Logical design is dependent on conceptual design, and physical design is dependent on logical design. Any changes to the conceptual design affect the logical design, leading to changes in the physical design.

Figure 4.3 illustrates the three processes within the planning phase.

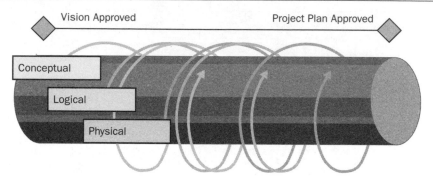

Figure 4.3.   The planning phase of the MSF Process Model

Table 4.1 summarizes the design processes of the planning phase.

Table 4.1.   The Three Design Processes

Type of design	Perspective	Purpose
Conceptual	View the problem from the perspective of the user and the business.	Defines the problem and solution in terms of usage scenarios.
Logical	View the solution from the perspective of the project team.	Defines the solution as a logical set of cooperating services.
Physical	View the solution from the perspective of the developers.	Defines the solution's services and technologies.

Note   Conceptual design can be broken down further into conceptual design research, conceptual design analysis, and conceptual design optimization. This chapter focuses on the three steps of the conceptual design process.

Roles and Responsibilities in the Planning Phase

Although the project team works as a whole during the planning phase, each role on the team has a different responsibility during the planning phase:

- *Product management* ensures that the plan meets the customer needs. This role is responsible for refining requirements, analyzing the current business state, optimizing the solution concept, and creating the conceptual design.

- *Program management* ensures that the resources can accomplish the project plan. This role is responsible for the overall design, with an emphasis on logical design and the functional specification. The project management team creates the project plans and schedules and is responsible for completing the planning phase.

- *Development* ensures that the plan is technically feasible. This role is responsible for creating the logical and physical design of the solution and adding it to the functional specification. This team also determines the time and effort required for developing and stabilizing the solution.

- *Testing* ensures that the plan meets the requirements. This role is responsible for evaluating the design to determine whether features can be tested and for providing a plan and schedule for testing them.

- *Release management* evaluates the design for ease of deployment, management, and support. In addition, this role plans for and schedules deployment of the solution.

- *User experience* ensures that users will be able to use the product. This role is responsible for analyzing user needs and creating performance support strategies and for evaluating the completed design for usability. This role also estimates the time and effort required to develop user support systems and conduct usability testing for all user interface deliverables.

Milestones and Deliverables of the Planning Phase

The planning phase culminates in the project plan approved milestone, which is the point at which the project team, the customer, and project stakeholders agree on the project deliverables and that the plan meets the requirements and is likely to be successful. The final deliverables at this milestone of the planning phase are:

- *Functional specification (baseline).* The functional specification represents what the product will be, based on input from the entire team. You will learn about the functional specification in Lesson 2.

- *Master project plan (baseline).* The master project plan is a collection of plans that addresses tasks performed by each of the six team roles to achieve the functionality described in the functional specification. It documents the strategies by which the various teams intend to complete their work.

- *Master project schedule (baseline).* The schedule applies a time frame to the master plan. The master project schedule synchronizes project schedules across the teams. It includes the time frame in which the teams intend to complete their work. Aggregating the individual schedules gives the team an overall view of the project schedule and is the first step toward determining a fixed ship date.

- *Updated master risk assessment document.* The master risk assessment document that was developed during the envisioning phase is reviewed and updated regularly, but particularly at the milestones. It describes the risks associated with developing the solution. Typically, multiple risk assessments are sorted to identify the highest risks that must be addressed and aggregated to give an overall risk assessment.

All of these documents are living documents, evolving as the project progresses. Although these documents can be modified, any modifications to the documents must first be approved by a committee of users and stakeholders.

Figure 4.4 shows the deliverables of the planning phase.

Summary of Milestones and Deliverables

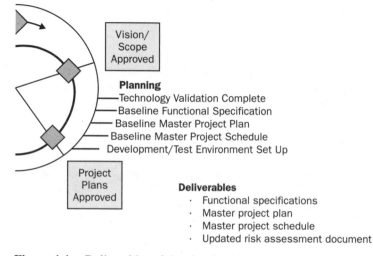

Figure 4.4.   Deliverables of the planning phase

Lesson 2: An Overview of the Functional Specification

During the planning phase, the focus of the project team begins to shift from problem definition to solution design. The planning phase of the MSF Process Model culminates in the project plan approved milestone. One of the primary deliverables at this milestone is the functional specification. The functional specification defines what will be built, how it will be built, and when it will be built. The project plan and schedule identify how the project will proceed and provide dates for various milestones in the project. In this lesson, you will learn about the goals and benefits of a functional specification. You will also learn about the risks of not creating a functional specification.

There is no finite beginning or ending point for the process of creating a functional specification. During the planning phase, each of the design processes—conceptual, logical, and physical—contributes different elements to the functional specification. With the completion of each task during the planning phase, the functional specification becomes more complete. The functional specification exists in a baseline version at the end of physical design and is updated throughout development as a best practice.

After this lesson, you will be able to

- Describe the purpose of a functional specification.
- Describe the goals and benefits of creating a functional specification.
- List the risks of not creating a functional specification.
- Describe the contents of a functional specification.

Estimated lesson time: 10 minutes

What Is a Functional Specification?

A *functional specification* is the virtual repository of project and design-related artifacts that are created during the planning phase of the MSF Process Model. The artifacts are a result of design activities during the conceptual design, logical design, and physical design processes of the planning phase. These artifacts can include Unified Modeling Language (UML) models such as use case diagrams, usage scenarios, candidate requirements (evolving), candidate features, and various information models.

> **More Info**   UML is a standard modeling language used to document projects that use object-oriented design. The following references provide more information about UML: *UML Distilled: A Brief Guide to the Standard Object Modeling Language, 2nd edition* by Martin Fowler and Kendall Scott (Addison-Wesley, 2000) and *Use Case Driven Object Modeling with UML: A Practical Approach* by Doug Rosenberg with Kendall Scott (Addison-Wesley, 1999).

It is important to remember that a functional specification is virtual in nature. Many of the conceptual, logical, and physical design artifacts are likely to be in electronic form and stored in the databases of various tools. The functional specification can manifest itself in different forms—electronic or paper; textual document or graphical; Microsoft Word document or Microsoft PowerPoint® presentation. Consequently, it is not easy to collate all these artifacts as a single physical document or deliverable. The functional specification is not just the work of one person or role but rather a joint effort by a number of roles on the team.

The functional specification describes the scope of the current version of the solution by listing which features will be a part of the solution. Excluded items should remain in the vision/scope document as potential features of a future version of the solution or as wants or items considered to be out of scope. The functional specification is used to record the decisions and agreements made regarding the functionality of the solution, its interface, design goals, and priorities.

You communicate the result of the design efforts of the team to the development team by using the functional specification. In addition to the development team, the testing team uses the functional specification to create test scripts, test plans, and data, and to test hardware requirements for the solution.

What Are the Goals of a Functional Specification?

Some of the goals of a functional specification are:

- *Consolidate a common understanding of the business and user requirements.* The features of a solution depend on the business and user requirements that the solution is going to address. For a small project, the number of requirements might be small and easily documented. For a large and complex project, the number and complexity of requirements increases. A functional specification helps the customer and the project team arrive at a common understanding of the requirements of the solution.
- *Break down the problem and modularize the solution logically.* For a complex project to be a success, it is important that the team identifies all parts of the problem clearly. Also, you need to break the solution into distinct, unambiguous parts. A functional specification helps you simplify a solution into logical

parts and document them. It also helps the team make changes to the design early in the development process. Making changes to the solution at this stage is less risky and less expensive than making them later in the process.

- *Provide a framework to plan, schedule, and build the solution.* The functional specification provides the program manager with a basis for identifying the team's tasks and creating cost estimates and budgets for the entire project. In addition, the program manager can correctly estimate the resources and time required by the project, and create project plans and schedules. The testing team uses the functional specification to create test cases and test scenarios early in the project life cycle. The release management team uses the functional specification for deploying the solution and supporting the development and test environments.

- *Serve as a contract between the team and the customer for what will be delivered.* In most organizations and on most projects, the functional specification serves as a contract between the team and the customer; it is the written evidence of what is to be developed and delivered. A functional specification is not necessarily a legal document, but it can serve as one. If third-party teams or other organizations are involved in the project, the functional specification can serve as an addendum to a project work order.

What Are the Risks of Not Creating a Functional Specification?

Sometimes, constraints such as budget and time prevent the team from creating and using the functional specification. Although the team can proceed to the developing phase of the MSF Process Model without a functional specification, the risks of the project increase significantly. Some of the risks of not creating the functional specification are:

- The team might develop a solution that does not completely address the customer requirements.

- The team might be unable to clearly define customer expectations and share a common understanding with the customer. Consequently, the team might not know whether they are developing the required solution.

- The team might not have enough detail to validate and verify that the solution meets customer expectations and is of the required quality level.

- The project manager might be unable to estimate the budget and schedule of the project accurately. The information in the functional specification helps the team estimate the effort and skills necessary for developing the solution.

Figure 4.5 illustrates the risks of not using the functional specification for developing a solution.

Figure 4.5.   Relationship between functional specification and output

Elements of the Functional Specification

The possible elements of a functional specification are listed below. Each element might be a separate document.

- *Conceptual design summary.* This section provides a summary of the conceptual design of the solution and includes information such as solution overview and solution architecture. The following artifacts from the conceptual design are used in the functional specification:

  - Use cases

  - Usage scenarios

  - Context models such as screen shots of existing systems and photocopies of current user manuals

  These artifacts can exist in various forms. For example, context models can be in the form of screen shots of an existing system or photocopies of current user manuals or reports; use cases can be in a use case documentation database; and conceptual user interface (UI) prototypes can be in electronic form.

- *Logical design summary.* This section provides a summary of the logical design and includes information such as users, objects, and attributes. The following artifacts from the logical design phase are included in the functional specification:

  - Task and task-sequence models

  - Logical object and service models

  - Conceptual models of the proposed solution

- UI screen flows
- Logical database model
- System architecture

- *Physical design summary.* This section provides a summary of the physical design document and includes information from key sections of the document, such as the application and infrastructure sections. The following artifacts from the physical design phase are included in the functional specification:
    - Component packaging
    - Component distribution topology
    - Technology usage guidelines
    - Infrastructure architecture and design
    - Description of UI screens
    - Physical database model

- *Standards and processes.* This section includes information about the standards and processes that the team uses as guidelines for performing various tasks for the project. In addition, this section includes details of quality and performance metrics that will be used. These metrics are gathered during tests and help achieve the goals defined by the requirements.

Depending on the size and scope of the project, you can include the following sections in the functional specification. To avoid unsynchronized versions, it is recommended that you use references to documents that exist separately rather than reproducing information. For example, do not include information in the functional specification that already exists in the vision/scope document or the risk assessment document.

- *Project vision/scope summary.* This section summarizes the business opportunity, the solution concept, and the scope of the project as documented in the vision/scope document.

- *Project history.* The section describes the important events and decisions that have been made up to the current date and that have helped deliver the project to its current state. The historical information ensures that the project team and the customer have the same understanding of the project. This information also helps to ensure a thorough understanding of the project.

- *Functional specification summary.* This summary is often useful for customers and new team members. You create the first version of the summary after user requirements have been gathered and analyzed and the UI design has been created. In addition to references to the other documents that make up the entire functional specification, this section typically contains screen shots that illustrate the proposed functionality of the solution.

- *Requirements summary.* This section provides a summary of the user, system, operations, and business requirements document. The business requirements summary describes what the customer, users, and stakeholders think the solution must do. The user requirements summary includes usage scenarios and describes who will use the solution, when the solution will be used, and how the solution will be used. The systems requirements summary includes information such as systems and services dependencies. The operation requirements summary includes information such as the security, manageability, and supportability requirements of an organization.

- *Usage scenario and use case studies summary.* This section provides a summary of the contents of the usage scenarios document. This summary includes a brief statement of each of the key use cases that are included in the document.

- *Assumptions and dependencies.* This section lists the project-oriented assumptions and dependencies. An example of a dependency might be the set of technical skills that is required for developing the solution. An example of an assumption might be that the deployment platform for the solution is the Microsoft Windows® operating system. You also need to identify tests that will challenge and validate these assumptions.

- *Security strategy summary.* This section describes the security strategy that will influence the design of the solution. The physical design document contains the specific security details in a per-feature and per-component format. This section contains a synopsis of the security strategy, along with references to the security plan.

- *Installation and setup requirements summary.* This section is a summary of the environmental requirements for installing the solution. This information is derived from the installation section of the deployment plan of the solution. The physical design document contains details on how these requirements will be addressed.

- *Removal requirements summary.* This section describes how the solution should be removed from its environment. This should include a definition of what must be considered prior to removing the solution. In addition, this section also covers information about data that must be backed up before uninstalling the solution, to ensure safe recovery and rebuilding later.

- *Integration requirements summary.* This section contains a summary of integration and interoperability requirements and the project goals related to these requirements. It includes a summary of the migration plan. The physical design document contains information about how integration will be delivered.

- *Supportability summary.* This section provides a summary of the supportability requirements and the project goals related to these requirements. This information is contained in the operations plan and the support plan. The physical design document describes how supportability will be delivered in the solution.

- *Legal requirements summary.* This section provides a summary of any legal requirements that must be taken into account. Legal requirements are typically defined by the customer's corporate policies and by regulatory agencies governing the customer's industry.

- *Risk summary.* This section describes the risks that might affect development and delivery of the solution. Along with each risk, this section contains information about the calculated exposure to the risk and a mitigation plan.

- *References.* This section describes any internal or external resources that provide supplementary information to the functional specification.

- *Appendixes.* This section is a collection of the outputs of the design process that the team used to develop the functional specification. It includes additional conceptual design details such as field surveys and user profiles, and physical design details such as existing server and client configurations.

Lesson 3: An Overview of the Conceptual Design Process

The planning phase of the MSF Process Model involves three design processes: conceptual, logical, and physical. The conceptual design starts during the envisioning phase of the MSF Process Model and continues throughout the planning phase. Because the MSF design process is evolutionary as well as iterative, conceptual design serves as the foundation for both logical and physical design.

In this lesson, you will learn about the conceptual design process. You will also learn about the goals and benefits of conceptual design.

After this lesson, you will be able to

- Define conceptual design.
- Describe the goals of conceptual design.
- Describe the steps in conceptual design.
- Describe the research step of conceptual design.

Estimated lesson time: 10 minutes

What Is Conceptual Design?

Conceptual design is the process of gathering, analyzing, and prioritizing business and user perspectives of the problem and the solution, and then creating a high-level representation of the solution.

Developing requirements

During information gathering, draft requirements are captured. It is important that the project team understands the difference between the different categories of requirements: *user*, *system*, *operation*, and *business*. Draft requirements can be gathered from the initial interviews or from other information that has been gathered. They can then be developed into more-precise statements as the business problem is better understood by the team. These requirements, called the *candidate* requirements, are later transformed from the language of the user into the language of requirements.

Note   You will learn more about transforming draft requirements to candidate requirements in Lesson 4.

Communicating requirements through modeling

To create an accurate and usable conceptual design of a solution, you need to set up an effective method of understanding and communicating the solution with all types of users. For this, you create models of the tasks covered by the scope of the solution. One way to model these tasks and their task sequences is to generate use cases and usage scenarios.

More Info   For more detailed information about writing use cases, you might find the following reference useful: *Writing Effective Use Cases* by Alistair Cockburn (Addison-Wesley, 2001).

Consider the example of a team that has been assigned to design an e-commerce Web site. To determine what the customer requires from the e-commerce Web site, the team asks the customer what lines of products will be sold on the site and how end users will use the site. To answer these questions, the customer must consider the product catalog and its maintenance, and the various activities that end users will perform on the site. The team can generate a set of tasks and describe them in use cases. For each activity that the customer describes, the architect creates a detailed usage scenario. Exceptions and alternatives that occur in an activity are also recorded in the usage scenario.

Conceptual design in the MSF Process Model

As defined by the MSF Process Model, conceptual design occurs during the planning phase. However, the project team might have begun conceptual design while drafting the vision document during the envisioning phase. After the team has established enough information to further gather and refine requirements, conceptual design can begin.

Figure 4.6 illustrates when the conceptual design occurs in the MSF Process Model.

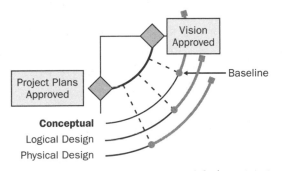

Figure 4.6.   When does conceptual design take place?

Remember that the design process is iterative. Consequently, the logical and physical designs might overlap with the conceptual design. These three design phases are not parallel; they have different starting points and baselines. Because of the iterative nature of the design process, conceptual design might be modified as a result of the logical and physical designs.

What Are the Goals of Conceptual Design?

Without a conceptual design, you might create a great solution to the wrong problem. Some of the goals of creating a conceptual design are:

- *Understanding the business problem to be solved.* Conceptual design involves understanding the problem to be solved and framing the future state of the process to the point of improving the business processes. It embodies a process for refining, documenting, and validating what the users and the business need from the solution.

- *Understanding the requirements of the business, the customer, and the end user.* Conceptual design helps the project team determine a project's needs in context, resulting in a view of the solution that focuses on both the process and the user. The view is not limited to a list of desirable functions; it also includes the broader context of business processes and activities.

- *Describing the target future state of the business.* Conceptual design also formalizes the target future state of the business activities. This future state becomes the basis for the next phases of the design process.

In conceptual design, the project team attempts to understand the context of the problem, records the business activities, and tries to portray their boundaries and their relationships. The entire functional specification is not created during conceptual design. However, the project team uses conceptual design to begin work on the functional specification.

Table 4.2 clarifies the scope of the conceptual design.

Table 4.2.   Scope of the Conceptual Design

Conceptual design is not	But it helps you to
The complete functional specification	Begin the functional specification
A definition of system components	Identify the parts of the business problem that will be addressed by the eventual components
A technology solution	Records the business activities and portray their boundaries and their relationships

What Are the Steps in Conceptual Design?

Conceptual design has the following three steps and associated baselines. Conceptual design is an iterative process and the steps are repeated as required.

1. *Research.* During this step, you perform the following tasks:
   - Obtaining answers to key questions
   - Identifying key business processes and activities
   - Prioritizing processes and activities
   - Validating, refining, and extending draft requirements, use cases, and usage scenarios created during the envisioning phase
2. *Analysis.* During this step, you perform the following tasks:
   - Reviewing the user and business research
   - Refining candidate requirements
   - Documenting and modeling the context, workflow, task sequence, and environmental relationships
3. *Optimization.* During this step, you perform the following tasks:

   - Optimizing the solution concept created during the envisioning phase
   - Validating and testing the improved business processes

   The optimization baseline leads to the baseline of the conceptual design.

Figure 4.7 illustrates the steps in the conceptual design.

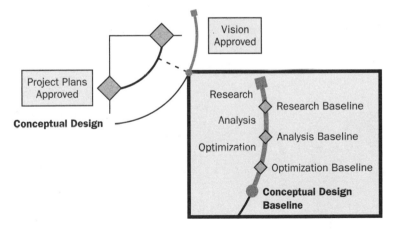

Figure 4.7.   Steps in conceptual design

During the research step of conceptual design, the team gathers more information to refine and validate data collected during the envisioning phase. Typically, the information gathered during the envisioning phase is high level and lacking in detail. During the first step of the conceptual design, the team needs to collect detailed information. For example, the team first identifies questions raised by the first iteration of information gathering; the team then continues to clarify the tasks, business processes, and workflow. As greater detail is discovered, the results are incorporated in the use cases and draft requirements.

More Info   You will learn about the analysis step of conceptual design in Lesson 4 and about the optimization step in Lesson 5.

Lesson 4: Building the Conceptual Design

After gathering detailed information about business and user requirements and business process, the team proceeds to the analysis step of conceptual design. At this step, the team analyzes the artifacts created during envisioning phase and elaborates and refines them.

In this lesson, you will learn how to use requirement restating to refine the information you have gathered. You will also learn how to categorize requirements and refine use cases and usage scenarios. In addition, you will learn how to make high-level architectural choices for the solution.

After this lesson, you will be able to

- Describe the analysis step of conceptual design.
- Restate requirements.
- Categorize requirements as user, system, operations, and business requirements.
- Refine use case diagrams.
- Select an appropriate application architecture for a solution.

Estimated lesson time: 20 minutes

What Is the Analysis Step in Conceptual Design?

In the analysis step of the conceptual design, you synthesize the information that you gathered in the research step and create detailed usage scenarios. The purpose of the analysis step is to:

- Review user and business processes and activities
- Document and model the context, workflow, task sequence, and environmental relationships of the business

Tasks in the analysis step

In the analysis step, you perform the following tasks:

- Synthesizing information
- Refining use case diagrams
- Selecting an appropriate application architecture for the solution
- Creating a conceptual model of the solution

Synthesizing information is the process of assimilating gathered data and interpreting the results. The team transforms the gathered data into meaningful information. To synthesize data, the project team performs the following tasks:

- Identify discrete pieces of information about what the user said and did.
- Record the detailed flow of the tasks that the user performed.
- Identify tools and pieces of information that were used.
- Identify exceptions and alternatives that occur while the user performs task.
- Model the relationship between business processes, business systems, and users.
- Model the current environment in which the user works and any possible changes to that environment.

Deliverables of the analysis step

Table 4.3 lists the key tasks and deliverables of the analysis step.

Table 4.3.   Tasks and Deliverables of Conceptual Design Analysis

Tasks	Deliverables

Synthesize gathered information	• Information models:
	  • Relationship between business processes, business systems, and users
	  • Workflow process
	  • Task sequence
	• Updated user profiles
	• Candidate requirements
	• Detailed use cases

Create usage scenarios	Current usage scenarios

How to Restate Requirements

When you restate requirements, keep the following criteria in mind:

- Requirements must be *well defined*. A well-defined requirement is a complete sentence and typically uses "shall," "may," "must," or "should."
- Requirements must be *concise*. Each requirement must address one item only.
- Requirements must be *testable*. Each requirement should have specific inputs resulting in known outputs.
- Requirements should be *organized in a hierarchy of related requirements*. You need to group related requirements together under a single high-level requirement to form feature sets.
- Requirements should be written in the language of the business and should not use jargon.

Table 4.4 shows potential requirement statements that the project team collected and formulated from the interview texts during the envisioning phase.

Table 4.4. Draft Requirement Statements in the Envisioning Phase

Requirement ID	Requirement
1	Identify best customers by product and location (profit analysis and geographical analysis); these are the customers on which the sales team should focus.
2	Identify decreases in a customer's sales.
3	Identify best customers.
4	Identify top buyers.

During the analysis step of conceptual design, the team restates the requirements to ensure that each requirement is a concise, complete, and testable statement. While the team is refining requirements, they might also discover new requirements. Restated versions of the requirements are listed in Table 4.5, based on the requirements in Table 4.4. The restated requirements are now concise, complete, and testable. Multiple related requirements are organized in a logical hierarchy.

Table 4.5. Restated Requirements

Requirement ID	Requirement
1.1	Must be able to analyze customer data
1.1.1	Must be able to analyze profit levels by product
1.1.2	Must be able to analyze profit levels by customer
1.1.3	Must be able to analyze profit levels by region
1.2	Must be able to sort (descending, ascending) customers
1.3.1	Must be able to sort (descending, ascending) customers by amount of sales
1.3.2	Must be able to sort (descending, ascending) customers by amount of sales of particular products
1.3.3	Must be able to sort (descending, ascending) customers by amount of sales in regions and amount of sales over a specified period of time
1.3.4	Must be able to sort (descending, ascending) customers by amount of sales over a specified period of time
1.4	Must be able to identify sales trends
1.4.1	Must be able to identify drop in sales
1.4.2	Must be able to identify drops in a customer's sales

Note Remember that at each step you must validate requirements with the customer.

How to Categorize Requirements

After refining requirements, you categorize them as user, system, operations, and business requirements.

User requirements

User requirements define the non-functional aspect of the user's interaction with the solution. They help you determine the user interface and performance expectations of the solution in terms of its reliability, availability, and accessibility. In addition, they help you identify the training that the users will need to effectively use the solution. A successful solution satisfies both the organization's need for technology and the user's expectations for employing that technology.

Examples of user requirements

Some of the user requirements might be:

- Sales representatives should not need to type any name they previously typed during any single sales call.
- A cashier should be able to complete more than one transaction per minute.
- A customer should be able to complete the purchase of a product on the shopping Web site within five minutes.

System requirements

System requirements specify the atomic transactions and their sequence in the system, and help the project team define how the new solution will interact with the existing systems. The project team also identifies the critical dependencies with external systems that must be managed. Before developing a new solution, the project team must understand the current infrastructure in the organization. This helps the project team to design and develop a solution that can be deployed in the organization with the minimum negative impact.

Examples of system requirements

Some of the system requirements might be:

- All enterprise line-of-business applications supporting near-real-time user notifications must either implement the approved notification component or have received a waiver during final design review.
- The solution should not require a user credential other than the credentials passed from logging on to the corporate network.

Operations requirements

Operations requirements describe what the solution must deliver to maximize operability and improve service delivery with reduced downtime and risks. It addresses the following key elements of operations:

- Security
- Availability and reliability
- Manageability
- Scalability
- Supportability

Examples of operations requirements

Consider the example of a music store that wants to implement an e-commerce Web site. Some of the operations requirements for this site include:

- *Availability and reliability.* Customers should be able to access the site and use its resources at any time within stated service levels.
- *Scalability and flexibility.* The solution should be able to handle varying volumes of users and transactions. In addition, the site must be designed so that it can be modified and upgraded without affecting availability or performance. Both the infrastructure and business processes must be scalable and flexible.
- *Performance manageability.* The site design should include a system for managing the total system throughput and response time within stated service levels.
- *Strong security.* The data, services, and devices in the system must be protected from unauthorized access. The system should also provide authentication and secure transactions.
- *Administrative manageability.* The site should allow the administrators to perform their tasks both onsite and remotely.
- *Recoverability.* The site should be able to recover from critical failure without major impact, or within stated service levels.

Business requirements

Business requirements describe the organization's needs and expectations for the solution. Business requirements define what the solution must deliver to capitalize on a business opportunity or to meet business challenges. To identify business requirements, you need to consider the organization as a valid entity with its own set of needs from the solution. These requirements exist at the managerial decision-making level and provide the context in which the solution will operate.

Examples of business requirements

Some examples of business requirements might be:

- Call-center managers must be able to view the last, current, and average call times for each telephone operator.
- Cashiers can override an item's price to a specified amount without the supervisor's code.
- The solution must be designed, built, and deployed as quickly as possible.
- The solution must be able to interact and communicate with other business processes, applications, and data sources.

Consider a music store that wants to increase the sales of its CDs and DVDs and sell to a larger segment of the market. The organization has decided to implement an online shopping site. Some of the business requirements of this organization are:

- After the user submits an order, inventory must be marked "for fulfillment" and removed from "available" status.
- The application must provide a method of applying a discount to orders over a specified amount.

How to Refine Use Cases Diagrams

During the envisioning phase, the project team creates a use cases diagram that specifies all high-level use cases in the organization. The purpose of this use cases diagram is to list the key use cases in the system, to define of the scope of solution, and to provide a basis for the solution concept. To create a conceptual model of the design, you need to refine the use cases that are within the scope of the solution by using the information gathered during the research step of conceptual design.

To refine the use cases diagram, you perform the following tasks:

- Create subordinate use cases.
- Create usage scenarios for each subordinate use case.
- Validate each use case and usage scenario against the original interviews, against other documentation, and with the user.
- Refine requirements with the validated use cases and usage scenario information.

Creating subordinate use cases

To create subordinate use cases, you revisit each use case in the use cases diagram that is within the scope of the project. You then identify each task associated with the use case, and model them as subordinate use cases for the higher-level use case. You also identify all actors that perform the tasks and the relationship between the various tasks and actors.

Figure 4.8 illustrates a refined use cases diagram. This diagram shows many subordinate use cases for the Manage Orders use case.

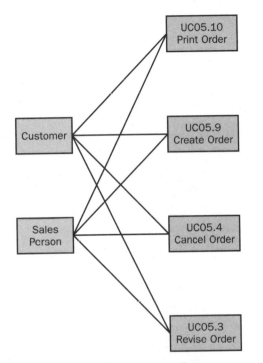

Figure 4.8.   Refined use case diagram

Usage scenarios for subordinate use cases

After creating subordinate use cases, you need to create usage scenarios for the new use cases. This step includes elaborating on the original usage scenario and adding a detailed scenario narrative; specifying the basic course; specifying an alternative course, if any; and describing the preconditions and postconditions.

The following is a sample usage scenario of a high-level use case included in the Adventure Works Cycles case study.

Use case title: Order Product Specifications

Abbreviated title: Order Product Specifications

Use case ID: UC 05.1

Requirements ID: 15.1

Intent: To provide full (not basic) product specification document to customer

Scenario narrative: While a customer is viewing an item in the catalog, the customer requests the product specifications.

Actors: Customer

Use case title: Order Product Specifications   *(continued)*

Preconditions: Customer is browsing through the product catalog.

Customer is viewing an item in the catalog.

Basic course:

1. Use case begins when a customer clicks Order Specifications for This Item
2. Customer selects the format of the specification.
3. Customer selects the shipping method.
4. Address is confirmed.
5. Use case ends when the order is complete, submitted, and ready to be fulfilled.

Alternative course:

Postconditions: Order is complete, submitted, and ready to be fulfilled. Customer is returned to last view in Browse Products.

Uses/extends: Customer Updates Profile, Customer Creates Profile, Submit Order

User implementation requests: None

Frequency: Occurs in 17 out of 100 sessions by Web customer.

Unresolved issues: None

Authority: Mike Danseglio

Modification history: Date: November 6, 2002

Author: Heidi Steen

Description: Initial version

One of the subordinate use cases for the Order Product Specifications use case is Order Product Specifications by Mail. The usage scenario for this subordinate use case is as follows.

Use case title: Order Product Specifications by Mail

Abbreviated title: Product Specifications by Mail

Use case ID: UC 05.1.1

Requirements ID: 15.1.1

Intent: Provide a means for a customer to receive the specification for a selected catalog item through the postal service.

Scenario narrative: A customer wants to receive a product specification through the postal service. The customer browses through the catalog (UC 05.1) and views the catalog item of interest. After choosing delivery by the postal service, the customer must specify a delivery address. If the customer has logged on with a valid account, the customer can select an address from a list of addresses on file. The customer can also specify an address in a form. After the request has been submitted, the customer receives a confirmation number for future reference.

Actors: Customer

Use case title: Order Product Specifications by Mail   *(continued)*

Preconditions:

- Customer is browsing through the product catalog.
- Customer is viewing an item in the catalog.

Basic Course:

1. Use case begins when a customer clicks Order Specifications for This Item
2. Customer selects the format of the specification, such as specification sheet or brochure.
3. Customer selects the shipping method, such as electronic, United States Postal Service, one-day delivery, or two-day delivery.
4. Address list from profile appears.
5. Customer chooses an address from a list of addresses.
6. Address is confirmed.
7. Customer submits the request.
8. Use case ends when the customer is given a confirmation number.

Alternative course:

1. Alternative course begins at 4.
2. 4a. Address does not exist in profile.
   4b. Go to Customer Updates Profile or Customer Creates Profile.
3. Use case resumes at 5.

Postconditions: Order is complete, submitted, and ready to be fulfilled. User is returned to last view in Browse Products.

Uses/extends: Extends UC 05.1, Order Product Specifications

User implementation requests: None

Frequency: Occurs in 17 out of 100 sessions by Web customer

Unresolved issues: None

Authority: Mike Danseglio

Modification history:

Date: December 6, 2002

Author: Heidi Steen

Description: Initial version

Validating use cases and usage scenarios

It is essential that the team validate the candidate requirements, use cases, and usage scenarios with users and other stakeholders. This step helps determine whether any steps in the process have not been documented. The features list is then developed based on the requirements. Revisions to the feature list are identified by elaborating on the use cases, and any additions are validated by the customer.

Remember that validation is an iterative process. It helps you identify gaps in requirements in addition to use cases and usage scenarios.

How to Select an Application Architecture

The key deliverable of the conceptual design is the conceptual model of the solution. To be able to create a conceptual model, you need to understand the services that the solution must provide.

Services in a solution

A *service* is defined as a unit of application logic that includes methods for implementing an operation, a function, or a transformation.

Services are mapped to actions and used to implement business rules, manipulate data, and enable actions such as adding, retrieving, viewing, and modifying data. Services are accessible across a network through a published interface that contains the interface specification. Customers are not concerned about how a service is implemented; they are concerned about the ability to perform the required actions.

Services can be either simple or complex. For example, services for creating, reading, updating, and deleting information are simple. You might also develop services to implement complex mathematical calculations.

The services that a solution typically provides are:

- *User services.* User services are units of application logic that provide the user interface in an application. The user services of an application manage the interaction between the application and its users. To design efficient user services, you need a thorough understanding of the users of the application, the tasks that they will perform, and the typical interactions they will have with the application to perform their activities.

- *Business services.* Business services are units of application logic that enforce business rules in the correct sequence. A business service hides the logic of implementing business rules and transforming data from the user services, other business services, and data services.

- *Data services.* Data services are units of application logic that provide the lowest visible level of detail for manipulating data. You use data services to implement business schema on the data store being used by the application. Data services are used to manage all kinds of data—static, structured, and dynamic. You use data services in all scenarios in which a user or business service needs to access or work with data.

- *System services.* System services are the units of application logic that provide functionality outside the business logic. Common system services include:
  - Backup services
  - Error handling services
  - Security services
  - Messaging services

Examples of services

Table 4.6 lists the various services in an order processing application.

Table 4.6.   Examples of Services

Services	Examples
User services	• Displaying the order service
	• Displaying the customer account service
	• Displaying product information service
Business services	• Order placing service
	• Updating customer account service
	• Retrieving product information service
	• Checking product inventory service
Data services	• Order information service
	• Customer account service
	• Product information service

Remember that you classify a service according to its function and not according to its location. The classification into user, business, or data service depends on what the service actually does, as opposed to where it is located. For example, a data service on the client workstation is still a data service.

Application architecture

You also need to know how the services are organized in the solution. The services are organized according to the application architecture. Application architecture consists of definitions, rules, and relationships that form the structure of an application. It shows how an application is structured but does not include implementation details. It focuses on the solution and not the technologies that will be used to implement the solution. To be able to develop a conceptual model of the solution, you need to select the application model and candidate application architecture that the solution will use.

The project team selects the architecture based on both the services that the solution must provide and users' expectations of the performance of the application. In addition, assumptions about the solution and constraints of the project affect the choice of the application architecture for the solution. Assumptions include the operating systems used in the system. Examples of constraints include budget, time, skills, and resources available for completing the project.

Some of the application architectures that are used are:

- Client/server architecture
- Layered architecture
- Stateless architecture
- Cache architecture
- Layered-client-cache-stateless-cache-server architecture

Client/server architecture

The *client/server architecture* is a two-tier approach that is based on a request-and-provide strategy. The client initiates a session with the server and controls the session, enlisting the server on demand. The client requests the server for one of its services. Upon receiving the request, the server performs the required operation and returns the result to the client.

The benefit of implementing this application architecture is that you can divide the processing required to accomplish a task between the two devices. The client can execute specialized processes and avoid overloading the server with processing requests.

However, one of the limitations of this architecture is that the clients depend heavily on the servers. If the client fails to communicate with the server, the client cannot perform even the most basic task. This is typical in solutions that must process a large number of requests. Such an application is not highly scalable.

Layered architecture

Layered architecture is an evolved version of the client/server architecture and is composed of hierarchical layers. The various services in the application are clearly positioned in specific layers in such a way that a service cannot communicate with other services except the ones in the adjacent layer. Layers encapsulate services and protect one service from another while providing a simplified set of interfaces for shared resources. User, business, and data services are examples of a layered architecture.

Benefits of layered architecture include improved system scalability and high security. You can balance services across available resources and various layers. In addition, layers allow you to implement security on well-defined boundaries with very little negative impact on communications between services within the system.

Layering adds overhead and latency that can negatively affect performance of the system as perceived by the user. You can mitigate the impact of this problem by adding shared caches to the system. However, this approach increases the complexity of the solution, the effort required to design and develop the solution, and the resources required to operate the solution.

Stateless architecture

Stateless architecture is a version of the client/server or layered architecture in which each client request contains all the information that is required by the server to understand and process the request. No information is stored on the client.

Some of the benefits of stateless systems are:

- *Improved visibility.* For example, a monitoring system does not need to read more than a single request to determine the full nature of the request
- *Reliability.* For example, the solution can easily recover from a partial failure
- *Scalability.* The resources used by the solution can be quickly released and easily pooled.

Note A stateless environment places an additional burden on clients to manage their own state. Because a lot of information is passed to the server for every request, the load on the communication channels is also increased.

Cache architecture

Caching is another approach in which the application provides a means for processing some client requests without forwarding the request to another device. To implement this kind of application architecture, you need to identify what can and cannot be cached. You also need to define ways to manage the lifetime of items in the cache.

Because caching avoids transferring request and response data between clients and servers, the application and network performance are greatly improved. In addition, this approach provides a high degree of scalability by creating local storage for frequently requested resources that would otherwise be queued to access a shared repository.

However, caching reduces the reliability of the solution. For example, the cached data might be outdated and so might not match the information that would be received if the request were processed by the server.

Layered-client-cache-stateless-cache-server architecture

Layered-client-cache-stateless-cache-server architecture is the browser-based version of the Windows Distributed interNet Applications (DNA) architecture. It combines the layered-client-server, client-cache, and cached-stateless-server approaches by adding proxies throughout the system as necessary.

This architecture allows you to create highly flexible and scalable applications by distributing processing and remaining stateless on the server. You can scale up and scale out the solution without affecting the transactional integrity of the solution. In addition, this architecture ensures the manageability and flexibility of the solution.

The layered-client-cache-stateless-cache-server architecture is complex and precariously balanced. Any deviation from the implied implementation can quickly deteriorate its portability, network, and user perceived performance.

Example of a conceptual model

Figure 4.9 illustrates the conceptual model of the solution in the Adventure Works Cycles case study. Notice that the model has multiple layers and that the various services of the solution are located in the solution's three layers.

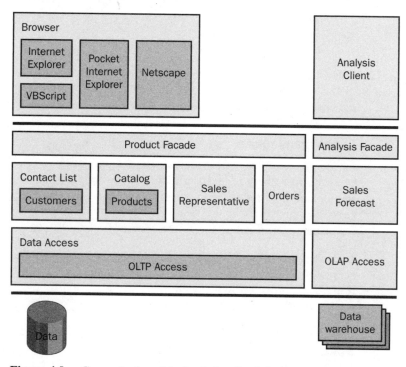

Figure 4.9.   Conceptual model of solution for Adventure Works Cycles

Lesson 5: Optimizing the Conceptual Design

The final step of conceptual design is optimization. During optimization, you begin designing the solution by evolving the solution concept as it will be in the final application.

Table 4.7 lists the tasks and deliverables of optimization.

Table 4.7.   Tasks and Deliverables of Conceptual Design Optimization

Task	Deliverable
Improve the process.	Description of problems addressed by solution.
Validate the design.	Validated future state of the solution.

In this lesson, you will learn how to optimize the process descriptions gathered during conceptual design. You will also learn how to evaluate the optimized processes and validate the conceptual design.

After this lesson, you will be able to

- Optimize processes.
- Evaluate optimized processes.
- Validate optimized processes.
- Validate the conceptual design.

Estimated time: 15 minutes

How to Optimize Processes

In addition to researching and analyzing current business processes, you determine which processes will be included in the solution and how the needs of those processes are met. The management or process owners, the users, and the project team must work together to arrive at a solution that focuses on both the processes and the users.

To design the future state, you examine the current state scenarios and eliminate inefficiencies, bottlenecks, and redundant effort. The future state is best designed by the project team and users together with the help of experts in business process reengineering.

Note   The project team and the business process reengineering team should design a target future state and redesign business processes only if these activities are included in the scope of the project.

Although many application development teams can do a great deal to design the future state, the involvement of business process reengineering experts is a best practice. To describe the future state, the team performs the following tasks:

- Envision the target future state.
  - Improve productivity of the current state.
  - Consider needs versus wants.
  - Balance business and user requirements.
  - Balance impact and technical feasibility.
- Redesign the current process to optimally support key business activities and processes, involving business process redesign experts as appropriate.
  - Optimize the entire process.
  - Integrate processes where possible.
  - Eliminate inefficiencies, bottlenecks, and redundancies.
- Build target future state usage scenarios that reflect the redesigned process.
- Validate future state scenarios with stakeholders.
- Iterate the redesign process as needed.

Instead of designing the future state from an analyst's perspective, redesign the solution from the users' perspective. You might find improvement opportunities in workflow activities, outdated or unproductive business policies, unchallenged bureaucracies, missed communication, and non-value-added roles that hinder and fragment the overall effectiveness of a business process. To identify the requirements from the user's perspective, keep in mind the following guidelines:

- Identify undesirable sequential activities, bottlenecks, and unnecessary steps in the process.
- Remove redundancies in the current environment.
- Integrate individual functional information systems into consolidated process-wide systems.
- Identify and remove all unnecessary paperwork.
- Determine the minimum performance level that must be achieved by a process. Try to design a process that achieves the same results with less effort.
- Reduce the wait time in a system by identifying steps that can be performed simultaneously instead of sequentially.
- Improve the system by providing users information such as feedback about performance to ensure that problems are resolved immediately.

Redesigning processes identified during design

The key objective of the project team, along with the business process reengineering experts, is to design an elegant solution that minimizes user effort as much as possible. There is no single method for redesigning a process effectively. The team can conduct brainstorming sessions that use various creativity techniques: metaphors, word and thought variation, creativity-barrier exploration, idea-generation exercises, open forum, and non-critical discussions. These ideas represent new approaches to the problem rather than detailed blueprints.

Key questions for the business process reengineers include:

- Where are the opportunities for user empowerment?
- Can certain decisions be delegated? If so, what is the impact of delegation on business activities?
- What can be done in software that is difficult to achieve in the physical world or on paper?
- What are the opportunities for automation or applying new technologies?

During the redesign process, explore multiple alternatives. It is important to encourage the creative process. Often, a problem has more than one solution.

A key principle in redesign is that every rule or assumption can be challenged. Also, you need to consider all elements of a process during redesign—inputs, outputs, performance levels, resources, control procedures, productivity, and timing. The following summary lists the key elements to consider when optimizing a process:

- Challenge rules and break assumptions that rules are unquestionable. For example, you can question a rule such as "In this company, all medical claim requests submitted by employees must be approved at the unit, departmental, and divisional levels."
- Align the process with performance goals. Think of performance in terms of meeting customer requirements and not just short-term profits.
- Design activities around products and services. The responsibilities of a user should be designed to meet the goals and objectives of the process and not be designed around a specific task.
- Replace bureaucracies and hierarchies with self-organized teams that work in parallel.
- Improve productivity by moving the focus from work fragmentations and task specialization toward task compression and integration.
- Determine where you can use technology to enable and support the redesigned process.
- Break the process into subprocesses and deal with each subprocess one process at a time.

Once the process is optimized and targeted as the goal, the focus shifts to redesigning the work. Redesigning work is based on what is necessary from a business standpoint, not what initially seems reasonable or accomplishable. The team needs to examine the conceptual model of the solution and reorganize it to make the process more efficient.

Also, the team might discover new use cases and need to incorporate them into the conceptual model. Based on the new use cases, several alternative process designs might be generated. Validate these alternatives with end users and business process experts by using techniques such as role playing. Based on the results of testing and validation, you can select an alternative for subsequent detailed design.

The process for redesigning work can be summarized as follows:

- Brainstorm for maximum ideas.
    - Use visualization.
    - Think creatively and break the rules.
    - Generate, evaluate, and challenge options.
- Supplement brainstorming with other techniques.
- Validate alternatives with end users and process experts.

How to Evaluate the Redesigned Process

You evaluate the redesigned process to determine whether there is any misunderstood or missing information about user requirements. You also confirm that no problems have occurred because of varying views of the solution among the team.

You also evaluate the cost and benefits of the solution in its current state. Many projects are canceled at this stage because evaluation indicates that the return on investment (ROI) of the new solution does not meet business criteria.

In addition, you need to determine the primary and secondary benefits. The specific benefits should be stated, and the stakeholders, including customers, should be identified.

Table 4.8 summarizes the evaluation criteria for most business solutions.

Table 4.8.   Evaluating Benefits and Costs of a Redesign

Evaluating benefits	Evaluating cost
Effectiveness and efficiency of whole and parts	Resources, work effort, and time
Beneficiaries of the solution	Operational costs of technical options and emerging technology
Organizational and cultural effects	Annual and recurring life-cycle costs
Potential revenue and savings	

How to Validate the Conceptual Design Model

After creating the conceptual design, validate it with users and other stakeholders. You can integrate validation directly into the process of evaluating user input. Validation enables you to get users' confirmation that the conceptual model and requirements represent their view of the business solution and that the solution addresses all use cases and usage scenarios.

You validate the conceptual design of the solution against the use cases, usage scenarios, business requirements, architecture, risks, available resources and time, and all other artifacts that you have developed. Users find it easier to validate a scenario because the scenario contains the context of the requirements.

The validation of the scenarios should also include a validation of the results from the prioritization activity. In other words, the priorities and volume of activity for the scenario should be verified. You get the conceptual design of the solution validated because validation:

- Reduces risk.
- Highlights missing information.
- Indicates diverging views and interpretations of the solution, especially between the business and users.
- Verifies the volume of activity.
- Assists in prioritization.
- Provides a baseline for proceeding to logical design.

The process for validating, testing, and redesigning can include the following steps:

1. Redesign the work.
2. Build a set of scenarios that support the work.
3. Build a prototype of the system.
4. Draw the user interface.
5. Obtain user and business feedback.
6. Repeat until users and the business are satisfied.

Repeat steps 5 and 6 as required.

Techniques for validating conceptual design

There are several techniques for validating scenarios. Some of those techniques include:

- *Walk through.* A facilitator guides users through the scenario and asks questions along the way to determine whether the users agree with individual actions and events.

- *Role playing.* A set of selected users executes multiple scenarios to evaluate the process and identify areas of refinement. This helps the team select one of the scenarios for detailed design.

- *Prototyping.* A prototype provides details of the process, process flow, organizational implications, and technology possibilities. Prototyping is an effective way to communicate the gathered and synthesized requirements to the user. You can create a prototype as an electronic application or in paper form as the functional specification summary. Prototypes should be reviewed and evaluated by the team and should allow management to decide about the final process design. The team also needs to prototype multiple user interfaces. Such prototypes are used to validate that the team has included appropriate information—not whether the dialog box looks right or whether the colors are correct.

Activity: Analyzing Requirements

In this activity, you will use what you learned in the lessons to work through the process of analyzing requirements.

Exercise 1: Refining Use Cases and Requirements

Open the Microsoft Visio® diagram named C04Ex1 in the \SolutionDocuments \Chapter04 folder on the CD. Look at the second tab: AWC Use Case - Ex1ToSolve.

1. What questions would you ask the customer's project staff to identify the subordinate use cases contained in Manage Orders?

   Questions you would ask might include:

   ■ What does it mean to manage orders?

   ■ What does the Sales Representative role do when managing orders? Name as many specific tasks as possible.

   ■ What does the Customer role do when managing orders? Name as many specific tasks as possible.

   ■ What are the differences between the tasks that the customer performs with orders and the tasks that the sales representative performs?

2. The customer gives you the following information:

   ■ Both the Customer and the Sales Representative roles need to create, print, change, and cancel orders by using the Web site and the devices the sales representative uses.

   ■ The Adventure Works Cycles project staff agree that a Help function is needed and that they want the user to be able to view a frequently asked questions (FAQ) section, get Help by means of a wizard, and have instant messaging (IM) sessions available.

   ■ The sales representative, but not the customer, can apply a discount to the order.

   Use this information and your requirements to enter the appropriate use cases on the third tab, Ch4 Manage Orders, in the Visio file. The Create Order and Revise Order use cases have been provided to give you a starting point.

To see one possible solution, see the C04Ex1_Answer document in the \Solution Documents\Chapter04 folder on the companion CD.

Exercise 2: Viewing a Conceptual Model Diagram

Open the Visio diagram named C04Ex2.vsd in the \SolutionDocuments\Chapter04 folder on the CD. Review the conceptual model. Open the requirements document C04Ex2.xls in the same folder. Review and revise the requirements statements and organize them into a loose hierarchy by using the conceptual model to guide you. For example, organize all requirements related to Revise Order together. Does the conceptual model allow the current requirements to be covered in the solution?

 To see one possible solution, see the C04Ex2_Answer.xls document in the \Solution Documents\Chapter04 folder on the companion CD.

Summary

- The planning phase results in the architecture and design of the solution, the plans to accomplish the development and deployment of the solution, and the schedules associated with tasks and resources.
- There are three design processes in the planning phase: conceptual, logical, and physical design.
- The program management team manages and is responsible for the planning phase.
- The key deliverables of the planning phase are:
    - The functional specification, which represents what the product will be, based on input from the entire team
    - The master project plan, which is a collection of plans for how each of the six team roles will perform their tasks to achieve the functionality described in the functional specification
    - The master project schedule, which specifies the time frame in which the teams intend to complete their work
    - The updated master risk assessment document, which describes the risks associated with creating the product
- A functional specification is the virtual repository of project and design-related artifacts that are created during the planning phase of the MSF Process Model.
- The goals of a functional specification are:
    - Consolidating a common understanding of the business and user requirements
    - Breaking the problem into logical modules
    - Providing a framework for planning, scheduling, and creating the solution
    - Serving as a contract between the team and customer about what will be delivered
- The functional specification consists of:
    - Conceptual design summary
    - Logical design summary
    - Physical design summary
    - Standards and processes used by the team
- Conceptual design is the process of gathering, analyzing, and prioritizing business and user perspectives of the problem and the solution, and then creating a preliminary version of the solution.

- The goals of creating a conceptual design are:
    - Determining the business problem to be solved
    - Determining the requirements of the business, the customer, and the end user
    - Describing the target future state of the business
- The process of conceptual design consists of three steps: research, analysis, and optimization.
- During the research step, the team gathers more information about the business requirements, the use cases, and the usage scenarios.
- The tasks performed during the analysis step are:
    - Synthesizing information
    - Refining the use cases diagram
    - Selecting an appropriate application architecture for the solution
    - Creating a conceptual model of the solution
- A business requirement must be:
    - Well defined
    - Concise
    - Testable
    - Grouped in a hierarchical manner
    - Written in a business language without jargon
- Business requirements can be categorized as:
    - User
    - System
    - Operations
    - Business
- To refine the use cases diagram, the project team:
    - Creates subordinate use cases
    - Creates usage scenarios for each subordinate use case
    - Validates each use case and usage scenario against refined requirements
- To create the conceptual design of the solution, you need to determine the services and the architecture of the solution.
- A solution can provide business, user, data, and system services.
- Application architecture consists of definitions, rules, and relationships that form the structure of an application.

- An application can be based on one of the following architectures:
    - Client/server architecture
    - Layered architecture
    - Stateless architecture
    - Cache architecture
    - Layered-client-cache-stateless-cache-server architecture
- During the optimization step of conceptual design, the team optimizes the solution and business processes and validates them against business requirements and use cases.
- To describe the future state of the system, the project team:
    - Envisions the target future state
    - Redesigns the current process to optimally support key business activities and processes
    - Builds target future state scenarios that reflect the redesigned process
    - Validates future state scenarios with stakeholders
    - Iterates the redesign process as needed
- To redesign a process, the project team:
    - Brainstorms for maximum number of ideas
    - Supplements brainstorming with other techniques
    - Validates alternatives with end users and process experts
- The project team validates the conceptual design of the solution against the use cases, usage scenarios, and business requirements.

Review

The following questions are intended to reinforce key information presented in this chapter. If you are unable to answer a question, review the lesson materials and try the question again. You can find answers to the questions in the appendix.

1. What is the purpose of the planning phase?

2. What is the difference between the responsibilities of the product management and project management roles during the planning phase?

3. What are the major deliverables of the planning phase?

4. How does a functional specification serve as a blueprint for the development team?

5. What are the goals of a functional specification?

6. What are the risks of not creating a functional specification?

7. What is the difference between the business and user requirements of the solution?

8. What are the benefits of creating a conceptual design?

9. A company plans to increase its sales by 15 percent during the next financial year by implementing an online shopping site. The company intends to provide its users a Web site that is fast, provides secure credit card processing, and is available at all times. Also, only registered users will be able to purchase products on the site. What are the user, system, operation, and business requirements for this site?

10. What are the goals of the analysis step of conceptual design?

11. What is the benefit of synthesizing information?

12. What are the tasks for creating the future state?

13. What are the benefits of validating the conceptual design?

14. What are the four service categories?

15. Study and categorize the following services.
    - Displaying the employee details service
    - Updating the employee details service
    - Employee information service
    - E-mail service

16. What are the characteristics of a refined business requirement?

17. How do you refine use cases during the analysis step of conceptual design?

18. What are the criteria for evaluating the cost of a solution?

C H A P T E R   5

Creating the Logical Design

About This Chapter

The planning phase consists of three levels of design—conceptual, logical, and physical. These design levels occur consecutively; however, they have overlapping start and end points. Therefore, the conceptual design process always starts before the logical design process, but conceptual design will be in process when the logical design process starts. Likewise, the logical design process always starts before the physical design process, but the logical design will be in process when the physical design process starts. Table 5.1 summarizes the design process in the planning phase.

Table 5.1.   The Three Design Processes

Type of design	Perspective	Purpose
Conceptual	View the problem from the perspective of the user and the business	Defines the problem and solution in terms of usage scenarios
Logical	View the solution from the perspective of the project team	Defines the solution as a logical set of cooperating objects and services
Physical	View the solution from the perspective of the developers	Defines the solution's services and technologies

In this chapter, you will learn about the logical design process of the planning phase. This chapter provides an overview of the purpose and benefits of logical design in addition to the team composition during this process. It describes how to create the logical design for a business solution and how to use tools and techniques for documenting the output. In addition, this chapter covers how to optimize the logical design.

Before You Begin

To complete the lessons in this chapter, you must

- Understand the Microsoft® Solutions Framework (MSF) Process Model.
- Be familiar with the outputs of the envisioning phase.
- Be familiar with the planning phase.
- Understand the three steps of conceptual design—research, analysis, and optimization.

Lesson 1: An Overview of Logical Design

In conceptual design, you describe the solution from the business and user perspectives. The next step is to describe the solution from the project team's perspective. This is done in the logical design process.

In this lesson, you will learn about the goals and purpose of logical design.

After this lesson, you will be able to
- Describe logical design.
- Describe the benefits of logical design.
- Describe the roles and responsibilities of team members during logical design.

Estimated lesson time: 10 minutes

What Is Logical Design?

Logical design is defined as the process of describing the solution in terms of its organization, its structure, and the interaction of its parts from the perspective of the project team. Logical design:

- Defines the constituent parts of a solution.
- Provides the framework that holds all parts of the solution together.
- Illustrates how the solution is put together and how it interacts with users and other solutions.

When creating a logical design, the team takes into account all the business, user, system, and operations requirements that identify the need for security, auditing, logging, scalability, state management, error handling, licensing, globalization, application architecture, and integration with other systems.

Planning   Because the MSF design process is evolutionary as well as iterative, logical design affects the physical design.

When does logical design take place?

When the project team begins to identify significant objects and entity attributes, it can start the logical design, so logical design can begin before conceptual design ends. The decision to start logical design is made on a case-by-case basis, depending on the project and the team. Figure 5.1 illustrates where the logical design fits within the MSF Process Model.

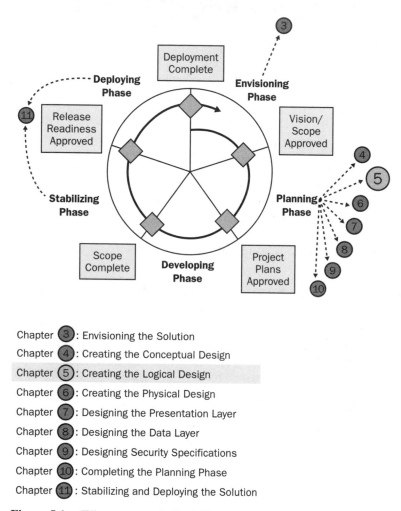

Chapter ③: Envisioning the Solution
Chapter ④: Creating the Conceptual Design
Chapter ⑤: Creating the Logical Design
Chapter ⑥: Creating the Physical Design
Chapter ⑦: Designing the Presentation Layer
Chapter ⑧: Designing the Data Layer
Chapter ⑨: Designing Security Specifications
Chapter ⑩: Completing the Planning Phase
Chapter ⑪: Stabilizing and Deploying the Solution

Figure 5.1. Where are you in the MSF design process?

When project teams proceed from conceptual to logical design, their perspectives change. During conceptual design, the project team defines the business problem based on the data it has gathered from the business and user communities. During logical design, the project team defines the solution elements from its own perspective. The members of the team identify what the solution needs to do. Based on that information, they define the behavior and organization of the solution.

Note   Logical design helps the team further refine the requirements that were initially created during the envisioning phase and refined during the conceptual design process.

A good logical design depends on a good conceptual design. If the project team creates a good logical design, it should be easy for a new team member to look at the design, identify important parts of the solution, and understand how the parts work together to solve the business problem. Most often, the work on the logical design overlaps the work on the physical design.

Note The project team optimizes the structure of the solution during the logical design and improves its operation during the physical design, thus leading to an iterative process between logical and physical design.

Logical design tasks

At a more detailed level, the logical design phase can be broken down into the following tasks:

- Logical design analysis, in which the team performs the following tasks:
    - Refining the list of candidate tools and technologies
    - Identifying business objects and services
    - Identifying important attributes and key relationships
- Logical design optimization, in which the team performs the following tasks:
    - Refining the logical design
    - Validating the logical design

Figure 5.2 illustrates the analysis and optimization tasks in logical design.

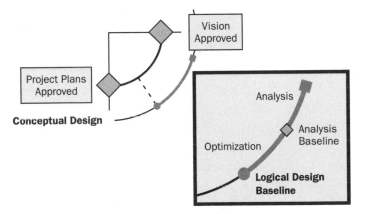

Figure 5.2. Tasks in logical design process

During logical design, the team might encounter some new requirements or features that have not been discovered previously. At this point, the team needs to go back to the customer to verify that these requirements or features are valid, and learn what the customer wants to do with this discovery. Depending on the customer's answer, the scope of the project might change. If the project scope changes, revise the documentation and models that have been created to incorporate the new requirements or features.

The primary purpose of logical design

The primary focus of the logical design is to identify what the system must do and explain it by using a set of elements. Logical design enables you to:

- Specify the business needs that should be supported by technology. The logical design is not a technology solution; however, it helps the project team specify the business needs that the solution must support.
- Identify technology constraints and opportunities. Although the logical design is independent of the physical implementation, the project team can start to identify constraints and opportunities that might affect the selection and implementation of a technology.
- Identify the appropriate technologies to be implemented. The team must understand the solution completely before the team selects the technology for implementing the solution. The logical design is not optimized for a selected physical model, but it helps the project team identify the most appropriate technologies for implementing the solution. Candidate technologies can be identified during logical design if the logical design demonstrates a good match to the technologies.
- Identify the areas of logical design that must be adjusted to accommodate infrastructure, operational, and deployment issues. Logical design is not affected by technologies required to develop the components. However, the logical design affects the physical design, and the physical design depends on technologies. Therefore, if the customer requires a Web-based solution for example, the project team should be aware of the deployment constraints during the logical design process.

Outputs of logical design

The outputs of the logical design process are:

- A logical object model
- A high-level user interface design
- A logical data model

Note   The logical object model and the logical data model document similar information in different ways. For most projects, one model is sufficient to document the logical design. However some teams might want to create both models as a precursor to physical design, and then validate one model with the other.

Each type of output is described in detail in Lesson 3.

The outputs of the logical design serve as a foundation for the physical design. To understand clearly what happens in the logical design process, consider the analogy of designing a house. During conceptual design, the customer and the architect list the customer requirements, such as entertainment, sleeping, dining, storage, and utility needs. During logical design, the architect creates the floor plan and identifies structural features such as doors, windows, roof, patio, and rooms. The architect also creates a complete layout of the house. Similarly, the project team works with users and the business customer during conceptual design to determine the requirements. Based on these requirements, the project team identifies the components of the solution and devises an overall framework into which the components then fit.

What Are the Benefits of Logical Design?

Creating a logical design for a solution has several benefits, such as helping to create a strong link between the members of the team who have technical knowledge and those who do not. The following list itemizes several of the benefits of logical design.

- Logical design helps manage the complexity of the project by defining the structure of the solution, describing the parts of the solution, and describing how the parts interact to solve the problem. Many projects fail because they are too complex and are not well designed before their implementation. Complexity can cause confusion, resulting in a poor design of the solution. Logical design helps the team understand and manage the inherent complexity of business processes.

- Logical design reflects and supports the requirements of conceptual design by verifying that the design will address the business problem. Logical design helps the team discover errors and inconsistencies in the conceptual design, eliminate redundancy in the requirements, and identify potential reuse in the scenarios. These discoveries can be applied back into the conceptual design and measured against the requirements to ensure that the solution will solve the problem.

- Logical design serves as a point of contact for organizing cross-functional cooperation among multiple systems in the enterprise and provides a coherent view of the entire project. The team can analyze the logical design to identify areas of reuse and make the design more efficient and maintainable.

- Logical design is used as the starting point for the physical design. Because logical design is an object model, the project team can determine the location and attributes of the objects for their physical representation.

What Are the Responsibilities of Team Roles During Logical Design?

During logical design, each team has a different set of responsibilities. For example, the program management team is responsible for developing the functional specification, facilitating communication and negotiation with the team, and maintaining project schedule and reporting project status. This team takes the primary responsibility for completing the logical design.

Figure 5.3 highlights the responsibilities of the various roles during logical design.

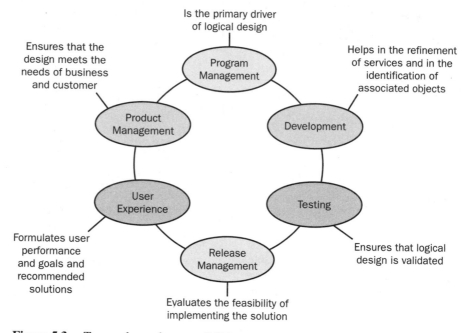

Figure 5.3.   Team roles and responsibilities

Table 5.2 summarizes the tasks that each team role performs during the logical design process.

Table 5.2.   Team Roles

Role	Primary task	Secondary task
Product management	Ensuring that the design meets the needs of the business and the customer	Managing customer expectations
Program management	Takes the primary responsibility for the logical design deliverables	Defining project plan, including resources, schedules, and risk assessments
Development	Identifying services and associated objects	Serving as technology consultants to evaluate and prototype technologies
Testing	Validating logical design models against conceptual design	Defining a high-level testing plan
User experience	Defining user performance goals and recommended solutions	Defining a high-level plan for user education
Release management	Evaluating the feasibility of implementing the solution	Defining infrastructure and deployment solutions

Lesson 2: Creating a Logical Design

During the analysis step of logical design, the team breaks the overall problem and its solution into smaller units called modules. A *module* is a logical unit used as an abstraction for the use cases and scenarios created in conceptual design. For each module, the team identifies objects, services, attributes, and relationships. The team also identifies candidate technologies for the solution during logical design.

In this lesson, you will learn how to identify candidate technologies for a business solution by considering the conceptual design, business objects, services, attributes of objects and services, and relationships between objects from use cases.

After this lesson, you will be able to

- Select candidate technologies.
- Identify candidate business objects from use cases.
- Identify services from use cases.
- Identify attributes from use cases.
- Identify relationships between objects from use cases.

Estimated lesson time: 20 minutes

How to Refine the List of Candidate Technologies in Logical Design

During conceptual design, the team begins to identify possible technologies that could be used to address parts of the solution. During logical design, the team further refines the list of candidate technologies already identified, while submitting additional candidate technologies to the list. In evaluating candidate technologies, the team addresses business considerations, enterprise architecture considerations, and technology considerations.

Business considerations

Some of the business considerations include:

- *Feasibility.* Determine whether the technology will actually meet the business needs and address the requirements.
- *Product cost.* Understand the complete product cost, which includes developer, server, and reseller licenses, and upgrade costs. The team also needs to consider costs for initial hardware and software, support, infrastructure, and training. A new product can be a short-term or long-term investment. A short-term

investment solves an immediate need temporarily, such as creating a small and simple client user interface until an intranet Web application is complete. Long-term investments are items that bring benefit for years, such as rewiring a workplace to support higher speed networks or purchasing leading-edge hardware for servers and workstations.

- *Experience.* Understand that the amount of experience users have with various technologies can have a large impact. Try to collect answers to questions such as "What experience is available in terms of training, consultation, and comfort level?"

- *Return on investment.* Each investment must correspond to a return on investment. Do not select a technology simply because it is new. The investment in new technologies should provide value to the business, such as an increase in revenue or a decrease in costs.

- *Maturity.* A mature product is accepted in the market, is well understood, is stable, and has knowledgeable support resources available.

- *Supportability.* When selecting a technology, it is important to realize that the technology will need to be supported along with the solution built. The team needs to consider the implications of providing required levels of support for the project and the enterprise.

Some other factors to consider when selecting candidate technologies are:

- Ease of deployment
- Competitive advantage
- Time needed to market the candidate technology
- Industry perception of the product
- Ability to integrate with existing systems

Enterprise architecture considerations

The application must fit within the goals and principles outlined by the enterprise architecture. In addition to looking at the existing enterprise architecture, the project team must consider any future plans for the enterprise architecture. For example, if the business is planning to use Microsoft Windows® Server 2003, align the selection of candidate technologies with this plan.

The enterprise architecture describes the current-state and future-state plans. The solution must fit within the constraints of the enterprise architecture. For example, a new technology such as streaming video might require enhanced networking capabilities. A new imaging system might require larger screens. Such changes require not only money to purchase new equipment, but also time to learn and implement the new technologies. If two technologies have an equivalent feature set, the best choice is the one that aligns more closely to the existing enterprise architecture.

The technology must work with the other systems within an organization. In addition, a communication interface must be defined so that other applications can easily interact with the new technology.

Technology considerations

Some of the technology considerations are:

- *Security*. Evaluate security considerations for a new solution in terms of authentication, access control, encryption, and auditing. Authentication and authorization are two separate steps in the process of granting users access to resources. *Authentication* determines whether an individual is who he or she claims to be; *authorization* permits the authenticated individual to perform permitted actions within the system. Security services also provide encryption to protect the information as it is transported or stored. *Auditing* creates a permanent record of actions that individuals are performing or attempting to perform within the system.

- *Services interaction standards*. Platforms and interaction standards are related. When the team selects a service interaction standard, it needs to evaluate cross-platform integration against power and performance. For example, the Microsoft .NET Framework simplifies application development in a distributed environment. Besides providing cross-language integration features, it reduces the performance problems of scripted or interpreted environments and provides a simplified model for component interaction.

- *Data access*. When selecting a data access service, consider performance, standardization, future direction, data access management, and the diversity of supported data stores. Candidate technologies for implementing a data access service might need to support industry standards. One of the requirements of data access services might be to allow the team to efficiently use the service regardless of the data store. Data access services should not force the development team to use a specific language or create a specific client interface. This independence from the requesting client allows the development team to use the most effective tools to process data, regardless of how the data is accessed.

- *Data storage*. Data storage systems are responsible for storing all of a business's information, such as employee, company, and customer information. When selecting a data store, evaluate multiple products. The decision should be based on the same structure and location of information. The location of the information is important. Data can be stored on a single computer, in a server farm, or distributed on client computers. The data storage location directly affects the performance of the application and how it is developed.

- *System services*. The project team should evaluate the system services that are required and identify the technologies that will provide those services. System services can also provide many high-availability services, such as fault tolerance and load balancing. In the past, many system services were programmed into each application, but many systems now offer system services independent of a specific application.

The following services are examples of system services:

- Transactional services provide the mechanisms and framework for a transaction-based application. In a transactional system, a sequence of steps can be grouped together as a single transaction. If any of the steps fails, the entire transaction fails and can be reversed or rolled back.

- Asynchronous communication services do not require immediate communication. These services provide a message-based form of execution. A requesting application can be guaranteed that a message will arrive at the remote system, but the requesting application is not dependent on a response within any given period.

- Messaging services are more than just electronic mail. They route information and deliver information that is not time dependent to many individuals. Queuing services are used to queue messages when the destination is not available. This allows the application to submit messages to a recipient regardless of the recipient's availability.

- *Development tools.* Development tools provide the ability to develop the various parts of an application, such as services and components. They provide integrated development environments, source code control, wizards, and code libraries. These tools can help decrease the time required to create applications. While evaluating development tools, the project team should consider several factors:

  - The first consideration is the skills of the developer. New tools require additional training and learning time for the development team and can affect schedule and resource constraints.

  - Specific project requirements might suggest a tool that requires team training or outsourcing to a third-party development team. Some development tools are easier to use than others. Consider the amount of time a particular development tool will require to implement a project. There is often a tradeoff involving the complexity of the development tool and the efficiency of the developed product. For example, assembly language can be used to develop an extremely fast application, but the development team would likely take much longer using assembly language than it would using a tool such as Microsoft Visual Basic® .NET.

  - Consider different languages for different tasks in the project. When choosing a development language, evaluate whether the language supports the design and implementation of loosely coupled components that can be replaced and upgraded as necessary. However, before implementing the use of different languages for different tasks, evaluate the current skills of the development team and the maintenance issues that might need to be addressed after the solution is deployed. For example, the .NET Framework programming model supports a range of programming languages. This also accelerates developer productivity because the developer can choose to develop in the development language of choice.

- Remember that the choice of development tools affects other technology decisions. For example, a specific operating system might be required for using the tool or for implementing solutions created by the tool. Microsoft ASP.NET provides a language-independent platform to create Web applications, but it is not platform independent. The applications must run on the Windows operating system.

- *Operating systems.* When selecting the operating system, the services that are provided by the operating system can significantly reduce the coding requirements of the application. Additionally, security and scalability needs can be met by the operating system. The choice of operating system might also depend on the types of devices, such as Handheld PCs, desktop computers, servers, and specialized devices particular to a specific industry.

Important   All technologies identified at this stage are documented in a technical specification section, which can be a part of any project document, such as a project plan or a functional specification document. This section is further refined during physical design when the team has identified the technologies that will be used to implement the solution.

How to Identify Candidate Business Objects

Objects are defined as the people or things described in the usage scenarios. Objects form the basis for services, attributes, and relationships.

Figure 5.4 shows the overall process of identifying objects, services, attributes, and relationships in the analysis step of logical design.

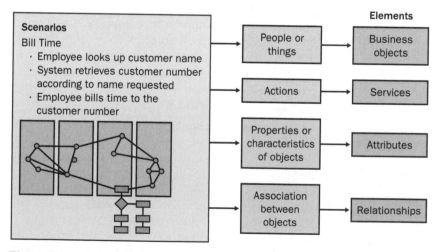

Figure 5.4.   Logical design analysis: identifying objects, services, attributes, and relationships

Identifying objects

You need to identify the business objects, or components, that will provide the functionality for the solution. Look at the usage scenarios you created during the conceptual design process to help you identify these objects. Figure 5.5 illustrates this process. When you have identified an object, you then need to identify the behaviors and attributes of the object in addition to its relationships with other objects.

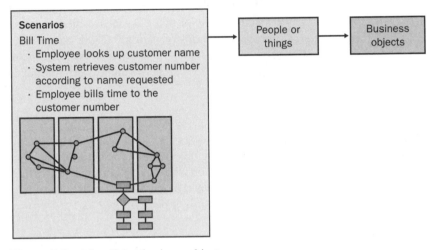

Figure 5.5.   Identifying business objects

Some usage scenarios might not explicitly contain objects, even though objects are necessary to perform the required business activities. The objects might be hidden within sentences, depending on how the usage scenario is written. Look for hidden references to structures, systems, devices, things, and events. To identify missing objects, think about the scenario in terms of required information and behavior that is not associated with an object.

Example of business objects

To clearly understand the concept of business objects, consider the following use cases:

- Employee completes a time sheet by recording the billable hours spent at work.
- Employee creates a contract with the customer.
- Employee reviews prior billings to the customer.
- Employee bills time to the customer number

After studying these use cases, you can identify the following business objects:

- *Employee.* Performs actions within the system.
- *Customer.* The recipient of actions performed by the employee.

- *Time sheet.* The means by which the employee identifies the amount of time spent on a project.
- *Contract.* The agreement between the employee and the customer.
- *Billings.* Invoices that the customer has received for work performed.
- *Customer number.* A means of identifying a specific customer in the system.

How to Identify Services

A *service* is a specific behavior that a business object must perform. It refers to an operation, a function, or a transformation that can be applied to or implemented by an object. You use services to implement business rules, manipulate data, and access information. A service can perform any activity that can be described by a set of rules.

Identifying services

To identify services for an object, examine the usage scenario again. To identify a service, determine what the object is supposed to do, the kind of data the object must maintain, and the actions that the object must perform. If an object maintains information, it also performs the operations on the information. Some examples of such actions that an object might perform include:

- Calculate total amount
- Determine the cost of shipping

Figure 5.6 illustrates identifying actions, and therefore services, from a usage scenario.

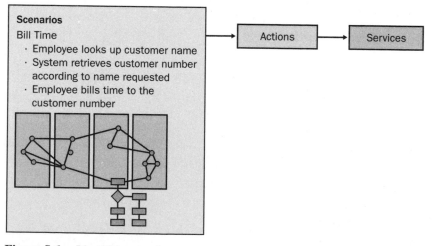

Figure 5.6. Identifying services

Assign the service that you identify to the associated object. This object is either the recipient of the action or is responsible for performing the action in the usage scenario. If it is difficult to identify the correct object for assigning a service, examine all possibilities by a walkthrough of the scenario. A walkthrough of the scenario involves working step by step through every requirement.

State the capabilities and responsibilities of a service in terms as broad as possible. In addition, you need an unambiguous name to identify the service. If you cannot assign a clear name to the service, it indicates that the purpose of the service is not clearly understood and needs more work in the conceptual design.

Examples of services

Figure 5.7 contains examples of services that can be identified from the sample usage scenario.

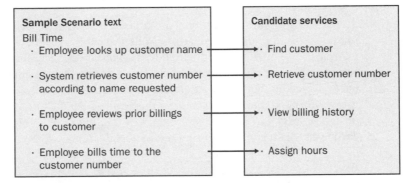

Figure 5.7.   Identifying services from a scenario

Consider the following usage scenarios:

- Employee looks up customer name. This usage scenario corresponds to the service *find customer* for the Employee business object.

- System retrieves customer name. This usage scenario corresponds to the service *retrieve customer number* for the Customer business object.

- Employee records billable hours on the time sheet. This usage scenario corresponds to the service *fill time sheets* for the Employee business object.

- Employee reviews prior billings to customer. This usage scenario corresponds to the service *view billing history* for the Employee business object.

- Employee bills time to the customer name. This usage scenario corresponds to the service *assign hours* for the Employee business object.

How to Identify Attributes

Attributes of an object are the definitions of data values that the object holds. Attributes are also known as *properties*. Each instance of an object maintains its own set of values. For example, for the Employee business object, one of the attributes is *given name*. In a particular instance, the value of the attribute *given name* is *John*. In another instance, the value of *given name* could be *Janet*. The set of values of an object's attributes at any given time is known as the *state of the object*.

Identifying attributes

To identify the attributes for an object, return to the usage scenario. Look for the words or phrases that further identify the object. For example, the length of a bridge, the name of a person, and the brand name and model of a computer indicate attributes.

The actual attributes of an object are often specified in greater detail than the information covered in usage scenarios. To identify the correct attributes, the project team uses its knowledge of the real world and experience in the problem domain. For example, the project team might derive the attribute *name* from a usage scenario. Based on their knowledge, the team members might modify this attribute to *given name* and *family name*. Often this level of detail is done during the physical design process. However, if sufficient information is available to start this process earlier, the team can start during the logical design.

Note   Although many attributes can be listed for an object, the project team should include only the relevant attributes. For example, the attributes *given name* and *family name* can be used for most solutions. However, attributes such as *height* and *weight* might only be relevant for, for example, a health care solution. To avoid the risk of omitting important attributes, document all the attributes at this stage of the design process. These attributes can be further refined at a later stage of analysis.

To identify the attributes of an object, the project team should consider each business object and attempt to answer the following questions:

- How is the object described in general and as part of this solution?
- How is the object described in the context of this solution's responsibilities?
- What information does the object contain?
- What information should the object maintain over time?
- What are the states in which the object can exist?

Each attribute is generally identified with an object. You need to clearly label each attribute to avoid confusion with other attributes. In addition, record the structure or type of the attribute, such as text or number.

Tip   In many cases, attributes are derived. The computation of such attributes should be recorded as a service of the object. After compiling the list of attributes, study all the attributes carefully. If some attributes are totally unrelated to the other attributes of a specific object, you might need to create a new business object.

Examples of attributes

Consider the following use cases in a usage scenario that describes the purchase order process.

- Customer has an account number, name, and address
- Customer must have an approved credit rating for work to be performed
- Depending on history, customer can request the last consultant that was on site

Based on these use cases, Table 5.3 identifies a business object with its attributes and associated values.

Table 5.3.   Example Object with Attributes and Values

Business object	Attributes	Values at one state
Customer	Account Number	10076
	Name	Contoso, Ltd.
	Address	123 East Main
	Credit	Approved
	Last Consultant	Greg Chapman

How to Identify Relationships

Relationships illustrate the way in which objects are linked to each other. Unified Modeling Language (UML) defines four types of relationships: dependency, generalizations, associations, and realizations.

- *Dependency.* A relationship between two objects in which a change to one object (independent) can affect the behavior or service of the other object (dependent). Use dependency when you want to show one object using another. For example, a water heater depends on pipes to carry hot water throughout a building. In UML diagrams, dependency between two logical objects is represented by a directional (that is, with an arrow) dashed line.

- *Association.* A structural relationship that describes a connection among objects. *Aggregation* is a special type of association that represents the relationship between a whole and its parts. For example, "Order contains details" is an example of an aggregation relationship. Typically in an aggregation relationship, the whole manages the lifetime of the parts. This form of relationship is called *composition*. Graphically, association is represented as a solid line. Aggregation is represented by a solid line with a hollow diamond on the end of the line that connects to the whole. Composition is represented in UML diagrams by a solid line with a filled-in diamond on the end of the line that connects to the whole.

- *Generalization.* A relationship between a general thing (called the parent) and the specialized or specific thing (called the child). For example, the Manager class is a specific type of the Employee class. A child inherits the properties of its parents, especially their attributes and operations. Generalization means that the child can substitute the parent object anywhere, but the opposite is not true. In UML diagrams, generalization is represented as a solid line with a hollow arrowhead pointing to the parent.

- *Realization.* A relationship between classes, in which one abstract class specifies a contract that another class needs to carry out. When you model, you find a lot of abstractions that represent things in the real world and things in your solution, such as a Customer class in a Web-based ordering system. Each of these abstractions can have multiple instances. In general, the modeling elements that can have instances are called *classes*. A class has structural and behavioral features. All instances of a class share the same behavior but can have different values for their attributes.

  Realization relationships exist between interfaces and the classes and components that realize these interfaces, and between use cases and collaborations. Graphically, generalization is represented as a cross between generalization and dependency relationship, with dashed lines and hollow arrowhead pointing to the parent.

Figure 5.8 illustrates the graphical representations of the four types of relationships.

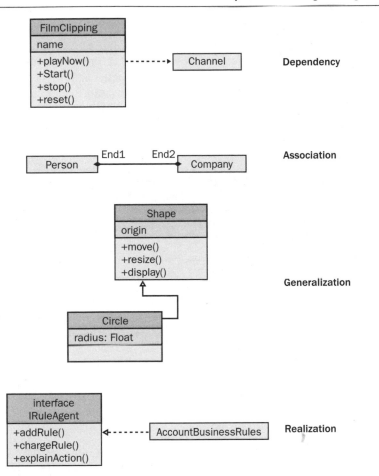

Figure 5.8.   Types of UML relationships

Figure 5.9 illustrates the two types of associations—the aggregation and composition relationships.

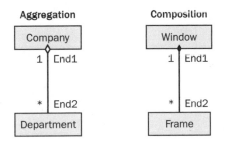

Figure 5.9.   Aggregation and composition relationships

Identifying relationships from use cases

To identify relationships from use cases, look at the usage scenario for information that describes physical location, directed action, communication, or ownership, or that indicates that a condition has been met. The project team reviews the scenario and determines which behaviors are associated with an object, and identifies relationships between two or more objects. Figure 5.10 illustrates how associations between objects indicate relationships.

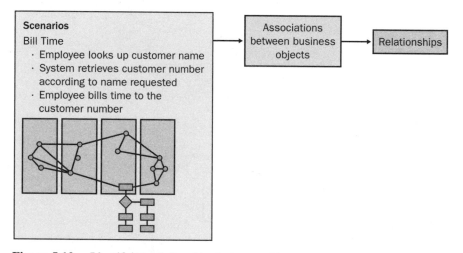

Figure 5.10. Identifying relationships between objects

Examples of relationships

Relationships represent how the actions of an object or a system affect another object or system, especially if a known state exists between the two. Figure 5.11 illustrates that relationships must exist between objects for a company to produce meaningful work and data.

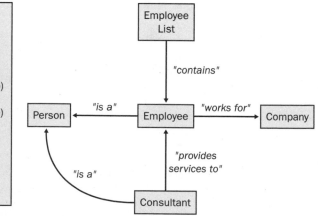

Figure 5.11. Examples of relationships

Some relationships between the objects are:

- The consultant and the customer are related because they are both people.
- The consultant and the customer are related because they interact with each other.
- The consultant performs services for the company, and the company requires the services of the consultant.
- A company has one or more divisions.

Additional relationships might exist in the system. For example, the consultants bring revenue to the company, and the accountants manage the company's money.

Lesson 3: Documenting Logical Design Output

During logical design, the team creates several outputs that will help in developing the solution design. The outputs include the logical object model, the logical data model, and a high-level user interface (UI) design. There are several tools for documenting and diagramming these outputs. This lesson discusses how to create and document the outputs of logical design.

For more information about diagramming the logical design, see Chapter 2, "Gathering and Analyzing Information."

After this lesson, you will be able to
- Use CRC cards to depict interactions between objects.
- Use sequence diagrams to depict interaction between objects.
- Create a logical object model to describe relationships between objects.
- Create a high-level UI design.
- Create a high-level database design.

Estimated lesson time: 20 minutes

How to Model Relationships

You can use several methods to document logical design outputs. Two such techniques are Class-Responsibility-Collaboration (CRC) cards and sequence diagrams.

Note   You can use CRC cards and sequence diagrams in combination to validate the objects and their relationships that you have identified during analysis.

Class-Responsibility-Collaboration cards

A CRC card helps teams focus on high-level responsibilities of a class instead of detailed methods and attributes. Project teams use the CRC card to brainstorm the responsibilities of a class; identify the responsibilities of a class to identify its services. The CRC card indicates all the classes with which a class must interact and identifies the relationships between classes. To validate CRC cards, the team recreates the usage scenarios by using the CRC cards.

Example of a CRC card

Order	
Roles: To maintain order information	
Responsibilities	**Collaboration**
Determine whether items are in stock	Get current stock information from Order Line
Determine price	
Check for valid payment	Get address from Customer
Dispatch to delivery address	
Issues	
Where do we store the price information?	

Sequence diagrams

A *sequence diagram* shows the actors and objects that participate in an interaction along with a chronological list of the events they generate. A vertical line in a sequence diagram represents an object's lifetime. An arrow between the lifetimes of two objects represents a message, which is a form of communication between two objects that conveys that an activity will take place. The receipt of a message instance is normally considered an instance of an event. The order in which these messages occur is shown top to bottom on the page.

In a solution design, the overall flow of control and sequence of behavior can be difficult to understand. Sequence diagrams help you see the sequence clearly.

Figure 5.12 is a sequence diagram for the logical design of the Adventure Works Cycles scenario.

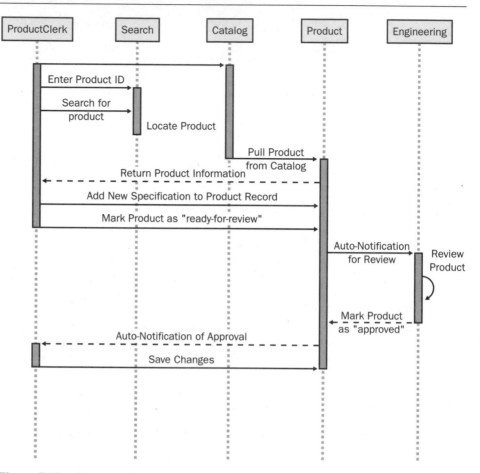

Figure 5.12.   Sequence diagram

How to Create the Logical Object Model

The primary output of the logical design process in solution design is the logical object model. The logical object model is created from the objects, services, attributes, and relationships that were created earlier in the logical design process.

Considerations for the logical object model

When creating the logical object model, it is important that you consider all the business and user requirements that are applicable to your scenario, such as security, globalization, localization, auditing and logging, error handling, integration with existing systems, and state management. It is also important to consider all the business constraints when creating a logical object model for a solution design.

Example of logical object model

Figure 5.13 is an example of the logical object model for the Adventure Works Cycles scenario. The object model takes into account the security and logging requirements identified during the conceptual design process.

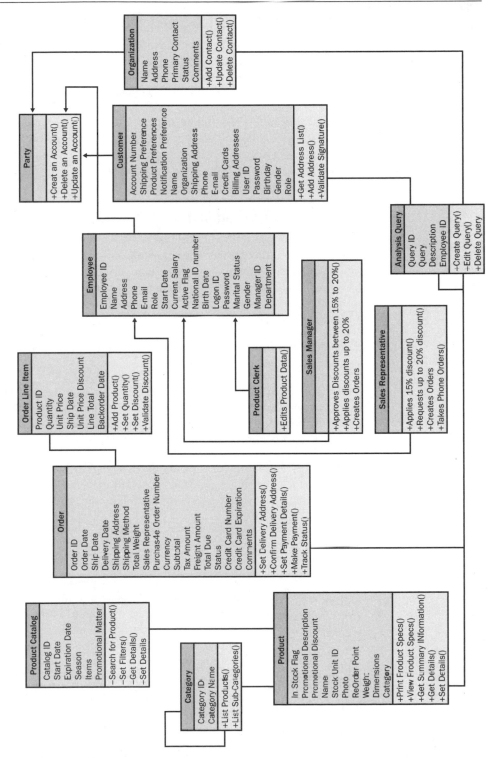

Figure 5.13.   Logical object model

How to Create a Logical Data Model

You can use either a logical object model or a logical data model to represent a logical design. However, a project team can create both models to represent a logical design in different ways. Both models might be necessary if one model represents a portion of the design more clearly than the other.

The logical design is the middle stage of the natural progression from conceptual design to physical design. When creating the logical data model, you convert the conceptual data needs identified during conceptual design into actual entities and relationships that will define how the data interacts. This information is then used to help model the physical design.

Identify entities and attributes

When you proceed to the logical stage of data design, one of your first tasks is to formulate entities from data requirements and other related information. An *entity* can be defined as any person, place, item, or concept that defines data or about which data will be collected and stored. An attribute is a characteristic that further defines and describes the properties of an instance of an entity. An entity can have multiple attributes.

Consider the following example, in which italicized words indicate possible candidates for entities:

"*Consultants* enter their *hours* onto a *time sheet* on a weekly basis. The time sheet is then forwarded to the *administrative assistant*, who types the *hours* into the invoicing program. The *administrative assistant* then sends *invoices* to the *customers* based on the *time* reported."

After identifying the entities, you must determine which of their attributes you want to gather. Attributes describe the solution's entities. For example, the attributes of a car might be its color, brand, model, and year of production.

When the physical design is implemented, the attributes might become the columns in the database tables.

Define tables

The objects that you identify in the analysis step of logical design are strong candidates for tables and might be transformed into tables in the database during physical design. Tables are meant for those objects about which you need to store information. For example, in a simple order processing system, objects such as customers, products, and catalog might be transformed into tables. In a more complicated system, objects might map to more than one table.

Define columns

The attributes of an object form the columns of the table associated with the object. For example, *given name*, *family name*, and *job title* can be the attributes (and therefore column names) for the Employee table. Each row in the table stores values for various fields for a specific instance of the object.

Define relationships

After identifying tables and their columns, you need to identify any association between tables. Such associations represent the relationship between objects. For example, a relationship exists between the objects Employee and Department—every Department has Employees and every Employee belongs to a Department. You can use cardinality and multiplicity to further define relationships.

Cardinality is an identifying property of a relationship. Cardinality allows you to specify the number of instances of an entity that are allowed on each side of a relationship. For example, one consultant can be assigned more than one project at a time. *Multiplicity* specifies the range of cardinalities an entity can assume.

You will learn more about defining object relationships in Chapter 8, "Designing the Data Layer."

Note   During logical design, if you have sufficient information to refine columns and define primary and foreign keys, you can create a logical data model that includes columns, primary keys, and foreign keys. However, this level of detail is typically recorded during the physical design process.

Figure 5.14 shows the logical database design that a team typically achieves during the logical design phase.

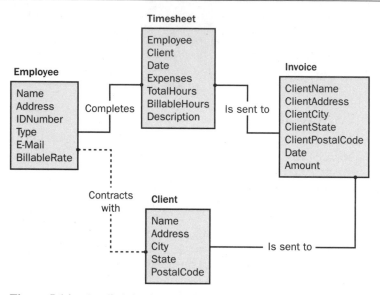

Figure 5.14.   Logical database design

How to Create a High-Level User Interface Design

Using the objects, services, attributes, and relationships identified during the analysis step of logical design, the team might decide to create a high-level user interface and database design. Creating a high-level user interface and database design enables the project team to describe the flow of processing that the end user will experience when the solution is ready for customers.

The list of objects and services gives the team an idea about the kind of functionality expected by the users. The team can use this information to design user interface elements such as buttons, text fields, and menu items.

Note   For most projects, a major portion of the user interface design is done during the physical design process. However, if the team members believe that they have sufficient information, they can create a high-level user interface design during the logical design process.

Consider the following usage scenario:

```
The Customer selects a Catalog to browse. The Categories and Products in
the
root of the selected catalog are displayed. The Customer can then select
a
Product to view its details or select a Category to view the Products and
subcategories in the selected category.
```

On the basis of this scenario, the team can create the following high-level design for the user interface:

- Products Information page that displays information about products, such as product description, pricing, and availability
- Customer Information page that displays information about the customer, such as registration and personal details

The scenario can be expanded to provide the customer with shopping features. Therefore, the user interface can also include the following:

- Order Information, Check Out, and Order Status pages
- A history of the previous transactions completed by the customer

Note   You will learn more about user interface design in Chapter 7, "Designing the Presentation Layer."

Lesson 4: Optimizing Logical Design

During the analysis step of logical design, the team analyzes the usage scenarios and defines the solution in terms of objects, services, attributes, and relationships between objects. After the analysis step, the team moves to the optimization step. In this step, the real challenge for the team is to refine and optimize the design by measuring it against the usage scenarios and requirements.

In this lesson, you will learn about refining the list of objects. You will also learn how to verify the business model and establish control in the logical design.

After this lesson, you will be able to

- Refine the list of objects identified during analysis.
- Verify the existing business model.
- Establish control in a logical design model.

Estimated lesson time: 15 minutes

How to Refine Objects

During the analysis step of logical design, the project team identifies objects. All objects might not be completely relevant to the solution. When the team refines objects, they determine whether the objects are relevant.

When refining objects, consider the following:

- If two objects express the same information or control the same activity, you might be able to combine them and give the combined object a more descriptive name.
- An object should be specific. Some candidate objects might be created by evaluating additional information from the scenarios. These objects are not necessarily incorrect, but they need to be made more tangible or real. In addition, you might want to examine these objects to determine whether they are within the scope of the project.
- If an attribute needs to exist independently in the solution, assign it as an object.
- You might need a new object to control or coordinate a set of services.
- You can also use services to refine the list of objects. For every service, identify the object on which the service acts.

How to Verify an Existing Logical Object Model

You can verify an existing logical object model by validating it against the set of requirements, by using individual object verification, and by the usage scenario walkthrough.

Validate against requirements

The most important task in optimizing and finalizing the logical design is to validate the logical object model against the existing set of requirements. Ensure that the logical object model documents each requirement that has been identified. If there are requirements that have not been documented, you need to fix the logical object model so that it addresses the missing requirements. After the logical object model captures all the requirements; you are ready to proceed to physical design.

Important   If the logical data model misses even a single requirement, it is considered incomplete.

Verify individual objects

In individual object verification, you identify an object's inputs and outputs and the capability or functionality that the object must provide. For any given input, you should be able to accurately predict the output and behavior and verify the independent parts of the object.

Individual object verification simplifies integration of systems because you can test the individual pieces of the system before integrating them into a single large product. If the constituent pieces have been verified and are correct, the project team can safely assemble the system.

Walk through the scenario

Although the individual object verification technique allows you to verify the independent aspects of a business object, the project team also needs to study how a set of objects solves the complex problems documented in the scenarios. A collection of objects that are interdependent in solving problems can be complex. You can verify the interdependence of objects by conducting a full walkthrough of the scenario, ensuring that all needs of the scenario are met by some combination of objects. Alternatively, you can implement role playing in the scenario. When using role playing, you assign individuals to represent objects and then walk through the scenarios. Role playing also exposes ambiguities that occur when various individuals have different interpretations of what a specific service must do.

By evaluating a scenario one step at a time, you can determine which services are required, and also the sequence in which the services are required in order to move the project team to a successful completion of the logical design. From the starting point of a usage scenario, determine all the objects from which the scenario needs services.

Any message sent between objects indicates a communication between those objects. To determine the type of communication, analyze the requests sent by each object and try to answer the following questions:

- Does the object have enough information to construct the request?
- Does the information content of the request come from either the object's internal data or from the request that triggered the operation?
- Does the object rely on the internal data of the supplier?
- Is information that is being passed from the consumer to the supplier linking the object to other parts of the system in an unintended way?

In addition, the project team should examine the input parameters of each request. You need to examine the input parameters and determine whether they provide context-sensitive information that the receiving object does not need. In addition, you need to identify any reliance on information regarding external context that can reduce the reusability of the object in other contexts. You can resolve these issues by shifting responsibilities between objects or by creating new objects.

For a walkthrough of a scenario, consider the following:

- Determine any dependencies of the operation on the existence or consistency of other business objects.
- Determine any consistency, sequencing, or concurrency issues. Is a sequential order of operation required in all or part of the transaction?
- Identify any critical timing. Is it critical to respond immediately, or can an activity be suspended?
- Consider any organizational issues, such as a transaction occurring in multiple functional areas.
- Look for business rules that are in more than one business object.
- Identify audit and control requirements. Identify who is accountable. Verify situations in which accountability is shared by two or more people.
- Estimate the frequency of an activity. How often does the activity occur? Is it uniform or periodic?
- Determine locations and cross-location dependencies.
- Determine whether the service that controls the transaction is dependent on services currently contained in other business objects.

How to Establish Control in Logical Design

Examining the object interactions for various scenarios illustrates that activities need to be performed in a specific sequence. One possible way to examine object interaction is by using state diagrams. Identifying the flow of control enables you to sequence object interactions. Control in logical design:

- Ensures the transactional integrity of a scenario
- Coordinates services across multiple objects
- Identifies cross-object interdependencies

For any activity to complete, specific ordering might be required. Multiple events might occur concurrently. Wait states that must be completed before continuing processing might exist for some services. Such issues determine the issues that the project team must consider during logical design to ensure that error-free actions are carried out at the right time and in the right order, relative to other activities in the system.

Control can be synchronous or asynchronous. *Synchronous control* refers to the situation in which object services are invoked and the calling object waits for control to be returned. In a synchronous scenario, control is transferred from the calling object to the called object, and the operation is executed immediately. The calling object is suspended until the called object completes its task. After the operation is completed, control is returned to the calling object.

In *asynchronous control*, a client can submit a request and then continue performing other tasks. The service will process the request and notify the client when processing completes. In this way, the client is not blocked from performing other, unrelated activities while the service is working on the client's request. The control of the overall process is not transferred from the calling object to the called object. This means that the called object must take responsibility for the integrity of its data resources that might be accessed simultaneously by multiple objects, and it must also maintain common resource coordination throughout the processing sequence.

Tip   In a distributed system, consider whether to create additional objects that handle the various aspects of control, sequencing, and dependency. You need to isolate dependencies and abstract those services that are likely to change frequently with changes in the business.

Control models

Figure 5.15 illustrates the two general models that are available for the control of objects.

High-level encapsulation   Controlling object

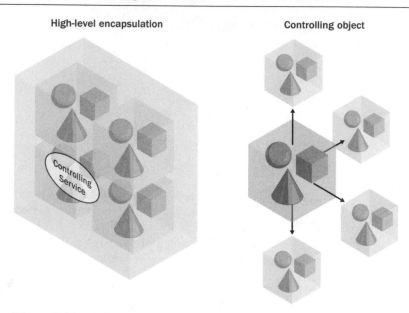

Figure 5.15.   Control models

The first model uses a high-level encapsulation of the objects to be controlled. The outer object has control and ownership of all of the logical resources required for the activity provided by the inner objects. Because the outer object contains everything that it needs to proceed with an activity, the design is simplified. This control and potential simplification results in a rigid structure for the activity.

For example, the inner objects can be used only by the other objects contained at the same level or by means of some service of the outer object. This can be thought of as a single-user model because only the single outer object can use the inner objects. The outer object is responsible for routing all incoming messages to the correct inner object.

The second model is more flexible, but it can be more difficult to design. In this model, you implement a controlling object at the same level as the resources that it needs to control. This model can be thought of as a multiple user model because the controlling object does not exclusively own the objects that it might be using. These objects can be used simultaneously by other parts of the system. The controlling object is not aware of any of these other potential interactions with the controlled objects. Maintaining the integrity of resources is more difficult in this model.

User interface in control

The two models of control—high-level encapsulation and controlling object—do not take into account the control that users have when they trigger events in objects. In interactive systems, the user interface places control with the users. In reality, however, most systems combine user control with control that is embedded in a set of controlling objects in the system.

Ultimately, joint control and dependency direct the sequence of events. Although you use objects to control transactions, users trigger the sequences of events.

Activity: Identifying Objects for the Logical Design

In this activity, you use what you learned in the lessons to identify objects for inclusion in the logical design.

Exercise 1: Identifying Objects from Use Cases

Following is a list of possible use cases for the company Web site project that Adventure Works Cycles is funding. Examine each use case and identify any objects that should be included in the logical design. You can find the answers to the questions in the appendix.

1. The shopping cart checks inventory to determine the availability of a particular product.

2. A new user creates an account in order to place orders.

3. A user adds a product to the shopping cart.

4. A user retrieves an order to check its status.

Exercise 2: Creating a Services Matrix

Open the files C05Ex2, Usage Scenario 06.1 View Catalog, Usage Scenario 06.1.1 Add Items in Catalog, and Usage Scenario 06.3.1 Edit Items in Catalog from the \SolutionDocuments\Chapter05 folder on the CD. Using the usage scenario documents, complete the service matrix in C05Ex2 for the Catalog Items business object. Be sure to identify the services, actors, responsibilities, and collaborations for each service, and to map each entry to one of the usage scenarios. To help you get started, an example of a service matrix has been provided in C05Ex2. One possible answer to this exercise can be found in C05Ex2_Answer in the \SolutionDocuments\Chapter05 folder on the CD.

Exercise 3: Creating a Sequence Diagram

Open the C05Ex3 Microsoft Visio® file from the \SolutionDocuments\Chapter05 folder on the CD, and click the Sequence Diagram tab. The page is blank. Assume that a customer has logged on to the online retail site for Adventure Works Cycles. Use the following use case to create a sequence diagram that shows the interaction between the objects. One possible answer to this exercise can be found in C05Ex3_Answer in the \SolutionDocuments\Chapter05 folder on the CD.

The customer opens a catalog, searches for items in the catalog, and adds an item to a new order.

Summary

- Logical design is defined as the process of describing the solution in terms of the organization, structure, syntax, and interaction of its parts from the perspective of the project team.
- The logical design phase consists of two overlapping steps:
    - Logical design analysis, during which the project team identifies business objects, services, attributes, and relationships between objects
    - Logical design optimization, during which the team verifies business objects and identifies implied business objects and scenarios
- The outputs of the logical design process are:
    - The logical object model, which is a set of objects with corresponding services, attributes, and relationships
    - A high-level user interface design
    - The logical data model
- Objects are the people or things described in the usage scenarios.
- A service is the behavior that a business object performs.
- Attributes are the definitions of data values that an object holds.
- Relationships illustrate the links between objects.
- A CRC card helps you focus on high-level responsibilities of a class instead of detailed methods and attributes. CRC cards also help identify relationships between different objects in the logical design.
- A sequence diagram shows the actors and objects that participate in an interaction and a chronologically arranged list of the events they generate.
- The list of objects and services helps the team to create a high-level user interface design of the solution.
- To create a database design, the team performs the following tasks:
    - Identify entities, attributes, and relationships
    - Define tables
    - Define columns
    - Define relationships
- To verify the design, validate the logical object model by comparing it to the existing requirements.
- To verify the design by using individual object verification, you identify an object's inputs and outputs and the capability or functionality that the object must provide.

- To verify the design by walkthrough of the usage scenario, you evaluate a scenario one step at a time and determine which services are required and the sequence in which they are required.
- Control enables you to sequence object interactions.
- Synchronous control refers to the situation in which object services are invoked and the calling object waits for control to be returned.
- Asynchronous control refers to the situation in which object services are invoked and the calling object continues to perform unrelated tasks until the service notifies the calling object of the results of the operation.
- In the high-level encapsulation method of control, the outer object has control and ownership of all of the logical resources required for the activity provided by the inner objects.
- In the controlling object method of control, a controlling object is defined at the same level as the resources that it needs to control.

Review

The following questions are intended to reinforce key information presented in this chapter. If you are unable to answer a question, review the lesson materials and try the question again. You can find answers to the questions in the appendix.

1. What are the two steps of logical design?

2. What are the outputs of the logical design?

3. Should you focus on technological issues during logical design?

4. What are the benefits of logical design?

5. How do you identify services in a usage scenario?

6. How do you identify attributes in a usage scenario?

7. What is a sequence diagram?

8. How do you design the tables and columns in a data store for a solution?

9. What is the purpose of refining the list of objects?

10. How do you verify the design by using individual object verification?

11. What is the purpose of control in logical design?

12. You are creating the logical design of a solution for a customer, and you discover a scenario that was not discovered in your previous analysis. What should you do with this new information?

13. What is the responsibility of the testing role during logical design?

C H A P T E R   6

Creating the Physical Design

About This Chapter

Along with conceptual and logical design, the project team creates a physical design of the solution during the planning phase. In this introduction to physical design, you will learn about the purpose of physical design, and the tasks and deliverables involved in completing the physical design. You will also learn about the four steps in creating a physical design: research, analysis, rationalization, and implementation.

More Info   As with the conceptual and logical designs, the outputs of the physical design step are documented in the functional specification, which is one of the outputs of the planning phase. You can learn more about the functional specification in Chapter 4, "Creating the Conceptual Design," and Chapter 10, "Completing the Planning Phase."

You will learn about creating the physical design for the presentation layer in Chapter 7, "Designing the Presentation Layer," and for the data layer in Chapter 8, "Designing the Data Layer."

Before You Begin

To complete the lessons in this chapter, you must

- Understand the Microsoft® Solutions Framework (MSF) Process Model.
- Be familiar with the outputs of the envisioning phase and the three steps of conceptual design: research, analysis, and optimization.
- Be familiar with the logical design phase in MSF.

Lesson 1: An Overview of Physical Design

Physical design is the last step in the planning phase of the MSF Process Model. The project team proceeds to physical design after all members agree that they have enough information from the logical design to begin physical design. During physical design, the team applies technology considerations and constraints to the conceptual and logical designs. Because the physical design evolves from the conceptual and logical designs, its success depends on the accuracy of the previous two designs. The reliance of physical design on the conceptual and logical designs ensures that the team will be able to complete a physical design that meets the business and user requirements.

Note To review the three design processes in the planning phase, refer to Table 5.1 in Chapter 5, "Creating the Logical Design."

In this lesson, you will learn about the purpose and goals of physical design. You will learn about the various steps that the team performs during physical design. You will also learn about the responsibilities of the various roles in physical design. In addition, this lesson covers the deliverables of physical design.

After this lesson, you will be able to

- Describe physical design.
- Describe the goals of physical design.
- List the steps in physical design.
- Describe the responsibilities of various team roles during physical design.
- List the deliverables of physical design.
- Describe the purpose and deliverables of the research step.

Estimated lesson time: 15 minutes

What Is Physical Design?

Physical design is the third design activity in the planning phase of the MSF Process Model. Physical design is the process of describing components, services, and technologies of the solution from the perspective of development requirements. Physical design defines the parts of the solution that will be developed, how they will be developed, and how they will interact with each other. Figure 6.1 illustrates where the physical design fits within the MSF Process Model.

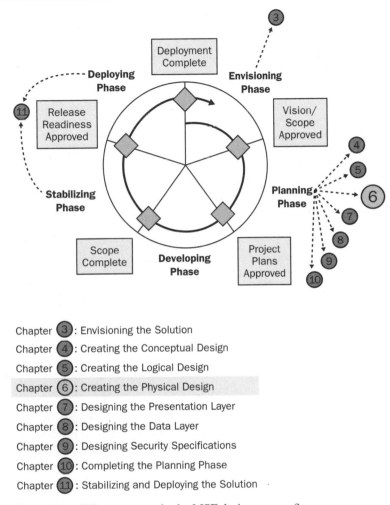

Figure 6.1.   Where are you in the MSF design process?

While working on the physical design, the team creates designs based on prior designs and refines the architecture of the solution that has been created up to this time. These designs apply real-world technology constraints to the logical model, including development tools and the deployment environment of the solution. In addition, the team tries to develop a solution that addresses design considerations such as security, availability, scalability, manageability, and performance. The team tries to achieve these goals in a manner that is appropriate to the project and its requirements.

The inputs to the physical design are all of the artifacts that have been created up to this time. This includes the logical object model, a high-level user interface design, and a logical data model generated during logical design. Artifacts such as the project plan might get minor updates and are referred to in setting the deadlines for the milestones of physical design.

During the physical design, the project team reduces the gap between the logical design of the solution and the implementation by defining the solution in terms of implementation details. The purposes of the conceptual design and logical design processes are to understand the business and its requirements and to design a solution that meets those requirements. The physical design process primarily addresses how to implement this design.

At the end of the physical design, the team delivers specifications for a set of components, Microsoft .NET assemblies, binaries, and link libraries; details of the user interface for the solution; the database schema; database objects such as triggers, indexes, and stored procedures; and details of any reports that will be used by the solution.

Figure 6.2 shows the purpose of the physical design process.

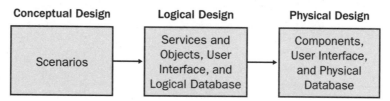

Figure 6.2.   What is physical design?

Consider the analogy of designing and building a house. In logical design, you determine requirements such as overall electrical capacity, levels of light, and plumbing fixtures required by the house. In physical design, you select the appliances that you will use, the electrical requirements for each device and the corresponding wiring, and circuit specifications.

To proceed from logical design to physical design, the team uses the layered services-based architecture.

Note   You can learn more about application architectures in Chapter 4, "Creating the Conceptual Design."

Scope of the physical design

Table 6.1 explains the scope of physical design.

Table 6.1.   Scope of the Physical Design

Physical design is not	But enables you to
Coding	• Create detailed component specifications for development • Determine where components should be located
Technology deployment	Identify technologies that can be used for developing the solution

During physical design, the project team develops the component specifications and deployment topology with which the development team will work to create the solution. The development team takes the target topology into consideration while building the solution.

Remember that in physical design you are still designing the solution and not developing a version of the solution that can be released and deployed.

Difference between logical and physical designs

Whereas during logical design the team views the problem from the perspective of the project team, during physical design the team views the problem from the perspective of the development team. During the logical design, the team documents the activities, constraints, and assumptions of the business. During the physical design, the team defines a solution addressing the constraints of the selected development technologies and deployment environment. In this sense, physical design views the design from a more technical viewpoint.

Basically, physical design is a refinement of the logical design that leads to the implementation of the design to create the solution.

What Are the Goals of Physical Design?

The project team creates the physical design with the following goals:

- *Identifying appropriate technologies for development.* During physical design, the project team evaluates technologies and determines the technologies that can be best used to develop the solution.

- *Transforming the logical design into physical design models.* During physical design, the team uses the outputs of logical design to produce a flexible specification based on components. This specification describes the application from the development team's perspective. The team describes the solution in just enough detail to allow the development team to begin creating the solution according to the requirements.

- *Providing a baseline for the development process.* In addition to creating models and strategies, the team defines the development roles, responsibilities, and processes.

- *Defining when the project plan approved milestone has been achieved.* The team reaches this milestone when the baseline physical design is complete. At the project plan approved milestone, the team re-assesses risk, updates priorities, and finishes estimates for resources and schedule.

What Are the Responsibilities of Team Roles During Physical Design?

During physical design, each team role has a different set of responsibilities. Table 6.2 summarizes the tasks for each team role during physical design.

Table 6.2.   Roles and Responsibilities in Physical Design

Role	Primary task	Secondary task
Product management	Managing customer expectations and creating the communications plan	Preparing for solution deployment
Program management	Managing the physical design process and creating the functional specification	Defining project plan, including resources, schedules, and risk assessments
Development	Creating the physical design deliverables: design models, development plans and schedules, and development estimates	Evaluating technologies, building prototypes if necessary, and preparing for the development environment
Testing	Evaluating and validating the functionality and consistency of the physical design against the usage scenarios	Defining detailed testing plans and preparing the testing and quality assurance (QA) environment
User experience	Evaluating physical design against user requirements and designing help solutions	Defining user education plan
Release management	Evaluating the infrastructure implications of the physical design	Defining infrastructure and operations requirements and deployment solutions

What Are the Deliverables of Physical Design?

At the end of the physical design phase, the project team has enough completed design documentation for the development team to begin creating the solution.

Specific documentation can vary from solution to solution. Some of the deliverables at the end of physical design include:

- *Class diagrams* of the solution.
- *Component models, sequence diagrams, or activity diagrams* of the solution.
- *Database schema* of the solution.
- *Baseline deployment model* that provides:
    - The network topology, which indicates hardware locations and interconnections.
    - The data and component topology, which indicates the locations of solution components, services, and data storage in relation to the network topology.
- *Component specifications* that include the internal structure of components and component interfaces.
- *Packaging and distribution strategy* that identifies the services to be packaged together in a component and specifies how the components will be distributed across the network topology. It might also include a preliminary deployment plan.
- *Programming model* that identifies implementation choices; choices in object state and connection modes; and guidelines for threading, error handling, security choices, and code documentation.

What Are the Steps in Physical Design?

Physical design is the last stage of the planning phase. The planning phase ends when the team reaches the project plan approved milestone. The project team completes the physical design before reaching this milestone.

Figure 6.3 shows the physical design in relationship to the conceptual and logical designs in the planning phase.

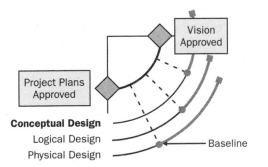

Figure 6.3.   When does physical design take place?

Figure 6.4 shows the four steps of physical design and their associated baselines.

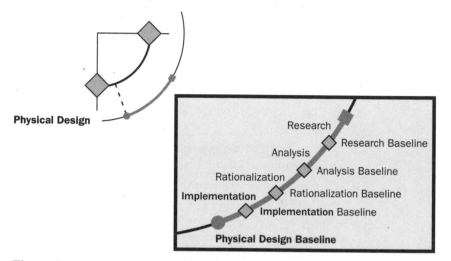

Figure 6.4.   Steps in physical design

The four steps in physical design are:

- *Research*, during which the team performs the following tasks:
    - Determining physical constraints and requirements
    - Identifying any infrastructure changes or concerns
- *Analysis*, during which the team performs the following tasks:
    - Developing a preliminary deployment model
    - Selecting technologies that will be used to develop the solution
- *Rationalization*, during which the team performs the following tasks:
    - Determining a packaging and deployment strategy
    - Packaging components and services
    - Distributing components across the network topology
- *Implementation*, during which the team performs the following tasks:
    - Determining a programming model
    - Specifying component interfaces, attributes, and services

Note   The implementation baseline leads into the baseline of the physical design.

What Is the Research Step in Physical Design?

During the physical design phase, the team focuses on creating technical solutions based on the logical design. To derive these technical solutions, the team must consider constraints such as the enterprise architecture, the business process, and the infrastructure. In addition, the team needs to consider the architectural and performance requirements of the solution, such as security, availability, scalability, and manageability. For example, perhaps the solution must be able to handle a specified number of transactions per second. During the research step of physical design, the team identifies these constraints and requirements.

Deliverables of the research step

The deliverables of the research step of physical design describe the current infrastructure of the business and provide the foundation for the analysis, rationalization, and specification steps of physical design. The deliverables of the research baseline include:

- Current network topology
- Current data topology
- Current component topology
- Physical application requirements
- Updated risk assessment and mitigation plans

Identifying physical requirements and constraints

Throughout the design process, you gather and analyze information about the requirements and constraints of the business. During physical design, you focus on the physical requirements and constraints that affect the development of the solution.

You gather physical requirements from sources such as the current business environment and the enterprise architecture. Some typical physical requirements of a solution are:

- Performance
- Cost and benefit
- Ease of use
- Deployability
- Supportability
- Reliability
- Reusability

Some typical physical constraints of a solution are:

- Budget
- Schedule
- Network topology
- Data topology
- Component topology
- Technology guidelines
- Security

Resolving conflicts between requirements and constraints

Often the requirements and constraints conflict with each other. By identifying these conflicts early in the design and addressing them, you can reduce potential problems early. If a problem occurs, you have a plan for mitigating it. For example, an application might require 100 megabits per second (Mbps) of bandwidth on the network, whereas the existing network infrastructure can support only 10 Mbps.

To resolve the conflict, you typically perform the following tasks:

- Identify the requirements that are absolutely necessary for the project. Identify conflicts among requirements and also analyze the impact of any constraints. Make as many tradeoff choices as possible before development begins.
- Identify the areas in the infrastructure where the requirements might conflict with the constraints.
- Analyze the gaps between the requirements and constraints and determine whether you need to make some kind of choice to resolve the conflict. For example, you might choose to upgrade the network to support 100-Mbps speeds. You must make these choices early in the design phase to avoid creating a solution that cannot be implemented.
- Brainstorm solutions with all groups associated with the project—business, users, project team, and development team.

You can address the gaps between requirements and constraints in the following ways:

- *Accept the gap without doing anything.* This implies that the gap is acceptable for the initial release of the solution. Clearly describe the consequences of accepting the gap. In addition, all stakeholders must reach a consensus that this is the appropriate choice.
- *Identify a way to work around the gap.* Working around the gap might not be the optimal solution in the long term. However, it may be necessary because of constraints such as limited project resources.
- *Defer addressing the requirement until later stages of the project.* The project team can decide to address a requirement in later stages of the project. The team can modify constraints by providing a business case for the change and identifying the impact of the change.

Lesson 2: Physical Design Analysis

During the analysis step of physical design, the team creates and refines the physical design models by using the logical design documentation. In addition, as in each phase, the team refines artifacts that are related both to the design and specifications (UML models, requirements, and use cases) in addition to those related to the project (risk documents, project plans and schedules, and the actors catalog). Physical design involves selecting candidate technologies for the implementation, based on the application requirements. After selecting the probable technologies, the team creates a preliminary deployment model.

In this lesson, you will learn how to refine Unified Modeling Language (UML) models. You will also learn how to select candidate technologies and create a preliminary deployment model.

After this lesson, you will be able to
- Refine logical design UML models.
- Create a preliminary deployment model.

Estimated lesson time: 10 minutes

How to Refine UML Models

At the end of the logical design, the team has UML models for objects, services, attributes, and relationships in the solution. Typically, the team uses the artifacts that best capture their intent and decisions to manage the complex parts of the project. This includes the following set of deliverables:

- Objects and services inventory
- Class diagrams
- Sequence diagrams
- Activity diagrams
- Component diagrams

During physical design, the team refines these models.

Objects and services inventory

In the analysis step of the physical design, examine the services inventory for the following tasks:

- Categorizing services based on the MSF services-based application model:
  - User services
  - Business services
  - Data services
  - System services
- Identifying hidden services

  The team tries to identify services that were not apparent during the logical design, such as system services or specific technical services for transforming data. Remember that each hidden service must be synchronized with development goals by validating it against requirements.

Class diagrams

Class diagrams are used in logical design to represent the static structure of the application object model. During physical design, the team performs the following tasks to refine UML class diagrams:

- Transforming logical objects into class definitions, including their interfaces.
- Identifying objects that were not apparent during logical design, such as services-based objects (also known as common services).
- Consolidating logical objects if necessary.
- Categorizing objects into a services-based model:
  - The *logical boundary objects* are potential user services.
  - The *logical control objects* are potential business services.
  - The *logical entity objects* are potential data services.

  There might be exceptions for these recommendations. Therefore, the team must carefully examine all relevant factors before making decisions.
- Refining the methods by focusing on parameters, considering the use of overloads, combining or dividing methods, and identifying how to handle passing values.
- Refining the attributes. Minimize the public attributes as much as possible for applications based on stateless server architecture. During physical design, the team focuses on internal protected attributes, which will be used by derived objects.

Figure 6.5 shows the class diagram for the Order components.

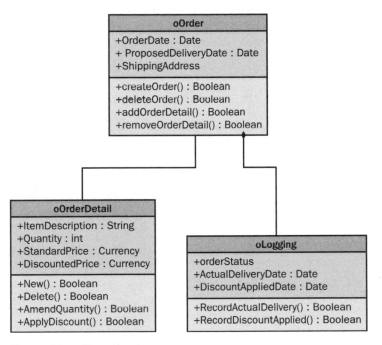

Figure 6.5.   Class diagram

Sequence diagrams

Sequence diagrams represent the interaction between objects and the dynamic aspect of the object model. They are usually used to clarify complex class relationships that might not be easily understood by reviewing the static methods and attributes of a group of classes. In the physical design, the team performs the following tasks:

- Updating classes based on the refined physical design classes
- Refining the sequence diagram to include interactions between the classes or services based on physical constraints or technology requirements
- Identifying additional messages (methods) that are triggered by the new physical classes

Figure 6.6 shows the sequence diagram for the Product and Catalog objects.

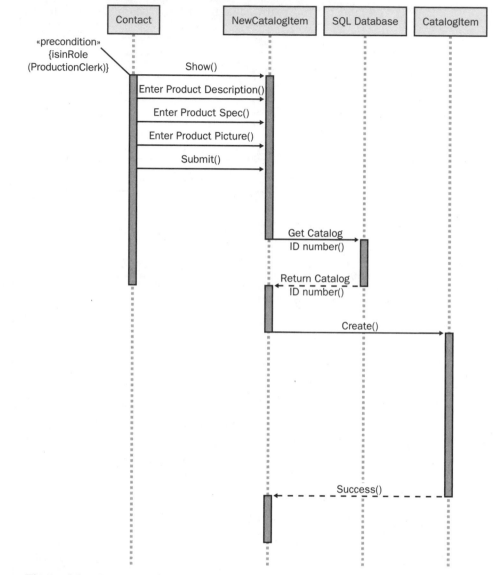

Figure 6.6. Sequence diagram

Activity diagrams

Activity diagrams are used to represent the state transition and flow of an application. You can use activity diagrams instead of sequence diagrams and vice versa. In the physical design, the project refines activity diagrams to:

- Include physical platform and technology requirements.
- Identify potential workflow processes.

Component diagrams

Component diagrams are used to represent the dependencies between components or component packages. As with sequence and activity diagrams, they are typically used in more complex situations. In the physical design, the project team might create component diagrams to:

- Clarify dependencies between components.
- Further define packaging decisions.

Figure 6.7 illustrates the component diagram for the Order process.

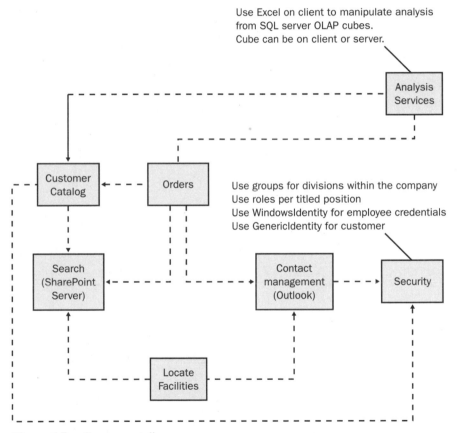

Figure 6.7.   Component diagram

How to Create a Preliminary Deployment Model

Taking artifacts such as the application architecture, the team structure, the project schedule, the requirements, the risks assessment document, and candidate technologies into consideration, the team can draft a *preliminary deployment model*. The preliminary deployment model includes network, data, and component topologies.

This model enables the project team and other stakeholders to review the design. Remember that during physical design the team proposes topologies for solutions that have not been selected yet.

Network topology

The network topology is an infrastructure map that indicates hardware locations and interconnections. The map shows workstations and servers and describes their functions. Additionally, the topology shows the network infrastructure that connects the computers.

Figure 6.8 illustrates a sample network topology for a solution.

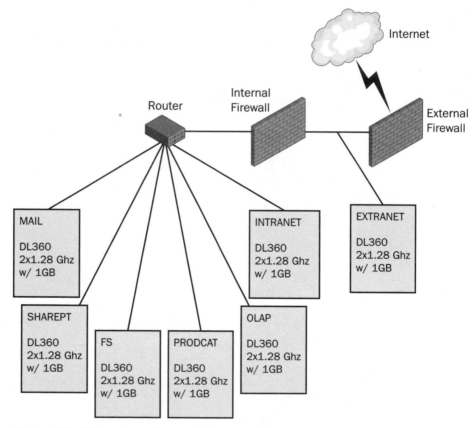

Figure 6.8.   Network topology

On the CD   The figure shows a sample network topology. For the complete network topology for the Adventure Works Cycles case study, refer to AWC - Network in the \SolutionDocuments\Chapter06 folder on the companion CD.

Component and Data Topology

The component and data topology is a map that indicates the locations of packages, components, and their services in relation to the network topology, in addition to data store locations. The map shows the physical distribution of the components and their locations across the various service layers. The current-state version should already exist if the team is not working on a completely new solution. You can add any new components and services required by the application at this time.

Figure 6.9 illustrates a sample component and data topology for Adventure Works Cycles.

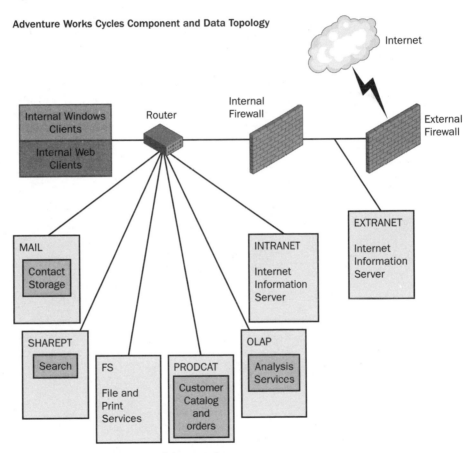

Figure 6.9.   Component and data topology

On the CD   The figure shows a sample component and data topology. For the complete component and data topology for the Adventure Works Cycles case study, refer to AWC Component Topology in the \SolutionDocuments\Chapter06 folder on the companion CD.

Lesson 3: Physical Design Rationalization

After selecting candidate technologies, the project team proceeds to the rationalization step of physical design. In this step, the project team designs services-based components for services-based applications and develops a distribution strategy for those components.

In this lesson, you will learn about the deliverables of the rationalization step. You will also learn how to develop strategies for distributing and packaging the services that have been designed. In addition, you will learn the effect of coupling and cohesion on the packaging strategy. You will also create a component topology and validate and refine the topology.

After this lesson, you will be able to

- Identify the deliverables of the rationalization baseline.
- Create distribution and packaging strategies.
- Describe cohesion and coupling.
- Transform services into components.
- Distribute preliminary components into layers.
- Create a deployment model.
- Validate and refine distribution and packaging.

Estimated lesson time: 10 minutes

What Are the Deliverables of Rationalization?

The rationalization step results in several deliverables. These deliverables describe the technologies, strategies, and topologies that you have designed for the solution.

The deliverables of the rationalization baseline include:

- A distribution and packaging strategy
- Services-based preliminary components
- Deployment models:
  - Future network topology
  - Future data topology
  - Future component topology
- A baseline deployment model

How to Create Distribution and Packaging Strategies

The *rationalization* step is an iterative process during which the project team tries to design an optimal solution. One of the goals of the rationalization step is the distribution of services and the packaging of those services into components.

The *distribution strategy* is a rationale for determining where the services will be located in the solution architecture. Distribution is services-based and not component-based.

The *packaging strategy* is a rationale for determining which services go into each component. You might have multiple strategies in a single solution. For example, a common practice is to divide the business services into business objects (commonly called a business facade layer) without incorporating the business rules directly in the class interfaces. This practice allows the team to create a business rules layer that incorporates most of the business rules (limiting discounts by authorization, for example). The business rules layer can then be changed and redeployed without modifying the business objects. Creating this layer limits the changes to interfaces that communicate with these objects. This strategy can be decided in advance.

To determine an appropriate overall distribution and packaging strategy, you must consider state management and performance of the solution.

State management

State management is the process by which the solution maintains state and page information over multiple requests for the same or different pages. Some methods of managing state in a Web-based solution are:

- *Hold state on client.* You can hold state on the client by using objects that retain values between multiple requests for the same information.

- *Structured Query Language (SQL) query strings.* A query string is information appended to the end of a page's URL, such as product number and its category ID.

- *Cookies.* A cookie is a small amount of data stored either in a text file on the client's file system or in memory in the client browser session.

- *Application state.* Application state is a global storage mechanism accessible from all pages in the Web application. You use it to store information that is required between server round trips and between pages.

- *Session state.* Session state is similar to application state but is limited to the current browser session. If different users are using the solution, each user has a different session state. In addition, if a user leaves the solution and returns later, the user will have a different session state.

Design considerations

Some of the design considerations include:

- *Scalability.* Scalability involves the ability to quickly and easily extend the solution to handle more transactions or more users.
- *Performance.* Performance of a system includes the response time of the system and the speed with which a system performs application tasks.
- *Manageability.* Manageability of a system includes the ease with which the system can be managed on all levels.
- *Reuse.* Reuse addresses the ease with which components can be reused by other applications.
- *Business context.* Business context involves separate business functions such as accounting or sales.
- *Granularity.* Granularity involves the number of services and objects packaged in a single component.

While defining a strategy for distributing and packaging the services of the business solution, the team must consider the solution and its physical requirements and constraints.

When using multiple strategies, the team should strive for a balance between the various requirements and constraints of the solution. For example, the team might decide to choose a strategy focusing primarily on the performance needs of the application. This might affect the scalability of the solution. In such a scenario, the team must decide how to handle this tradeoff.

What Are Cohesion and Coupling?

One of the features of a good component plan is high cohesion and loose coupling. *Cohesion* is the relationship among different internal elements of a component. *Coupling* is the relationship of a component with other components.

Cohesion

A component whose services are closely related is said to have high cohesion. The reliability of a component is directly dependent on the close relation between its services. Cohesion can be both beneficial and detrimental, depending on the cause of the cohesion. Cohesion can be:

- *Functional.* A unit performs only one task. This is the strongest type of cohesion.
- *Sequential.* A unit contains operations that must be performed in a specific order and that must share the same data.

- *Communicational.* Operations in a unit use the same data but are not related in any other way. This type of cohesion minimizes communication overhead in the application.
- *Temporal.* Operations are combined because they are all performed simultaneously.

Not all cohesion is beneficial. Other types of cohesion can result in a solution that is poorly organized and difficult to understand, debug, and modify. Ineffective types of cohesion include the following:

- *Procedural.* Operations are grouped together because they are executed in a specific order. Unlike sequential cohesion, the operations do not share data.
- *Coincidental.* Operations are grouped without any apparent interrelationship.

Coupling

Coupling can be tight or loose. When a component is tightly coupled, the component depends heavily on external components to accomplish its function. When a component is loosely coupled, the component is not dependent or is less dependent on external components.

Typically, the looser the link that binds components to each other, the easier it is for the developer to use individual components without causing problems. A component should depend as little as possible on other components. If a dependency exists, the connection between the dependent components must be as clear as possible so that you can easily define interfaces. Another reason to represent the dependencies clearly in design is to ensure that future decisions do not cause a series of failures in the design.

How to Package Components

The primary focus of the physical design rationalization is distributing and packaging services. In the first step of this process, you package the services into layers: user, business, and data.

To begin the process of distribution, identify the high-level services in the physical object model and break them into their individual, layer-based services.

For each business object, group the resulting low-level services into three layers: the user services layer, the business services layer, and the data services layer.

Figure 6.10 illustrates the three service layers.

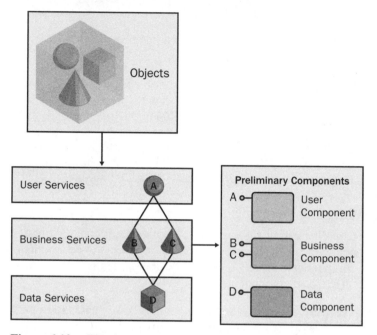

Figure 6.10.   The three service layers

How to Distribute Preliminary Components

After packaging services into components, you distribute the components across the network topology and create a component topology. To start the distribution process, the team identifies categories of services—user, business, and data—for each node in the network topology. These categories serve as the baseline for distribution. The distribution strategy evolves as the design is validated against the solution requirements.

Figure 6.11 illustrates the three layers of services and the corresponding components in a sample application.

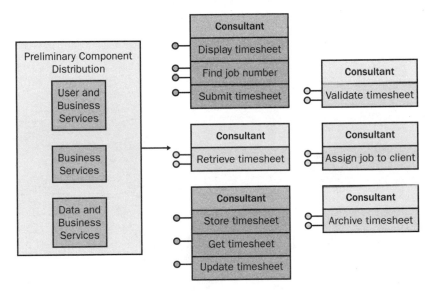

Figure 6.11. Distributing preliminary components

To help with the distribution of layers, use the following guidelines:

- Distribute user services to the Web servers or to the client computers.
- Distribute business services to application servers or Web servers.
- Distribute data services to the data locations identified in the data topology, including database servers or other locations where the data services will reside.
- After identifying where service layers will reside, distribute the preliminary components into their indicated service layers. This represents the initial component topology that will evolve throughout the rationalization process.

Figure 6.12 illustrates the logical partitioning of the three service layers in the component model of a generic order processing system.

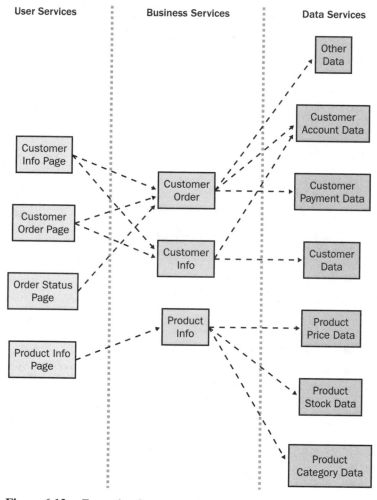

Figure 6.12.   Example of a component model

Note   The illustration shows a sample logical partitioning of the three service layers.

How to Create a Deployment Model

The deployment model shows the mapping of the application and its services to the actual server topology. The purpose of the deployment model is to allow the development team and the release management team to design and plan the server topology and configuration.

Figure 6.13 shows an example of a deployment model.

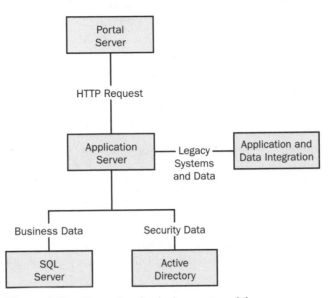

Figure 6.13.   Example of a deployment model

There are five sets of servers:

- Application servers that host Web applications and components
- Database servers that host business databases
- Portal servers that handle all portal functionality, including all HTTP requests from the application servers
- Directory or security servers that manage security data, such as enhanced employee data
- Application and data integration servers that support the optional Microsoft BizTalk Server and the Microsoft Host Integration Server

How to Validate and Refine Distribution and Packaging

After creating the component and deployment models, the project team validates and refines these models.

Validating component and deployment models

During the physical design, the team should validate the component topology against the strategies and requirements of the solution. Validation occurs on an ongoing basis. This enables the team to iterate the design as required.

The project team arrives at an optimal solution by iterating through the process of validation and testing, and by using prototypes to test and tune the packaging and distribution of the components. The team should stop iterating through the solution when only marginal improvements can be made to the solution.

Refining component and deployment models

The key to refining the component topology is to work with services, not components. To evolve the component topology, undo the preliminary component packaging and redistribute the services to meet the needs of the solution.

For example, a requirement states that users must be able to scroll through an entire list without interruption. For best performance, the project team might choose to distribute some of the data services on the client.

After the services have been redistributed, you need to repackage the services. At each location, package the services according to the strategies identified earlier. For example, if ease of deployment is the main goal, the project team might choose to have only one component on the client computer rather than many small components.

Tip   Always take the concepts of cohesion and coupling into consideration when repackaging and redistributing. High cohesion and loose coupling are the ideal, but that ideal might not be practical given the requirements of the solution.

Lesson 4: Physical Design Implementation

During the implementation step of physical design, the team specifies the programming model that the development team will use, the interfaces for each component, and the internal structure of each component. The deliverables of physical design implementation include a programming model; component specifications for interfaces, attributes, and services; and a baseline component specification. The level of detail for each of these deliverables depends on the level of interaction between project management and the development team.

In this lesson, you will learn about the implementation step of physical design. You will learn about the programming model. You will also learn how to specify component interfaces and define the internal structure of components. In addition, you will learn about designing the user interface (UI) and database models.

After this lesson, you will be able to

- Describe the programming model.
- List the guidelines for designing component interfaces.
- Create the internal structure of a component.
- Describe the physical UI model.
- Describe the database model.

Estimated lesson time: 10 minutes

What Is the Programming Model?

Because physical design presents the solution from the developer's perspective, the project team should provide the developers with specifications for component design and technology selection. Component specification provides the development team with enough detail to develop the components of the solution. The specification includes interfaces and the scope of various services and attributes of components. The specification is directly related to the programming model selected for implementation.

A programming model describes how components will be structured. It is based on the goals of the solution and the technologies being implemented.

Purpose of the programming model

The programming model describes how the development team can use the selected technologies. It consists of the programming specifications or standards that will be followed during implementation of the project. The programming model sets specific guidelines to provide consistent component implementation and to increase the maintainability of the components.

The standards prescribed by a programming model might vary for different aspects and service layers of an application. Physical design standards reflect the implementation of the guidelines prescribed by the architecture. If the team decides to implement a stateless server and a stateful client, all attributes are eliminated from class definitions in the physical design. The stateful client might use disconnected .NET datasets as the preferred means of transferring subsets of information to the client.

Design considerations for the programming model

There are several aspects of the programming model that you should consider, including the following:

- *Implementation technologies.* Implementation technologies consist of the programming languages, application programming interfaces (APIs), servers and server technologies, and other technologies that are required for implementing a solution. To efficiently use these technologies, you must use a specific programming model. For example, COM+ 2.0 requires single-entrant, single-threaded, in-process components.

- *Stateful versus stateless objects.* The state that an object maintains can directly affect its performance, scalability, and implementation complexity. Stateful objects retain information that was used in one or more client calls; stateless objects do not maintain transaction-related information. When creating stateful objects, especially in Web-based solutions, the team must determine where and how the state will be maintained; in contrast, stateless objects typically send and receive all necessary information when the objects are invoked or when objects complete the transaction.

- *In-process versus out-of-process function calls.* In-process components perform all execution within a single process, thus eliminating marshalling overhead and increasing performance. Out-of-process components perform their tasks in a process that is separate from that of the invoking client, thus incurring marshalling overhead and degrading performance.

- *Cohesion and coupling.* Cohesive components are closely related to other objects with regards to their functionality. Coupling refers to the strength of component interconnections and interactions. In determining how to apply these principles to a programming model, you should design highly cohesive components and loosely coupled objects. If an object is highly cohesive, its methods and properties are tightly related, and the objects within a component are related. Loosely coupled objects are not highly dependent on the interface, state, or the status of other objects. The communication between loosely coupled objects is implemented by means of messages.

- *Connected versus connectionless modes.* In distributed component environments, various components participating in the service must have real-time, live connections to each other to function properly. If these real-time connections are severed, the components involved in the interaction fail. Because real-time components must typically be run in connected mode, components written to run in a connectionless environment must be able to reestablish connections as required.

- *Synchronous versus asynchronous programming models.* A synchronous programming model blocks the calling component from proceeding with other work until the called interface has completed the requested service and returned control to the calling component. An asynchronous programming model allows components to send messages to other components and then continue functioning without waiting for an immediate reply. A component designed to use an asynchronous programming model is more difficult to program, although technologies such as COM+ Queued Components greatly simplify asynchronous programming. A component that uses an asynchronous programming model lends itself to more scalability because individual components are not blocked and do not need to wait for another process to complete before proceeding.

- *Threading model.* Choosing the threading model for a component is a difficult task because the appropriate model depends on the function of the component. A component that performs extensive input and output (I/O) processing might support free threading to provide maximum response to clients by allowing interface calls during I/O latency. In addition, an object that interacts with the user might support apartment threading to synchronize incoming Component Object Model (COM) calls with its window operations.

- *Error handling.* Because no component performs perfectly or within a perfect environment, components need an error-handling strategy. Certain programming and deployment model decisions constrain the number of error-handling options available. For example, an error message written to a log file on the client might be difficult to retrieve and pass to someone trying to identify system-wide problems.

- *Security.* Security for components and services can be addressed in four basic ways:

  - Component-based security is at the method level, interface level, or component level.

  - Database-based security is handled after data is involved.

  - User context–based security is an interactive method, using system security, or a fixed security within the application.

  - Role-based security involves groups, such as a general manager group.

- *Distribution.* Carefully consider the method for distributing the application. Remember that three logical layers do not necessarily translate into three physically distributed tiers. For example, some business services tend to reside on the client, so you should use as many physical tiers as are required to meet the needs of your application and the enterprise's business goals, possibly even distributing all components to a single location.

Although not a part of the programming model itself, the skills and experience of the technical people who will implement the programming model are an important consideration.

Note   Typically, there is not just one programming model for all components. An application might use many programming models, depending on the requirements of the various components.

How to Specify Component Interfaces

After describing the programming model, the project team defines how the components will interact. This interaction is documented by the component's interfaces, which describe how to access their services and attributes. An interface can represent one or more services. The interface provides a means for requesting a service to perform an operation and a means for receiving information about the resulting attributes. The external structures of the component are outlined in the component interfaces. A component interface:

- Represents the supplier and consumer relationship between components
- Is a means to access the underlying services
- Represents a set of related methods that are a part of a service
- Includes underlying object attributes for a stateful component

The specification of a component interface typically includes all of the ways a component can be accessed and examples of how the component can be used for each means of access. This specification is complete only when the development team finishes creating the component.

When you create component interfaces, remember that:

- A published interface is considered as permanent as possible.
- A modification of an existing interface should be published either as a new component or as a new interface.
- The data types of published attributes must be supported by the service interface consumer.

The only way to access the underlying services within a component is to use the component's published interface. A poorly defined interface can negatively affect other parts of the solution.

Most programming languages allow developers to use Interface Definition Language (IDL) interface definitions when coding components. These definitions help to ensure consistency and change control when multiple developers are coding components.

Each implementation language varies in the syntax and complexity required to define a component's interface. Languages such as Microsoft Visual Basic® often hide much of the interface complexities from developers, whereas languages such as Microsoft Visual C++® provide more control and access to the interfaces. This added control increases coding complexity. Remember that the physical design remains the same, regardless of the implementation language. During physical design, the team can provide a fully-qualified method signature in pseudocode, IDL, or the selected programming language. However, the development team will convert these specifications to a concrete implementation with the selected tools, languages, and technologies during the developing phase.

The Physical Design UI Model

The presentation layer enables users to interact with a system. It provides a communication mechanism between the user and the business services layer of the system. There are two types of users: human users who require an interface through which they can interact with the system, and other computer systems. Although other computer systems do not require a user interface, they require an intermediary to the system with which they will interact. Typically, this intermediary is the user services layer or a Web services interface that facilitates communication between the two layers.

Note   A user interface provides a visual means for humans to interact with systems. User services provide the navigation, validation, and error-processing logic.

To design the user interface and user services layer, the project team uses the outputs of the conceptual design. These outputs include:

- Solution requirements and constraints
- Future-state usage scenarios
- Workflow models
- User profiles
- Task descriptions
- User terminology and concepts

More Info   You will learn more about user interface design in Chapter 7, "Designing the Presentation Layer."

The Physical Design Database Model

During logical design, the database team explores different ways in which the information needs of the conceptual design can be structured in a logical model for a database. The primitive definition for a database is simply an organized collection of data values.

During physical design, the database team must consider:

- Physical database constraints, such as memory and disk size
- Performance tuning considerations, such as deadlock detection, indexing, and hot spots
- Primary keys and foreign keys
- Trigger design
- Stored procedure guidelines
- Application object model considerations
- Indexing specifications
- Partitioning data
- Data migration from the previous database systems
- Operational considerations, such as cluster failover, backup process, and update process

---

More Info   You will learn more about database design in Chapter 8, "Designing the Data Layer."

Activity: Working on the Physical Design

In this activity, you use what you learned in the lessons to create a class model and then create a component model diagram.

Exercise 1: Creating a Class Model

Open the C06Ex1 Microsoft Visio® file from the \SolutionDocuments\Chapter06\ folder on the compact disc, and examine the logical design. Using these diagrams, design a physical class model that is derived from the Catalog, CatalogItem, ManageCatalogItems, and Search objects. You might need to delete or add objects or their attributes and operations. You can see one possible answer to this exercise in C06Ex1_Answer, which is located in the \SolutionDocuments\Chapter06 folder on the CD.

Following are some of the possible discoveries and decisions that have been made in C06Ex1_Answer.

The ManageCatalogItems logical object functionality can best be handled by the Catalog object's operations: addCatalogItem, removeCatalogItem, countSelected-Items, and so on, so it has been deleted from the diagram.

The customer needs to be able to select items for purchase from the catalog while still browsing the catalog. The group of selected items might change in many ways before it is submitted as an order. To meet these needs, a new object is added to the design: the ShoppingCart object.

Exercise 2: Creating a Component Model Diagram

Open the C06Ex2 Visio file from the \SolutionDocuments\Chapter06\ folder on the CD, and then click the Component Model tab. The page is blank. Create a component model for the objects identified in Exercise 1, "Creating a Class Model." Assume the following:

- Sales representatives maintain customer contact information in Microsoft Outlook®.

- Information about Web customers are maintained in a Microsoft SQL Server™ database and managed by using an authorization component.

You can see one possible answer to this exercise in C06Ex2_Answer, which is located in the \SolutionDocuments\Chapter06 folder on the CD.

Summary

- During physical design, the project team defines the services and technologies that will be provided by the solution.
- Physical design is defined as the process of describing the components, services, and technologies of the solution from the perspective of the development team.
- The goals of physical design are:
    - Transforming the logical design into specifications for a set of components
    - Providing a baseline for implementing the design
    - Identifying appropriate technologies for development
    - Creating a structural view of the solution from the perspective of the development team
- There are four steps in physical design: research, analysis, rationalization, and implementation.
- The new deliverables of physical design include:
    - Class diagrams
    - Sequence diagrams
    - Baseline deployment model
    - Programming model
    - Component specifications
- The deliverables of the research baseline include:
    - Current network topology
    - Current data topology
    - Current component topology
    - Physical application requirements
    - Risk assessment and mitigation plan
- During the research step of physical design, the project team identifies the requirements and constraints of the solution and tries to reduce the gap between the two.
- During the analysis step of physical design, the project team refines the UML model created during the logical design, which includes an objects and services inventory, class diagrams, sequence diagrams, and activity diagrams.
- During the analysis step of physical design, the project team creates a preliminary deployment model that includes network, data, and component topologies.
- The network topology is an infrastructure map that indicates hardware locations and interconnections.

- The data topology is a map that indicates data store locations in relation to the network topology.
- The component topology is a map that indicates the locations of components and their services in relation to the network topology.
- The deliverables of the rationalization step include:
  - Distribution and packaging strategy
  - Services-based preliminary components
  - Deployment models
  - Baseline deployment model
- The distribution strategy is a rationale for determining where services will be located in the solution architecture. Distribution is services-based, not component-based.
- The packaging strategy is a rationale for determining which services will go into each component. You might have multiple strategies in a single solution.
- Cohesion is the relationship among various internal elements of a component.
- Coupling is the relationship of a component with other components.
- To distribute services, identify the high-level services in the business object model, and break them into their individual, layer-based services.
- To package services, group the low-level services into three components: the user services component, the business services component, and the data services component.
- The deployment model links the application and its services to the actual server topology.
- The team must validate the component topology against the strategies and requirements of the solution.
- To refine the component and deployment model, the team must undo the preliminary component packaging and redistribute the services to meet the needs of the solution.
- During the implementation step of physical design, the team specifies the programming model that the development team will use, the interfaces for each component, and the internal structure of each component.
- A programming model describes how components will be structured based on the goals of the solution and the technologies being implemented.
- A component's interface describes how to access its services and attributes.
- The presentation layer enables users to interact with a business system and provides a communication mechanism between the user and the business services layer of the system.

Review

The following questions are intended to reinforce key information presented in this chapter. If you are unable to answer a question, review the lesson materials and try the question again. You can find answers to the questions in the appendix.

1. What are the goals of physical design?

2. What is the difference between conceptual, logical, and physical designs?

3. What does the development team do during physical design?

4. What does the deployment model include?

5. What does the project team do during the research step of physical design?

6. How does the project team handle the gap between requirements and constraints?

7. During the analysis step of physical design, how does the project team use the list of objects and services created during logical design?

8. How does the project team refine the class diagrams during the analysis step of physical design?

9. How do you select the candidate technologies for the solution?

10. What is the difference between the network topology and the data topology of the deployment model?

11. What is the difference between the distribution strategy and the packaging strategy?

12. What is the difference between cohesion and coupling?

13. What is the purpose of a programming model?

14. What is a component interface?

15. What are the various types of users of the user services layer of an application?

C H A P T E R 7

Designing the Presentation Layer

About This Chapter

You have learned the process of designing a business solution, focusing on the envisioning phase and planning phase, which includes the conceptual, logical, and physical design processes. However, the design of any system that will be used by users is not complete without a way for users to interact with that system. User interaction takes place by means of the application's *presentation layer*. You design the user interface of an application during the physical design process.

Figure 7.1 illustrates where the design of the presentation layer fits into the MSF Process Model.

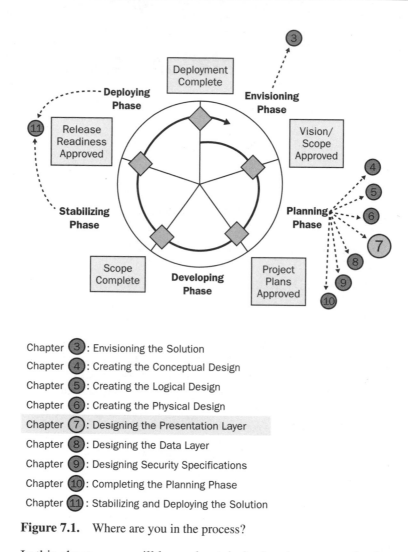

Chapter ③ : Envisioning the Solution
Chapter ④ : Creating the Conceptual Design
Chapter ⑤ : Creating the Logical Design
Chapter ⑥ : Creating the Physical Design
Chapter ⑦ : Designing the Presentation Layer
Chapter ⑧ : Designing the Data Layer
Chapter ⑨ : Designing Security Specifications
Chapter ⑩ : Completing the Planning Phase
Chapter ⑪ : Stabilizing and Deploying the Solution

Figure 7.1. Where are you in the process?

In this chapter, you will learn about designing the presentation layer of an application. You will also learn about the two pieces of the presentation layer—the user interface (UI) components and the user process components—and how to design them.

Before You Begin

To complete the lessons in this chapter, you must

- Understand the MSF Process Model.
- Be familiar with the MSF design process.

Lesson 1: Basics of User Interface Design

In this lesson, you will learn about the basics of user interface design, including the various types of user interfaces, the goals of the user interface design process, and the characteristics of a good user interface design.

After this lesson, you will be able to

- Explain the functions of user interface components.
- Determine the guidelines for user interface design.
- Identify some metaphors and elements that can be used in user interface design.
- Distinguish between a well-designed and poorly designed user interface.

Estimated lesson time: 20 minutes

What Is the Presentation Layer?

The *presentation layer* is the part of the business application that provides a communication mechanism between the user and the business service layer of the system.

Elements of the presentation layer

Simple presentation layers contain *user interface components* that are hosted in a graphical user interface (GUI) such as Microsoft Windows® Forms or Microsoft ASP.NET Web Forms. For more complex user interactions, you can design *user process components* to orchestrate the UI elements and control the user interaction, as shown in Figure 7.2.

User process components are especially useful when there is a specific process that must be followed and access to that process varies depending on the user. For example, a retail application might require two user interfaces: one for the e-commerce Web site that customers use, and another for the Windows Forms–based applications that the sales representatives use. Both types of users perform similar tasks by using these user interfaces. Both user interfaces must provide the ability to view the available products, add products to a shopping cart, and specify payment details as part of a checkout process. This process can be abstracted in a separate user process component to make the application easier to maintain.

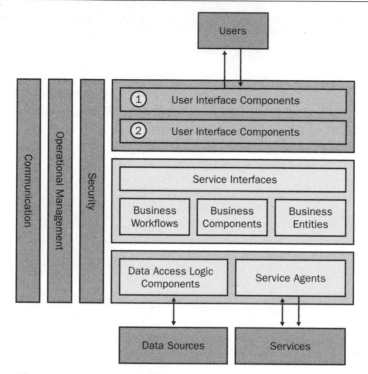

Figure 7.2.   Presentation layer

Inputs to the presentation layer design

The information that you researched, analyzed, and optimized during the envisioning and planning phases is the input for the design of the presentation layer. This information includes:

- Solution requirements and constraints
- Usage scenarios
- Workflow models
- User profiles
- Task descriptions

What Is a User Interface Component?

The first area of the presentation layer that you will learn about is the user interface. In some ways, this interface could be considered the most important part of the business application because, to most users, it *is* the application. A well-designed user interface helps to ensure the success and acceptance of a business application.

User interface components manage interaction with the user. They display data to the user, acquire data from the user, interpret events that are caused by user actions, change the state of the user interface, and help users view progress in their tasks.

User interface components perform view or control roles, or both, in the Model-View-Controller (MVC) pattern. The MVC pattern divides an application, or even an application's interface, into three parts: the model (application object), the view (representation to the user), and the controller (user control).

Tip   Separation of model, view, and controller provides greater flexibility and possibility for reuse.

A component plays a view role when it displays data to users. Control functions are called when the user performs an action that changes the state of the related business data in the user interface process. A control function is a method that performs an action based on the user interface component that the user acted on, and the data that was provided at the time the action was initiated.

What Are the Functions of the User Interface Components?

User interface components display data to users, acquire and validate data from user input, and interpret user actions that indicate the user wants to perform an operation on the data. Additionally, the user interface should filter the available actions to let users perform only the operations that are appropriate at a certain point in time.

User interface components perform the following functions:

- Acquire data from users and assist in its entry by providing visual cues (such as ToolTips), validation, and the appropriate controls for the task.
- Capture events from the user and call controller functions to notify the user interface components to change the way they display data, either by initiating an action on the current user process or by changing the data of the current user process.
- Restrict the types of input a user can enter. For example, the Age field might limit user entries to whole numeric values.
- Perform data entry validation, for example, by restricting the range of values that can be entered in a particular field, or by ensuring that mandatory data is entered.
- Perform simple mapping and transformations of the information provided by the user controls to values needed by the underlying components to do their work. For example, a user interface component might display a product name but pass the product ID to underlying components.

- Perform formatting of values (such as formatting dates appropriately).

- Perform any localization work on the rendered data, for example, using resource strings to display column headers in a grid in the appropriate language for the user's locale.

- Provide the user with status information, for example, by indicating when an application is working in disconnected or connected mode.

- Customize the appearance of an application based on user preferences or the kind of client device used.

Note   In addition to the listed functions, user interface components also help manage the flow of actions needed to perform a task, control resource usage, group information to aid user understanding, convert tabular data into graphical form to help users interpret it, and support local caching for performance improvements.

Guidelines for User Interface Design

Designing a user interface that provides a good user experience requires knowledge and understanding of the users' needs and workflow. You accumulate this information during the envisioning and planning phases.

Guidelines

The design of the interface must implement the users' tasks in a way that is intuitive to the user. This goal is accomplished by including users in all stages of the design of the user interface. Prototyping, beta testing, and early adoption programs are methods for involving the user during the design and implementation of the UI.

The success or failure of an application might depend on the user interface. If users have difficulty using the interface, they see their difficulties as a failure of the application. Designing and developing a user interface that truly meets the needs of users involves asking user-focused questions and incorporating the answers in your design.

Designer's questions

Some design questions to consider include:

- How are users going to interact with the system?
- Does the interface represent the concepts and terminologies of the users?
- Are appropriate metaphors used in the design of the user interface?
- Do the users have the control that they require to override automated processes when needed?
- Can users easily find the features required to complete common tasks?
- Is the workflow correct and complete?
- Does the interface optimize the workflow of the users?

- Can users easily access help for specific problems?
- Are users able to customize the UI to meet their particular needs?
- Are there alternative ways to perform a specific task in case a problem arises, for example, if a mouse gets disconnected from the computer?

What Features Does a Well-Designed Interface Include?

Users judge an application by its interface. If the interface fails to provide a good experience to the users, the overall effort of application development is wasted. However, do not compromise functionality to make the application interface user-friendly. Getting users to accept an interface requires that the users' needs and workflow be taken as a primary consideration during its design and development. You want to ensure that the UI is accessible by all users, including users with physical, visual, or auditory disabilities.

The following features help make an interface effective.

- *Intuitive design.* Design the interface so that a user can intuitively understand how to use it. An intuitive design helps a user become familiar with the interface more quickly. The interface should guide the user's interactions with the application. To make an effective interface, label controls appropriately and make Help context-sensitive.
- *Optimum screen space utilization.* Determine the content of the interface by planning the amount of information that is displayed and the amount of input required from the user. When possible, place all related information and input controls on the same screen. Sometimes, there is too much information for one screen. In such cases, provide tabbed panes or child windows. You could also provide a wizard that guides a user through the data input process.
- *Appearance.* You can use factors, such as the frequency and length of time that a user will interact with a specific piece of the interface, to determine the appearance of the interface.

  For example, when you design Windows-based applications for data entry, do not use bright colors because bright colors strain the eyes. Also, refrain from using colors to indicate specific things, such as red for error messages, because the user might change the color settings because of accessibility or cultural requirements.

  You can, however, use bright colors for Web-based interfaces to make them attractive. For example, when designing confirmation and status pages, you might use bright colors to attract the user's attention to the information. Users tend to spend more time on data input screens than they do on confirmation and status screens. Following accepted guidelines and standards, such as those in the article *Official Guidelines for User Interface Developers and Designers* on MSDN® (*http://msdn.microsoft.com/library/en-us/dnwue/html/welcome.asp*), will help you succeed in designing a usable user interface.

More Info   For more information about designing user interfaces for applications that run on the Windows operating system, see *Microsoft Windows User Experience* (Microsoft Press, 1999).

- *Ease of navigation.* Because different users prefer different ways of accessing components on an interface, design the components so they are easily accessible by using the TAB key, the arrow keys, and other keyboard shortcuts, in addition to the mouse. Sometimes, as in the preceding data entry example, faster navigation is more important than guided navigation. When designing keyboard shortcuts into the UI, associate the shortcut keys with the action being performed. For example, if you are creating a shortcut that will fill in default data for a product description, a shortcut such as CTRL+ALT+D might be more intuitive than CTRL+ALT+P.

- *Controlled navigation.* Although it is important for an interface to provide easy navigation, it is also important to maintain the order in which the components can be accessed. For example, in interfaces that are designed for the purpose of data entry and modifications, you might require that the values be entered in a specific order. However, be wary of taking away the user's feeling of control over the input process.

  One of the key benefits of Windows-based applications is that they typically do not constrain a user to an input sequence, so users have more control. You should also consider adding *breadcrumb trail navigation* functionality to the interface. This type of navigation shows the path the user has navigated to get to the current position. To see an example of a Web site that uses the breadcrumb trail navigation functionality, see the article *The Developing Phase*, on MSDN, at *http://msdn.microsoft.com/library/en-us/dnsolac/html/m05_develphase1.asp*.

- *Populating default value.* If the interface includes fields that always take default values, it is better to provide the default values automatically, therefore avoiding the user having to enter anything whenever possible.

- *Input validation.* It is important to validate the user input before the application processes the input. You need to determine when validation should occur. For example, determine whether validation should occur every time the user moves the focus from one input field to another, or whether it should occur when the user submits the inputs. Sometimes both approaches can be required if there are data dependencies between fields.

- *Menus, toolbars, and Help.* Design the interface to provide access to all of the application's functionality by means of menus and toolbars. In addition, a Help feature should provide complete information about what a user can do with the application.

Note   Although menus and toolbars are the primary methods for input, most frequently used features of an application should also have alternative methods of access, such as keyboard shortcuts, in case the primary input device becomes unusable.

- *Efficient event handling.* The event-handling code that you write for the components of the interface controls the interaction of the user with the interface. It is important that the execution of such code does not cause the user to wait a long time for the application to respond.

Lesson 2: Designing the User Interface

Now that you have learned the basics of designing a user interface, the next step is to learn about the process. In this lesson, you will learn about the process of designing a user interface, and about the deliverables of this process.

After this lesson, you will be able to

- Create an initial user interface design.
- Distinguish between a high-fidelity and a low-fidelity design.
- Design user assistance for an application.
- Select an appropriate user interface model for an application.
- Identify the technology options and considerations for a client environment.
- Validate a user interface design.
- Identify the deliverables of the user interface design process.

Estimated lesson time: 35 minutes

How to Create an Initial User Interface Design

The first part of designing a user interface is creating an initial design that the users can review. This initial design can be either low fidelity (for example, created with a pencil on paper) or high fidelity (for example, a prototype created with a tool such as Microsoft Visual Basic®), as shown in Figure 7.3.

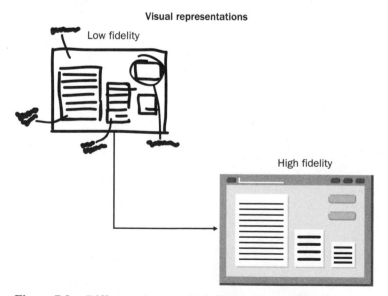

Figure 7.3.   Difference between high fidelity and low fidelity

A *low-fidelity design* shows the main structure and features of the UI and illustrates the navigation path. This type of design is useful for brainstorming sessions where you will receive immediate feedback. It provides one way to quickly identify design problems and explore alternative designs.

A *high-fidelity design* provides detailed information about screen layout and interface elements. This type of design is often based on a low-fidelity design. Compared to a low-fidelity design, a high fidelity design is relatively quick to implement and adjust.

In addition, you can create a *navigation map* for the user interface. A navigation map shows which component is called for each UI event. To keep the focus on the workflow, do not yet include field validation or error processing.

By involving the users early in the design process and keeping them involved throughout the design process, you mitigate the risk of design flaws and increase the likelihood of designing an interface that the users will find acceptable.

Planning   Consider providing a low-fidelity representation, rather than a prototype, to the users. When the initial design is being created, it is better to create a low-fidelity design. Later, when the design is more complete, you can create prototypes to give a detailed representation of the design to the customers. This approach reinforces that what they are reviewing is truly a design and that they can have an influence on the final version.

These initial designs should use the elements that were agreed upon with the users. They should also incorporate the terminology and concepts of the users. The glossary that you create during the envisioning and planning phases serves as a good starting point for the terminology. However, for a better understanding of the terminologies and concepts, you need to talk to the users.

How to Provide User Assistance

User assistance is frequently neglected, or poorly implemented, in computer applications. There are several options available for providing user assistance in applications.

Online Help

Online Help refers to any help that is immediately available upon user request while the user is interacting with the system. This assistance can be installed with the application, located on a CD, or located on an intranet or the Internet. Online Help is an important part of all applications and provides an effective way to answer user queries.

Online Help can be either context-sensitive or in a reference format. *Context-sensitive* Help provides information about a specific field or area of the UI. Other Help formats allow the user to read the Help contents in a specific order (by topic or an alphabetized list) or to search for information.

Tip   When designing your Help system, try to include topics that provide answers to task-oriented questions. Task-oriented Help is most useful for less-experienced users.

ToolTips

A *ToolTip* is a small label that is displayed when a user moves the mouse over a control or an option in the user interface. The label provides a description of the function of the control. ToolTips are normally used in conjunction with toolbars, but they also work well in many other parts of the interface.

Tip   As with other parts of the interface, ensure that the text clearly conveys the intended message to the user.

Status displays

Status displays are a useful way to provide instructions or messages that might not fit easily into a ToolTip. To provide status displays, you can use a status bar control or a label control.

Wizards

A *wizard* is a user assistance device that guides the user step-by-step through a procedure. Wizards are mostly used to provide task-specific assistance. They help a user complete a difficult task that would otherwise require a lot of time to learn and accomplish. Wizards are also used to provide advanced information to a user who has enough experience with basic steps but wants additional or advanced information.

Accessibility aids

Accessibility aids are specialized programs and devices that help people with disabilities use applications more effectively. There are many types of aids. Some examples include:

- Screen enlargers that enlarge portions of the screen
- Screen-reading software that presents graphics and text as speech
- Speech recognition systems that provide input by using your voice instead of the keyboard or mouse

When designing accessible applications, you should follow certain guidelines. Some examples of accessibility guidelines include:

- Applications must be compatible with specific system color, size, font, sound, and input settings.

   This guideline provides a consistent user interface across all applications on the user's system.

- Applications must provide keyboard access to all features.

   This guideline allows the user to interact with the application without requiring a pointing device, such as a mouse.

- Applications must not convey information by sound alone.

   This guideline requires that applications that convey information by sound must provide additional means of expressing this information, such as on-screen messages.

More Info   For more information about the guidelines for designing accessible applications, see the MSDN Library (*http://msdn.microsoft.com*), and the Microsoft Accessibility Web site at *http://www.microsoft.com/enable*.

How to Select a User Interface Model

When designing an application, it is important to select the best user interface model because the user interface can affect deployment, how users interact and relate to the data, and how the state is maintained while the application is interacting with the user. Some of the common user interface implementation models and technologies include:

- Windows-based user interfaces
- Web-based user interfaces
- Mobile device user interfaces
- Document-based user interfaces

Windows desktop user interfaces

Windows-based user interfaces are used when you need to provide users with disconnected or offline capabilities and rich user interactions. Windows user interfaces provide a wide range of state management and persistence options, and local processing power. There are three main categories of standalone user interfaces:

- *Full-featured workstation/Tablet PC user interfaces created with Windows Forms.* These UIs involve creating an application with Windows Forms and Windows controls. In these applications, the application provides all or most of the data rendering functionality. These UIs give the developer total control over the user experience and the appearance and functionality of the application.

- *Embedded HTML.* You can implement the entire user interface by using Windows Forms, or you can use additional embedded Hypertext Markup Language (HTML) in your Windows-based applications. Embedded HTML provides greater run-time flexibility (because the HTML can be loaded from external resources or even a database in connected scenarios) and user customization. Extra coding is necessary to load the HTML, display it, and connect the events from the control with your application functions.

> **Important**   Careful planning is needed to ensure that malicious scripts cannot be introduced through the embedded HTML.

- *Application add-ins.* For some applications, the use cases developed during the planning phases might suggest that the user interface of the application could be better implemented as an add-in for other applications, such as Microsoft Office, AutoDesk AutoCAD software, customer relationship management (CRM) solutions, engineering tools, and so on. In such cases, the developers can use all the data access and display logic of the host application and just provide their business-specific code to gather the data and work with their business logic.

- *Remote access.* By using programs such as Windows XP Remote Desktop Connection and Windows Terminal Services, remote users can access remote computers and run applications on them remotely. The only information passed between the client computer and the remote user is the user interface. All other functionality, such as data validation and computations done by the CPU, is performed on the remote computer.

Web-based user interfaces

In Microsoft .NET, you develop Web-based user interfaces with ASP.NET. ASP.NET provides a rich environment in which you can create complex Web-based interfaces that support the following features:

- Consistent development environment
- User interface data binding
- Component-based UIs with controls
- Integrated .NET security model
- Rich caching and state management options
- Availability, performance, and scalability of Web processing

Mobile device user interfaces

Mobile devices such as handheld computers, Wireless Application Protocol (WAP) phones, and Handheld PCs are becoming increasingly popular, and building user interfaces for a mobile device has several challenges.

A user interface for a mobile device needs to be able to display information on a much smaller screen than other common applications, and must offer acceptable usability for the devices being targeted. Because user interaction can be difficult on mobile devices, design your mobile user interfaces with minimal data input requirements. A common strategy is to allow users to pre-register data by means of a workstation-based client, and then select the data when using a mobile client. For example, an e-commerce application might allow users to register credit card details by means of a Web site so that a pre-registered credit card can be selected from a list when orders are placed from a mobile device, thus avoiding the requirement to enter full credit card details by using a mobile phone keypad.

Document-based user interfaces

In some applications, you might benefit from having users enter or view data in document form. Document-based user interfaces include:

- *Showing data.* The application allows users to view their data in a document, such as showing customer data as a Microsoft Word form, a sales report as a Microsoft Excel worksheet, or a project timeline as a Microsoft Project Gantt chart.
- *Gathering data.* You can allow sales representatives to complete Word forms with customer information, allow accountants to enter data into Excel worksheets, or let designers enter design data with Microsoft Visio®.

How to Select the Client Environment

The selection of a client environment for the user interface of a business application is determined by how the user will be using the application, in addition to how the user will be connected to the systems that support the application.

When users are on a local area network (LAN) or a high-speed wide area network (WAN), the main choice of client is a feature-rich environment known as a *rich client*. For these users, the communication speed between their computers and the system they are accessing is not a primary issue. This type of client also has the greatest number of options for development and implementation. Additionally, the processing of the application can easily be distributed between the servers and the clients.

Another choice of clients is the *thin client*. However, thin clients, such as Web browsers and remote desktop connections, are most frequently used for remote or distributed users, or users with slower connections such as a dial-up modem. These users are frequently concerned with communication speed and require a user interface that sends the minimum amount of information possible over their connections. These users might benefit from a rich client if the business requires functionality that is not available otherwise.

You should take the following factors into account when deciding whether to create a thin-client or a rich-client application.

Note   This choice between thin and rich clients is also known as the choice between reach clients and rich clients.

- *Client devices.* An application that must be used on a wide variety of client devices is ideally suited to being a thin-client application. If the application must run on Windows-based computers but must also run on computers and are not running Windows, or on PDAs, telephones, or interactive televisions, the application will typically be a thin client.

  You must use special care in these situations when using heterogeneous systems because the client might have limitations. For example, a browser might be unable to host ActiveX® controls, or it might not have a Java Virtual Machine. When an application can be hosted in an unknown browser, the ASP.NET server controls can be used because the server will determine the browser's capabilities and render the controls accordingly. If mobile devices are to be targeted, Mobile Internet Controls must be used for the same reason.

- *Graphics.* If an application makes heavy use of highly dynamic graphics, such as computer-aided design (CAD) or video applications, then you need to use a rich client.

  If an application is not heavily graphical and it can avoid using animations and other cosmetic graphical effects, it can work well as a thin client. Dynamic HTML can be used to provide some localized effects, but doing so increases the size of each page. The features that you use depend on the capabilities of the browser that you are targeting.

- *Interaction.* If an application is highly interactive and provides the user with a rich experience, it is best suited to being a rich client. Highly interactive applications are those that present a dynamic user interface that changes frequently based on user input (for example, a word processor, a game, or a CAD application), allows drag-and-drop operations, performs immediate inter-control validations, and so on.

- *Network bandwidth.* A thin-client application generally uses much more network bandwidth than a locally hosted rich client. This is especially true if the interface uses Web server controls because many mouse clicks result in a round trip to the Web server. This is also true for Terminal Services clients and remote desktop connections because, in the case of remote clients, user interface rendering and responses need to travel across the network. Therefore, if network bandwidth is an issue, a rich client is the preferred choice.

- *Disconnected client.* If the client must be able to operate while disconnected from the corporate network, then you use a rich client. This would include applications used by mobile personnel, or by personnel working from customer locations.

- *CPU-intensive operations.*   If users need to perform operations that require a lot of CPU-intensive work (for example, CAD and graphics applications), these operations should occur on the end-user's computer; otherwise the operations could quickly overload the server. CPU-intensive applications are best suited to a rich-client environment.

- *Database locking.*   If the application requires a high degree of concurrency control, a rich client is essential. For example, if an application must use pessimistic locking, it cannot be a thin client because the locks are released after each page has been processed.

- *Local resources.*   If an application needs access to local resources, such as files (storage), the registry (configuration), databases (storage), or any other local devices, a rich client might be more suitable.

- *Security.*   In a highly secure environment, a thin-client application has the following benefits:
  - Privileged operations can be confined to the server.
  - Code that could be misused by a malicious user is kept away from workstation computers (as long as active content is avoided).
  - The workstation can be locked down.
  - Sensitive data is not stored outside the data center.

The following advantages apply to rich-client applications hosted by Terminal Services:

- Authorization: user-based and code access security-based
- Authentication
- Secure communication and state management
- Auditing

How to Create a User Interface Prototype

After you have made the design decisions for the user interface, you are ready to create a user interface prototype from the gathered interviews, requirements document, use cases, usage scenarios, and activity diagrams created during the planning phase.

Example usage scenario

To learn how to create a user interface prototype, consider the example of the Adventure Works Cycles scenario. The following is a usage scenario that was created based on the use cases defined during early stages of planning for sales representatives and sales managers.

Adventure Works Cycles Usage Scenario

Use case title: UC 05.5.1 Apply Discount to Product

Abbreviated title: Apply Discount to Product

Use case ID: UC 05.5.1

Requirements ID: 2.1.1, 2.1.2, 2.1.3

Description: A sales representative is creating an order for a specific customer. The representative wants to offer the customer a discount on one or more products in the order. This affects the total order price, and it is the recalculated price that the customer will then pay. Sales managers can also apply discounts to orders.

Sales representatives are currently authorized to apply a discount of up to 15 percent without approval. Sales managers can apply a discount of up to 20 percent.

Actors: Sales Representative, Sales Manager

Preconditions:

- Actor has access rights to view customer and sales data
- An order is in the process of being created

Task sequence	*Exceptions*
1. Actor chooses to apply a discount to an order	Product is not in current view
2. Application requests which order is to be discounted	
3. Actor selects the order to be discounted	Any piece of data is not available
4. Application presents order information (including any existing discounts) and requests discount amount	
5. Actor enters discount amount	
6. Application validates discount amount and presents order information with updated total price	• If discount amount is over a certain threshold, system reports this fact • Use case continues at Step 5 of main path to enable actor to re-enter discount amount
7. Information is passed to a method of delivery	

Postconditions:

Uses/Extends:

1. EXTENDS UC 05.5 Apply Discount to Order

Unresolved issues:

Sales Managers have authority to supply a higher level of discount than sales representatives. This is captured in extended use case UC 5.5.1.1.

Adventure Works Cycles Usage Scenario   *(continued)*

Authority: Mike Danseglio

Modification history:

Date: December 19, 2002

Author: Yan Li

Description: Initial version

Tip   When designing the user interface, keep in mind the preconditions, the basic course, the alternative courses, and the extensions specified in the usage scenarios. All these factors need to be addressed by the UI.

Example requirements

Following are some of the requirements that were identified and refined during the planning phase for Adventure Works Cycles:

- Sales representative should be allowed to search the site for information across all products or within a specific catalog.
- Sales representative should be allowed to view the categories of the product.
- Sales representative should be allowed to view product details such as pricing and information about promotions.
- Sales representative should be allowed to view product specifications.
- Additional navigation links should appear on the page. These links include Home, About Adventure Works Cycles, Track Orders, Shipping Rates and Policies, Contact Us, and a copyright notice.
- Sales representative should be allowed to view the customer reviews about the product.
- Sales representative should be allowed to provide discounts of up to 15 percent to the customers.
- Sales representative can provide discounts from 16 through 20 percent to the customers with prior approval from a sales manager.
- Sales manager should be allowed to search the site for information across all products or within a specific catalog.
- Sales manager should be able to view the categories of the product.
- Sales manager should be able to view product details such as pricing and information about promotions.
- Sales manager should be able to view product specifications.

- Sales manager should be able to view the customer reviews about the product.
- Sales manager should be able to provide discounts of up to 20 percent to the customers.
- Sales manager can approve discounts of up to 20 percent to the customers.

You need to address the above requirements when you design the user interface for Adventure Works Cycles Web site.

Example UI prototypes

Figure 7.4 is an example of a UI prototype that was created to address the requirements derived from use cases and usage scenarios. This prototype shows the information that a sales representative needs on the product information page.

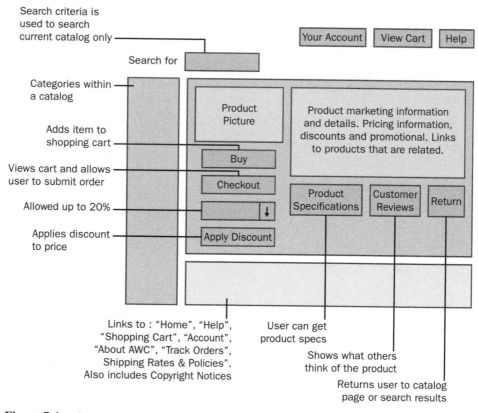

Figure 7.4. A prototype of the product information page for sales representatives

Figure 7.5 is another example of a UI prototype. This prototype shows the information that a sales manager needs on the product information page.

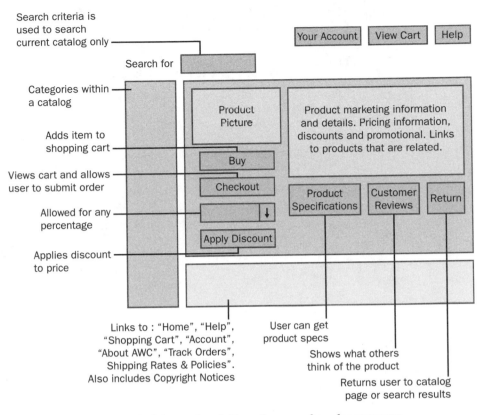

Figure 7.5.   A prototype of the product information page for sales managers

How to Validate User Interface Design

As part of the design process, validate that the user interface is addressing the requirements of the users.

After you create the UI prototypes, you need to map the UI back to the requirements, use cases, usage scenarios, and logical design. Ensure that all the requirements are addressed by the user interface. If a requirement has not been addressed in the user interface, you need to address it and incorporate that in the design before you present the prototypes to the customers.

The navigation and flow are validated to ensure that the flow is as expected. The maps should be compared to the future-state usage scenarios to confirm that the user interface is able to handle the scenarios.

The final step of the validation process is to review the design with the users and obtain their agreement that it satisfies their requirements.

The next step is to create prototypes of limited functionality so that the user interface can be validated in usability tests.

What Are the Deliverables of the UI Design Process?

Like all the other processes of designing a business solution, the UI design process has deliverables:

- The project team, customer, and users should have an agreement on the guidelines for the design, including the elements that are being used in the application. The guidelines, and an identification of common interface elements, should be documented for the development team.
- The design should include descriptions of how the interface will provide appropriate feedback (such as progress bars) and user assistance (such as ToolTips) to the user.
- The design produced should be testable by storyboarding and by comparing it against the future-state usage scenarios.

Lesson 3: Designing User Process Components

User interaction with your application might follow a predictable process. For example, the Adventure Works Cycles Web site might require users to enter product details, view the total price, enter payment details, and finally enter delivery address information. This process involves displaying and accepting input from a number of user interface elements, and the state for the process (the products that have been ordered, the credit card details, and so on) must be maintained between each transition from one step in the process to another. To help coordinate the user process and handle the state management required when displaying multiple user interface pages or forms, you can create user process components.

In this lesson, you will learn about the functions of user process components and how to design them.

After this lesson, you will be able to

- Explain the function of user process components.
- Separate the user interface from user processes.
- Design user processes.

Estimated lesson time: 20 minutes

Functions of User Process Components

Separating the user interaction functionality into user interface and user process components provides the following advantages:

- Long-running user interaction state is more easily persisted, allowing a user session to be abandoned and resumed, possibly even using a different user interface. For example, a customer could add some items to a shopping cart by using the Web-based user interface, and then later call a sales representative to complete the order.
- The same user process can be reused by multiple user interfaces. For example, in the retail application, the same user process could be used to add a product to a shopping cart from both the Web-based user interface and the Windows Forms–based application.

Figure 7.6 shows how the user interface and user process can be abstracted from one another.

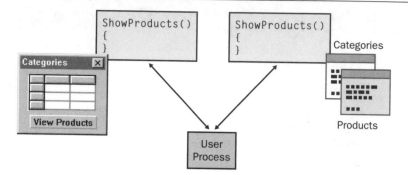

Figure 7.6. User interfaces and user process components

User process components are typically implemented as classes that expose methods that can be called by user interfaces. Each method encapsulates the logic necessary to perform a specific action in the user process. The user interface creates an instance of the user process component and uses it to transition through the steps of the process.

User process components coordinate the display of user interface elements. They are abstracted from the data rendering and acquisition functionality provided in the user interface components. You should design them with globalization in mind, to allow for localization to be implemented in the user interface. For example, you should endeavor to use culture-neutral data formats and use Unicode string formats internally to make it easier to consume the user process components from a localized user interface.

User process components:

- Provide a simple way to combine user interface elements into user interaction flows without requiring you to redevelop data flow and control logic.
- Separate the conceptual user interaction flow from the implementation or device in which it occurs.
- Encapsulate how exceptions can affect the user process flow.
- Keep track of the current state of the user interaction.
- Keep internal data related to application business logic and their internal state, persisting the data as required.

How to Separate a User Process from the User Interface

Before you design a user process component, separate user process components from user interface components. It is important to determine what functions can be done by the user interface and what needs to be handled by the user process components.

To separate a user process from the user interface, perform the following tasks:

1. Identify the business process or processes that the user process will help to accomplish. Identify how the user sees this as a task. You can usually do this by consulting the sequence diagrams, use cases, and usage scenarios that you created as part of your requirements analysis.
2. Identify the data needed by the business processes. The user process will need to be able to work with this data when necessary.
3. Identify additional state you will need to maintain throughout the user activity to assist rendering and data capture in the user interface.
4. Design the visual flow of the user process and the way that each user interface element receives or gives control flow.

Note   Implementing a user interaction with user process components is not a trivial task. Before committing to this approach, you should carefully evaluate whether your application requires the level of orchestration and abstraction provided by user process components.

What Are the Guidelines for Designing User Processes?

Use the following guidelines when designing user processes for an application:

- Decide whether you need to manage user processes as separate components from the user interface components. Separate user processes are generally only needed in applications with a high number of user interface dialog boxes, or in applications in which the user processes might be subject to customization and might benefit from a add-in approach.
- Choose where to store the state of the user process:
    - If the process is running in a connected fashion, store interim state for long-running processes in a central Microsoft SQL Server™ database; in disconnected scenarios, store it in local XML files, isolated storage, or local Microsoft SQL Server 2000 Desktop Engine (MSDE) databases. On Handheld PC devices, you can store state in a Microsoft SQL Server CE database.
    - If the process is not long-running and does not need to be recovered in case of a problem, you should persist the state in memory. For user interfaces created for rich clients, you might want to keep the state in memory. For Web applications, you can choose to store the user process state in the Session object of ASP.NET. If you are running in a server farm, you should store the session in a central state server or a SQL Server database. A server farm is a grouping of several Web servers used for load balancing. When you implement a Web site on a server farm, the processing load is distributed across different Web servers. ASP.NET will remove unnecessary SQL Server–stored session to prevent the buildup of unwanted data.

- Design your user process components so that they are serializable. This will help you implement any persistence scheme.
- Include exception handling in user process components, and propagate exceptions to the user interface. Exceptions that are thrown by the user process components should be caught by user interface components.

Activity: Creating the User Interface

In this activity, you use what you learned in the lessons to work through the process of creating a user interface.

You have been assigned the task of creating a prototype of the product information management tool. The product clerks will use this tool to manage products for the online shopping application. The prototype should be designed in Microsoft PowerPoint®. The requirements for the management tool are as follows:

- The tool should allow the clerk to look up products by supplying a product identification number or by searching the product database. For searching, clerks should be allowed to specify the catalog in which they want to search, or search for the product across all catalogs.

- The information for each product should be broken down into separate sections, such as name, description, part number, catalog, pricing, entry date, expiration data, last modified date, pictures, specifications, promotions, and discount. Rather than displaying all this information on a single screen, the clerk should be allowed to select the type of information and work with that specific data.

- When the clerk wants to add a new product, a new product record must be created and a new product ID must be supplied. The clerk fills in each section of information for the product. Some sections might be optional while others are mandatory. After all the information has been entered, the clerk must explicitly save the new information to the database.

- When the clerk wants to edit an existing product, the clerk must look up the product in the database, explicitly indicate that changes will be made to the information, select each section of information to change, and make the changes. After all the changes have been made, the clerk must explicitly save the changes to the database.

- For each section of information, the clerk should be allowed to cancel edits. This should cancel the edits on only that section of data. For example, if the clerk makes changes to the description of a product and then makes changes to the promotional information for the product, the clerk can cancel the changes to the promotional information without affecting the changes made to the description of the product.

- For each product record that has been added or changed, the user should be allowed to cancel all the entries and changes made since the user last saved the product record.

- When clerks want to delete an existing product, they must look up the product in the database, explicitly indicate that the record will be deleted, and confirm that the record should be deleted. The record is deleted from the database by changing its expiration date to a date that occurred in the past.

Be sure to point out the functionality that can be accessed on the page and what each area of the user interface provides to the user. After you have designed the user interface, compare it to the preceding requirements. To see one possible solution to this exercise, open C07Ex1_Answer.ppt, which is located in the \Solution-Documents\Chapter07\ folder on the CD.

Summary

- Design of any application is not complete without a way for users to interact with the system. User interaction takes place through the application's presentation layer. The presentation layer is the part of the application that provides a communication mechanism between the user and the business service layer of the system.

- The most simple presentation layers contain user interface components, such as Windows Forms or ASP.NET Web Forms. For more complex user interactions, you can design user process components to orchestrate the user interface elements and control the user interaction.

- User interface components display data to users, acquire and validate data from user input, and interpret user gestures that indicate the user wants to perform an operation on the data. Additionally, the user interface should filter the available actions to let users perform only the operations that are appropriate at a certain point in time.

- The features of a good user interface include:
  - Intuitive design
  - Optimum screen space utilization
  - Ease of navigation
  - Controlled navigation
  - Input validation
  - Menus, toolbars, and Help
  - Efficient event handling

- There are several types of user interface models:
  - Windows desktop user interfaces
  - Web-based user interfaces
  - Mobile device user interfaces
  - Document-based user interfaces

- User assistance in an application can be provided by using any or all of the following options:
  - Online Help
  - ToolTips
  - Status displays
  - Wizards
  - Accessibility aids

- User process components are typically implemented as .NET classes that expose methods that can be called by user interfaces. User process components coordinate the display of user interface elements. They are abstracted from the data rendering and acquisition functionality provided in the user interface components.

Review

The following questions are intended to reinforce key information presented in this chapter. If you are unable to answer a question, review the lesson materials and try the question again. You can find answers to the questions in the appendix.

1. What is the function of the presentation layer in the business application architecture?

2. What are the features of a good user interface?

3. What are the differences between a high-fidelity and low-fidelity design?

4. What are some of the options that application developers can use to design user assistance for an application?

5. What are the various types of user interface models, and when should you use them?

6. Describe the difference between a user interface component and a user process component. Describe a situation in which you would use a user process component.

7. How do you separate user interface from user process?

8. Your design calls for the use of Windows Terminal Services. What kind of user interface will you create to implement this design?

9. During the envisioning and planning phases, you determined that the users of the solution will be using a wide variety of hardware, will be located at various remote locations, and will not all have access to the company's intranet. What type of client lends itself to these constraints?

10. After your design of the user interface is complete, what are some of the ways you can validate the design before implementing it?

C H A P T E R   8

Designing the Data Layer

About This Chapter

During the planning phase of the Microsoft® Solutions Framework (MSF) Process Model, the project team designs the data layer of the solution, along with the presentation and business layers. In this chapter, you will learn about designing the data layer for a solution. You will also learn about optimizing data access and implementing data validation in the solution.

Before You Begin

To complete the lessons in this chapter, you must

- Be familiar with the various phases of the MSF Process Model.
- Understand the envisioning phase of the MSF Process Model.
- Understand the tasks and deliverables of the conceptual and logical design processes of the planning phase.
- Understand how to design the presentation layer and business layer of a solution in the physical design process.

Lesson 1: Designing the Data Store

The *data layer* of a solution consists of a data store and data services. The *data store* is typically a database in which data is organized and stored. In this lesson, you will learn about data models and how data is structured in various data models. You will learn how to identify entities and attributes in a data model. You will also learn how to derive tables and columns for a data store and implement relationships among various entities.

After this lesson, you will be able to

- Describe a database schema.
- Identify entities and attributes.
- Identify tables and columns for a data store.
- Implement relationships.

Estimated lesson time: 20 minutes

What Is a Database Schema?

Throughout the planning phase, the project team focuses on analyzing requirements and designing the solution that meets those requirements. Therefore, in addition to identifying the features of the solution, the project team analyzes the data requirements of the solution and specifies how data will be structured, stored, accessed, and validated in the solution.

Research and analysis of data requirements begins during the conceptual design process. These requirements help determine what actually needs to be stored and processed by the business solution. During logical design, the project team derives a set of data entities from sources that include the logical object model, usage scenarios, and data artifacts such as data schema, triggers, constraints, and topology from any existing data store. During physical design, the team defines tables, relationships, field data types, indexes, and procedures to create a database schema, and finalizes data services. In addition, the team plans how to provide for data migration, backup and recovery, and failover support.

Definition of database schema

A *database* is defined as a collection of data values that are organized in a specific manner. A *database schema* specifies how data is organized in a database. During the physical design process, the members of the project team create a database schema so that they can focus on what must be built before they focus on how to build it.

During the logical design process, the team describes the entities and attributes that will be stored in the database, and how the users will access, manipulate, and browse through the data. During the physical design, the team creates the database schema that provides specifications for creating, reading, updating, and deleting data that is used in a solution.

When the team begins to design the database schema, the schema has a close relationship with the logical object model. The schema defines the main entities of interest to the problem, the attributes of those entities, and the relationships between entities. Most data modeling techniques define an entity as an abstraction of something in the real world. You learned to derive entities and attributes of those entities while defining the object model for a solution.

Note The final production schema might not resemble the logical object model.

Figure 8.1 shows part of the database schema for the Adventure Works Cycles system.

Typically, database objects are modeled in an entity relationship (ER) diagram. The ER diagram consists of entities, attributes, and relationships. It provides a high-level logical view of the data. In an ER model, all data is viewed as stating facts about entities and relationships.

Note You will learn more about entities, attributes, and relationships in the subsequent topics in this chapter.

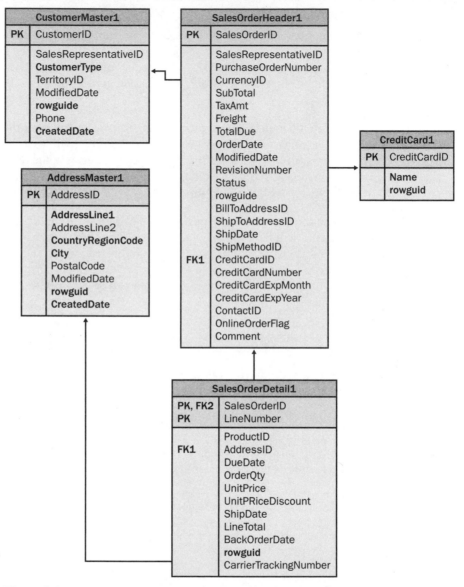

Figure 8.1.   Partial database schema for the Adventure Works Cycles system

Types of physical data models

In addition to defining the logical database design, you must select a technology for physically storing data. The physical data model of a *database management system* (DBMS) defines the internal structure that the DBMS uses to keep track of data. The structure reflects the types of database tables that you can create, as well as the speed of access and versatility of the database. The various types of physical data models that commonly exist are:

- *Flat-file.* A flat-file database stores all data in a single file as a set of rows and columns. There is no relationship between multiple flat-file databases because each database exists without knowledge of any other database. They can provide fast updates and retrieval because they support an indexing method called the *indexed sequential access method* (ISAM). Legacy mainframe databases, as well as smaller PC-based databases, implement ISAM storage technology.

- *Hierarchical.* Hierarchical databases store a wide range of information in a variety of formats. Therefore, they are extensible and flexible. You use this type of database when information storage requirements vary greatly. An example of a hierarchical database is Microsoft Exchange, which can store varying types of information in a format that facilitates messaging and collaboration applications that require many types of information to be encapsulated in messages.

- *Relational.* In a relational model database, data is stored in multiple tables and columns. Relational databases combine the advantages of both flat-file and hierarchical databases by providing good performance and flexibility of storage. The relational model tends to be the most popular because tables can be linked together with unique values. It is important to understand, however, that the other models are still in use and that developers who are working in enterprise environments will likely need to interface with one of these other types of databases at some time. The relational model focuses on storing data, retrieving data, and maintaining data integrity. Related items of data can be retrieved efficiently by using Structured Query Language (SQL), regardless of whether the items are stored in one table or in many tables. Data integrity is maintained by applying rules and constraints.

- *Object-oriented.* In an object-oriented database, database objects appear as programming language objects, in one or more existing programming languages. The *object-oriented database management system* (ODBMS) extends the language with transparently persistent data, concurrency control, data recovery, associative queries, and other database capabilities. You use an ODBMS if you need to store complex data and require high performance. Complex data is characterized by lack of natural, unique identification, many-to-many relationships, and frequent use of type codes as used in relational models.

At Adventure Works Cycles, the data storage technology currently being used is Microsoft SQL Server 7.0. After looking at the long-term requirements for data storage, the project team chose Microsoft SQL Server 9.0 for this solution. The completed application will convert the existing data store to allow for several improvements. Therefore, the physical model selected for the Adventure Works Cycles system is the relational model. The physical model reflects the target implementation environment.

How to Identify Entities and Attributes

In the logical design process, the project team analyzes use cases and usage scenarios to identify entities and attributes. These entities and attributes form the basis for logical design and are used in the physical design process to model the physical design of the solution. The logical design helps ensure that the data design for the solution represents and maps to the conceptual requirements. However, the actual structures that are used to store the data are optimized for the environment in which the physical data model will be implemented.

Guidelines for deriving entities

When identifying entities for the purpose of logical data design, keep in mind that entities are:

- Objects about which information will be stored. Some examples of entities are Product, Order, and Customer.
- The starting point for the logical data design. The identification of these entities is the first step in the design of a database.
- The equivalent of rows in one or more database tables. An instance of an entity corresponds to a row of a table.

Consider the following use cases:

```
Employee creates a contract with the client.
Employee reviews prior billings to the client.
```

Based on these use cases, you identify the following objects:

- *Employee.* The employee performs actions within the system.
- *Client.* Client is the recipient of actions that are performed by the employee.
- *Contract.* The agreement between the employee and the client.
- *Billings.* Invoices that the client has received for work performed.

In addition to being objects in the object model of the solution, the preceding entities are used in the logical data design. The database for the solution must store information for every instance of the Employee, Client, Contract, and Billings entities that are within the scope of the solution. Remember that the entity description helps determine relationships between the entities.

Characteristics of attributes

After identifying the entities, you must determine the attributes that you want to capture in the database. Attributes have the following characteristics:

- Attributes describe a solution entity. For example, the attributes of a car can include its color, make, model, and year of production. Although size is a characteristic of a car, it is not related to the solution and is not included as an attribute.
- Attributes exist only when attached to an entity. For example, the attribute of color does not describe anything tangible unless the color is applied to an object.

- Attributes define the columns in database tables. When the physical design is implemented, the attributes become the columns in the database tables. They are fully described by type, length, and any applicable relationships.

For example, the entity Client has the attributes account number, name, and address. You must store this information for each instance of the Client entity.

How to Identify Tables and Columns

During physical design, the outputs of logical design are used to produce components, user interface specifications, and physical database design. The entities, attributes, and constraints derived during logical design are mapped to tables, fields, relationships, and constraints in a database. This database physically represents the logical model.

Definition of tables

Tables are the physical representation of entities in a relational database. Tables can store a wide variety of data. A table can contain names, addresses, pictures, audio files, video files, Microsoft Word documents, and so on. Because of this flexibility, a database can be used to store not only simple text data, but also the knowledge base of a business, no matter what form that knowledge takes. A database represents the relationships between various data items.

The data in a table is stored in *rows*, or records. Each record must be unique. Records in a relational database can be manipulated by using Extensible Markup Language (XML). XML can be used to transmit data between databases, and different enterprises, without aligning the table structures of the two communicating databases.

A traditional method of manipulating relational data is by using the American National Standards Institute (ANSI) standard relational database language, which is referred to as SQL. SQL is an English-like language that abstracts the operations that are performed on a database into easily readable statements, such as Insert, Update, and Delete. Most databases adhere to the ANSI SQL standard, although the version and enhancements that are used vary from product to product.

Tip   Tables can be linked to other tables within the same database file. This capability allows one type of data to be joined to another type and allows data normalization.

Definition of columns

The data in each record is stored in *columns*, or fields, that are specified from the attributes of the table's defining entity. Each field contains one distinct item of data, such as a customer name.

Example of tables and columns

Consider the Adventure Works Cycles system. One of the entities in the system, *SalesOrderDetail,* maintains details about an order placed by a customer. The attributes of this entity include SalesOrderID, ProductID, AddressID, UnitPrice, and DueDate. Corresponding to this entity and its attributes, the Adventure Works Cycles database includes a table named SalesOrderDetail that contains the following columns: SalesOrderID, ProductID, AddressID, UnitPrice, and DueDate.

Purpose of data types

Data types specify the kind of data that is stored in a field. Every field within a database must have a data type. The data type allows you, and the database engine itself, to verify that a value entered in a field is valid for the information that the field represents. Remember that a valid data type does not ensure valid data. For example, an integer data type field can store numeric data. According to the business rules, the field values can range from 1 through 20. If a user inputs 25, the value is a valid entry by type but it is not valid data.

The data types that are allowed for a given field depend on the data types that are supported by the hosting DBMS. When defining your tables, choose data types that will optimize performance, conserve disk space, and allow for growth. Most DBMSs support two major classifications of data types:

- *System-supplied data types.* Every DBMS contains its own data types. Examples of system-supplied types are *Integer, Character*, and *Binary*. Some DBMSs contain variations of these types as well as additional types.

- *User-defined data types.* Some DBMSs allow you to define your own data types based on the system-supplied types. For example, in Microsoft SQL Server, you can define a state data type with a length of 2 that is based on the character data type. Defining this data type helps maintain conformity across all tables that include a state field. In every table, any field of state data type would be consistent and identical.

Table 8.1 shows a set of common data types, each of which is a variation on a generic character, number, or binary data type.

Table 8.1.   Common Data Types

Data type	Description
Binary	Fixed or variable length binary data
String	Fixed or variable length character data
Date	Date and time data
Float	Floating point numeric data (from -1.79E+308 through 1.79E+308 in Microsoft SQL Server 2000)
Decimal	Fixed precision and scale numeric data (from $-10^{38} + 1$ through $10^{38} - 1$ in SQL Server 2000)

Table 8.1.   Common Data Types   *(continued)*

Data type	Description
Integer	Integer (whole number) data. Different DBMSs have different variations with upper limits at 255, 32,767, or 2,147,483,647
(Long) Integer	Integer value of longer ranges than the Integer type listed above
Monetary	Currency values with fixed scale
(Double) Float	Float value with double-precision data range over regular Float data type

Data types also specify how data is displayed. For example, fields of the Float, Money, and Integer data types all store numeric data. However, each type of data is stored, calculated, and displayed in a different format. Because their data is stored in different formats, different data types consume different amounts of storage space.

Note   The double variants of a data type can store a number that is twice as large or store a fraction to more decimal places, but they typically use twice as much storage space.

During physical design, you must consider the requirements of each data object and choose the smallest possible data type that will accommodate every possible value for that object or attribute. Each data storage technology—including Microsoft SQL Server, Oracle Database, Sybase Adaptive Server Enterprise, IBM DB2 and Informix, and the NCR Teradata Warehouse—defines its own data types.

Table 8.2 illustrates the columns and their data types, using SQL data types, of the ProductMaster table in the Adventure Works Cycles database.

Table 8.2.   ProductMaster Table

Columns	Data type	Allow nulls
ProductID	uniqueidentifier	Not allowed
Name	text	Not allowed
ProductNumber	text(25)	Allowed
DiscontinuedFlag	bit	Allowed
MakeFlag	bit	Not Allowed
StandardCost	money	Allowed
FinishedGoodsFlag	bit	Not Allowed
Color	text(15)	Allowed
CreatedDate	datetime	Not Allowed
ModifiedDate	datetime	Allowed
SafetyStockLevel	smallint	Allowed
ReorderPoint	smallint	Allowed

Table 8.2.   ProductMaster Table   *(continued)*

Columns	Data type	Allow nulls
ListPrice	money	Allowed
Size	text(50)	Allowed
SizeUnitMeasureCode	char(3)	Allowed
ProductPhotoID	int	Allowed
rowguid	LongBinary	Allowed
WeightUnitMeasureCode	char(3)	Allowed
Weight	float	Allowed
DaysToManufacture	int	Allowed
ProductLine	char(2)	Allowed
DealerPrice	money	Allowed
Class	char(2)	Allowed
Style	char(2)	Allowed
ProductDescriptionID	int	Allowed
ProductSubCategoryID	smallint	Allowed
ProductModelID	int	Allowed

Types of keys

Keys are an important part of a relational database. Keys uniquely identify each instance of an entity within the data model. Keys also provide the mechanism for tying entities together.

A relational database might use several types of keys:

- *Primary keys* that uniquely identify each row of data in a table. To assign the primary key of a table, identify the attribute that is unique for each instance of the entity. For example, SalesOrderID is unique for each order and is the primary key for the SalesOrderHeader table. In some cases, you might need to create a new attribute to accomplish this. Most DBMSs provide several mechanisms for creating primary keys, including auto-generation of unique identifiers and the ability to create *composite keys*, which enforces uniqueness across two columns, such as SalesOrderID and LineNumber in the SalesOrderDetail table).

Note   Another frequent practice is to use *smart keys*, in which the key has some relation to the domain data—for example, using BLDG001 to identify records in a table storing building information.

- *Foreign keys* that link two tables. For example, ProductID is a foreign key in the SalesOrderDetail table. The attribute ProductID is the primary key in the ProductMaster table and links the SalesOrderDetail and ProductMaster tables. This allows the SalesOrderDetail table to refer to a product by its unique ID, thereby avoiding redundant product data such as name and description in the two tables.

On the CD   For the complete database schema of the Adventure Works Cycles database, refer to Adventure Works Cycles Data Schema.vsd in the \SolutionDocuments\Chapter08 folder on the CD.

How to Implement Relationships

Various relationships can exist between database tables. Just as the entities and attributes that are identified during logical design are represented as tables and columns in physical design, the relationships that are identified during logical design must be represented in the database during physical design.

In the physical database design, you represent relationships between entities by adding the keys from one entity table to other entity tables so that the entities are bound together by the common key value.

A relationship can represent one of the following multiplicities:

- One-to-one relationship
- One-to-many relationship
- Many-to-many relationship

One-to-one relationship

In a *one-to-one relationship*, an instance of one entity is directly related to the corresponding instance of the other entity. For example, every department can have only one faculty member as the head of the department. In addition, a faculty member can be the head of only one department. If both entities are required for the relationship, the entities and their relationship can be represented in one of three ways:

- *As one table.* You can combine two entities into one table and use the primary keys as a composite key of the combined tables. The advantage of combining the entities into one table is that you do not need to maintain separate tables. This technique eliminates the need for query parsers to deal with a join condition. It also uses space storage more efficiently. The disadvantage is that if the relationship changes some time in the future, reversing this design decision might be costly.

- *As two tables.* You can keep each entity in its own table and add the primary key of one entity as a foreign key of the other entity. Often, there is an implied parent-child relationship between entities. In such situations, you should add the primary key of the parent entity as a foreign key in the child entity because the child entity needs the parent entity to exist. This arrangement forces the database to allow only unique entries in each key field and helps to ensure that each instance of one entity can relate to only one instance of the other entity.

- *As multiple tables.* If the relationship between the entities is optional and the parent entity can exist without a related instance of the child entity, you should create a separate table for each entity and use foreign keys to implement the relationship. For example, consider an organization that assigns cars to employees and provides insurance policies for both the driver and the car. There might be a situation when no car is assigned to an employee or a car has no assigned driver. In addition, the insurance policy might not exist as yet. Therefore, the relationship between the three entities is optional. You can use three tables and create a join table containing all three keys or implement two foreign keys in each table.

Figure 8.2 illustrates the one-to-one relationship between two tables.

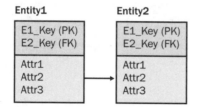

Entity1

| E1_Key (PK) |
| E2_Key (FK) |
| Attr1 |
| Attr2 |
| Attr3 |

Entity2

| E1_Key (PK) |
| E2_Key (FK) |
| Attr1 |
| Attr2 |
| Attr3 |

Figure 8.2.   One-to-one relationship

One-to-many relationship

The physical design of a *one-to-many relationship* requires that you define tables for a parent entity such as Customer and a child entity such as Order, where many child entities can exist for each parent entity. It requires the use of foreign keys in the child entity that determines the existence of the relationship. Enforcing the relationship involves confirming that the foreign key is a valid parent entity.

Note   A one-to-many relationship is used frequently in data design because it tends to use storage space efficiently.

Figure 8.3 illustrates the one-to-many relationship between two tables.

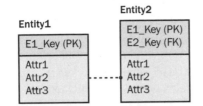

Figure 8.3.   One-to-many relationship

Many-to-many relationships

Most relational database systems, including SQL Server, cannot directly represent a *many-to-many relationship*, except by using denormalization. (You will learn more about normalization in Lesson 2.) Many DBMSs work around this problem by using a new table, called a *join table*, to hold information that maintains the relationship between the entities.

In Figure 8.4, the Employee and Client entities have a many-to-many relationship. A single Employee can contract with many Clients, and a single Client can have contracts with many Employees. Because this relationship cannot be expressed directly, each entity's primary key is used as a foreign key in a separate Contracts table. This foreign key pair uniquely identifies the relationship between the Employee table and the Client table.

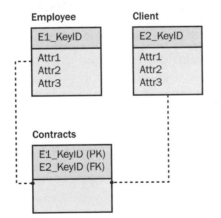

Figure 8.4.   Many-to-many relationship

Lesson 2: Optimizing Data Access

The goal of optimization is to minimize the response time for each query and to maximize the throughput of the entire database server by minimizing network traffic, disk I/O, and processor time. This goal is achieved by understanding the application's requirements, the logical and physical structure of the data, and the trade-offs between conflicting uses of the database, such as a large number of write-intensive insertions and heavy read-intensive queries.

In this lesson, you will learn about the guidelines for optimizing data access. You will also learn about optimizing data access by indexing, partitioning, normalizing, and denormalizing data.

After this lesson, you will be able to

- List the best practices for optimizing data access.
- Describe the impact of indexing data.
- Describe the purpose of partitioning data.
- Describe the purpose of normalizing data.

Estimated lesson time: 10 minutes

What Are the Best Practices for Optimizing Data Access?

Performance issues should be considered throughout the development cycle and not at the end when the system is implemented. Data access performance affects the overall performance of the application. You can achieve significant performance improvements by optimizing both application and database design from the beginning.

Optimize the application

When you design an application that accesses a database, consider the following coding guidelines:

- Minimize roundtrip requests for result sets.
- Minimize the amount of data involved in a result set.
- Reduce concurrency (multiple users editing the same record) and resolve conflicts efficiently.
- Carefully evaluate the tradeoffs between managing data results on the client or on the server, especially for Web-based applications.

Stress test the application

The only way you can understand the behavior of your application is to run it under a moderate load with a test tool such as the Microsoft Web Application Stress tool, and then execute the application. You cannot adequately determine where bottlenecks exist in your application unless you test it under load. It is usually a better practice to stress test your application than it is to stress test your users.

Use transactions wisely

Transactions should be short-lived and incorporate only what is required. Distributed transactions require significant overhead that can adversely impact application performance. As such, they should be used only when necessary.

Communicate effectively across boundaries

Any cross-boundary communication that occurs between applications or processes adversely impacts performance. You can minimize this impact by minimizing the number of transitions that occur. For example, it is more efficient to call a method requiring six input parameters than it is to set six properties and then call the method. This design pattern promotes the use of a stateless business logic layer.

Optimize the database

The most commonly used techniques to optimize data access include:

- Indexing data
- Partitioning data
- Normalizing data

Note   You will learn about these techniques in detail in the next few topics in this lesson.

To remove bottlenecks while accessing and writing to the database, you can perform the following steps:

- Identify potential indexes, but do not index excessively.
- If using Microsoft SQL Server, use SQL Server Profiler and Index Tuning Wizard.
- Monitor total processor usage; desired range is 75 to 80 percent processor time.
- Analyze query plans by using Query Analyzer to optimize queries.
- Use stored procedures to maximize performance.
- Normalize data that is written frequently.
- Denormalize data that is read frequently.

How to Index Data

You need to optimize a system for both accessing and updating data. Indexing is one of the most commonly used techniques for optimizing data access. An *index* is an ordered list of rows in a table that a DBMS can use to accelerate lookup operations.

Purpose of an index

An index is structured like a tree and maintains a sorted list of a specific set of data. Queries performed on indexed data are much faster and more efficient than queries on data that is not indexed. Rather than scanning an entire table each time a value is needed, the DBMS can use the index to quickly lead the query to the direct location of the required data because the index records the location of the data in the table.

Benefits of indexing

Some of the benefits of indexing include:

- *Faster data access.* Indexes in databases are similar to indexes in books. In a book, an index allows you to find information quickly without reading the entire book. In a database, an index allows the DBMS to find data in a table without scanning the entire table.
- *Data integrity.* Some DBMSs allow indexes to ensure the uniqueness of each record of a table.

Types of indexes

To optimize retrieval of data, you can use two types of indexes:

- *Clustered.* A clustered index physically reorders the rows of data in the table to match the order of the index. It is a very high-performance index for read operations. A clustered index is usually defined as a table's primary index. (Most DBMSs allow only one clustered index per table.) For example, the SalesOrderDetail table uses the columns SalesOrderID and LineNumber as the clustered index. One limitation of clustered indexes is that they can slow down writes because rows might be physically rearranged frequently.
- *Nonclustered.* A nonclustered index simply maintains a small table of index information about a column or group of columns. A table can have many nonclustered indexes.

How to Partition Data

Often, the number of records stored in a table increases to a level at which data optimization techniques can no longer help improve data access speed. In such a situation, you must partition the tables. You can implement horizontal or vertical partitioning of large data tables to increase processing speed.

Horizontal partitioning

In *horizontal partitioning*, you divide a table containing many rows into multiple tables containing the same columns. However, each table contains a subset of the data. For example, one table might contain all customer names with last names beginning with the letters A through M, and another table contains all customer names with last names beginning with the letters N through Z.

Vertical partitioning

In *vertical partitioning*, you divide a table containing many columns into multiple tables containing rows with equivalent unique identifiers. For example, one table might contain read-only data, whereas the other table contains updateable data. In a large data environment, partitioning can extend across several database servers to further distribute the workload.

How to Normalize Data

Normalization is the process of progressively refining a logical model to eliminate duplicate data from a database. Normalization usually involves dividing a database into two or more tables and defining relationships among these tables.

Database theorists have evolved standards of increasingly restrictive constraints, or *normal forms*, on the layout of databases. Applying these normal forms results in a normalized database. These standards have generated at least five commonly accepted normal form levels, each progressively more restrictive on data duplication than the preceding one.

Tip   Typically, you work toward achieving the third normal form because it is a compromise between too little normalization and too much.

Benefits of normalization

Normalized databases typically include more tables with fewer columns than non-normalized databases. Normalizing a database accomplishes the following:

- Minimized duplication of information

    A normalized database contains less duplicate information than a non-normalized database. For example, you need to store timesheet and invoice information in a database. Storing timesheet information in the Invoice table would eventually cause this table to include a large amount of redundant data, such as employee, job, task, and client information. Normalizing the database results in separate, related tables for timesheets and invoices, thus avoiding duplication.

- Reduced data inconsistencies

  Normalization reduces data inconsistencies by maintaining table relationships. For example, if a client's telephone number is stored in multiple tables or in multiple records within the same table, and the number changes, the telephone number might not be changed in all locations. If a client's telephone number is stored only once in one table, there is minimal chance of data inconsistency.

- Faster data modification, including insertions, updates, and deletions

  Normalization speeds up the data modification process in a database. For example, removing client names and address information from the Invoice table results in less data to track and manipulate when working with an invoice. The removed data is not lost because it still exists in the Client table. Additionally, reducing duplicated information improves performance during updates because fewer values must be modified in the tables.

Note   Normalization can reduce performance for write operations due to locking conflicts and the potential of increased row sizes after the write.

The first normal form

The first step in normalizing a database is to ensure that the tables are in first normal form. To accomplish this step, the tables must adhere to the following criteria:

- Tables must be two-dimensional and have data organized as columns and rows. Entities specified in the logical data model are transformed into database tables represented in a two-dimensional table, similar to a spreadsheet.
- Each cell must contain one value.
- Each column must have a single meaning. For example, you cannot have a dual-purpose column such as Order Date/Delivery Date.

Figure 8.5 shows the Timesheet table, which was not originally in first normal form. The original Timesheet table had no unique identifier and not all of its attributes were singularly tied to one piece of information. Also, each column in the Timesheet table could have multiple meanings. In the first normal form, the Employee attribute can be divided into two distinct attributes: EmployeeFirstName and EmployeeLastName.

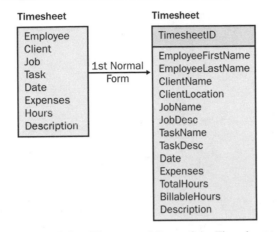

Figure 8.5.   First normal form of the Timesheet table

The second normal form

The second normal form is a bridge process that eventually leads to the third normal form. To move a data design to second normal form, you must look at several instances of an entity and move any redundant data within an entity's attributes to a separate table.

- Eliminate redundant data within an entity.
- Move attributes that depend on only part of a multivalue key to a separate table.
- Consolidate information when possible.

Figure 8.6 shows the Timesheet table. If a client moves to a different city, the client database must be updated, as well as every timesheet that references that client. The solution is to remove the client information from the Timesheet table and replace the information in the Timesheet table with a ClientID foreign key that corresponds to the ClientID primary key of the Clients table. The Timesheet table can then find the client's name and address by means of the foreign key relationship. When the address of a client changes, the change is recorded in the Client table only. Similarly, the second normal form replaces the employee information with an EmployeeID foreign key that links the timesheet to the individual employee who enters information into the timesheet. The second normal form also eliminates any other duplicate information. The JobName and JobDesc attributes have been replaced with a single attribute, JobDesc, because the job description would likely contain the job name. This logic also applies to the TaskName and TaskDesc attributes.

Timesheet

TimesheetID
EmployeeFirstName
EmployeeLastName
ClientName
ClientLocation
JobName
JobDesc
TaskName
TaskDesc
Date
Expenses
TotalHours
BillableHours
Description

2nd Normal Form →

Timesheet

TimesheetID
EmployeeID
ClientID
JobDesc
Date
Expenses
TotalHours
BillableHours
Description

Figure 8.6.   Second normal form of the Timesheet table

The third normal form

Third normal form is the level to which most design teams strive to normalize their data designs. Third normal form eliminates any columns that do not depend on a key value for their existence. Any data not directly related to the entity is generally moved to another table. Third normal form is generally the final form that you should implement.

- Eliminate any columns that do not depend on a key value for their existence.
- Generally, move any data not directly related to the entity to another table.
- Reduce or eliminate update and deletion anomalies.
- Verify that no redundant data remains.

Third normal form helps to avoid update and deletion anomalies because all data can be reached by means of foreign key values, and redundant data within each table no longer exists. This level of normalization greatly increases database robustness and generates a more optimized design.

Figure 8.7 shows the Timesheet entity that has been normalized to third normal form. All attributes that do not depend on the primary key have been moved into separate tables, and foreign keys now take the place of unrelated data. This form, like second normal form, further eliminates update and deletion anomalies because all data can be directly referenced from one point, instead of residing in multiple tables within the database.

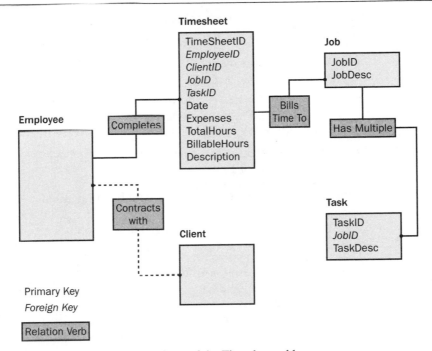

Figure 8.7.   Third normal form of the Timesheet table

Denormalization of Tables

Optimizing the physical data design for updates is a common practice. In many systems, data changes frequently, and having a system optimized for this activity is important.

A database design that is based solely on normalization rules produces a large number of narrow tables. This design technique reduces data redundancy and decreases the number of pages on disk that are required to store the data. However, complex joins are required to retrieve data.

Denormalization is the process of reversing normalization to generate tables with more fields that require fewer joins. Depending on the type of queries and updates that are being performed on the database, denormalization can dramatically increase its overall performance. For this reason, denormalization is a common optimization technique even though some DBMS systems include an optimizer that enables joins to be performed efficiently.

When deciding whether to use denormalization as an optimization technique, keep the following issues in mind:

- The data becomes more redundant. Related data is moved into one table to increase query performance and reduce disk access times.
- The number of tables is reduced, which makes query programming and administration easier. The disadvantage is that the data is located in fewer places, thus creating tables with more fields and possibly duplicating data across tables.
- Data that appears in more than one place can get out of synchronization if it is updated in one table and not others.

Although there are tradeoffs between a highly normalized physical data design and an intelligently denormalized design, a strategy of selective and intelligent denormalization most often results in the greatest performance gains.

Data that is over-normalized can cause performance issues in certain types of applications and can adversely affect read and write operations. Normalizing the ER model is a major step in creating the logical database design. The goal of normalization is to ensure that there is only one way to know a fact. It eliminates redundancy in the data and ensures that the correct business rules are recorded. The logical database design is implementation-independent—without details of a specific DBMS. However, for this discussion, a relational model is assumed.

During physical design, the database team must consider the following:

- Physical database constraints, such as memory and disk size.
- Performance tuning considerations, such as deadlock detection, indexing, and hot spots.
- Primary keys and foreign keys.
- Design of triggers.
- Stored procedures guidelines.
- Normalization. Although the third normal form is often appropriate, evaluate fourth and fifth normal forms if justified by the target data.
- Application object model considerations. Some tables that do not appear in the logical data model might be required to support the application.
- Data migration from any legacy database systems.
- Quality of existing data.
- Operational considerations, such as cluster/failover, backup process, and update/deployment process.

Lesson 3: Implementing Data Validation

In addition to the performance of the database, you need to ensure the quality of the data stored by the database. This means that the database implements data integrity and stores valid data that conforms to the business rules.

In this lesson, you will learn about data integrity requirements of the solution. You will also learn how to identify business rules and implement them in the database and the business layer.

After this lesson, you will be able to

- Define data integrity.
- Identify data integrity requirements.
- Identify business rules.
- Implement business rules in a database.
- Implement business rules as components.

Estimated lesson time: 15 minutes

What Is Data Integrity?

Data integrity refers to the consistency and accuracy of data. An important step in database planning is deciding how to ensure this integrity. You can implement three types of data integrity in a database: domain, entity, and referential.

Domain integrity

Domain integrity specifies a set of valid data values for a column and determines whether null values are to be allowed. You can enforce domain integrity by implementing validity checking and restricting the data type, format, or range of possible values that are allowed in a column. For example, you must store discount rates. According to business rules, the discount rate must be between 2 percent and 18 percent. In addition, the discount rate cannot be zero because it causes errors in calculations.

Entity integrity

Entity integrity requires that each row in a table has a unique identifier, known as the *primary key value*. Whether the primary key value can be changed, or whether an entire row can be deleted, depends on the level of referential integrity that is required between the primary key of the table and the foreign keys of any other tables. For example, a customer record must have a primary key. If there is a business need for the key to be changed, such as a merger, or for the record to be inactivated but not deleted, the business rules determine your choices in entity and referential integrity.

When used together, domain and entity integrity help to ensure that each entity in a physical design maintains consistency. When planning for databases in your design, you must consider consistency among entities and data validity within the entities as important additional aspects of data integrity.

Referential integrity

The domain and entity integrity categories suffice for enforcing data integrity in a single table. However, many databases contain multiple tables with parent and child entities and are related. When both entities in a relationship must exist and must have a valid link with one another, *referential integrity* ensures that these conditions are met. Referential integrity ensures that the relationships between the primary keys (in the parent entity's table) and foreign keys (in the child entity's table) are always maintained.

As a result of the restrictions that referential integrity imposes on tables, it is important that you consider what to do when a primary key must be updated or deleted. If the primary key value in the parent entity is changed or deleted, the instance of that entity is modified. Consequently, all child entities that referenced the parent entity must be modified as appropriate. By cascading through all related child tables and updating or deleting data as necessary, the database can maintain referential integrity.

Data validation

It is important to have valid data. Domain, entity, and referential integrity ensure that data exists where necessary and that entities follow a basic set of rules for existence. None of these data integrity categories, however, can determine whether the data is valid. You can ensure that the data is correct by checking it using the following methods:

- *Range checking* involves making sure that the data's value is within a set of limits determined by the functional specification.
- *Data format checking* involves making sure that the data conforms to a set of format specifications, such as currency formatting, telephone number formatting, or length-of-character strings.
- *Data type checking* involves making sure that the data belongs to the proper data type and that an invalid data type is not used to represent the data when it is written to the database.

To ensure that queries return correct information, you must make sure that the information being stored is valid. You can validate data in two ways:

- *Client-side checks* can ensure that invalid data is not posted to a database. These checks can be coded in many ways, including in scripts, in the user interface controls, as part of an executable program, or as part of a Web page. For example, if a field on a Web page denotes a monetary value, validation controls on the page can ensure that the information in that field is the proper data type and format.

- *Server-side checks*, which are executed by the DBMS engine, can be implemented with field data types, default values, and constraints. These checks can also ensure that invalid data is not stored in the database.

The methods or combination of methods that you use depends on the objectives and requirements of the solution. Although more difficult to maintain than server-side checks, client-side checks can help decrease the processing load on the DBMS server. Server-side checks might present a bottleneck if the server has to validate many client requests. Remember that a strong test process is needed to verify that the business rules have been correctly implemented while maintaining a high quality of user experience.

How to Identify Data Integrity Requirements

Identifying data integrity requirements helps ensure that all logical and physical requirements for a solution are met and that the physical design supports the full intent of your specification.

When attempting to identify the data integrity requirements of a solution, you must start with the data requirements specified during the solution's design. When you examine the data requirements, identify areas within the requirements in which uniqueness, or limits and constraints, has been specified or deemed necessary to help ensure that entities can exist and be implemented correctly.

If limits and constraints are specified, you must determine whether the limits and constraints are bound to an entity or to a relationship between entities. Consider the following examples:

- You need to determine whether a particular task can exist without a related job number. If it cannot exist without a job number, you must implement a data integrity requirement to ensure that no instance of that task is created without a corresponding job number.

- A consultant must submit a weekly timesheet for a client. No timesheet can duplicate another timesheet, and no two timesheets can represent the same time or work performed by a consultant. Therefore, a data integrity requirement exists for guaranteeing the uniqueness of timesheet information. Each timesheet within the database must be represented by a unique attribute or a combination of unique attributes.

Finally, you must implement referential integrity requirements to ensure that all relationships are maintained. For example, if a customer wants to be removed from the database, a referential integrity requirement must ensure that the customer cannot be deleted as long as payment has not been received for any outstanding invoices.

How to Identify Business Rules

Business rules form a foundation for encapsulating logic from the data requirements into the solution. Business rules represent logic specified within a solution.

The data development team already identified many of the business rules for the solution while identifying requirements. The team must reexamine the solution's data requirements for the criteria that the data integrity rules must satisfy. The team should also review any existing process documentation, use cases, and usage scenarios to identify the data-centric processes that are currently being executed and the processes that must be executed in the future.

While identifying business rules, consider the following criteria:

- *Conditions that must be satisfied for data to be considered valid.* For example, issues that you might consider when determining applicable business rules include whether a product can be shipped to a customer if no payment has been received.

- *Conditions that must be avoided.* For example, issues you might consider include whether product pricing can drop below certain levels or whether inventory levels for products can drop below zero.

- *Sequences in which events must occur.* For example, you must determine what to do when an inventory product drops below zero or when payment for an order is received.

You can implement business rules and data integrity requirements by using the following methods:

- *Directly in the database.* Most DBMSs provide automated processes that can be bound to tables and columns to enforce business rules and data integrity requirements.

- *Programmatically within or outside the database.* You can code business rules and data integrity requirements into client applications, create components that can be deployed on application servers, or use programming logic and languages that are part of the database engine.

The primary distinction between these two methods is that the former involves rules that are automatically processed by the database engine, whereas the latter involves rules that must be called or invoked by an application's logic.

Determining where to implement rules is often based on the nature of the required programming logic. Most relational database engines now execute automatic methods that incorporate simple and commonly required application logic. This logic applies to specific business rule tasks and resides in a single location. It is also easily updated and efficient to execute. If more complex logic is required, it can be implemented as application code that can reside in any of the three service layers: user, business, or data.

How to Implement Business Rules in a Database

If you choose to implement business rules directly in the database, the DBMS performs much of the work for you by using its automatic and built-in checks.

Within the database engine, business rules and data integrity requirements can be enforced through a set of criteria that data must either meet or not meet. Usually, most of the data integrity requirements are implemented by using the automatic controls and properties of the database engine. This automatic control involves the specification, or declaration, of the criteria at the time an object (such as a field, table, index, or key) is created.

Database features for implementing business rules

Enforcing data integrity through built-in database features has some distinct benefits: integrity is enforced automatically, and the criteria do not have to be maintained or updated unless they change. You can use the following database features to enforce data integrity:

- *Data types.* Setting appropriate data types for the fields in a database ensures that incorrect types of data cannot be added to the table. For example, if a data type of Date is specified, the database rejects any string or numeric value that is not in a date format. Data types ensure that the format of the data is valid, but it cannot ensure that the value is valid.

- *Default values.* Default values specify the values to be used for a field when the values have not been explicitly supplied in INSERT statements. By using default values in your table definitions, you can ensure that a field value is valid even when a user does not explicitly supply it.

- *Data validation rules.* Data validation rules encapsulate logic for specifying data values that are acceptable in a table's fields. They can specify the length of a field, an input mask, or a range of valid values. For example, you can use data validation rules for making simple comparisons.

- *Keys.* Most database engines can automatically monitor referential integrity between tables. The primary and foreign key relationships from the physical model directly correspond to the database engine's key settings. These key settings automatically enforce referential integrity between linked tables.

- *Triggers.* Triggers are sets of programmatic statements that are explicitly defined for a particular table. When a specific action (such as an insert, update, or delete) occurs in that table, the trigger causes the statements to automatically run. For example, a trigger can verify data in other tables or perform an automatic update to a different table.

Programmatic implementation of business rules

The team's analysis will determine that certain business rules are best implemented in the business layer and others in the data layer. You can implement business rules programmatically in the data layer by using the following methods:

- *Stored procedures.* Stored procedures are named collections of SQL statements that are stored on the DBMS. They are precompiled, eliminating the need for the query analyzer to parse the statement every time the stored procedure is called. By using stored procedures, you can write one piece of code that performs an action, store it, and call it repeatedly as necessary.

  Stored procedures are useful for controlling changes to a table. For example, instead of granting a user update rights to a specific table, you can allow updates to the table only through stored procedures. You can then determine whether the modifications are valid and then either disregard or apply the change.

  The flow of a process can also be handled through the use of stored procedures. For example, you can change or reorder several tables by using a stored procedure. You can also use stored procedures to perform administrative tasks.

- *Scripts.* Typically, you write a script in a database to automate a process that is either impractical or inefficiently handled by the DBMS engine. For example, you might write a script that maintains a database by importing a series of mainframe downloads, re-indexing the database, and then copying a report file to another file server.

The script logic can be written in any of several languages. Each script executes outside the memory space of the DBMS and might perform more tasks than simply manipulating data. Scripts are generally used in a command-line environment or as part of a batch process that performs other tasks.

How to Implement Data Validation in Components

In a multitier application, a data service acts as an intermediary between the application's business services and its data store. Therefore, if there are any changes to the data store, the application's business services do not need to be changed. Data services perform basic tasks such as creating, retrieving, updating, and deleting data. Data services are also used to manipulate data within the database and to implement data integrity. You can design and develop components to implement data services in an application.

Components are executable collections of code that reside on a server or within another program. Components are similar to scripts, but allow for tighter integration with development environments, database engines, and custom code.

You can enforce data integrity through logic that is encapsulated in a component and is called or invoked as needed. The criteria for the logic are determined by the business rules, including any additional data integrity requirements that have been identified for the solution.

Typically, components are deployed on application servers, on a separate computer. Some of the benefits of deploying components on application servers include:

- *Easier maintenance.* Because the code is stored in only one or a few locations, it is much easier to maintain than if it were included in the application itself. The increased cost of an application server might be offset by the maintainability of the system. Any necessary changes can be made on only one or a few computers, as opposed to possibly thousands of clients.
- *Scalability.* As the load on the system increases, additional application servers can be added to distribute the load.

Implementing business rules by using components can increase the overall cost of the solution. The added cost is associated not only with the hardware and software of the computers serving as the application server, but also in the development costs of creating and maintaining the code that will serve the data access requests.

Activity: Creating a Data Schema

In this activity, you use what you learned in the lesson to create a data schema.

Exercise 1: Creating a Data Schema

This exercise builds on the Adventure Works Cycles scenario. Customers of Adventure Works Cycles use the Sales Order form to order products. Some of the considerations for order processing are:

- The customer provides a purchase order number to start an order.
- An order can be revised.
- Discounts are applied per item in an order.

You need to design a data schema for capturing all information in the Sales Order form. The data schema should include:

- One or more tables that store order-related data
- Primary and foreign keys
- Data types for all columns
- Indexes
- Fields needed for data or business requirements

To get started with this exercise, use the data schema that is provided on the P08 Schema Starter tab in the file C08Ex1.vsd in the \SolutionDocuments\Chapter08 folder on the CD. To view the Sales Order form, open the file C08Ex1.doc in the \SolutionDocuments\Chapter08 folder on the CD.

You can view one of the probable solutions to this exercise in the file C08Ex1_ShortAnswer.vsd in the \SolutionDocuments\Chapter08 folder on the CD. You can also design a detailed data schema as illustrated in the file C08Ex1_LongAnswer.vsd in the \SolutionDocuments\Chapter08 folder on the CD. To view the data schema for the complete Adventure Works Cycles system, open the file Adventure Works Cycles Data Schema.vsd in the \SolutionDocs\Chapter08 folder on the CD.

Summary

- In the planning phase, the project team analyzes the data requirements of the solution and specifies how data will be structured, stored, accessed, and validated in the solution.

- A database schema reflects the entities of the problem, attributes of the entities, and the relationships between entities.

- The physical data model of a DBMS defines the internal structure that the DBMS uses to keep track of data.

- The three physical data models that are typically used are flat files, the hierarchical model, and the relational model.

- The entities and attributes that are derived during logical design are mapped to tables, fields, and relationships in a database.

- Tables are the physical representation of entities in a relational database.

- Columns are the physical representation of attributes in a relational database.

- Data types specify the kind of data that is stored in a field and how the data is displayed.

- Keys uniquely identify each instance of an entity within the data model.

- Primary keys uniquely identify each row of data in a table.

- Foreign keys link two tables in a database.

- Relationships between entities are represented by adding the keys of one entity table to other entity tables.

- To optimize the performance of a database, you need to:
    - Optimize your database.
    - Stress test the application.
    - Use transactions wisely.
    - Communicate effectively across borders.

- An index is an ordered list of rows in a table that a DBMS can use to accelerate lookup operations.

- You can optimize processing speed of huge tables by partitioning data, either vertically or horizontally.

- In horizontal partitioning, you segment a table containing a large number of rows into multiple tables containing the same columns.

- In vertical partitioning, you segment a table containing a large number of columns into multiple tables containing rows with equivalent unique identifiers.

- Normalization is the process of progressively refining a logical model to eliminate duplicate data and wasted space from a database.

- Normalization results in reduced data inconsistencies and faster data modification.

- Denormalization is the process of reversing normalization to generate tables with more fields that require fewer joins, which can improve query processing.

- Data integrity refers to the consistency and accuracy of data.

- Domain integrity specifies a set of legitimate data values for a column and determines whether null values are to be allowed.

- Entity integrity requires that each row in a table has a unique identifier, known as the primary key value.

- Referential integrity ensures that the relationships between the primary keys (in the parent entity's table) and foreign keys (in the child entity's table) are always maintained.

- Identifying data integrity requirements helps ensure that all logical and physical requirements for a solution are met and that the physical design supports the full intent of your specification.

- Identifying business rules includes identifying conditions that must be met, conditions that must be avoided, and sequences in which events must occur.

- You can implement business rules in a database by using the built-in checks of the DBMS engine, such as data types, data validation rules, default values, keys, and triggers.

- You can implement business rules in a database programmatically by using stored procedures and scripts.

- You can implement business rules by using components that are deployed on application servers.

Review

The following questions are intended to reinforce key information presented in this chapter. If you are unable to answer a question, review the lesson materials and try the question again. You can find answers to the questions in the appendix.

1. How is the data model designed during the planning phase?

2. What is the purpose of the database schema?

3. What are the characteristics of attributes?

4. What is the purpose of specifying data types in a database?

5. How do most DBMSs support a many-to-many relationship?

6. How do you optimize transactions for good system performance?

7. What is the impact of indexing on data access?

8. What is the difference between horizontal and vertical partitioning?

9. What are the benefits of normalization?

10. What is denormalization?

11. What are the three types of data integrity that can be enforced in a database?

12. How do you identify data integrity requirements?

13. What are the criteria for identifying business rules?

14. How do keys implement referential integrity?

15. What are the benefits of using components to implement business rules?

C H A P T E R   9

Designing Security Specifications

About This Chapter

In this chapter, you will learn how to design security in an application. Designing security features and policies is one of the most important aspects of application development. As the amount of money that is spent on securing corporate networks increases, so do the losses that are accrued by businesses in terms of stolen intellectual property, system downtime, lost productivity, damage to reputation, and lost consumer confidence. It is possible, however, to defend your business applications in this hostile environment by adding the appropriate authentication and authorization schemes, ensuring data integrity with encryption, and performing data validation.

Before You Begin

To complete the lessons in this chapter, you must have

- A general understanding of Microsoft® technologies.
- Familiarity with security concepts.

Lesson 1: Overview of Security in Application Development

You can secure your application by employing several security mechanisms, such as firewalls, proxies, secure channels, and authentication schemes. However, all it takes for a security breach to occur is for an attacker to find one weakness in your system. In this lesson, you will learn about some common security weaknesses in applications and how some malicious users exploit these security weaknesses. You will also learn about some drawbacks of the traditional security models. You will then learn about some important principles of secure coding.

After this lesson, you will be able to

- Identify some of the common security vulnerabilities of applications.
- Identify some of the drawbacks of traditional security models.
- Explain some of the security principles for designing secure applications.
- Define some security terms.

Estimated lesson time: 15 minutes

Common Types of Security Vulnerabilities

Malicious attackers use various methods to exploit system vulnerabilities to achieve their goals. Vulnerabilities are weak points or loopholes in security that an attacker exploits to gain access to an organization's network or to resources on the network. Some vulnerabilities, such as weak passwords, are not the result of application or software development design decisions. However, it is important for an organization to be aware of such security weaknesses to better protect its systems. Common vulnerabilities of applications include:

- *Weak passwords.* A weak password might give an attacker access not only to a computer, but to the entire network to which the computer is connected.
- *Misconfigured software.* Often the manner in which software is configured makes the system vulnerable. If services are configured to use the local system account or are given more permissions than required, attackers can exploit the services to gain access to the system and perform malicious actions on the system.
- *Social engineering,* A common form of discovering passwords that generally occurs when users are not aware of security issues and can be deceived into revealing their passwords. For example, an attacker posing as a help desk administrator might persuade a user to reveal his or her password under the pretext of performing an administrative task.

- *Internet connections.* The default installation of Internet Information Services (IIS) version 5.0 often enables more services and ports than are necessary for the operation of a specific application. These additional services and ports provide more opportunities for potential attacks. For example, modem connections bypass firewalls that protect networks from outside intruders. If an intruder can identify the modem telephone number and password, the intruder can connect to any computer on the network.

- *Unencrypted data transfer.* If the data sent between a server and the users is in clear text, there is a possibility that the data can be intercepted, read, and altered during transmission by an attacker.

- *Buffer overrun.* Malicious users probe applications looking for ways to trigger a buffer overrun because they can use a buffer overrun to cause an application or an operating system to crash. They can then find more security weaknesses by reading error messages.

- *SQL injection.* SQL injection occurs when developers dynamically build SQL statements by using user input. The attacker can modify the SQL statement and make it perform operations that were not intended.

- *Secrets in code.* Many security problems are created when a malicious user is able to find secrets that are embedded in code, such as passwords and encryption keys.

More Info   For more information about security issues, refer to the *Microsoft Windows Security Resource Kit* (Microsoft Press, 2003).

Drawbacks of Traditional Security Models

Traditional security models do not adequately meet the security challenges presented by the networked computing environment. Most traditional security models restrict access to resources based on the identity of the user who is running the code. There is no specific mechanism in this model to restrict resources based on the identity of the code.

Security that is based on user identity is circumvented if a trusted user unknowingly runs malicious code. A trusted user can inadvertently launch malicious code by:

- Opening an e-mail attachment.
- Running a script that is embedded on a Web page.
- Opening a file that was downloaded from the Internet.

Principles for Creating Security Strategies

To design a secure application, you should be familiar with the following principles of security and employ them when creating security strategies:

- *Rely on tested and proven security systems.* Whenever possible, you should rely on tested and proven security systems rather than creating your own custom solution. Use industry-proven algorithms, techniques, platform-supplied infrastructure, and vendor-tested and supported technologies. If you decide to develop a custom security infrastructure, validate your approach and techniques with expert auditing and security review organizations before and after implementing them.

- *Never trust external input.* You should validate all data that is entered by users or submitted by other services.

- *Assume that external systems are not secure.* If your application receives unencrypted sensitive data from an external system, assume that the information is compromised.

- *Apply the principle of least privilege.* Do not enable more attributes on service accounts than those minimally needed by the application. Access resources with accounts that have the minimal permissions required.

- *Reduce available components and data.* Risk will increase with the number of components and amount of data you have made available through the application, so you should make available only the functionality that you expect others to use.

- *Default to a secure mode.* Do not enable services, account rights, and technologies that you do not explicitly need. When you deploy the application on client or server computers, its default configuration should be secure.

- *Do not rely on security by obscurity.* Encrypting data implies having keys and a proven encryption algorithm. Secure data storage will prevent access under all circumstances. Mixing up strings, storing information in unexpected file paths, and so on, is not security.

- *Follow STRIDE principles.* Each letter in the STRIDE acronym specifies a different category of security threat: spoofing identity, tampering, repudiation, information disclosure, denial of service, and elevation of privilege. These are classes of security vulnerabilities a system needs to protect itself against.

More Info   For more information about security practices, see *Writing Secure Code* by Michael Howard and David LeBlanc (Microsoft Press, 2002).

Lesson 2: Planning for Application Security

Before you start planning for security features in an application, you must understand the kinds of threats an application is likely to encounter so that you can specify and develop the appropriate security features. Planning for security in applications involves the following tasks:

- *Identify the threats to the application (Threat modeling).* This is the most important task in planning for security. Without first identifying the threats, the security policies cannot be determined. When assessing threats to your application, gather the following information:
    - What are the assets of the organization that need to be protected?
    - What are the threats to each of the assets?
- *Create a security policy to prevent or minimize the threat.* After most of the threats are identified, you need to categorize these threats and define a strategy for each type of threat. You will learn more about mitigation techniques later in this lesson.

    You can use various techniques to identify and categorize threats. One commonly used technique of identifying threats is STRIDE. In this lesson, you will learn about threat modeling with STRIDE.

After this lesson, you will be able to

- Identify the security tasks performed during various stages of the Microsoft Solutions Framework (MSF) design process.
- Explain threat modeling.
- Create a threat model.
- Use the threat model to respond to a threat.

Estimated lesson time: 15 minutes

Security in the Application Development Process

Application security fails most often because security is not planned from the very beginning of product design. If you wait to think about security until the late phases of development, security will be less effective and development and maintenance costs will be higher.

The planning and implementation of security features should persist throughout product development. Table 9.1 shows each phase in the MSF Process Model and the corresponding security initiative.

Table 9.1.   Security Initiatives and the MSF Process Model

Phase	Security initiative
Envisioning	Gather security requirements. The team talks to the customers and stakeholders to learn about sensitive data and operations, privileges each user needs, and how the application currently manages these security requirements. From this information, security requirements are established and listed in the requirements document.
Planning	Create a threat model, discussed in the What Is the STRIDE Threat Model? section, to anticipate security threats. In the functional specification, propose security features that mitigate each identified risk.
Developing	Implement security features as identified in the functional specification.
Stabilizing	Conduct security testing. Revise the threat model if new information about threats is uncovered by research, testing, and customer feedback.
Deploying	Monitor security threats to an application.

After the solution is released to the customer, security and any attacks to the solution are monitored to ensure that the product remains secure. If any breaches occur, the problem is resolved and the circumstances are noted for the next version of the product.

What Is the STRIDE Threat Model?

The STRIDE threat model is a technique used for identifying and categorizing threats to an application. Each letter in the STRIDE acronym specifies a different category of security threat: spoofing identity, tampering, repudiation, information disclosure, denial of service, and elevation of privilege. Most security threats combine more than one element of the STRIDE model:

- **Spoofing identity**   A malicious user poses as a trusted entity. For example, a malicious user might obtain the password of a trusted user to gain access to restricted materials or to send an e-mail message that appears to come from a trusted source.

  Note   IP spoofing is a special case of spoofing identity. It happens when a malicious user inserts a false Internet Protocol (IP) address into an Internet transmission so that the transmission appears to originate from a trusted source. In this way, the malicious user can gain unauthorized access to a computer system.

- **Tampering**   A user gains unauthorized access to a computer and then changes its operation, configuration, or data. Tampering can be either malicious or accidental. For example, accidental tampering can occur when users inadvertently delete files on a network or change a database that they should not have permission to change.

- **Repudiation**   A system administrator or security agent is unable to prove that a user—malicious or otherwise—has performed some action. For example, a malicious user can repudiate having attacked a system because the system did not adequately log events leading to the attack.

- **Information disclosure**   An unauthorized user views private data, such as a file that contains a credit card number and expiration date.

- **Denial of service**   Any attack that attempts to shut down or prevent access to a computing resource. Denial-of-service (DoS) attacks can cause:

  - An application or the operating system to stop functioning

  - The CPU to engage in long, pointless calculations

  - System memory to be consumed so that the functioning of applications and the operating system is impaired

  - Network bandwidth reduction

- **Elevation of privilege**   A user gains access to greater privileges than the administrator intended, creating the opportunity for a malicious user to launch attacks of every other category of security threat.

How to Create a Threat Model

Creating a threat model is a first step in building a secure application. This process involves the following tasks:

1. Arrange for a brainstorming meeting.

   Invite experienced developers and members of every MSF role to the brainstorming session to identify potential threats.

2. List all the possible threats.

   During the brainstorming meeting, provide participants with a proposed list of features and describe the architecture of the product. Instruct the participants to think of threats that might occur between application components and to connections between your application and other systems.

3. Apply the STRIDE security categories.

   After you create an initial listing of possible security threats, use the STRIDE threat model to categorize the threats.

4. Create notes.

   For each security threat, your group should create a note that includes the following information:

   - Type of threat
   - Impact of the attack to the organization in terms of cost and effort
   - The technique that will be used by the attacker to carry out the threat
   - The likelihood of the attack taking place
   - Possible techniques to mitigate this attack

5. Conduct research.

   Inevitably, factual and technical questions will be raised during the brainstorming process. If you conduct your meeting in a facility that can access the Internet, you might be able to resolve research questions during the meeting.

6. Rank the risk of each threat.

   Assign each threat a risk rank by dividing the criticality of the threat by its chance of occurrence.

Example

Figure 9.1 depicts a Web-based expense report application. You will create a threat model for this application.

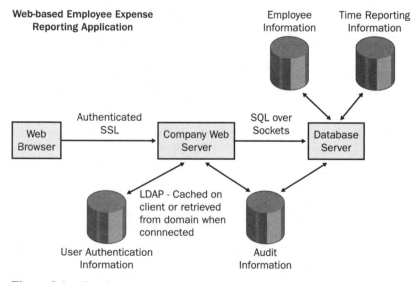

Figure 9.1. Employee expense report application

Threats and their categories

Table 9.2 lists possible threats to the expense report application that were identified during a brainstorming meeting. It also lists their categorization based on the STRIDE model.

Table 9.2.   Threats to the Expense Report Application.

Threat	Category
The time reporting and employee information databases are vulnerable to direct access, which could allow unauthorized users to view and modify confidential data such as historical data.	T, I
The database server can become unavailable if it is flooded with Transmission Control Protocol/Internet Protocol (TCP/IP) packets.	D
Audit logs can be viewed, modified, and deleted by unauthorized users or applications.	T, R
Lightweight Directory Access Protocol (LDAP) authentication packets can be intercepted and viewed. Based on the information in each packet, the perpetrator might be able to figure out how to impersonate another user on the system. For example, the perpetrator might be a computer operator but might be able to act as the chief financial officer.	S, I, E
The data that is exchanged between the Web browser and the Web server is vulnerable to being viewed by an unauthorized user. This might compromise sensitive information such as passwords, employee IDs, employee information, salary information, and time reporting information.	T, I
The Web server can be become unavailable. If the Web server is shut down, an unauthorized server can be installed in its place, therefore compromising information that is sent from the browser.	S, T, I, D, E
The Web pages that are rendered to the browser might be altered to include viruses and worms. If the browser displays the Web page, the virus or worm can be invoked and possibly damage the user's machine.	T, D

How to Use a Threat Model

After you have identified the threats, you must decide how to respond to each threat identified in the threat modeling exercise. You can respond to a threat in several ways:

- *Inform users about the threat.* If a security weakness is created when the user performs some action, it can be appropriate to warn the user. For example, in Microsoft Windows XP, users who choose the option that displays protected operating system files are warned that doing so poses a risk to those files. In this case, the threat of tampering results primarily from enabling the user to access and potentially damage operating system files.

- *Remove features.* If you know of a feature that will introduce a significant security risk, and the risk cannot be mitigated effectively, consider whether the feature is worth including in the final version of the product.
- *Identify a mitigation technique.* If you must include a feature that introduces a security risk, you must choose a technique that mitigates the risk. There are several techniques for mitigating threats.

Incorporating Mitigation Techniques

Mitigation techniques can be divided into two categories, general techniques and techniques for the STRIDE model. Table 9.3 describes some of the general mitigation techniques used for resolving threats.

Table 9.3.   Mitigation Techniques

Technique	Description
Authentication and authorization	Authentication is the process by which an entity verifies that another entity is who or what it claims to be. Authorization is the process of determining access to resources.
Secure communication	You must ensure that communication between the tiers of your application is secure to avoid attacks in which data is tampered with while it is being transmitted or is being stored in a queue. For secure communication use:
	Secure Sockets Layer (SSL). SSL is used to establish an encrypted communication channel between client and server.
	IPSec. IPSec can be used to secure the data sent between two computers; for example, an application server and a database server.
	Virtual private networks (VPNs). A VPN lets you establish a point-to-point IP transport over the Internet (or other networks).
Quality of service(QoS)	Implements profiling on the messages that are sent to your system.
Throttling	Limits the number of messages sent to your system. If there is no control over the rate at which messages are sent, a target can be inundated with more messages than it can handle.
Auditing	The process of collecting information about user activities and important events and storing the information for analysis at a later stage. Auditing is also commonly known as *logging*. Windows event logs allow your applications to record information about important events. You can use these records to audit access to your system and troubleshoot problems.

Table 9.3.   Mitigation Techniques *(continued)*

Technique	Description
Filtering	The process of intercepting and evaluating messages sent to your system.
Least privilege	Provides users with the minimum level of privilege that will allow their work to be completed, and no more.

Table 9.4 includes a partial list of threat mitigation techniques as applied to various STRIDE threats.

Table 9.4.   Mitigation Techniques for STRIDE Threats

Mitigation technique	Type of threat
Authentication	S, D
Protect secrets	S, I
Audit trails	R
Do not store secrets	S, I
Privacy protocols	I
Authorization	T, I, D
Hashes	T
Message authentication codes	T
Digital signatures	T, R
Tamper-resistant protocols	T, R
Time stamps	R
Filtering	D
Throttling	D
Quality of service	D
Run with least privilege	E

More Info   For more information about threat modeling and mitigation technologies for some common threats, see *Writing Secure Code* by Michael Howard and David LeBlanc (Microsoft Press, 2002).

Lesson 3: Using .NET Framework Security Features

This lesson describes the important security features in the .NET Framework.

More Info   For more information about creating secure Microsoft ASP.NET applications, see the article "Building Secure ASP.NET Applications: Authentication, Authorization, and Secure Communication" under .NET Security on the MSDN® Web site (*http://msdn.microsoft.com*).

After this lesson, you will be able to

- Define type safety verification.
- Define code signing.
- Define encryption and data signing.
- Define code-access security.
- Define role-based security.
- Define isolated storage.
- Explain the security features of .NET Web technologies.

Estimated lesson time: 20 minutes

What Is Type Safety Verification?

Type safety verification plays a crucial role in assembly isolation and security enforcement.

Definition of type-safe code

Any code that accesses only the memory it is authorized to access is called type-safe code. For example, type-safe code does not access values from the private fields of another object.

Code that is not type-safe can cause security threats to an application. For example, unsafe code might access and alter native (unmanaged) code and perform malicious operations. Because the code is unsafe, the runtime is unable to prevent the code from accessing the native code. However, when code is type-safe, the security enforcement mechanism of the runtime ensures that it does not access native code unless it has permission to do so. Before it can run, all code that is not type-safe must have been granted a security permission with the *SkipVerification* member. This permission is granted only to code that is trusted at a very high level.

Definition of type safety verification

During just-in-time (JIT) compilation, Microsoft intermediate language (MSIL) code is compiled into native machine code. As this process occurs, a default verification process examines the metadata and MSIL code of a method to verify that they are well formed and type-safe.

Type-safe components can run in the same process even if they are trusted at different levels. For code that is verifiably type-safe, the runtime can rely on the following statements being true:

- A reference to a type is compatible with the type being referenced.
- Only appropriately defined operations are invoked on an object.
- Methods are called by means of defined interfaces so that security checks cannot be bypassed.

These restrictions provide assurances that security restrictions on code can be enforced reliably. Also, multiple instances of different type-safe assemblies can run safely in the same process, because they are guaranteed not to interfere with each other's memory.

What Is Code Signing?

To make any source reliable for software download, you need to consider the following:

- *Ensure authenticity.* Ensures that users know the origin of the code and helps to prevent malicious users from impersonating the identity of a publisher.
- *Ensure integrity.* Verifies that the code has not been changed by unauthorized sources since it was published.

Definition of code signing

Signing code with a strong name defines the unique identity of code and guarantees that code has not been compromised. Code signing is the process of providing a set of code with credentials that authenticate the publisher of the code. The credentials of the code can be verified prior to installing and running the code.

Code signing in the .NET Framework

.NET Framework code signing relies on strong name signatures. The .NET Framework also supports Authenticode® digital certificates and signatures.

What Is Encryption and Data Signing?

Data signing and encryption are processes that are used to protect data contents from being discovered and to verify that data has not been compromised.

Definition of encryption and decryption

Encryption is the process of disguising data before it is sent or stored. Before it is encrypted, the content is referred to as *plaintext*. Data that has undergone encryption is called *ciphertext*. A plaintext message that is converted to ciphertext is completely unreadable. *Decryption* is the process of unscrambling ciphertext into readable plaintext. The processes of encrypting and decrypting data rely on the techniques of hashing and signing data.

Definition of cryptographic hashing

Hashing is the process of matching data of any length to a fixed-length byte sequence. The fixed-length byte sequence is called a *hash*. A hash is obtained by applying a mathematical function, called a hashing algorithm, to an arbitrary amount of data. Cryptographic hashes that are created with the cryptography functions of the .NET Framework approach statistical uniqueness; a different two-byte sequence does not hash to the same value.

Definition of signed data

Signed data is a standards-based data type. Signed data consists of any type of content plus encrypted hashes of the content for zero or more signers. The hashes are used to confirm the identity of a data signer and to confirm that the message has not been modified since it was signed.

What Is Code-Access Security?

Windows operating system security ensures that unauthorized users are not allowed access to the computer system. However, Windows operating systems security alone cannot ensure against the possibility of authorized users downloading and running malicious code.

Definition of code-access security

The .NET Framework provides code-access security to help protect computer systems from malicious or faulty code and to provide a way to allow mobile code to run safely.

Code-access security allows code to be trusted to varying degrees, depending on the code's origin, code's evidence (such as its strong name signature), and on other aspects of the code's identity. For example, code that is downloaded from your organization's intranet and published by your organization might be trusted to a greater degree than code that is downloaded from the Internet and published by an unknown entity.

Requesting level of privilege required

The .NET Framework allows you to include features in your application that request a specific level of security privilege from the operating system. This request specifies the level of privilege your application:

- Requires to run
- Can make use of but is not required for the application to run
- Does not need and should be expressly excluded from ever being granted permission to access

What Is Role-Based Security?

Role-based security relates mostly to the spoofing identity security threat by preventing unauthorized users from performing operations that they are not authorized to perform. Role-based security allows code to verify the identity and role membership of the user.

Tip The .NET Framework includes classes to identify Windows users and groups, in addition to classes to help implement role-based security for other authentication schemes.

Figure 9.2 depicts the role-based security model.

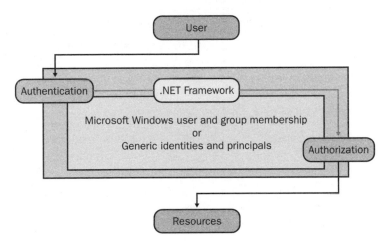

Figure 9.2. Role-based security

Authentication

Authentication is the process of discovering and verifying the identity of a user by examining the user's credentials and then validating those credentials against some authority. A variety of authentication mechanisms are used, some of which can be used with .NET Framework role-based security.

Examples of commonly used authentication mechanisms include the operating system, Passport, and application-defined mechanisms, such as NTLM and Kerberos version 5 authentication.

Authorization

Authorization is the process of determining whether a user is allowed to perform a requested action. Authorization occurs after authentication and uses information about a user's identity and roles to determine what resources that user can access. You can use .NET Framework role-based security to implement authorization.

What Is Isolated Storage?

A common requirement of applications is to store data, such as user preference information or application state, on the client.

One challenge to storing data successfully is the possibility that the storage location will be accessed or corrupted, either intentionally or unintentionally. Without a standard system in place to manage these problems, developing improvised techniques that minimize storage conflicts can be complex and the results can be unreliable. Therefore, it is important to protect your data by providing isolated storage.

Isolated storage allows developers to use an isolated virtual file system on the client to save data. When using isolated storage, applications save data to a unique data compartment that is associated with some aspect of the code's identity, such as its Web site, publisher, or signature.

The data compartment is an abstraction, not a specific storage location. It consists of one or more isolated storage files, called *stores*. The actual directory location of the data is contained in a store. To the developer, the location of the actual data is transparent. A quota can be used to limit the amount of isolated storage that an assembly uses.

Access permission to a store can be based on identity of:

- User
- Assembly
- Application

Security Features of .NET Technologies

.NET Web applications implement one or more of the logical services by using technologies such as Microsoft ASP.NET, Enterprise Services, XML Web services, remoting, Microsoft ADO.NET, and Microsoft SQL Server. To create effective security strategies, you need to understand how to fine-tune the various security features within each product and technology area, and how to make them work together.

ASP.NET security

ASP.NET provides a useful tool for application developers to use to create Web pages. When a Web site records a user's credit card information, the file or database that stores such information must be secured from public access. ASP.NET, in conjunction with IIS, can authenticate user credentials such as names and passwords by using any of the following means of authentication:

- Windows: basic, digest, or integrated Windows authentication (NTLM or Kerberos)
- Passport authentication
- Forms
- Client certificates

ASP.NET implements authentication by means of authentication providers. ASP.NET supports the following authentication providers:

- *Forms authentication.* A system by which unauthenticated requests are redirected to a Hypertext Markup Language (HTML) form by using HTTP client-side redirection. The user provides credentials and submits the form. If the application authenticates the request, the system issues a cookie that contains the credentials, or a key for reacquiring the identity.
- *Passport authentication.* A centralized authentication service provided by Microsoft that offers a single logon and core profile services for member sites.
- *Windows authentication.* A system used by ASP.NET in conjunction with IIS authentication. Authentication is performed by IIS in one of three ways: basic, digest, or integrated Windows authentication. When IIS authentication is complete, ASP.NET uses the authenticated identity to authorize access.

More Info   For more information about ASP.NET security, see "ASP.NET Security" under the section "Building Secure ASP.NET Applications" on the MSDN Web site (*http://msdn.microsoft.com*).

Enterprises Services security

Traditional COM+ services such as distributed transactions, just-in-time activation, object pooling, and concurrency management are available to .NET components. In the .NET environment, such services are referred to as Enterprise Services.

The authentication, authorization, and secure communication features supported by Enterprise Services applications are shown in Figure 9.3. The client application shown in Figure 9.3 is an ASP.NET Web application.

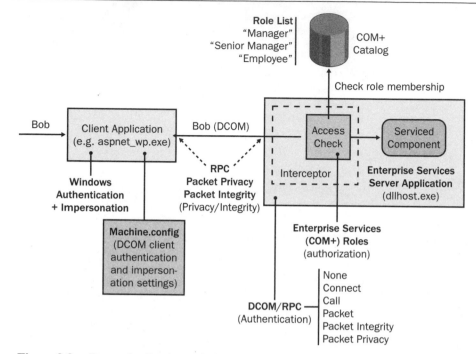

Figure 9.3.   Enterprise Services role-based security architecture

---

More Info   For more information about Enterprise Services security, see "Enterprise Services Security" under the section "Building Secure ASP.NET Applications" on the MSDN Web site (*http://msdn.microsoft.com*).

Web services security

Web services enable the exchange of data and the remote invocation of application logic by using SOAP-based message exchanges to move data through firewalls and between heterogeneous systems. Web service security can be used at three levels:

- Platform/transport-level (point-to-point) security
- Application-level (custom) security
- Message-level (end-to-end) security

More Info   For more information about Web services security, see "Web Services Security" under the section "Building Secure ASP.NET Applications" on the MSDN Web site (*http://msdn.microsoft.com*).

.NET remoting security

.NET remoting allows you to access remote and distributed objects across process and machine boundaries. Remoting does not have its own security model. Authentication and authorization between the client and server is performed by the channel and host process.

ADO.NET and SQL Server

ADO.NET provides data access services. It is designed for distributed Web applications, and supports disconnected scenarios. When you build Web-based applications, it is essential that you use a secure approach to accessing and storing data. ADO.NET and SQL Server provide several security features that can be used to ensure secure data access.

Figure 9.4 shows the remote application tier model together with the set of security services provided by the various technologies.

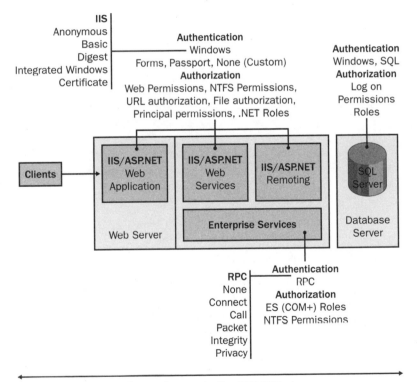

Figure 9.4.   Security architecture

Table 9.5 summarizes the authentication, authorization, and secure communications features provided by .NET technologies.

Table 9.5.   Security Features and .NET Technologies

Technology	Authentication	Authorization	Secure communication
ASP.NET	• None (custom) • Windows • Forms • Passport	• File authorization • URL authorization • Principal permissions • .NET roles	
Web services	• Windows • None (custom) • Message-level authentication	• File authorization • URL authorization • Principal permissions • .NET roles	• SSL and message-level encryption
Remoting	• Windows	• File authorization • URL authorization • Principal permissions • .NET roles	• SSL and message-level encryption
Enterprise Services	• Windows	• Enterprise Services (COM+) roles • NTFS permissions	• Remote Procedure Call (RPC) Encryption
SQL Server	• Windows (Kerberos/NTLM) • SQL authentication	• Server logons • Database logons • Fixed database roles • User-defined roles • Application roles • Object permissions	• SSL

Lesson 4: Designing Authorization, Authentication, and Auditing Strategies

Designing an authorization and authentication strategy for an application is a challenging task. Proper authorization and authentication design during the early phases of your application development helps to mitigate many serious security risks. In many cases, you will also need to implement auditing functionality to track user and business activity in the application for security purposes.

In this lesson, you will learn the general process for designing authorization and authentication strategies. You will then learn how to design authorization, authentication, and auditing for the application tiers.

After this lesson, you will be able to

- Identify the process of designing authorization and authentication strategies.
- Design authorization strategies for user interface and user process components.
- Design authorization strategies for business components and data access components.
- Design authentication strategies for user interface and user process components.
- Design authentication strategies for data access components.
- Design auditing strategies.

Estimated lesson time: 25 minutes

How to Design Authorization and Authentication Strategies

To design authentication and authorization strategies for your application, you need to perform the following steps:

1. Identify resources.
2. Select an authorization strategy.
3. Select the identities used for resource access.
4. Consider whether identity should flow through the system.
5. Select an authentication approach.
6. Decide how to flow identity through the system.

Identify resources

Identify the resources that the application provides to the clients. Examples of resources include:

- Web server resources such as Web pages, Web services, and static resources (HTML pages and images)
- Database resources such as per-user data or application-wide data
- Network resources such as remote file system resources and data from directory stores such as Active Directory®

Select an authorization strategy

The two basic authorization strategies are:

- *Role based.* Users are associated with roles; if a user is authorized to perform the requested operation, the application uses fixed identities with which to access resources.
- *Resource based.* Individual resources are secured by using Windows access control lists (ACLs). The application impersonates the caller prior to accessing resources, which allows the operating system to perform standard access checks.

Choose the identities used for resource access

Choose the identity or identities that should be used to access resources across the layers of your application.

- *Original caller's identity.* Assumes an impersonation or delegation model in which the original caller identity can be obtained and then flowed through each layer of your system. The delegation factor is a key criterion used to determine your authentication mechanism.
- *Process identity.* This is the default case. Local resource access and downstream calls are made using the current process identity. The feasibility of this approach depends on the boundary being crossed, because the process identity must be recognized by the destination system.
- *Service account.* Uses a fixed service account. For example, for database access this might be a fixed user name and password presented by the component connecting to the database. When a fixed Windows identity is required, use an Enterprise Services server application.
- *Custom identity.* When you do not have Windows accounts to work with, you can construct your own identities that can contain details that relate to your own specific security context. These could include role lists, unique identifiers, or any other type of custom information.

Consider identity flow

To support per-user authorization, auditing, and per-user data retrieval, you might need to flow the original caller's identity through various application tiers and across multiple computer boundaries. For example, if a back-end resource manager needs to perform per-caller authorization, the caller's identity must be passed to that resource manager.

Based on resource manager authorization requirements and the auditing requirements of your system, identify which identities need to be passed through your application.

Select an authentication approach

Two key factors that influence the choice of the authentication approach are the nature of your application's user base (the types of browsers they are using and whether they have Windows accounts), and your application's impersonation/delegation and auditing requirements.

You have a variety of options for authentication in your .NET-connected Web applications. For example, you can choose to use one of the supported IIS authentication mechanisms, or you might decide to perform authentication in your application code. Consider some or all of the following factors when choosing an authentication method:

- Server and client operating systems
- The client browser type
- The number of users, and the location and type of the user name and password database
- Deployment considerations, such as whether your application is Internet- or intranet-based and whether it is located behind a firewall
- The application type, such as whether the application is an interactive Web site or a non-interactive Web service
- Sensitivity of the data you are protecting
- Performance and scalability factors
- Application authorization requirements, such as making your application available to all users, or restricting certain areas to registered users and other areas to administrators only

Some of the ASP.NET and IIS authentication types include:

- Forms
- Passport
- Integrated Windows (Kerberos or NTLM)
- Basic
- Digest

Decide how to flow identity

You can flow identity (to provide security context) at the application level or you can flow identity and security context at the operating system level. To flow identity at the application level, use method and stored procedure parameters. Application identity flow supports:

- Per-user data retrieval using trusted query parameters, as shown in the following code:

```
SELECT x,y FROM SomeTable WHERE username='jane'
```

- Custom auditing within any application tier

Operating system identity flow supports:

- Platform level auditing (for example, Windows auditing and SQL Server auditing)
- Per-user authorization based on Windows identities

To flow identity at the operating system level, you can use the impersonation/delegation model. In some circumstances, you can use Kerberos delegation, while in cases where the environment does not support Kerberos, you might need to use other approaches, such as using Basic authentication. With Basic authentication, the user's credentials are available to the server application and can be used to access downstream network resources.

How to Design Authorization Strategies for User Interface Components

User interface components show data to users and gather data from them. You perform authorization at this level if you want to hide specific data fields from the user, show specific data fields to the user, or enable or disable controls for user input.

Authorization for user interface components

If the user is not supposed to see a certain piece of information, the most secure option is to avoid passing that piece of information to the presentation components in the first place.

It is common to perform some level of personalization of the user interface or menu so that users can see only the panes, Web elements, or menu entries that they can act on depending on their roles. A user interface .exe file usually starts the application. You should set code-access permissions on the user interface assemblies if you do not want to let it (or the local components it calls) access sensitive resources such as files.

Planning   Consider the security context in which the presentation components of the application will run, and test them in an appropriately restricted environment.

Authorization in user process components

User process components manage data and control flow between user processes. You should perform authorization at this level if you need to:

- Control whether a user can start a user interface interaction process at all.
- Add and remove steps or full user interface components in a user interaction flow based on who is executing it. For example, each sales representative might see data for only the appropriate region, so there is no need to present a step to choose the region of a sales report.

User process components are typically consumed only from user interface components. You can use code-access security to restrict who is calling them. You can also use code-access security to restrict how user process components interact with each other. This approach is especially important in portal scenarios when it is critical that a user process implemented as an add-in cannot gather unauthorized information from other user processes and elements.

How to Design Authorization Strategies for Business Components

Like the other tiers of an application, you can set authorization for business components. Use the following guidelines when setting authorization:

- Try to make the business process authorization independent of user context, especially if you plan to use many communication mechanisms as queues and Web services.
- Use role-based security as much as possible rather than relying on user accounts. Roll-based security provides better scalability, eases administration, and avoids problems with user names that support many canonical representations. You can define roles for serviced components in an Enterprise Services–based application, or you can use Windows groups or custom roles for .NET components that are not running in Enterprise Services.

How to Design Authorization Strategies for Data Access Components

Data access components are the last components that expose business functionality before your application data. You need to perform authorization at this level if you need to share the data access components with developers of business processes that you do not fully trust and if you want to protect access to powerful functions made available by the data stores.

To perform authorization, you can use Enterprise Services roles and .NET *PrincipalPermission* attributes, if you are using Windows authentication. Use .NET roles and attributes if you are not using a Windows security context.

If you are flowing the same user context into your data store, you can use the database's authorization functionality, for example, granting or revoking access to stored procedures.

Because data access components are typically called only by other application components, they are a good candidate for restricting callers to the necessary set of assemblies—usually a combination of assemblies with components of the user interface layer, business process components, and business entities (if present).

How to Design Authentication Strategies for User Interface Components

User interface components need to authenticate the user if the application needs to perform authorization, auditing, or personalization.

Authentication for Web-based UI

A wide range of authentication mechanisms are available for Web-based user interfaces (UIs). To choose the right one for your scenario, see Figure 9.5.

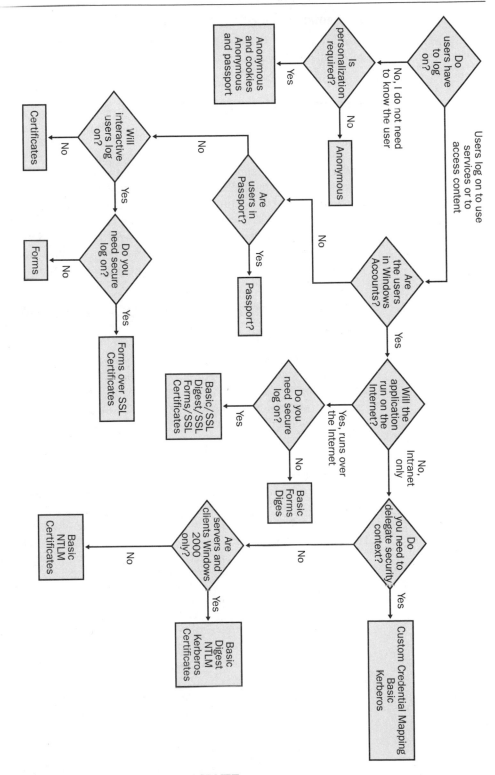

Figure 9.5.   Authentication in ASP.NET

Authentication for Windows-based UI

Windows-based user interfaces usually either rely on a custom authentication mechanism (in which the application prompts for a user name and password), or they authenticate users by using their Windows logons.

Authentication for user process components

User process components do not perform authentication; they rely on the security context set at application start.

The user process components should run in the same user context as the user interface itself, so that all authentication tasks are delegated to the user interface or even the rendering infrastructure. For example, in ASP.NET, any request to an ASPX page results in IIS requesting authentication credentials or ASP.NET redirecting the user to a forms-based authentication page. This operation is handled transparently to any user process layer and does not interrupt state flow, even when an authenticated session expires and needs to be reestablished.

How to Design Authentication Strategies for Data Access Components

Data access components are designed to be used by other components in the application or service. They are not usually meant to be called from scripts or other applications, so you can design them to rely on the security context set by the caller or the authentication mechanism of your remoting strategy. Data access components can authenticate with the database in two main ways: using service accounts and impersonating the caller.

Service accounts

Use one or a limited set of service accounts that represent roles or user type. In most cases, it will be just one service account, but you can use more if you need more control over authorization. For example, in the order processing application you could access your database as "TheOrderApplication," or log on selectively as "OrderProcessingManager" or "OrderProcessingClerk," depending on the role of the caller identity.

Use service accounts when:

- You connect to the underlying data source from an environment in which impersonation of the initial caller is unavailable (for example, Microsoft BizTalk® Server).
- You have very limited change control over the accounts that can log on to the other system, for example, when logging on to a relational database management system, which is strictly managed by the database administrator.

- The data store you are accessing has a different authentication mechanism than the rest of your application, for example, when you are logging on to a Web service across the Internet.

Do not use service accounts when:

- You do not have a secure way of storing and maintaining service credentials.
- You need to access the data store with specific user resources because of security policies, for example, when you need access to data or objects in SQL Server on behalf of users.
- The data store audits activities, and these audits need to correspond to individual users.

Impersonating the caller

You are impersonating the caller when you access a data store with a set of accounts that correspond one-to-one with your application user base. For example, if Jane logs on to your application, and your data access components access a database, you are impersonating Jane if you log on to this database with Jane's credentials.

You need caller impersonation when:

- The data store performs authorization based on the logged on user.
- The data store needs to audit the activities of each individual end user.

How to Design Auditing Strategies

To audit your business activities, you need a secure storage location. In fact, auditing can be thought of as secure logging. If you are implementing your own auditing solution, you must ensure that audit entries are tamperproof or at least tamper-evident (achieved with digital signatures) and that storage location is secured (for example, either connection strings cannot be changed or storage files cannot be replaced, or both). Your auditing mechanism can use document signing, platform authentication, and code-access security to ensure that spurious entries cannot be logged by malicious code.

Auditing in user interface and user process components

The activity that occurs in user interface components is not usually audited. Activities that are audited at the user interface include global events such as logon, logoff, password changes, and all security exceptions in general.

Because user process components represent user activities, which can be stopped, abandoned, and so on, it is not common to audit them. As always, you might want to audit security-related exceptions.

Auditing in business process components

Auditing is most often performed for business processes. You will want to know who performed key business activities and when the activities occurred.

If you are auditing within the context of a transaction to a transactional resource manager such as SQL Server, you will want to have a new transaction started by your auditing component so that the failures in the original transaction tree do not roll back the audit entry.

Auditing in data access components

Data access components are the closest custom business logic layer to the data store. The data layer is a good location for implementing auditing.

The data access components in your application will usually invoke stored procedures that actually do the data-intensive work, so you might want to also audit inside the data base management system (RDBMS).

More Info   For information about how to implement auditing in SQL Server, see "Auditing SQL Server Activity" in the SQL Server 2000 SDK on the MSDN Web site (*http://msdn.microsoft.com*).

Activity: Threat Modeling and Mitigation

In this activity, you use what you learned in the lessons to work through threat modeling exercises.

Exercise 1: Identifying Potential Threats

The sales staff at Adventure Works Cycles can create orders for their customers in two ways. The first way allows the sales staff to use the public Web site in a manner similar to how the customers place orders. However, the sales staff will need to provide their credentials, which will allow discounts to be applied to the order. The second way is accomplished by means of the Handheld PCs and laptop computers that each sales representative has and a Windows Forms application that is installed on each laptop. The sales representative creates the order either on the Handheld PC or the laptop and obtains the customer's signature by means of the Handheld PC. Later, the sales representative can connect to the network and upload the order to the order entry application.

 Both ways of creating orders can be subject to a number of security threats. Open the C09Ex1.ppt file in the \SolutionDocuments\Chapter09 folder on the CD and examine the high-level architecture diagram for the Windows Forms application. Using the STRIDE threat model, identify some of the security threats to the application.

One possible answer to this exercise can be found in C09Ex1_Answer.ppt in the \SolutionDocuments\Chapter09 folder on the CD.

Exercise 2: Applying Mitigation Technologies

Using the possible threats you identified in Exercise 1, list some technologies that would help to mitigate these threats.

 One possible answer to this exercise can be found in C09Ex2_Answer.ppt in the \SolutionDocuments\Chapter09 folder on the CD.

Summary

- Common types of security vulnerabilities include:
    - Weak passwords
    - Misconfigured software
    - Social engineering
    - Internet connections
    - Unencrypted data transfer
    - Buffer overrun
    - SQL injection
    - Secrets in code
- Principles for building security strategies include:
    - Rely on tested and proven security systems.
    - Never trust external input.
    - Assume that external systems are non-secure.
    - Apply the principle of least privilege.
    - Reduce available components and data.
    - Default to a secure mode.
    - Do not rely on security by obscurity.
    - Follow STRIDE principles.
- The STRIDE model is a threat model. Each letter in the STRIDE acronym specifies a different category of security threat: spoofing identity, tampering, repudiation, information disclosure, denial of service, and elevation of privilege.
- The steps to create a threat model are:
    - Arrange for a brainstorming meeting.
    - Apply the STRIDE security categories.
    - List all possible threats.
    - Create notes.
    - Research.
    - Rank the risk of each threat.
- The important security features of .NET Framework include:
    - Type safety verification
    - Code signing
    - Encryption and data signing
    - Code-access security
    - Role-based security
    - Isolated storage

- To design an authentication and authorization strategy for your application, you need to perform the following steps:
  - Identify resources.
  - Select an authorization strategy.
  - Select the identities used for resource access.
  - Consider identity flow.
  - Select an authentication approach.
  - Decide how to flow identity.

Review

The following questions are intended to reinforce key information presented in this chapter. If you are unable to answer a question, review the lesson materials and try the question again. You can find answers to the questions in the appendix.

1. What are some of the drawbacks of traditional security models?

2. What are some of the principles of secure coding?

3. Which of the following statements about buffer overruns is true? (Select all that apply.)
   - Type safety verification was designed to eliminate buffer overruns.
   - A buffer overrun can cause an application to stop responding or to malfunction.
   - A buffer overrun can be exploited by a malicious user to run arbitrary code.
   - The error message that results from a buffer overrun can pose a security threat.

4. During which MSF phase should the threat model be created?
   - Planning
   - Developing
   - Stabilizing

5. What is the STRIDE model?

6. Read the following security attack scenario, and then decide which elements of the STRIDE model are implicit in the attack.

   Carl sees that Bob has left his workstation unattended and unlocked. Carl sits down at Bob's workstation and opens Bob's e-mail application. Carl, pretending to be Bob, sends an e-mail message to Alice. Carl quits the e-mail client and then walks away unobserved.

7. What is code-access security?

8. What is role-based security?

9. Which are the authentication providers supported by ASP.NET?

10. What are the three types of security provided by Web services?

11. What are the steps for designing an authorization and authentication strategy for an application?

C H A P T E R   1 0

Completing the Planning Phase

About This Chapter

The planning phase encompasses the greater part of the architecture and design of a solution. It also results in plans to accomplish the development and deployment of the solution, and the schedules associated with tasks and resources. These plans help the project team to work on the subsequent phases of the project.

In this chapter, you will learn about the tasks and plans that the project team works on to complete the planning phase of the project.

Before You Begin

To complete the lessons in this chapter, you must

- Understand the MSF Process Model.
- Be able to create use cases, usage scenarios, and use case diagrams.
- Be familiar with the outputs of the envisioning phase, such as vision/scope, project structure, and risk analysis documents.
- Be familiar with tasks and outputs of the three design processes of the planning phase—conceptual, logical, and physical design.

Lesson 1: Incorporating Design Considerations

During the planning phase, several elements affect and shape the design of the application. Some of these elements might be non-negotiable and finite resources, such as time, money, and workforce. Other elements, such as available technologies, knowledge, and skills, are dynamic and vary throughout the development life cycle. While these elements influence the design of an application to some extent, the business problem dictates the capabilities the application must have for a satisfactory solution.

In this lesson, you will learn about the capabilities and considerations that might be addressed by a solution. You will learn about design considerations such as scalability, availability, reliability, performance, interoperability, and globalization and localization. You will also learn the techniques for incorporating these design considerations into a solution.

After this lesson, you will be able to

- Design a solution for scalability.
- Design a solution for availability.
- Design a solution for reliability.
- Design a solution for performance.
- Design a solution for interoperability.
- Design localization and globalization specifications for a solution.

Estimated lesson time: 25 minutes

How to Design for Scalability

Scalability is defined as the capability to increase resources to produce an increase in the service capacity. In a scalable application, you can add resources to manage additional demands without modifying the application itself.

A scalable application requires a balance between the software and hardware used to implement the application. You might add resources to either software or hardware to increase the scalability of the application. Adding these resources might produce a benefit; however, it could also have a negative or null effect, with the application showing no significant increase in service capacity. For example, you might implement load balancing in an application. This will help only minimally if the application has been written to make synchronous method calls or to retrieve lengthy datasets in response to a user's request.

Common approaches

The two most common approaches to scalability are:

- *Scaling up*. Refers to achieving scalability by improving the existing server's processing hardware. Scaling up includes adding more memory, more or faster processors, or migrating the application to a more powerful computer. The primary goal of scaling up an application is to increase the hardware resources available to the application. Typically, you can scale up an application without changing the source code. In addition, the administrative effort does not change drastically. However, the benefit of scaling up tapers off eventually until the actual maximum processing capability of the machine is reached.

Figure 10.1 illustrates the effect scaling up has on the service capacity of an application.

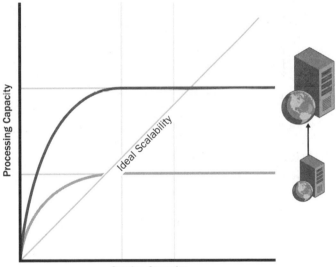

Figure 10.1.   Scaling up an application

- *Scaling out*. Refers to distributing the processing load across more than one server. Although scaling out is achieved by using multiple computers, the collection of computers continues to act as the original device configuration from the end-user perspective. Again, the balance between software and hardware is important. The application should be able to execute without needing information about the server on which it is executing. This concept is called *location transparency*. Scaling out also increases the fault tolerance of the application.

Figure 10.2 illustrates the effect scaling out has on the service capacity of an application.

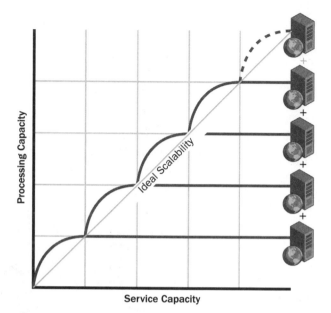

Figure 10.2.   Scaling out an application

Designing for scalability

Good design is the foundation of a highly scalable application. The planning phase has the greatest impact on the scalability of an application.

Figure 10.3 illustrates the role of design, code tuning, product tuning, and hardware tuning in the scalability of an application. Design has more impact on the scalability of an application than the other three factors. As you move up the pyramid, the impact of various factors decreases. The pyramid illustrates that effective design adds more scalability to an application than increased hardware resources.

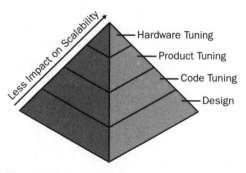

Figure 10.3.   Scalability pyramid

To design for scalability, use the following guidelines:

- *Design processes such that they do not wait.* A process should never wait longer than necessary. A process can be categorized as *synchronous* or *asynchronous*. A synchronous process waits for another process to complete before it continues. Such processes must wait for another process to succeed or fail completely before performing another operation. Applications that implement synchronous processes encounter bottlenecks for resources. These bottlenecks affect both the performance and the scalability of the application. One way to achieve scalability is to implement asynchronous processes. In applications that have asynchronous processes, long-running operations can be queued for completion later by a separate process.

- *Design processes so that processes do not compete for resources.* One of the biggest causes of scalability problems is competition for resources such as memory, processor cycles, bandwidth, or database connections. Plan your resource usage to minimize these problems:

  - Sequence resource usage to use the most plentiful resources first and the least plentiful resources last.

  - Acquire resources as late as possible. The shorter the amount of time a process uses a resource, the sooner the resource becomes available to another process.

- *Design processes for commutability.* Two or more operations are called *commutative* if they can execute in any order and still obtain the same result. Typically, operations that do not involve transactions are commutative. For example, a busy e-commerce site that continuously updates the inventory of its products might experience contention for record locks. To prevent this, each inventory increment and decrement could become a record in a separate inventory transaction table. Periodically, the database could add the rows of this table for each product and then update the product records with the net change in inventory.

- *Design components for interchangeability.* An interchangeable component is designed to release its resources, move into a pool managed by a resource manager, and be re-initialized for use by a new client. Design the component so that no client-specific state persists from client to client. In addition, the component should support aggregation and not be bound to a specific thread. Resource pooling schemes such as COM+ component pooling and Open Database Connectivity (ODBC) connection pooling use interchangeable resources. For example, you can use the Component Services Administration tool to enable object pooling, set minimum and maximum pool size, and create timeout settings. For more information, refer to *Improving Performance with Object Pooling* in the Platform SDK: COM+ (Component Services documentation in MSDN).

- *Partition resources and activities.* Minimize relationships between resources and activities by partitioning them. This helps you avoid the risk of bottlenecks. Partitioning activities can also ease the load on critical resources such as the processor and bandwidth. For example, using Secure Sockets Layer (SSL) to provide a secure connection results in significant overhead. Therefore, you might decide to use SSL only for pages that require a high level of security and use dedicated Web servers to handle SSL sessions. You can also partition resources and activities by creating many small components rather than a few large components, and by limiting cross-device communication. However, partitioning can make a system more complex. Dividing resources that have dependencies can add significant overheads to an operation.

How to Design for Availability

Though all applications are available at least some of the time, Web-based applications and mission-critical enterprise applications must provide services at all times. If your enterprise application needs to work 24 hours a day, 7 days a week, you need to design for high availability. Advances in hardware and software have increased the quality of high-availability applications.

Definition of availability

Availability is a measure of how often the application is available to handle service requests as compared to the planned run time. Availability also takes into account repair time because an application that is being repaired is not available for use.

Note   Availability does not address business continuation issues such as backups and alternative sites.

Table 10.1 shows the measurements used for calculating availability.

Table 10.1.   **Measurement Types for Calculating Availability**

Name	Calculation	Definition
Mean Time Between Failure (MTBF)	Hours / Failure Count	Average length of time the application runs before failing
Mean Time To Recovery (MTTR)	Repair Hours / Failure Count	Average length of time needed to repair and restore service after a failure

The formula for calculating availability is:

```
Availability = (MTBF / (MTBF + MTTR)) × 100
```

For example, the typical availability requirement for the Adventure Works Cycles application is that the site is available 24 hours a day, 7 days a week. If you assume 1000 continuous hours as a checkpoint, two 1-hour failures during this time period results in availability of:

```
((1000 / 2) / ((1000 / 2) + 1)) × 100 = (500 / 501) × 100 = .998 × 100 =
99.8%.
```

A popular way to describe availability is by the *nines*, for example, three nines for 99.9 percent availability. However, the implication of measuring by nines is often misunderstood. You need to do the arithmetic to discover that three nines (99.9 percent availability) represent about 8.5 hours of service outage in a single year. The next level, four nines (99.99 percent), represents about 1 hour of service outage in a year. Five nines (99.999 percent) represent about 5 minutes of outage per year.

Planning availability levels

To determine the level of availability that is appropriate for your application, you need to answer a few questions, such as:

- Who are the customers of the application? What are their expectations from the application?
- How much downtime is acceptable?
- Do internal company processes depend on the service?
- What is the schedule and budget for developing the application?

Techniques for availability

Designing for availability includes anticipating, detecting, and resolving hardware or software failures before they result in service errors, faults, or data corruption, thereby minimizing downtime. To ensure availability, provide multiple routes to application services and data. Use only tested, proven processes (both automated and people-based) that support the application throughout its life cycle.

In addition to unplanned downtime, planned downtime must be reduced. Planned downtime can include maintenance changes, operating system upgrades, backups, or any other activity that temporarily removes the application from service.

Availability of an application also depends on its reliability. For a highly available and reliable application, you need a reliable foundation: good application design, rigorous testing, and certification. Some of the techniques used for designing for availability include:

- *Reduce planned downtime.* To avoid planned downtime, use *rolling upgrades*. For example, to update a component on a clustered server, you can move the server's resource groups to another server, take the server offline, update the component, and then bring the server online. Meanwhile, the other servers handle the workload, and the application experiences no downtime. You can use this strategy in an application that scales out.

- *Reduce unplanned downtime with clustering.* Clustering is a technology for creating high-availability applications. A cluster consists of multiple computers that are physically networked and logically connected using cluster software. By using clustering, a multiple server Web site can withstand failures with no interruption in service. When the active server fails, the workload is automatically moved to a passive server, current client processes are switched over, and the failed application service is restarted automatically. If a resource fails, customers connected to that server cluster might experience a slight delay, but the service will be completed. Cluster software can provide failover support for applications, file and print services, databases, and messaging systems that have been designed as cluster-aware and assigned to a cluster.

- *Use network load balancing.* Network load balancing (NLB) is used to distribute traffic evenly across available servers. NLB also helps increase the availability of an application: if a server fails, you can use NLB to redefine the cluster and direct traffic to the other servers. NLB is especially beneficial for e-commerce applications that link external clients with transactions to data servers. As client traffic increases, you can scale out the Web server farm by adding up to 32 servers in a single cluster. NLB automatically detects server failures and redirects client traffic to the remaining servers, all the time maintaining continuous, unbroken client service.

- *Use redundant array of independent disks (RAID) for data stores.* RAID uses multiple hard disks to store data in multiple places. If a disk fails, the application is transferred to a mirrored data image and the application continues running. The failed disk can be replaced without stopping the application.

- *Isolate mission-critical applications.* An application is constantly performing tasks and requesting resources such as network communications, data access, or process threads. Each of these resource requests can affect the performance and availability of applications sharing the same resources. If an application shares these services on the same servers, the workload and throughput characteristics for these servers might change unfavorably. It is recommended that mission-critical applications use dedicated infrastructures and private networks.

- *Use queuing.* Queuing enables your application to communicate with other applications by sending and receiving asynchronous messages. Queuing guarantees message delivery; it does not matter whether the necessary connectivity currently exists (with mobile applications, for example). Queuing removes a failure point from the application. Queuing is also a solution for managing peak workloads that can require a lot of hardware. In addition, by increasing the number of routes for successful message delivery, an application can increase the chances for successful and immediate message completion.

How to Design for Reliability

The reliability of an application refers to the ability of the application to provide accurate results. Reliability and availability are closely related. While availability measures the capacity to handle all requests and to recover from a failure with the least loss of access to the application, reliability measures how long the application can execute and produce expected results without failing. Users bypass unreliable Web sites, resulting in lost revenue and reduced future sales. In addition, the expense of repairing corrupted data increases the cost of application failure. Unreliable systems are also difficult to maintain or improve because the failure points are typically hidden throughout the system.

Reasons for application failure

An application is a collection of hardware, operating system services, software components, and human processes that together provide pre-specified business services. Reliability of the entire application depends on the reliability of the individual components. Because all components in a system are related, failure of one component can affect the reliability of other components.

Application failures can occur for many reasons:

- Erroneous code
- Inadequate testing
- Change management problems
- Operational errors
- Lack of ongoing monitoring and analysis
- Lack of quality software engineering processes
- Interaction with external services or applications
- Changing operating conditions, such as usage level or workload changes
- Unusual events, such as security failures and broadcast storms
- Hardware failures (disks, controllers, network devices, servers, power supplies, memory, and CPUs)
- Environmental problems (power, cooling, fire, flood, dust, and natural disasters)

Designing for reliability

To design for reliability, you need to examine the application's expected usage pattern, create a reliability profile, and create a solution that meets the profile. You must examine how a particular service is provided, evaluate failure scenarios, and design preferred alternatives. In addition, you need to consider the application's interactions with other applications.

It is difficult to identify reliability problems and solutions for a system that has not been developed. However, you can begin by analyzing the currently running applications in the organization. Such analysis reveals the failure frequency and distribution, root causes, and possible improvements for existing systems. You can use this information to design a reliable solution.

A reliable solution ensures error-free data input, data transformations, state management, and non-corrupting recovery from any failure conditions. Creating a high-reliability application depends on the entire software development lifecycle, from the planning phase, through development and testing, to deployment and stabilizing. The following tasks can help you create a reliable application:

- Putting reliability requirements in the specification
- Using a good architectural infrastructure
- Including management information in the application
- Using redundancy
- Using quality development tools
- Using reliability checks that are provided by the application
- Implementing error handling
- Reducing the application's functionality instead of completely failing the application

How to Design for Performance

An application's performance is defined by metrics such as transaction throughput and resource utilization. A user might define an application's performance in terms of its response time.

Performance goals and metrics

Before designing for performance, you need to determine performance goals of the application and metrics for measuring performance. To determine performance goals, you need to answer questions such as:

- *What is the business goal?* For example, if the business goal of the solution is to handle more orders each week, you could begin with the expected increase in revenue and convert the figure into a performance goal for each functional area.

- *What is the critical functionality of the solution?* Identifying critical features allows you to prioritize the system design. You might decide to degrade the performance of a low priority feature to maintain or increase the performance of a higher priority feature.

- *What are the features required by different sets of users?* You can create profiles according to the various expectations of the organization and the end users of the solution. Because of varying expectations, the performance requirements of the application can differ. You need to determine the relationship between each functional area and performance goal. For example, the database stores all information about orders placed by the customer. From the customer's perspective, the application should quickly update the database. The organization expects the solution to store valid data quickly. Therefore, the performance goal of the solution is to ensure fast inserts and updates to the database. Creating profiles helps in partitioning and developing accurate tests for the solution.

> **Note**   For the purposes of testing, the performance goal must be expressed in a way that is measurable in your testing routines. You need to identify performance metrics for the application. For example, the performance goal of fast inserts and updates to a database can be measured in terms of transactions per second.

Designing for performance

You must define performance requirements before the team proceeds to the developing phase. To define a good performance requirement, you must identify project constraints, determine services that the application will perform, and specify the load on the application.

- *Identifying constraints.* Constraints in the project include budget, schedule, infrastructure, and the choice of development tools or technologies. For example, you might need to deploy an application by a specific date. You might also need to use a specific development tool because the team has expertise in that tool only. You might not be able to design and develop applications that are processor intensive because the client computers do not have adequate hardware. You need to design an application so that it meets its performance goals within the limitations of the constraints. Instead of changing some aspects of a project to improve performance, you can modify aspects of the project that are not constrained to determine how you can improve performance. For example, can the team be trained so that they can create components by using a different tool? Can data access be improved by changing the data access technology?

- *Determining features.* The features of an application correspond to use cases and usage scenarios. You can identify the usage scenarios that affect the performance of the application and, for each such scenario, specify what the user does and what the application does in response, including how databases and other system services are accessed. In addition, you need to determine how often each feature will be used. This information can help you create tests for measuring performance that resemble actual usage of the application as closely as possible.

- *Specifying the load.* You can specify the load of an application as the number of clients that will use the application. In addition, you can examine how the load might vary over time. For example, the number of requests for an e-commerce site will be higher during certain times of year. You can use the load to define the performance metrics of the application.

How to Design for Interoperability

Typically, medium and large organizations have heterogeneous computing environments. For example, many organizations deploy distributed *n*-tier client/server applications that require access to data or transactions on existing systems. In addition, your application might need to interact with applications that have been developed using proprietary or third-party software.

Reasons for interoperability

You need to design for interoperability because interoperability:

- *Reduces operational cost and complexity.* Customers can continue to work in mixed environments for the foreseeable future. The ability for different systems to operate in the same environment together reduces the cost of developing and supporting a heterogeneous infrastructure.
- *Enables optimal deployments.* Customers might have business requirements that can be delivered with specific applications and platforms. An interoperable application enables the organization to continue using the diverse applications that address its specific requirements.
- *Uses existing investments.* Typically, customers have a large and diverse range of systems installed in their environments and move to a new platform gradually. Therefore, new applications must be able to interact with previous applications. In addition, existing applications might be made Web-aware and need to allow access from an intranet or the Internet to systems hosted on environments such as an IBM mainframe. This extends the functionality of existing applications and protects the investments that the organizations have made.

Designing for interoperability

To integrate heterogeneous applications, you need to consider the following types of interoperability:

- *Network interoperability.* Refers to the ability of multiple vendor systems to communicate with each other without having to use common protocols. In the past, applications might have been designed for predefined protocols such as Transmission Control Protocol/Internet Protocol (TCP/IP), Internetwork Packet Exchange /Sequenced Package Exchange (IPX/SPX), or Systems Network Architecture (SNA). Implementing technologies or standards such as Hypertext Transfer Protocol (HTTP), Extensible Markup Language (XML), SOAP, Web Services Description Language (WSDL), and XML Web services to make use of the Internet can make your applications independent of programming language, platform, and device.
- *Data interoperability.* Refers to the ability of applications to access and use data stored in both structured and unstructured storage systems such as databases, file systems, and e-mail stores. Enterprise applications often require the sharing of data between disparate data sources and multiple applications. Published data exchange standards, such as cascading style sheets, ODBC, and XML, allow data access to both Windows-based and non-Windows-based data sources.
- *Applications interoperability.* Refers to the infrastructure required to ensure interoperability between new *n*-tier applications and existing applications, business logic, and data. As you create new *n*-tier applications, they will need to work with a wide variety of existing applications. One of the methods of

enabling application interoperability is by using Common Language Specification (CLS). CLS is a standard that is currently met by more than twenty different languages to allow the interoperability of services created in any CLS-compliant language.

You can enable interoperability in Microsoft .NET-connected applications to access and use traditional Active Server Pages (ASP) and Component Object Model (COM) applications that you are not yet ready to migrate to .NET–connected solutions. In addition, XML was specifically created to allow applications to exchange data easily and without conversion code that would need to be created for each instance or type of data exchange.

- *Management interoperability.* Refers to the tasks of user account management, performance monitoring, and tuning for heterogeneous applications in the organization.

How to Design for Globalization and Localization

Globalization and localization are processes that you use for developing world-ready applications. During the planning phase, you need to clearly identify and document globalization and localization requirements so that the design of the application can address these requirements.

Note   In the Microsoft .NET Framework, three namespaces have been provided to make your application easy to globalize and localize. They are the System.Globalization namespace, the System.Resources namespace, and the System.Text namespace.

Definition of globalization

Globalization is the process of designing and developing an application that can operate in multiple cultures and locales. Globalization involves:

- Identifying the cultures and locales that must be supported
- Designing features that support those cultures and locales
- Writing code that executes properly in all the supported cultures and locales

Globalization enables you to create applications that can accept, display, and output information in different language scripts that are appropriate for various geographical areas. To globalize these functions, you use the concept of cultures and locales. A culture and locale is a set of rules and a set of data that are specific to a given language and geographical area. These rules and data include information about:

- Character classification
- Date and time formatting
- Numeric, currency, weight, and measure conventions
- Sorting rules

Definition of localization

Localization is the process of adapting a globalized application to a specific culture and locale, using separate resources for each culture that is to be globalized. A resource file contains culture-specific user interface items that are provided to an application as a text file, a *.resx* file, or a *.resources* file. An application prepared for localization has two conceptual blocks: the *data block* and the *code block*. The data block (usually contained in resource files) contains all user-interface string resources. The code block contains the application code that is applicable for all cultures and locales and accesses the correct resource file for the culture currently selected in the operating system.

To create a localized version of the application, you change the data block and combine it with the code block, which essentially remains the same. You need to have a basic understanding of relevant character sets commonly used in modern software development and the issues associated with them. Although all computers store text as numbers, different systems can store the same text by using different numbers.

To successfully create a localized version of an application, ensure that:

- The code block is separate from the data block.
- The application code can read data accurately, regardless of the culture and locale.

Issues in globalization and localization

Some of the issues that you need to consider while planning for globalization and localization are:

- *Language issues.* Language issues are the result of differences in how languages around the world differ in display, alphabets, grammar, and syntactical rules. For example, various languages are read and written left-to-right, right-to-left, or top-to-bottom.

- *Formatting issues.* Formatting issues are the primary source of discrepancies when working with applications originally written for another language, culture, and locale. During globalization and localization, you need to pay attention to factors such as addresses, currency types, dates, paper sizes, telephone numbers, time formats, and units of measure. Developers can use the National Language Support (NLS) application programming interfaces (APIs) in Microsoft® Windows® or the System.Globalization namespace to handle most of these issues automatically.

- *String-related issues.* Strings are the text displayed in the various elements in an application's user interface, such as message boxes, dialog boxes, title bars, status bars, and menus. For example, message boxes typically concatenate strings of standard text and context-specific texts. In different languages, the concatenated string might not be grammatically correct.

- *User interface issues.* You should pay special attention to the design of the following user interface (UI) components:

  - *Messages.* The length of messages might differ in different languages.

  - *Menus and dialog boxes.* Menus and dialog boxes might become larger as a result of localization.

  - *Icons and bitmaps.* Icons and bitmaps must use symbols that are internationally accepted and convey the same meaning, regardless of the culture or locale.

  - *Access and shortcut keys.* The keyboards used in the different locales might not have the same characters and keys. You need to ensure that access keys and shortcut keys are supported in the keyboards used in the destination locales.

  - *UI controls.* UI controls should not be hidden or used as a parts of strings.

Best practices for globalization and localization

The following best practices provide a checklist of the issues associated with developing world-ready software.

- *Technical issues.*

  - Use Unicode as your character-encoding standard to represent text. All applications process data, whether text or numerical. Different cultures and locales might use different data encoding techniques. *Unicode* is a 16-bit international character-encoding standard that covers values for more than 45,000 characters. It allows each character in all the required cultures and locales to be represented uniquely.

  - Implement a multilingual user interface. If you design the user interface to open in the default UI language, and offer the option to change to other languages, users who speak different languages can quickly switch to the preferred interface.

  - Examine Windows messages that indicate changes in the input language, and use that information to check spelling, select fonts, and so on.

  - Detect the culture that your application uses to handle dates, currencies, and numeric differences and change it to correspond to the culture that application supports. In the .NET Framework, *culture* refers to the user's language, which can be combined with that user's location. By specifying a culture, it is possible to use a set of common preferences for certain information, such as strings, date formats, and number formats, that corresponds to the user's language and location conventions.

- *Cultural and political issues.* Examples of cultural and political issues include disputes related to maps, which can induce governments to prevent distribution in specific regions. These issues do not prevent the application from running. However, they can create negative feelings about the application and customers might seek alternatives from other companies. To avoid such issues:

    - Avoid slang expressions, colloquialisms, and obscure phrasing in all text.

    - Avoid images in bitmaps and icons that are ethnocentric or offensive in other cultures and locales.

    - Avoid maps that include controversial regional or national boundaries.

- *User interface issues.*

    - Store all user interface elements in resource files, message files, or a private database so that they are separate from the program source code.

    - Place only those strings that require localization in resource files. Leave non-localized strings as string constants in the source code.

    - Use the same resource identifiers throughout the life of the project. Changing identifiers makes it difficult to update localized resources from one version of the application to another.

    - If the same string is used in multiple contexts, make multiple copies of the string. The same string might have different translations in different contexts.

    - Allocate text buffers dynamically because text size might change when text is translated.

    - Be aware that dialog boxes might expand because of localization.

    - Avoid text in bitmaps and icons.

    - Do not create a text message dynamically at run time.

    - Avoid composing text that uses multiple insertion parameters in a format string.

    - If localizing to a Middle Eastern language such as Arabic or Hebrew, use the right-to-left layout APIs to lay out text in the application from right to left.

    - Test localized applications on all language variants of the operating system.

Lesson 2: Planning for Administrative Features

Administrative features are an important part of a solution. In this lesson, you will learn how to design and plan administrative features such as monitoring, data migration, and the licensing specifications of a solution.

After this lesson, you will be able to

- Plan for monitoring in a solution.
- Plan for data migration.
- Create licensing specifications.

Estimated lesson time: 10 minutes

How to Plan for Monitoring

Application monitoring is used to ensure that the application is functioning correctly and performing at an optimal level. Automated monitoring enables identification of failure conditions and potential problems. Monitoring helps to reduce the time needed to recover from failures.

Typically, application monitoring is the responsibility of administrators and operators within the operations team. It is critical for an operations team to establish guidelines and procedures for application monitoring. Communicating these procedures to the development team allows both teams to work together to log and monitor information that can assist problem discovery and problem diagnosis. This process is ongoing and requires revision; both the operations and development teams should strive to continually refine monitoring processes.

Error logging is closely related to monitoring and is a development function. You should design an appropriate strategy for error management at an early stage during the design phase. The development team must communicate with the operations team to inform them of the types of error logs generated by the application. The operations team must inform the development team of the various mechanisms that are available for monitoring errors. Together, both teams must decide on the appropriate logging mechanisms and then develop and monitor applications accordingly.

The monitoring plan

The monitoring plan defines the process by which the operational environment will monitor the solution. It describes what will be monitored, how it will be monitored, and how the results of monitoring will be reported and used. Organizations use automated procedures to monitor many aspects of a solution.

The plan provides details of the monitoring process, which will be incorporated into the functional specification. Once incorporated into the functional specification, the monitoring process (manual and automated) is included in the solution design. Monitoring ensures that operators are made aware that a failure has occurred so that they can initiate procedures to restore service. Additionally, some organizations monitor their servers' performance characteristics to identify usage trends. This process allows organizations to identify the conditions that contribute to system failure and to take action to prevent those conditions from occurring.

Elements of the monitoring plan

Some of the key sections of the monitoring plan are:

- *Resource threshold monitoring.* Identifies the solution resources that will be monitored. This section also includes the threshold values of each of the resources. A threshold value might be, for example, when processor usage increases to more than 80 percent.

- *Performance monitoring.* Defines the performance metrics to be gathered for the performance of the solution and the individual components of the solution. This section indicates the events that will be recorded and monitored, their frequency of occurrence, start and end times, and success and failure status. For example, you can record the logon attempts made by users, and the number of repeated failed logon attempts by the same user.

- *Trend analysis.* Defines the analysis that will take place on the data collected during performance monitoring. You can use this information for predicting the performance of the application under varying situations. For example, you can predict the number of users for various parts of the day and determine how the application will perform under varying loads.

- *Detecting failures.* Describes how the development, operations, and maintenance teams will use the functional specification and user acceptance criteria to detect failure incidents. You use the functional specification to determine the success criteria for the solution. This information is also included in the user acceptance criteria. For example, if shoppers must be able to browse items and select them from a list, and the list does not display any items, the event is marked as a failure.

- *Error detection.* Describes the processes, methods, and tools teams will use to detect and diagnose solution errors. These errors are typically identified and resolved by the development, operations, and maintenance teams without the knowledge of the users.

- *Event logs.* Describes the logs that will provide a system for capturing and reviewing significant application and system events. For example, you can use Microsoft SQL Server™ logs for an application that uses a SQL Server database.

- *Notifications.* Describes how the operations team will be notified when monitoring and exception trapping has detected solution failures. Notification methods can include pagers and e-mail.

■ *Tools.* Describes the tools teams can use to detect, diagnose, and correct errors and to improve a solution's performance. The team can use tools such as Microsoft Systems Management Server and System Monitor.

How to Plan for Data Migration

When data from earlier or existing sources is identified as a part of the new solution, data migration becomes a critical element. Without well-tested migration paths, new solutions can fail because earlier components can introduce risks that were never accounted for during planning. If data from earlier systems cannot be migrated successfully to the new solution, the new solution cannot be deployed and a return on investment cannot begin.

The migration plan describes the migration from existing systems or applications to the new solution. Migration is often more important in infrastructure deployment than it is in application development projects, but application development projects usually include some sort of migration.

The migration plan includes the following sections:

■ *Migration strategies.* Describes the strategy or strategies that will guide the migration process. These strategies do not need to be mutually exclusive but can describe different pieces of the overall migration. Strategy can be organized around releases (related to the business or to development or technology maturity) or organized around solution components. These strategies also need to take into account moving earlier systems into the new solution environment. You might have multiple migration strategy sections if you need to migrate both business objects and data.

■ *Tools.* Identifies the tools that will be used to support the migration strategy. These tools can include conversion tools, installation tools, testing tools, and training tools.

■ *Migration guidelines.* Describes the guidelines that must be followed within the environment, such as how migrated data will be validated or in what order data must be migrated.

■ *Migration process.* Describes how the migration will be conducted. It includes the preparatory activities in addition to the migration stages necessary to complete the migration process.

■ *Test environment.* Describes the test environment that replicates the production environment. This includes all environmental attributes that must be in place.

■ *Rollback plan.* Describes how a customer can roll back to the prior configuration if problems occur during migration.

How to Create Licensing Specifications

It is a good practice to determine purchasing requirements early in the project for both hardware and software that will be required by the solution. Purchasing specifications developed early in the process ensure that there is sufficient time for the approval process and that vendors have sufficient time to deliver hardware so as not to affect the schedule. An important part of purchasing specifications is licensing specifications.

You need to provide licensing specifications for both the developing and deploying phases. During the developing phase, the team will work with selected technologies and software products. You must ensure that you have sufficient licenses of the required products.

Depending on the type of solution and the number of users who will use the solution, you need to specify the number of licenses of any software that might be used.

For example, if your application can be deployed only on Windows XP, you need the appropriate number of Windows XP licenses for all users to install and run the application.

Lesson 3: Planning for Future Phases

The MSF Process Model consists of five phases: envisioning, planning, developing, stabilizing, and deploying. During the planning phase, you plan what will be developed, how it will be developed, and who will develop it. You also create plans for the activities that must be performed in the subsequent phases.

In this lesson, you will learn to plan for tasks in the subsequent phases of the project.

After this lesson, you will be able to

- Create plans for the developing phase.
- Create plans for the stabilizing phase.
- Create plans for the deploying phase.

Estimated lesson time: 5 minutes

How to Plan for the Developing Phase

Before the team actually begins developing the solution, it is important to verify that the infrastructure of the development and test environments is ready. The test environment should ideally represent the production environment, but the team must balance the level of representation with the associated costs. It is important to maintain separation between the production environment and the development and test environments to prevent occurrences in development and test from affecting live production systems.

The development plan

During the planning phase, the project team creates a master project plan and a master project schedule. In addition, the team can create a development plan and a development schedule. The development plan describes the solution development process used for the project, in addition to the tasks necessary to create and assemble the components of the solution. This plan complements the functional specification that provides the technical details of what will be developed. The plan also provides consistent guidelines and processes to the teams creating the solution.

Having the development process documented indicates that the team has discussed and agreed on a consistent structure and direction to be used during the development process. This documentation allows developers to focus on creating the solution. Development guidelines and standards promote meaningful communication among the various teams, because they will use a common approach and common processes. The guidelines and standards also facilitate reuse among different groups and minimize the dependency upon one individual or group.

The development role in the MSF Team Model creates the development plan and the development schedule. The focus of the development role during this process is to consider how key aspects of the development process should be undertaken.

Elements of the development plan

Some of the key sections of the development plan are:

- *Development objectives.* Defines the primary drivers that were used to create the development approach and the key objectives of that approach.

- *Overall delivery strategy.* Describes the overall approach to delivering the solution. Examples of delivery strategy include staged delivery, depth-first, breadth-first, and features then performance.

- *Tradeoff approach.* Defines the approach for making design and implementation of tradeoff decisions. For example, you might agree to trade features for schedule improvements or to trade features for performance.

- *Key design goals.* Identifies the key design goals and the priority of each goal. Examples of design goals include interoperability and security.

- *Development and build environment.* Describes the development and build environment and how it will be managed. Include information on items such as source code control tools, design tool requirements, operating systems, or other software installed.

- *Guidelines and standards.* Lists and provides references to all standards and guidelines to be used for the project.

- *Versioning and source control.* Describes how versioning and source control will be managed. This section includes identification of the specific tools that will be used and how developers are expected to use them.

- *Build process.* Describes the incremental and iterative approach for developing code and for builds of hardware and software components. It also describes how the build process will be implemented and how often it will be implemented.

- *Components.* Provides a high-level description of the set of solution components and how they will be developed.

- *Configuration and development management tools.* Identifies all the development tools the team will use during the project. This includes tools for all steps in the project: development, testing, documentation, support, operations, and deployment.

- *Design patterns.* Identifies the design patterns or templates that the team will use for this project and their sources. The team can acquire design patterns from both external and internal sources or create new design patterns.

- *Development team training.* Identifies the training necessary to ensure that the development team will successfully develop the solution.

■ *Development team support.* Identifies the various types of support the development team will require, the sources of that support, the amount of support of each type that the team will require, and the estimated schedule for support.

How to Plan for the Stabilizing Phase

During the stabilizing phase, the testing team conducts tests on a solution whose features are complete. Testing during this phase emphasizes usage and operation under realistic environmental conditions. The team focuses on resolving and prioritizing bugs and preparing the solution for release.

During the planning phase, the team typically creates the following plans that will be used during the stabilizing phase:

■ The test plan
■ The pilot plan

The test plan

The test plan describes the strategy and approach used to plan, organize, and manage the project's testing activities. It identifies testing objectives, methodologies and tools, expected results, responsibilities, and resource requirements. This document is the primary plan for the testing team. A test plan ensures that the testing process will be conducted in a thorough and organized manner and will enable the team to determine the stability of the solution. A continuous understanding of the solution's status builds confidence in team members and stakeholders as the solution is developed and stabilized.

The testing role in the MSF Team Model is responsible for creating the test plan. This team is also responsible for setting the quality expectations and incorporating them into the testing plan.

The test plan breaks the testing process into different elements, including:

■ Code component testing
■ Database testing
■ Infrastructure testing
■ Security testing
■ Integration testing
■ User acceptance and usability testing
■ Stress, capacity, and performance testing
■ Regression testing

Elements of the test plan

The key sections of a test plan are:

- *Test approach and assumptions.* Describes at a high level the approach, activities, and techniques to be followed in testing the solution. If different approaches are required for the solution's various components, you need to specify which components will be tested by each approach.

- *Major test responsibilities.* Identifies the teams and individuals who will manage and implement the testing process.

- *Features and functionality to test.* Identifies at a high level all features and functionality that will be tested.

- *Expected results of tests.* Describes the results that should be demonstrated by the tests. This information includes expectations of both the solution team and the testers. This section also defines whether the results must be exactly as anticipated or whether a range of results is acceptable.

- *Deliverables.* Describes the materials that must be made available or created to conduct the tests and that will be developed from the tests to describe test results.

- *Testing procedures and walkthrough.* Describes the steps the testing team will perform to ensure quality tests.

- *Tracking and reporting status.* Defines the information that test team members will communicate during the testing process. This section defines the specific test status information that will be created and distributed. This information normally includes status information for each test case and the probability of completing the test cycle on schedule.

- *Bug reporting tools and methods.* Describes the overall bug reporting strategy and methodology. This section also defines what will qualify as a bug in the code, product features, and documentation.

- *Schedules.* Identifies the major test cycles, tasks, milestones, and deliverables. This section also describes who is responsible for each test cycle and its tasks. In addition, it identifies the expected start and completion date for each test cycle and the tasks within that cycle.

For the test plan for the Adventure Works Cycles case study, refer to the AWC Test Plan document in the \SolutionDocuments\Chapter10 folder on the companion CD.

Note   Testing is covered in detail in Chapter 11, "Stabilizing and Deploying the Solution."

The pilot plan

The pilot plan describes how the team will move the candidate release version of the solution to a staging area and test it. The goal of the pilot is to simulate the equipment, software, and components that the solution will use when it is active.

This plan also identifies how issues discovered during the pilot will be solved. The pilot plan includes details about how to evaluate the pilot; the results of the evaluation will facilitate a decision whether to move the solution to production.

Project teams often conduct one or more pilots to prove the feasibility of solution approaches, to experiment with different solutions, and to obtain user feedback and acceptance on proposed solutions. Pilot solutions implement only those subsets or segments of requirements or the functional specification that are necessary to validate the solution.

Note   Some projects might not conduct a pilot.

The pilot plan provides the means to validate the business requirements and the technical specification prior to deploying the solution into production. Planning the details of the pilot ensures that the participating project teams identify their roles and responsibilities and resource requirements specific to pilot development, testing, and deployment activities.

Note   You can learn more about creating pilot plans in Chapter 11, "Stabilizing and Deploying the Solution."

How to Plan for the Deploying Phase

During the deploying phase, the team deploys the solution technology and components, stabilizes the deployment, transitions the project to operations and support, and obtains final customer approval of the project.

The deployment plan

During the planning phase, the team typically creates the deployment plan. The deployment plan describes the factors necessary for a relatively problem-free deployment and transition to ongoing operations. It includes the processes of preparing, installing, training, stabilizing, and transferring the solution to operations. These processes include details of installation scenarios, monitoring for stability, and verifying the soundness of the new solution. This plan guides the implementation of the solution into production. This plan also provides detailed deployment guidelines and helps drive the solution's deploying phase. Deployment is the beginning of the realization of business value for a given solution. A detailed and verified deployment plan accelerates value realization for both the customer and the project team.

The release management role of the MSF Team Model is responsible for designing and implementing the solution's deployment plan. Release management is also responsible for specifying the solution infrastructure and ensuring that the solution continues to run as expected after it has been deployed.

Elements of the deployment plan

Some of the key sections of the deployment plan are:

- *Deployment scope*. Describes the solution architecture and scale of deployment.
- *Seats*. Describes the magnitude of the deployment in terms of sites, number of workstations, countries and regions, and other relevant size factors.
- *Components*. Lists and describes the components to be deployed and any critical dependencies among them.
- *Architecture*. Describes the solution's architecture and how it might affect deployment.
- *Deployment schedule*. Identifies the critical dates and anticipated schedule for the deploying phase.
- *Installation*. Defines how the overall deployment will occur.
- *Deployment resources*. Identifies the workforce that will be needed to complete the deployment and the sources of the personnel.
- *Solution support*. Describes how the users will be supported during the deployment.
- *Help desk*. Describes the support provided to users and applications by the help desk team, including support for direct user questions and application issues, and also in-depth support for new or difficult issues.
- *Desktop*. Describes any changes in current workstation application support that might be required during deployment.
- *Servers*. Describes any changes in current server support that might be required during deployment.
- *Telecommunications*. Describes any changes in current telecommunication support that might be required during deployment.
- *Coordination of training*. Describes how end-user and support staff training is coordinated with the deployment schedule.
- *Site installation process*. Describes the four phases of site installation: preparing, installing, training, and stabilizing.

Lesson 4: Creating the Technical Specification

To begin creating the solution, the development team uses the technical specification document. In this lesson, you will learn about technical specification and the components of a technical specification document.

After this lesson, you will be able to

- Describe the purpose of technical specification.
- List the elements of a technical specification document.

Estimated lesson time: 5 minutes

What Is the Technical Specification?

The technical specification is a set of reference documents that usually include the artifacts of physical design, such as class specifications, component models, metrics, and network and component topologies. During the developing phase, the developers use the technical specification to scope and define their work products. The technical specification includes interface definitions, registry entries, bytes required to install, dynamic-link library (DLL) and assembly names, strong names, keys, and all identified elements that will affect deployment. When elements of the solution are completed during development, the technical specification is updated to ensure that it documents the solution.

Elements of a Technical Specification Document

The sections of a technical specification include:

- *Architecture overview*. Describes the architecture that will be implemented by the solution.
- *Object model*. Describes the object model of the solution. This section includes a description of all objects in the solution and their functionality.
- *Interfaces*. Contains the code and details of methods of each interface in the solution.
- *Code flow*. Describes the operation of each method in the solution.
- *Error codes*. Describes the error codes used for error handling in the solution.
- *Error logging*. Describes how various errors will be handled and logged in the solution.
- *Configuration*. Describes how the solution will be registered on the destination computer. This section includes registry keys and their settings.

- *Supporting documentation.* Lists the documents that describe the solution, such as the functional specification, and their locations.
- *Issues.* Describes any known issues with the solution. Typically, the probable date of resolution for each is also specified in this section.

For the technical specification for the Adventure Works Cycles case study, refer to AWC Technical Specification.doc in the \SolutionDocuments\Chapter10 folder on the companion CD. This is a draft version of the technical specification document, as it would look prior to the developing phase. This document is updated throughout the developing phase.

Activity: Reviewing a Test Plan and Technical Specification

In this activity, you use what you learned in the lessons to work through a review of a test plan and a technical specification.

Exercise 1: Reviewing a Test Plan

Open the document named AWC Test Plan.doc in the \SolutionDocuments\Chapter10 folder on the companion CD.

1. Review the test plan and then list three ways that use cases and usage scenarios are used in the testing process for AdventureWorks Cycles.

2. How will bugs be approved and documented for action for the solution?

3. Which user accounts must be configured on the test environment servers?

4. Why is the following threat important to list under threats to testing?

   Availability of sales staff for testing. The test team should be overseen by at least one sales representative. Mitigation: Gain prior agreement from the vice president of sales for two sales representatives to be assigned to test the application

Exercise 2: Reviewing a Technical Specification

Open the document named AWC Technical Specification.doc in the \SolutionDocuments\Chapter10 folder on the companion CD. Answer the following questions:

1. What are the parameters for the *addOrderDetail* method?

2. Will two types of client interfaces be available in the application?

3. Why is the Interfaces section still to be determined?

Summary

- Scalability is defined as the capability to increase resources to yield a linear increase in service capacity.
- You can either scale up or scale out an application.
- Guidelines for scaling include:
    - Design processes so that they do not wait
    - Design processes so that they do not fight for resources
    - Design processes for commutability
    - Design components for interchangeability
    - Partition resources and activities
- Availability is a measure of how often an application is available for use.
- To decide the availability level of an application, you need to answer the following questions:
    - Who are the customers and what are their expectations?
    - How much downtime is acceptable?
    - Do internal company processes depend on the application?
    - What are the schedule and budget for developing the application?
- Guidelines for designing for availability of a solution include:
    - Reduce planned downtime
    - Reduce unplanned downtime by using clustering
    - Use network load balancing
    - Use RAID for data stores
    - Isolate mission-critical applications
    - Use queuing
- The process of designing for reliability involves reviewing the application's expected usage pattern, specifying the required reliability profile, and engineering the software architecture with the intention of meeting the profile.

- To create a good reliability design, you need to perform the following tasks:
    - Put reliability requirements in the specification.
    - Use a good architectural infrastructure.
    - Include management information in the application.
    - Use redundancy.
    - Use quality development tools.
    - Use reliability checks that are provided by the application.
    - Use consistent error handling.
    - Reduce the application's functionality instead of completely failing the application.
- An application's performance is defined by key application metrics, such as transaction throughput and resource utilization.
- To determine performance goals, you need to answer questions such as the following:
    - What is the business goal?
    - What is the critical functionality of the solution?
    - What are the features required by different sets of users?
- To integrate heterogeneous applications, you need to consider the following types of interoperability:
    - Network interoperability, which provides the core foundation for interoperability between systems
    - Data interoperability, which delivers the ability for users and applications to access and query information stored in both structured and unstructured storage engines
    - Applications interoperability, which provides the key infrastructure required to ensure interoperability between new and existing applications
    - Management interoperability, which focuses on reducing the burden of administration of multiple systems, including user accounts management
- Globalization is the process of designing and developing a software product that functions in multiple cultures and locales.
- Localization is the process of adapting a globalized application to a particular culture and locale.
- Application monitoring is used to ensure that the application is functioning correctly and performing at the optimal level.
- The monitoring plan describes what will be monitored, how the application will be monitored, and how the results of monitoring will be reported and used.

- The migration plan describes the migration from existing systems or applications to the new solution.
- You need to provide licensing specifications for both the developing and deploying phases.
- The development plan describes the solution development process used for the project.
- The test plan describes the strategy and approach used to plan, organize, and manage the project's testing activities, and identifies testing objectives, methodologies and tools, expected results, responsibilities, and resource requirements.
- The pilot plan describes elements of the solution that will be delivered as a pilot and provides the details necessary to conduct the pilot successfully.
- The deployment plan describes the factors necessary for a smooth deployment and transition to ongoing operations and includes the processes of preparing, installing, training, stabilizing, and transferring the solution to operations.
- The technical specification is a set of reference documents that usually include the artifacts of physical design, such as class specifications, component models, metrics, and network and component topologies.

Review

The following questions are intended to reinforce key information presented in this chapter. If you are unable to answer a question, review the lesson materials and try the question again. You can find answers to the questions in the appendix.

1. How do you scale up an application?

2. What do you need to take into consideration while designing for scalability?

3. What do you need to take into consideration while designing for availability?

4. How does clustering enhance the availability of an application?

5. How do you reduce planned downtime of an application?

6. Why is reliability an important design consideration for an application?

7. How do you design for reliability of an application?

8. How do you define a performance requirement?

9. Why do you need to design for interoperability?

10. How do you prepare an application for globalization?

11. What is the purpose of a monitoring plan?

12. What is the purpose of the migration strategies section of the migration plan?

13. Why do you need to provide licensing specifications for both the development and the deployment phase?

14. What is the purpose of the development plan?

15. What is the purpose of the test plan?

16. Who creates the deployment plan?

17. What is a technical specification?

C H A P T E R   1 1

Stabilizing and Deploying the Solution

About This Chapter

After the development phase of a project is complete, the project enters its stabilizing and deploying phases. The goal of the stabilizing phase of the Microsoft® Solutions Framework (MSF) Process Model is to improve the quality of the solution to meet the acceptance criteria for release to production. During the deploying phase, the solution is deployed to the production environment.

Before You Begin

To complete the lessons in this chapter, you must have

- General understanding of Microsoft technologies.
- Understanding of the MSF process and its phases.

Lesson 1: The MSF Stabilizing Phase

During the stabilizing phase, testing is conducted on a solution whose features are complete. Testing starts early in the MSF process with activities such as defining the success criteria and the testing approach during the envisioning phase, and creating a testing plan during the planning phase. However, it is during the stabilizing phase that the Testing team completes the tasks and creates the deliverables that move the feature-complete build to a state in which the defined quality level is reached and the solution is ready for full production deployment.

Testing during this phase emphasizes usage and operation under realistic environmental conditions. The team focuses on resolving and prioritizing bugs and preparing the solution for release.

The two main tasks in the stabilizing phase are:

- *Testing the solution.* The team implements the test plans that were created during the planning phase, which were enhanced and tested during the development phase.
- *Conducting the pilot.* The team moves a solution pilot from development to a staging area to test the solution with actual users and real scenarios. The pilot is conducted before the deploying phase is begun.

After this lesson, you will be able to

- Explain the deliverables of the MSF stabilizing phase.
- Explain the interim milestones of the MSF stabilizing phase.
- Explain the team roles and responsibilities during the stabilizing phase.

Estimated lesson time: 15 minutes

MSF Stabilizing Phase Deliverables

The goal of the MSF stabilizing phase is to improve the quality of a solution and to stabilize it for release to production. During this phase, the team conducts testing on a feature-complete solution. The testing in this phase also includes testing the accuracy of supporting documentation, training, and other non-code elements.

The following are the deliverables of the stabilizing phase:

- Pilot review
- Release-ready versions of:
    - Source code and executables
    - Scripts and installation documentation
    - End-user Help and training materials
    - Operations documentation
    - Release notes
- Testing and bug reports
- Project documents

MSF Phase Interim Milestones

In addition to the deliverables, the stabilizing phase has interim milestones. The interim milestones of the stabilizing phase are:

- Bug convergence
- Zero-bug bounce
- Release candidates
- Golden release

Bug convergence

Bug convergence is the point at which the team makes visible progress against the active bug count. It is the point at which the rate of bugs that are resolved exceeds the rate of bugs that are found.

Figure 11.1 illustrates bug convergence.

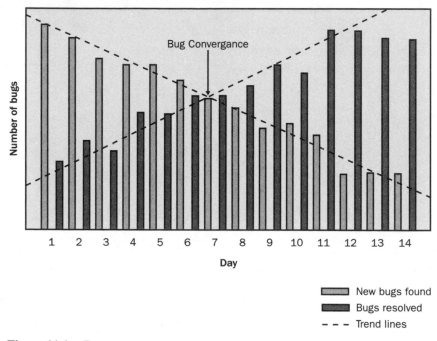

Figure 11.1.   Bug convergence

Because the bug rate will still vary—even after it starts its overall decline—bug convergence usually manifests itself as a trend rather than a fixed point in time. After bug convergence, the number of bugs should continue to decrease until zero-bug release.

Zero-bug bounce

Zero-bug bounce (ZBB) is the point in the project when development resolves all the bugs raised by Testing and there are no active bugs—for the moment. Figure 11.2 illustrates ZBB.

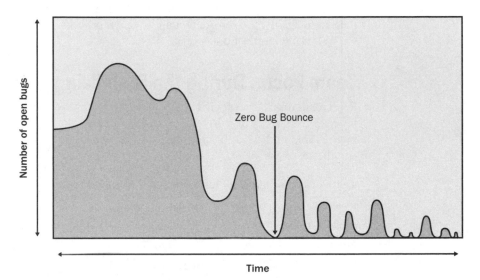

Figure 11.2.   Zero-bug bounce

After zero-bug bounce, the bug peaks should become noticeably smaller and should continue to decrease until the product is stable enough to release.

Careful bug prioritization is vital because every bug that is fixed creates the risk of creating a new bug, or regression issue. Achieving zero-bug bounce is a clear sign that the team is in the final stage as it progresses toward a stable product.

Note   New bugs will certainly be found after this milestone is reached. But it does mark the first time that the team can honestly report that there are no active bugs—even if it is only for the moment—and it focuses the team on working to stay at that point.

Release candidates

After the first achievement of zero-bug bounce, a series of *release candidates* are prepared for release to the pilot group. Each of these releases is marked as an interim milestone. The release candidates are made available to a preselected group of users so they can test it. The users provide feedback to the project team, and the project team in turn continues to improve the product and resolve bugs that appear during the pilot. As each new release candidate is built, there should be fewer bugs to report, prioritize, and resolve. Each release candidate indicates that the team is nearing the end of deployment.

Golden release

Golden release is the release of the product to production. Golden release is a milestone in the stabilizing phase, which is identified by the combination of *zero-defect* and *success criteria* metrics. At golden release, the team must select the release candidate that they will release to production. The team uses the testing data that is measured against the zero-defect and success criteria metrics and the tradeoff triangle to make this selection.

Team Focus During the Stabilizing Phase

Each team role has a specific focus and responsibilities during stabilization. The primary team roles that drive the stabilizing phase are testing and release management. Table 11.1 describes the roles and responsibilities of each team during the stabilizing phase.

Table 11.1. Stabilizing Phase Roles and Responsibilities

Role	Focus
Product management	Communications plan execution; production launch planning
Program management	Project tracking; bug priority
Development	Bug resolution; code optimization
User experience	Stabilization of user performance materials, training materials, user assistance materials
Testing	Testing; bug reporting and status; configuration testing
Release management	Pilot setup and support; deployment planning; operations and support training

Lesson 2: Testing and Piloting for Stabilization

The testing process is designed to identify and address potential solution issues prior to deployment. Testing certifies that the solution components meet the project plan's goals for schedule and quality. It should also verify that the solution components meet the agreed-upon feature set.

The development team designs, documents, and writes code that is tested through unit testing and daily builds. This team tracks development progress against a project schedule, resolves reported bugs, and documents testing results.

The testing team designs and documents test specifications and test cases, writes automated scripts, and runs acceptance tests on components that are submitted for formal testing. This team assesses and reports on overall solution quality and feature completeness, and certifies when the solution features, functions, and components meet the project goals.

After this lesson, you will be able to

- Identify the best practices of testing.
- Explain the types of testing in the MSF process.
- Explain the testing terms.
- Explain the issue and bug tracking process.
- Identify some of the tasks involved in testing.
- Explain the process of conducting a pilot.
- Close the stabilizing phase.

Estimated lesson time: 40 minutes

Testing Best Practices

There are some testing best practices that the testing team should consider implementing when testing a solution.

Success criteria

Judging whether a project has been successful is almost impossible without something to measure the project's results against. The creation of *success criteria* involves defining conditions under which the proposed solution will achieve its goals. Success criteria are sometimes referred to as *key performance indicators.*

Note   Although defined here, success criteria for a project needs to be established during the envisioning and planning phases.

Zero-defect mindset

Zero-defect mindset means that the project team commits to producing the highest quality product possible. Each team member is individually responsible for helping achieve the desired level of quality. The zero-defect mindset does not mean that the deployed solution must be perfect with literally no defects; rather, it specifies a pre-determined quality bar for the deliverables.

Testing Types

MSF defines two types of testing: coverage testing and usage testing.

Coverage testing

Coverage testing is low-level technical testing. For example, when a developer writes a section of code or a subject matter expert creates an automated unattended installation, he or she typically performs low-level testing to ensure that the solution meets the functional specification. In MSF, this type of testing is called coverage testing; in Microsoft product groups, it is also referred to as *prefix testing*.

Of course, if developers or subject matter experts are the only groups to perform coverage testing, risk is increased. Their closeness to the work and the pressures to deliver a finished product make it difficult for them to identify all issues and bugs in the solution. This is where *external coverage testing* can help. External coverage testing is low-level testing that is performed by a tester other than a developer or subject matter expert. Often this external coverage testing is automated to promote consistency and speed.

A typical strategy that is used for performing the coverage testing role is to use the *buddy tester* principle. Buddy testing involves using developers who are not working directly on the creation of a particular code segment, and employing them to perform coverage testing on their colleague's code. This strategy works well because the skills that are required by coverage testers are on the same level as the skills that are required for development.

Usage testing

Usage testing is high-level testing that is often performed by potential users of the solution or subsets of this group. This type of testing is very important because it ensures that issues and bugs that are related to user performance enhancement are captured and addressed. Automated scripts and check lists are a best practice in this area because they provide repeatability and prescriptive direction to the usage tester, which will improve accuracy.

Testing Terms

Before you learn more about testing a solution, it is important to be familiar with some basic testing terms.

Check-in tests

Check-in testing ensures that tested code is behaving acceptably. This type of testing is performed by developers or testers before the code is checked in to the change control system. Check-in testing can be thought of as the aggregation of all internal coverage tests that are performed by developers before the code is checked in to the change control system.

Unit tests

A unit test is a form of developer-performed internal *coverage testing* or *prefix testing* that takes advantage of automated testing. The philosophy behind unit testing is to perform testing on isolated features (one small piece at a time).

Functional tests

Functional tests are normally specified by the users of the solution and are created by the testing team. These tests are often automated tests and are normally conducted by the testing team. They focus on testing end-to-end functionality rather than isolated features.

Build verification tests

The objective of build verification testing is to identify errors during the build process. It can be thought of as the identification of compilation errors, as opposed to run-time errors, of all solution components. This type of testing can be performed by both developers and testers. For some projects, a specific team might perform these tests.

Regression tests

Regression testing is the process of repeating identical actions or steps that were performed using an earlier build of a product on a new build or version of the product. The goal of this process is to determine the following:

- Is the problem you previously reported still present?
- Has the problem been completely resolved?
- Did the resolution cause other or related problems?

Configuration tests

Most software-based solutions can be installed and configured in many different ways. The aim of configuration testing is to conduct solution tests in each of the possible solution configurations. Each of these configurations has the potential to affect the behavior of the solution and might result in the identification of new issues or bugs.

Compatibility tests

Often there is a requirement for the solution under development to integrate and interoperate with existing systems or software solutions. This form of testing focuses on integration or interoperability of the solution under development with existing systems.

This type of test often involves groups that are external to the project team. The external team must be identified as early as possible so its involvement can be planned for. Also, performing these tests in a completely isolated environment might not be possible.

Stress tests

Stress tests, also known as *load tests,* are specifically designed to identify issues or bugs that might present themselves when the solution under development is highly stressed. By stressing the solution, which most commonly entails loading the solution beyond the level that it was designed to handle, new issues or bugs might be seen.

Performance tests

Performance testing focuses on predicted performance improvements by the solution under development. These tests are often performed in conjunction with stress or loading tests. For example, if a design goal of the solution under development is to increase e-mail message throughput by 15 percent, tests would be devised to measure this predicted increase.

Documentation and Help file tests

This form of testing focuses on testing all developed support documents or systems. The documents and Help files are compared with the solution to discover any discrepancies. For example, testers might look for incorrect instructions, outdated text and screen shots, typographic errors, and so on.

Alpha and beta tests

In the MSF testing discipline, *alpha code* broadly refers to all code produced in the developing phase of the MSF Process Model, whereas *beta code* is all code tested in the stabilizing phase. Therefore, during the developing phase of the MSF Process Model tests are performed on alpha code, whereas during the stabilizing phase of the MSF Process Model tests are performed on beta code.

Parallel testing

Parallel testing is a common usage testing strategy. Parallel usage testing is testing both the current solution and the new solution, under development, side-by-side at the same time. The advantage of parallel usage testing is that it provides a quick check on expected solution behavior. For example, data is entered into the current solution and behaviors are observed. Then, the same data is entered into the new solution and its behavior is observed. These two observed behaviors can then be compared and used as usage testing data.

Planning   Parallel testing can be automated to quickly help validate the results without involving production users. However, the disadvantage of parallel testing is that if parallel testing cannot be automated, it doubles the work load of production users.

How to Categorize and Track Bugs

It is impossible to release a high quality solution to production without data from an issue or bug tracking system. Without a bug tracking system, the team cannot judge whether the zero-defect criteria have been met.

Categorization process

The MSF issue or bug categorization process builds on the risk categorization system of the MSF risk management process. In the MSF risk categorization system, team members are asked to estimate risk probability and impact, and these two variables are multiplied together to derive the risk exposure value, which is used in turn to prioritize these risks.

The issue or bug categorization prioritization system is a similar system. A risk is something that has not yet occurred, so probability of occurrence and impact of the risk to the project are appropriate variables to estimate. However, issues or bugs are things that have happened or exist now. The important variables to an individual issue or a bug are:

- *Repeatability.* A variable that measures how repeatable the issue or bug is. Repeatability is the percentage of the time the issue or bug manifests itself. Is the issue or bug 100 percent repeatable, or can it be reproduced only 10 percent of the time? Note that zero is not a valid metric here because it would mean the issue or bug is never repeatable.

- *Visibility.* A variable that measures the situation or environment that must be established before the issue or bug manifests itself. For example, if the issue or bug occurs only when the user holds down the Shift key while right-clicking the mouse and viewing the File menu, the percentage of obscurity is high. A highly obscure issue or bug is not very visible and therefore not as compelling as a highly visible issue or bug.

- *Severity.* A variable that measures how much impact the issue or bug will produce in the solution, in the code, or to the users. For example, when an issue or bug occurs, does it crash the operating system or application, or does it cause one pixel of color to change on a menu bar? To be able to assign severity, the project team needs to define a list of problematic situations, with associated severity. For example, if the system crashes with loss of data and no workaround, it is severity 10; if it crashes with loss of data but with a workaround, it could be severity 9.

These three variables are estimated and assigned to each issue or bug by the project team and are used to derive the issue or bug priority. Table 11.2 describes the symmetrical scales to assign a value to each variable.

Table 11.2.   Variables for Categorizing Bugs

Variable	Scale
Repeatability	A percentage in the range of 10% (integer value '0.1') through 100% (integer value '1'), where 100% indicates that the issue or bug is reproducible on every test run.
Visibility	A percentage in the range of 10% (integer value '0.1') through 100% (integer value '1'), where 10% indicates that the issue or bug is visible under only the most obscure conditions. Issues or bugs that manifest themselves in environments with simple conditions are said to be highly visible.
Severity	An integer in the range of 1 through 10, where classification 10 issues or bugs present the most impact to the solution or code.

The priority of a bug can be calculated by using the following formula:

```
(Repeatability + Visibility) * Severity = Priority
```

Table 11.3 provides an example of this priority calculation displayed in a matrix.

Table 11.3.   Bug Prioritization Matrix

Description	Repeatability	Visibility	Severity	Priority	Submitted By	Assigned To
Description	1	1	10	20.0	Name	Name
Description	0.9	0.9	9	16.2	Name	Name
Description	0.8	0.8	8	12.8	Name	Name
Description	0.7	0.7	7	9.8	Name	Name
Description	0.6	0.6	6	7.2	Name	Name
Description	0.5	0.5	5	5.0	Name	Name
Description	0.4	0.4	4	3.2	Name	Name

Issue or bug tracking process

The bug tracking process, shown in Figure 11.3, is driven by the development and testing roles.

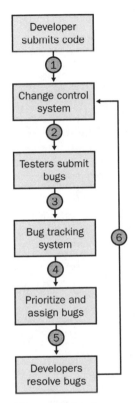

Figure 11.3.   Issue or bug tracking process

The steps in the bug tracking process are:

1. Developers develop code, perform internal coverage testing, and then check this code into the change control system.

2. Testers perform the daily or periodic build and external coverage testing on all submitted code.

3. Testers submit issues or bugs into the issue or bug tracking system, entering issue or bug descriptions and Repeatability, Severity, and Visibility variables.

4. The development and test leads conduct a Prioritization or Issue/Bug Prioritizing meeting and:

   - Calculate the priority of each issue or bug. This task is referred to in the MSF Testing Method as *Issue/Bug Prioritizing.*

   - Assign issues or bugs that exceed the zero-defect criteria to developers for correction.

   - Retire issues or bugs from a previous cycle of the sub-process that were corrected.

5. Assigned developers resolve or correct issue or bug.

6. Developers perform internal coverage testing and then check this code into the change control system.

This is a continuous process that starts again when developers develop code and check it into the change control system.

Testing Tasks

Two important tasks in the MSF Testing Method are *code reviews* and *development environment construction*. These two project tasks are very important to the successful implementation of the MSF Testing Method.

Code reviews

The MSF Testing Method defines three types of code reviews:

- *Comprehensive.* A comprehensive code review is a formal review in which the developer is asked to present or walk through his or her code with the rest of the development team.

- *Casual.* A casual code review is a peer-based review that is conducted by other developers from the direct development team. This is a particularly good strategy to mentor junior developers.

- *Independent.* An independent code review is a review that is conducted by a third-party organization with the goal of providing a fresh set of eyes to review the code.

Testing environment construction

Before any development and therefore testing work can proceed, it is important that a development and testing environment is designed and built. This environment must be separated from the production environment and be capable of accommodating both development and testing requirements. Typical testing requirements are:

- *Build hardware* to enable the testers to perform the daily and periodic builds.

- *Automate testing* to facilitate the automation of as many test functions as possible.

- *Create change control systems*; these systems must be in place and accessible to the testers.

- *Create issue or bug tracking systems*; these systems must be in place and accessible to the testers.

How to Conduct a Pilot

A *pilot* is a test of the solution in the production environment, and a trial of the solution by installers, systems support staff, and end users. The primary purposes of a pilot are to demonstrate that the design works in the production environment as expected and that it meets the organization's business requirements. A secondary purpose is to give the deployment team a chance to practice and refine the deployment process.

A pilot tests the solution under live conditions and takes various forms depending on the type of project.

- In an enterprise, a pilot can consist of a group of users or a set of servers in a data center.
- In Web development, a pilot can take the form of hosting site files on staging servers or folders that are live on the Internet, only with a test Web address.
- Commercial software vendors, such as Microsoft, often release products to a special group of early adopters prior to final release.

These various forms of piloting have one element in common—the tests occur in a live production environment. The pilot is not complete until the team ensures that the proposed solution is viable in the production environment and every component of the solution is ready for deployment.

Process

The pilot is the last major step before full-scale deployment of the solution. Prior to the pilot, integration testing must be completed in the test lab environment.

The pilot provides an opportunity for users to provide feedback about how features work. This feedback must be used to resolve any issues or to create a contingency plan. The feedback can help the team determine the level of support they are likely to need after full deployment. Some of the feedback can also contribute to the next version of the product.

Important   Ultimately, the pilot leads to a decision either to proceed with a full deployment or to delay deployment so you can resolve problems that could jeopardize deployment.

The pilot process is iterative. It starts with planning tasks, such as creating a pilot plan and preparing users and sites, and then moves to implementing the pilot, evaluating the results, fixing problems, and deploying another version until reaching the scope and quality that indicate the readiness for a full deployment.

Figure 11.4 illustrates the primary steps for planning and conducting a pilot.

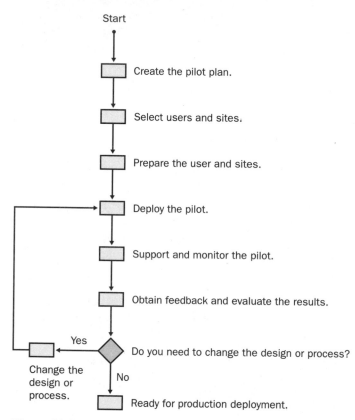

Figure 11.4.   Conducting a pilot

Preparing for the pilot

A pilot deployment needs to be rehearsed to minimize the risk of disruption for the pilot group. At this stage, the development team is performing last-minute checks and ensuring that nothing has changed since pre-production testing. The following tasks need to be completed before starting the pilot:

- The development team and the pilot participants must clearly identify and agree on the success criteria of the pilot. The criteria should map back to the success criteria for the development effort.

- A support structure and issue-resolution process must be in place. This process might require that support staff be trained. The procedures used for issue resolution during a pilot can vary significantly from those used during deployment and when in full production.

- To identify any issues and confirm that the deployment process will work, it is necessary to implement a trial run or a rehearsal of all the elements of the deployment.

■   It is necessary to obtain customer approval of the pilot plan. Work on the pilot plan starts early during the planning phase so that the communication channels are in place and the participants are prepared by the time the test team is ready to deploy the pilot.

Tip   The pilot sets the tone for the full deployment, so it is important that the plan is developed carefully and communicated effectively to the participants, and that the results are evaluated thoroughly.

A recommended pilot plan includes the following:

■   Scope and objectives

■   Participating users, locations, and contact information

■   Training plan for pilot users

■   Support plan for the pilot

■   Communication plan for the pilot

■   Known risks and contingency plans

■   Rollback plan

■   Schedule for deploying and conducting the pilot

Implementing the pilot

Avoid the mistake of making pilot testing too easy. As much as possible, try every use case and scenario that will arise in production, including operations tasks, by including various use cases and scenarios in the rollout group. It is also recommended that you intentionally cause the pilot to fail so that you can test rollback procedures, disaster recovery, and business continuity planning.

Evaluating the results

At the end of the pilot, its success is evaluated and the next step is recommended. The project team then needs to decide whether to continue the project beyond the pilot. To help with the evaluation and recommendation, analyze information from a variety of sources. For example, obtain information from:

■   Web site feedback forms

■   Sessions with business managers

■   Problem reports

■   End-user surveys

■   Observations of the IT project team

■   Solution and operating system logs

It is important to obtain information about both the design and the deployment processes. Review what worked and what did not work so that it is possible to revise and refine the plan. Example of information to be gathered includes:

- Training required for using the solution
- Rollout process
- Support required for the solution
- Communications
- Problems encountered
- Suggestions for improvements

The feedback is used to validate that the delivered design meets the design specification, as well as the business requirements. The pilot is then evaluated to answer the following questions:

- Did the pilot meet the success criteria you defined before the pilot began?
- If metrics were established to measure your success, how did the pilot measure up?

After the data is evaluated, the team must make a decision. The team can select one of following strategies:

- *Stagger forward.* Prepare another release candidate and release it to the original group and then to additional groups in serial fashion. The release to more than one group might have been part of the original plan or might have been a contingency triggered by an unacceptable first pilot.
- *Roll back.* Return the pilot group to their pre-pilot state.
- *Suspend the pilot.* Put the solution on hold or cancel it.
- *Patch and continue.* Fix the build that the pilot is running and continue.
- *Proceed to deployment phase.* Move forward to deploy the pilot build to the full live production environment.

Outputs of conducting a pilot

As cycles of the pilot tests are completed, the team prepares reports detailing each lesson learned and how new information or issues are resolved. The following can result from performing the pilot testing:

- The identification of additional risks
- The identification of frequently asked questions for training purposes
- The identification of user errors for training and documentation purposes
- The ability to secure buy-in and support from pilot users
- Documentation of concerns and issue resolutions
- Updates to documentation—particularly Help files and deployment plans
- Determination of whether all success criteria were met

How to Close the Stabilizing Phase

Closing the stabilizing phase requires completing a milestone approval process. The team needs to document the results of the different tasks it has performed in this phase to submit the project to management for approval.

The stabilizing phase culminates in the *release readiness approved* milestone. This milestone occurs when the team has addressed all outstanding issues and has released the solution and made it available for full deployment. This milestone is the opportunity for customers and users, operations and support personnel, and key project stakeholders to evaluate the solution and identify any remaining issues they need to address before beginning the transition to deployment and, ultimately, release.

After all of the stabilization tasks are complete, the team must formally agree that the project has reached the milestone of release readiness. As the team progresses from the release milestone to the next phase of deploying, responsibility for on-going management and support of the solution officially transfers from the project team to the operations and support teams. By agreeing, team members signify that they are satisfied with the work that is performed in their areas of responsibility.

Project teams usually mark the completion of a milestone with a formal sign-off. Key stakeholders, typically representatives of each team role and any important customer representatives who are not on the project team, signal their approval of the milestone by signing or initialing a document stating that the milestone is complete. The sign-off document becomes a project deliverable and is archived for future reference.

Lesson 3: The MSF Deploying Phase

At the end of the stabilizing phase, the *release readiness approved* milestone indicates the solution's readiness for deployment into the production environment.

During the deploying phase, the team deploys the solution technology and components, stabilizes the deployment, moves the project to operations and support, and obtains final customer approval of the project. After the deployment, the team conducts a project review and a customer satisfaction survey. Stabilizing activities might continue during this period as the project components are transferred from a test or staging environment to a production environment.

After this lesson, you will be able to

- Describe the dynamics of the team composition during deployment.
- Explain the goal, milestones, and deliverables of the MSF deploying phase.

Estimated lesson time: 15 minutes

MSF Deploying Phase Milestones and Deliverables

The main deploying tasks include preparing for deployment and then deploying the solution. After deployment, stabilization, and transfer to operations, the project team conducts a project review.

The deploying phase culminates in the *deployment complete* milestone. Deliverables during this phase are:

- Operations and support information systems
- Procedures and processes
- Knowledge base, reports, and logbooks
- Repository of all versions of documents, configurations, scripts, and code
- Project closeout report
    - Project documents
    - Customer survey
    - Next steps

Team Focus During the Deploying Phase

After completing the stabilizing phase, the project team can migrate to the deploying phase in a variety of ways. One deployment option is to use the organization's operations team to handle the actual deployment. If the operations team manages the entire deployment, representatives from the development team usually remain on the project for a period of time after going live to mitigate potential problems during the transfer of ownership. Another option is to combine members from each group and create a separate deployment team. The release management role is responsible for coordinating the required activities that ensure a successful deployment.

Table 11.4 lists the focus and responsibility areas of each team role during deploying.

Table 11.4.   Deploying Phase Roles and Responsibilities

Role	Responsibility
Product management	Customer feedback, assessment, sign-off
Program management	Solution/scope comparison; stabilization management
Development	Problem resolution; escalation support
User experience	Training; training schedule management
Testing	Performance testing; problem identification, definition, resolution, and reporting
Release management	Site deployment management; change approval

Deployment Scenarios

Some of the solution scenarios for deployment include Web applications and services, client/server applications, packaged applications, enterprise infrastructure, and mobile applications.

The MSF process model works regardless of the type of project you are trying to deploy. However, the complexity and length of the deploying phase varies depending on what you are deploying. For example, a Web application can be deployed with ease and minimal impact to physical locations, geographies, and workstations, whereas an infrastructure project that involves rolling out workstations is a longer and more complicated process. It is essential to make sure the team's solution scenario for deployment is appropriate for the project type.

In addition to the solution scenarios, it is necessary to consider the types of hardware and operating system requirements when deploying a solution. A solution needs a different type of solution scenario depending on whether it is to be deployed to a datacenter, to a group of enterprise servers, or to mobile devices. Some of the hardware and operating system requirements for solution scenarios include:

- Enterprise servers
- Datacenter (Internet, department, global)
- Web services
- Clients (desktop, mobile)

Lesson 4: Deploying to a Production Environment

This lesson focuses on the considerations that are involved in deploying a solution to a production environment and the steps that are taken in the deployment.

After this lesson, you will be able to

- Explain how to plan for deployment.
- Distinguish between core and site-specific components.
- Deploy core components.
- Deploy site-specific components.
- Explain how to prepare for the transition to operations.
- Describe the steps for deploying the solution to a production environment.
- Explain the closeout activities for the deploying phase.

Estimated lesson time: 30 minutes

How to Plan for Deployment

During development and especially as the stabilizing phase nears completion, the release management lead assigns deployment tasks to staff members. These individuals review the project status and test results, and update the deployment plan, which is initially created during the planning phase. The team creates task-based procedures that help ensure a successful deployment.

Staging and production environments

To be ready for deployment, the physical infrastructure, system software, and application software are tested, installed, and configured in their respective environments.

Documentation

The project team and operations representatives revisit and update the following documentation:

- *Deployment diagrams* that are created during the planning phase.
- A *test plan* that includes coverage for areas that are exposed in real use. The operation team needs to update the test plans that were created during the planning phase.
- A *security plan* that the operations team uses to ensure that all personnel are aware of the security standards and rules to which the project adheres.

- A *backup plan* that will prevent the loss of data. During the planning phase, the team creates a plan for processes that the team will use for file and data backups to prevent loss of data. This is updated when planning for deployment.

- A *plan for analyzing system performance and site usage.* The operations team is responsible for the site's daily maintenance and routine care.

- A *plan for log handling* and other administrative tasks.

- A *disaster recovery plan.* During the planning phase, the team creates a disaster recovery plan that establishes what the team expects to happen to the solution, its equipment, personnel, and data should a crisis occur. During the planning process for deployment, the team will review the document and validate and update its contents.

- A *business contingency plan.* During the planning phase, the team creates a business contingency plan, establishing what will happen if the business activities halt. When planning for deployment, the team reviews and validates the contents of the business contingency plan.

- *Training information.* The team must ensure that support personnel who will maintain or update the solution are properly trained, and that proper channels or regulations are provided in the event of a disaster.

Deployment plan review

The deployment plan is created during the planning phase and revised throughout the development process. However, when planning for deployment, the release manager might need to make changes to the deployment plan because of changes made to the solution during development and stabilization. The release manager must review and revise the deployment plan and confirm that the team has accomplished the following tasks:

- The deployment strategy is reviewed and approved.

- Setup, installation, configuration, test, operation, and support procedures are available, reviewed, and approved.

- Deployment procedures are documented, reviewed, and approved.

- Hardware and software components are available and tested.

- The deployment team has clearly defined roles, and the assigned personnel are trained and available.

- There is a plan and ample resources for ownership transfer to the operations team.

Customer sign-off

The solution's key stakeholders review the collateral documentation and solution and confirm that the solution is ready for deployment. The project team prepares an affidavit reiterating that the key stakeholders have reviewed the solution and the accompanying collateral documentation, and that they find the solution to be final and acceptable in the current state.

Core Components vs. Site-Specific Components

For efficient deployment of solutions, it is important to group components as core components and site-specific components.

Core components

Core components are components located at a central location that enable interoperability of the overall solution. Core components are usually the enabling technology of the enterprise solution. Examples of core components are:

- Domain controllers
- Network routers
- Database servers
- Mail routers
- Remote access servers

Site-specific components

Components that are located at individual locations and enable users to access and use the solution are called site-specific components. Examples of site-specific components are:

- Local routers
- File print servers
- Client applications, such as Microsoft Office XP

In most cases, core components must be deployed before site-specific components are deployed. For example, when Microsoft Exchange Server is deployed, the core backbone, which supports all sites, must be in place first, and only then can the site components be deployed.

How to Deploy Core Components

Deploying core components involves selecting an appropriate deployment strategy and then performing the deployment. Selecting a deployment strategy requires a thorough understanding of both the solution and the needs of the customer.

A core component is often shared by multiple locations; it is a critical or enabling part of the overall solution. For virtually any solution, you must deploy some core components before users can use the solution. When considering how to deploy a solution, it is necessary to identify those components that are not functionally vital to the overall solution and to decide on an effective strategy for deploying them. For many projects, the cost of deploying all core components first is excessive and unnecessary.

Tip   Devices that are functionally redundant and exist only to provide capacity usually do not need to be installed before deploying to the sites.

You can use two main strategies for deploying core components:

- *Serial.* All core components are deployed prior to any site deployments. This approach has less risk and is adequate for short deployments and small environments.
- *Parallel.* Core components are deployed as needed in parallel to support each site deployment. This is a more cost-effective approach for larger environments or for deployments that will extend over a longer period.

Depending on the solution scenario, the core technology might need to be deployed before or in parallel with site deployments.

How to Deploy Site-Specific Components

Site deployment represents a process within a process. It involves the execution of a well-thought-out plan for installing the solution. Figure 11.5 depicts the process of deploying site-specific components.

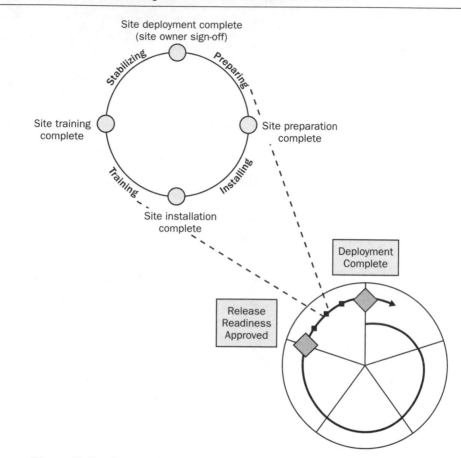

Figure 11.5.   Site-specific deployment process

Sites can be deployed serially by fewer teams or in parallel by more teams. Parallel site deployment requires more coordination and provides less opportunity to deal with the ramp-up of usage. However, a more serialized deployment can introduce confusion to the users, especially when the new solution must coexist with an existing system.

Site deployment also involves the use of the system by users in a production environment. The team must take steps to ensure that the necessary operations and support infrastructures exist for these users as they gain access to the system. Site deployment involves four phases:

- Preparing the site deployment
- Installing the site deployment
- Training during site deployment
- Stabilizing the site deployment

Preparing for the site deployment

Preparing for site deployment involves three distinct activities: taking inventories, scheduling, and informing. A coordinator often performs these activities off-site. The coordinator validates all the deployment information collected during planning, creates a final schedule for the actual site deployment, and informs the team about when the deployment will occur. This phase is performed to validate the information about the site to make sure that nothing significant has changed since the site survey was performed during the planning phase. It is also used to verify that all required equipment for the deployment has been delivered to the site.

Installing the site deployment

To minimize disruption and confusion about the process, the team does not install the solution until all preparations are made. In some cases, last-minute issues that are uncovered during the preparatory phase might indicate the need to revisit the site after the issues are resolved.

Note   In some cases, the team might choose to delay activation until the solution is stable and users have undergone training.

During installation, the following tasks are performed:

- Installing or upgrading required hardware or software
- Validating that the installed systems function as expected
- Activating the system for user access

During deployment, the team should have a support mechanism in place in case it encounters problems. Generally, developers and testers on the core project team should be ready to support the site deployment team.

Training during site deployment

It is the responsibility of the deployment team to ensure that all users receive suitable training. During the planning phase, the project team developed a training plan that prescribes the appropriate level and type of training for all users. Training can be delivered before, during, or after installation.

Use the following guidelines for training during site deployment:

- Deliver appropriate training to each user
- Vary training based on user background and experience
- Include a variety of media as defined in the training plan
- Train local support staff

Avoid the temptation to employ a one-size-fits-all strategy. If the training strategy requires all users to undergo the same training process, novice users will be forced to learn too quickly, and more experienced users will feel held back. Consider alternatives to the traditional courseware approach to training, such as coaching sessions and a mentoring program.

Stabilizing the site deployment

Stabilization is an important part of the site deployment process. It is never a good idea to install a solution and then simply walk away from the deployment. It is the responsibility of the deployment team to remain with the project until the team is comfortable putting it into production. For this to occur, the team must focus on the success criteria, obtain the customer's approval, and collect user feedback to ensure satisfaction and evolve the site deployment process. Each site deployment should go through the sign-off process. During the planning phase, a person at the site should have been designated to have the authority to sign off on the site deployment.

What Is the Quiet Period?

The quiet period begins when deployments are complete. During the quiet period, the team begins transferring responsibility to operations and support. A quiet period of 15 to 30 days is needed to generate statistically useful data. The quiet period also serves as a baseline for the service-level agreement.

The operations plan and acceptance criteria established by the project team during the planning phase define service levels for the solution. These levels serve as a baseline for the service-level agreement (SLA), which operations begins monitoring when responsibility is transferred to them.

A service-level agreement is defined as an agreement between the service provider and the customer that defines the responsibilities of all participating parties and that binds the service provider to provide a particular service of a specific agreed-upon quality and quantity. It constrains the demands that customers can place on the service to those limits that are defined by the agreement.

How to Transfer the Project to Operations and Support

Disengaging from the project includes transferring operations and support functions to permanent staff. In many cases, the resources to manage the new systems already exist. In other cases, it might be necessary to design new support systems.

Some of the tasks that need to be performed during transferring the project to operations and support include:

- *Activate report systems.* Ensure that you transfer call volume and issue resolution to the help desk. Transfer system faults, corrective actions, and trend analysis to operations.
- *Publish knowledge base.* The knowledge base provides easy access to corrective knowledge and can be used by support teams and users.
- *Validate operations.* Before disengaging from the project, verify that the operations are being performed.

Note   It is very important for the project team to transition responsibility for the deployment to a support group at the customer's company. If the project team cannot transition the responsibility, the project team will become the support group. The customer will continue to rely on the project team for help with questions and support issues.

Closeout Activities

After deployment is complete and ownership and responsibility have been transferred to operations and support, the team performs closeout activities for the project.

When the team has obtained customer sign-off, the project is officially complete, and the team has reached the deployment complete milestone. The following are the closeout activities:

- *Survey customer satisfaction.* The customer satisfaction survey provides an important opportunity for the team to receive feedback from the customer. It is a necessary component of the closeout report and represents validation of the entire project. At a minimum, the persons who are surveyed should include project sponsors and key stakeholders.
- *Prepare closeout report.* The closeout report is the final physical deliverable of the deployment. It includes final versions of all the major deliverables: the vision/scope document, the functional specification, and so on.

  Typically, the closeout report also includes a summary of information solicited from the customers and users and a summary of the known next steps. Essentially, the closeout report answers the question, "Where do we go from here?"

- *Conduct project review.* Typically, the team conducts two types of project reviews: team and customer. Most technology projects end with a meeting, or *project review*, in which team members review the project and identify areas that could be improved in future projects.

  The project review is an opportunity for the entire team to reflect on the process and outcomes of the implementation. The team documents this reflection as action items in the next project plan.

  Important   In addition, customer reviews are conducted with sponsors and key stakeholders to determine customer satisfaction levels, outstanding issues, and next steps.

- *Obtain customer approval.* Upon project closeout, the product manager obtains the final sign-off from the customer, signaling the customer's approval of the solution and permission to disengage from the project.

Activity: Prioritizing Bugs

In this activity, you use what you learned in the lessons to assign and prioritize bugs.

The project testing team has been testing the E-Commerce Web application and has identified a number of bugs. The following is a list of the identified bugs without any priority assigned to them:

- In 12 out of 75 tests, the browser stopped responding when the user submitted an order. The order status on the server showed that it was submitted, but the user never received a confirmation or an order number in these instances.
- If a sales representative applies a discount that is greater than 15 percent, the system accepts it without approval from a manager.
- When the user is viewing the order confirmation page and he or she clicks Keep Shopping, the account logon page appears. This seems to occur only for users whose user names are longer than 8 characters. In the test database, this equates to 20 users out of 172.
- When the customer logs on, the background of the Help page changes from white to off-white.
- In 50 tests, the Track Orders page twice displayed order details for the wrong order.
- Performing a load test of 1000 simultaneous users showed a degradation of 18 percent in performance. Average number of users to simultaneously access the E-Commerce Web site in production is estimated to be 300.
- The copyright notice does not appear on the Order Confirmation page.
- In 130 tests, the home page failed to load 6 times. Performing a refresh successfully loaded the home page.
- Every time the home page appears, the View Cart button is missing. This happens even after something is placed in the cart.
- In 40 tests, there were 2 instances in which the sales manager was unable to apply a discount that was greater than 15 percent to an order. In all 40 tests, the same sales manager account was used, but different products were added to the orders.
- In 8 out of 50 tests, error HTTP 404 - File Not Found occurred when the user clicked Keep Shopping on the Order Confirmation page.
- The list of catalogs does not appear when viewing product details for bicycle helmets.
- If the sales manager is viewing product details and he or she presses the Enter key, the Help topics home page appears in the browser.
- In 25 tests, the Order Confirmation page failed to appear 3 times.

- In 25 tests, the Track Orders page failed to show the order details 16 times.
- Every time the production clerk attempts to connect to the administration site over SSL, the following error message appears: "The page cannot be displayed. The page you are looking for is currently unavailable. The Web site might be experiencing technical difficulties, or you may need to adjust your browser settings." The production clerk cannot access the data to manage the online catalog.

Estimate the repeatability, visibility, and severity of each of the preceding bugs. You might have to guess at some of the values based on the amount of information you have available. Then, using the formula discussed in the chapter, compute the priority of each of the bugs.

Open the C11Ex1.doc file in the \SolutionDocuments\Chapter11 folder on the companion CD to complete this exercise. One possible answer to this exercise can be found in C11Ex1_Answer.doc in the \SolutionDocuments\Chapter11 folder.

Summary

- The purpose of the stabilizing phase is to reduce the risks of releasing the solution to production.
- A successful stabilizing phase requires that the team make the transition from a mindset focused on building features to one focused on getting the solution to a known state of quality.
- The goals of the deploying phase are:
    - Place the solution into a production environment.
    - Facilitate the smooth transfer of the solution from the project team to the operations team.
    - Secure customer approval that the project is complete.
- Steps in the site deployment process are preparing, installing, training, and obtaining sign-off.
- The project team can disengage from the project only after sign-off from the customer.
- Deliverables of the deploying phase are operations and support information systems, repository of all versions of documentation and code, and project closeout reports.

Review

The following questions are intended to reinforce key information presented in this chapter. If you are unable to answer a question, review the lesson materials and try the question again. You can find answers to the questions in the appendix.

1. What are some of the specific goals of the stabilizing phase?

2. How does ongoing analysis of bug convergence provide warning signs about the stability of the project?

3. Why is zero-bug bounce a positive indicator for the project?

4. What is a release candidate, and what are some of its features?

5. What is a pilot, and what are its goals?

6. Why should pilot testing not be too easy?

7. What are the deliverables of the deploying phase?

8. Which person or group is the best candidate to deploy the solution?

9. What are some examples of core components? What arc some examples of site components?

10. What is the quiet period, and what are some of its features?

11. What type of documents result from completing closeout activities?

12. Which MSF role handles the final sign-off from the customer?

13. What are the two types of project reviews that MSF advocates at the end of the deployment phase?

A P P E N D I X   A

Questions and Answers

Chapter 1   Introduction to Designing Business Solutions
Review

Page 35   **1. Describe the differences between the waterfall model and the spiral model, and describe how MSF uses both in the MSF Process Model.**

The waterfall model is based on milestones. For a milestone to be achieved, all the tasks related to that phase must be completed. The next phase of development cannot be started until the milestone from the previous phase is completed. The clearly identifiable milestones of this model make it is easy to monitor the progress of the project and the schedule, and to assign responsibilities and accountability to the appropriate resources. The waterfall model is more applicable to projects that have clearly defined requirements and are not liable to modifications in the future.

The spiral model was created with the intention of being able to refine the product requirements and project estimates on a regular basis. Each time the project goes through an iteration of the spiral model, the development team can assess the project and plan for the next iteration. However, because the spiral model has no clear checkpoints, monitoring the progress of the project is difficult. The spiral model is suited best for rapid development of small projects.

The MSF Process Model incorporates the milestone approach of the waterfall model with the iterative approach of the spiral model. By using the process model, the development team takes an iterative approach to building a solution, while tracking the progress of each iteration by using milestones.

Page 35   **2. In the MSF Team Model, who is responsible for the design process?**

The program management role is responsible for the design process.

Page 35   **3. The tradeoff triangle describes the three types of tradeoffs that a project team and the customer can make. What is a fourth tradeoff that could be considered but that should never be compromised?**

Quality is another tradeoff that could be considered in addition to features, resources, and schedule. However, quality should be the last tradeoff to be compromised because of the poor results that would ensue.

Page 35   **4. Using the following statement, complete the tradeoff matrix below.**

"Given a fixed feature set, we will choose resources and adjust the schedule as necessary."

	Fixed	Chosen	Adjustable
Resources		X	
Schedule			X
Features	X		

Page 35   **5. Describe the purpose of performing daily builds in the MSF Process Model.**

Daily builds allow the development team and the customer to understand the current state of the project and to measure the stability of the project on a frequent basis. Daily builds can be applied to both software development projects and hardware infrastructure projects.

Page 36   **6. When you reach the release readiness milestone, what phase have you completed?**

The stabilizing phase is complete when the project team reaches the release readiness milestone and the solution has been validated by the project team and the customer.

Page 36   **7. During which phase of the MSF Process Model is the initial risk assessment document created?**

During the envisioning phase, risk assessment begins and a risk assessment document is created. However, risk assessment is an ongoing process that occurs throughout the duration of the project. Therefore, the risk assessment document will continue to undergo changes and updates while the project progresses. In addition, as the project progresses, risk mitigation plans are created as a part of risk assessment.

Page 36   **8. When are test cases established in the MSF Process Model?**

The majority of work on test cases is performed during the developing phase. However, the testing role is involved in the project from the very beginning.

Page 36   **9. List several types of tests that are performed during the stabilizing phase.**

Following is a list of the types of tests that will be conducted during the stabilizing phase:
- Component testing
- Database testing
- Infrastructure testing
- Security testing
- Integration testing
- User acceptance and usability testing
- Stress, capacity, and performance testing
- Regression testing
- Recording the number of bugs

Page 36   **10.** **Why is it important to create a vision statement for the project during the envisioning phase?**

The vision statement communicates the direction for guiding the team toward its business goals. Everyone on the project team must agree to and support the vision of the solution. This agreement and support is fundamental to the success of the project. If members of the team do not agree with the vision statement, the success of the project is at risk.

Page 36   **11.** **What are some of the key tasks that are performed during the planning phase?**

- Creation of the functional specification
- Creation of the development, testing, and staging environments
- Development of the project plans
- Creation of the project schedule
- Development of the solution design and architecture

Page 36   **12.** **Describe the *quiet period* and the activities that occur during this period.**

The quiet period is the time between the deployment stable interim milestone and the deployment complete interim milestone of the deploying phase. During this period, the effectiveness and performance of the solution are measured. The results of this activity lead to an estimate of the effort needed to maintain the solution for continued operations.

Chapter 2   Gathering and Analyzing Information Review

Page 82   **1.** **What is the difference between the interviewing and focus-group techniques of gathering information?**

An interview is a one-on-one meeting between a member of the project team and a user or stakeholder. The interviewer asks the user or stakeholder questions related to work and processes.

A focus group is a form of group interview, in which a group of individuals discuss a process or an activity in the presence of a facilitator. The group of individuals represents all the relevant users and stakeholders of the process. You should use focus groups when many people must be interviewed in a short period. In addition, the various people in a focus group can help each other fill any information gaps.

Page 82   **2.   When should you use for prototyping instead of shadowing to gather information?**

Shadowing is the process of gathering information by observing a user performing day-to-day tasks in the actual work environment. You can ask the user questions related to the work. However, some activities cannot be understood by watching. You might need to document the actions that the user performed, such as keystrokes. In such a situation, you must use prototyping.

Page 82   **3.   How do you identify the most effective information gathering technique for a project?**

To identify the most effective information gathering technique, you consider the advantages and disadvantages of each technique. You identify the type of information to be collected and the amount of time you have to collect the information. If you want to gather information quickly, use interviewing or focus groups instead of surveys.

Page 82   **4.   What is the purpose of creating use cases?**

You create use cases to:

- Identify the business process and all activities from start to finish.
- Document the context and environmental issues.
- Document relationship between business needs and user requirements.
- Describe needs and requirements in the context of use.
- Focus users and the development team.

Page 82   **5.   What is an actors catalog?**

The actors catalog contains a list of actors used in the use cases. It contains information such as actor name, actor responsibilities, and the sources from which the actor was identified.

Page 82   **6.   What is ORM?**

ORM is a modeling language that allows to you to present information as elementary facts. An elementary fact asserts that an object has a property and that one or more objects participate in a relationship. ORM expresses the model in terms of natural concepts, like objects and roles. ORM is based on the assumption that objects play roles in real life.

Page 83   **7.   What is UML?**

UML is a simple, extensible, and expressive visual modeling language. It is a set of notations and rules for modeling software systems of varying complexities. UML enables the creation of simple, well-documented, and easy-to-understand software models.

Page 83   **8.   What are the purposes of the various UML views?**

The five UML views are:

- The user view, which represents the goals and objectives of the system from the viewpoint of various users and their requirements from the system.

- The structural view, which represents the static or idle state of the system.
- The behavioral view, which represents the dynamic state of the system.
- The implementation view, which represents the distribution of the logical elements of the system.
- The environment view, which represents the distribution of the physical elements of the system.

Page 83   **9.   What is an actor in a use case?**

An actor is an entity that interacts with the system to be built for the purpose of completing an event. An actor can be:

- A user of the system.
- An entity, such as another system or a database, that resides outside the system.

Page 83   **10.   What is the purpose of a usage scenario?**

A usage scenario describes in detail a particular instance of a use case. You need to create many usage scenarios to completely describe a use case.

Page 83   **11.   What are the steps in creating a usage scenario?**

To create a usage scenario, you perform the following steps:

- Determine the preconditions for the usage scenario, specifying information that must exist before a scenario can be executed.
- Identify the postconditions for the usage scenario, which describe what must be accomplished upon completion of the usage scenario.
- Break the activity into discrete steps.
- Identify exceptions that might occur for any step. You might need to develop usage scenarios for these exceptions.
- Identify the requirement that this particular usage scenario addresses, for tracking and traceability.

Chapter 3   Envisioning the Solution
Review

Page 120   **1.   What is the purpose of envisioning?**

The overall purpose of envisioning is to develop a common vision of the goals of the solution and share it with the customers. Specifically, some of the purposes served by envisioning are as follows:

- Achieving an early understanding of the goals and constraints of the project among the customers and the team
- Analyzing the feasibility of the solution and gaining approval from key stakeholders
- Defining the scope of the project
- Estimating the resources that are required to complete the project
- Identifying the major milestones for the project

Page 120   **2. What are the responsibilities of the various roles during the envisioning phase?**

Responsibilities of the various roles are as follows:

■ The product management role is responsible for ensuring that the customer requirements are addressed by the project team.

■ The program management role is responsible for developing the project design goals and solution concept.

■ The development role is responsible for providing the technical implications of the proposed solution and the feasibility of the solution concept.

■ The user experience role is responsible for analyzing the performance needs and support issues of the end users of the solution.

■ The testing role is responsible for defining the quality requirements of the solution and how the specified level of quality can be achieved.

■ The release management role is responsible for identifying all that is required for deploying the solution.

Page 120   **3. What are the outputs of the envisioning phase?**

The key outputs of the envisioning phase are as follows:

■ The vision/scope document, which describes the goals and constraints of the project

■ The project structure document, which describes the organization of the team and the standards used by the team for documentation

■ The risk assessment document, which lists the risks associated with the project, their impact, and corresponding mitigation plans

Page 120   **4. What is the purpose of specifying the project scope?**

You create the project scope to specify what the project will and will not accomplish. Therefore, you identify the features that the customer considers essential in the solution and focus on successfully including them in the solution. To accomplish this, you need to analyze all project variables and make the appropriate tradeoffs. Some of the benefits of defining the scope of the project are that scope enables the team to focus on the work that must be done. Defining the scope also helps the team to clearly identify all tasks in the project.

Page 120   **5. How does the envisioning phase end?**

The envisioning phase ends at the vision/scope approved milestone. This milestone involves a meeting and follow-up conversations in which key stakeholders, customers, and representatives of each role in the team approve the vision/scope document to indicate that they have a formal agreement about the goals and objectives of the project and solution. They "sign off" on this document to indicate that all parties believe the team can proceed with the project.

Page 120   **6.   What kinds of change management decisions are recorded in the project structure document?**

In the change management section of the project structure document, you record the processes that the team will follow to handle changes in the project. Some of the decisions that are made include:

- How will you define change on the project?
- What is the release date? Who will determine the release date, and how will it be determined? What will the basis be for determining the release date?
- Who will define the change management process that will be used?
- How will proposed changes be identified and tracked? Who will track this information?
- How will you assess the impact of a change? How much deviation are you willing to accept before major rescheduling?

Page 120   **7.   What is the difference between business goals and design goals?**

Business goals use business language to describe what the customer wants to change in the business by using the solution. Design goals represent the attributes of the solution that the project team is going to develop. The project team uses the design goals to illustrate what they want to accomplish with the solution.

Page 121   **8.   What are the guidelines for creating user profiles?**

While creating user profiles, remember the following:

- Identify the goals and expectations of the users of the solution.
- Identify the factors that might affect the ability of the user to use the solution.
- To help provide required support, identify problems that users might have had with similar products or solutions and methods.
- Determine whether the solution will be used globally.
- Identify the number of users at each location where the solution will be implemented, the infrastructure at each location, and the network bandwidth available at each location.
- Identify how the information flows between users of the solution. Identify the volume and importance of the communication.
- Analyze the hierarchical structure of the organization and its implications on information flow between different levels of the hierarchy.
- Analyze the scope of user functions.
- Analyze policies that might affect the implementation of the solution.

Page 121   **9.   What are the essential components of a risk assessment document?**

A risk document must contain the following:

- Risk statements, which capture the nature of the risk
- Risk probability, which describes the likelihood of the occurrence of the risk
- Risk severity, which specifies the impact of the risk
- Risk exposure, which specifies the overall threat of the risk
- Mitigation plans, which describe the efforts for preventing or minimizing the risk
- Contingency plans and triggers, which specify the steps that you need to take when a risk occurs and when to take those steps
- Risk ownership, which specifies the team member who is responsible for monitoring the risk

Page 121   **10. What are the guidelines for assessing risks for a project?**

You must use a consistent scale to calculate the probability for every risk and its impact. If you express the impact of some risks by using a number and others by using financial terms, you cannot compare the exposure of the different risks. In addition, you need to rank the risks according to their exposure. Review this list frequently during the life of the project and update the list according to the importance of the risks.

Chapter 4   Creating the Conceptual Design Review

Page 168   **1.   What is the purpose of the planning phase?**

The purpose of the planning phase is to achieve a detailed and validated understanding of the problem to be solved and to define a solution that addresses the problem. This is the solution that is most likely to be successful given the assumptions and constraints as understood by the team.

Page 168   **2.   What is the difference between the responsibilities of the product management and project management roles during the planning phase?**

During the planning phase, product management represents the users and ensures that the product addresses their needs. Project management ensures that the solution is created to specifications defined by the product manager.

Page 168   **3.   What are the major deliverables of the planning phase?**

The major deliverables of the planning phase are:

- The functional specification, which describes what will be built and how it will be built.
- The master project plan document, which presents how the solution will be built by the various teams involved in the project.

- The master project schedule, which specifies the time frame during which the project team will build and deploy the solution.
- The updated master risk assessment document, which lists the risks associated with the project and their mitigation plans.

Page 168

4. How does a functional specification serve as a blueprint for the development team?

The functional specification identifies what the solution is going to be. This enables the development team to formulate development strategies and estimate the time and effort required to develop the solution.

Page 168

5. What are the goals of a functional specification?

The goals of a functional specification are:

- Consolidating a common understanding of the business and user requirements.
- Articulating a logical way to break down a problem and modularize the solution.
- Providing a framework to plan, schedule, and develop the solution on time.
- Serving as a contract between the team and the customer about what will be delivered.

Page 168

6. What are the risks of not creating a functional specification?

Some of the risks of not creating a functional specification are:

- The solution might not address the customer requirements.
- The project manager might not correctly estimate the time and effort required to complete the project.
- The team might be unable to define customer expectations clearly or share a common understanding of the solution with the customer.
- The team might not have enough information to validate that the solution meets the customer requirements.

Page 168

7. What is the difference between the business and user requirements of the solution?

The business requirements of the solution are specified by the customer. These requirements focus on meeting the business goals and objectives.

The user requirements are provided by the end user of the solution and focus on using the solution to effectively perform day-to-day tasks.

Page 169

8. What are the benefits of creating a conceptual design?

The conceptual design helps you:

- Develop part of the functional specification.
- Develop an effective user interface.
- Determine how different components work together in a solution.
- Design a solution that addresses both business and user needs.

Page 169   **9.** **A company plans to increase its sales by 15 percent during the next financial year by implementing an online shopping site. The company intends to provide its users a Web site that is fast, provides secure credit card processing, and is available at all times. Also, only registered users will be able to purchase products on the site. What are the user, system, operation, and business requirements for this site?**

The requirements for this site are:

- Business requirement: A Web site that improves the annual sales by 15 percent.
- User requirements:
  - Users can complete their purchases in five minutes.
  - Users can access only their own credit card details.
- System requirement: Only registered users will be able to purchase products on the site.
- Operation requirement: The users must be able to access the site at all times.

Page 169   **10.** **What are the goals of the analysis step of conceptual design?**

The goals of the analysis step are to:

- Review the user and business processes and activities.
- Create scenarios to illustrate context, workflow, task sequence, and environmental relationships in the business.

Page 169   **11.** **What is the benefit of synthesizing information?**

When you synthesize information, you present the information to the entire team and receive their perspectives about user requirements and solutions. You also ensure that all team members have a common understanding of user requirements and expectations.

Page 169   **12.** **What are the tasks for creating the future state?**

To create future state usage, the team performs the following tasks:

- Envision the desired future state.
- Redesign the current process to optimally support key business activities and processes.
- Create accurate target future state scenarios.
- Validate future state scenarios by using iteration.

Page 169   **13.** **What are the benefits of validating the conceptual design?**

Some of the benefits of validation include:

- Reducing risk.
- Highlighting missing information.
- Indicating diverging views and interpretations of the solution, especially between the business and users.
- Verifying the volume of activity.

- Assisting in prioritization.
- Providing a baseline for proceeding to logical design.

Page 169   **14.   What are the four service categories?**

The four service categories are:

- User services that provide the user interface in an application
- Business services that enforce business rules in the correct sequence
- Data services that provide the lowest visible level of detail for manipulating data
- System services that provide functionality outside the business logic

Page 170   **15.   Study and categorize the following services.**

- Displaying the employee details service
- Updating the employee details service
- Employee information service
- E-mail service

The categorized services are:

- Displaying the employee details service: User service
- Updating the employee details service: Business service
- Employee information service: Data service
- E-mail service: System service

Page 170   **16.   What are the characteristics of a refined business requirement?**

A business requirement must be:

- Well defined.
- Concise.
- Testable.
- Grouped in a hierarchical manner.
- Written in business language without jargon.

Page 170   **17.   How do you refine use cases during the analysis step of conceptual design?**

To refine the use cases diagram, you perform the following tasks:

- Create subordinate use cases.
- Create usage scenarios for each subordinate use case.
- Validate each use case and usage scenario against refined requirements.

Page 170   **18.   What are the criteria for evaluating the cost of a solution?**

The criteria are:

- Resources, work effort, and time
- Operational costs of technical options and emerging technologies
- Annual and recurring life cycle costs

Chapter 5   Creating the Logical Design
Activity

Page 208   **1.   The shopping cart checks inventory to determine the availability of a particular product.**

Objects include shopping cart, inventory, and product.

Page 208   **2.   A new user creates an account in order to place orders.**

Objects include user, account, and orders.

Page 208   **3.   A user adds a product to the shopping cart.**

Objects include user, product, and shopping cart.

Page 208   **4.   A user retrieves an order to check its status.**

Objects include user and order.

Chapter 5   Creating the Logical Design
Review

Page 212   **1.   What are the two steps of logical design?**

- Analysis, during which you identify objects, services, attributes, and relationships
- Optimization, during which you refine the object list, verify the design, and implement control

Page 212   **2.   What are the outputs of the logical design?**

- The logical object model, which is a set of objects with corresponding services, attributes, and relationships
- A high-level user interface design
- The logical data model

Page 212   **3.   Should you focus on technological issues during logical design?**

Though logical design is considered to be technology independent, it is a good practice to consider physical constraints and opportunities during logical design to validate that the design can be implemented. Experienced teams and designers typically use the optimization step of logical design to identify the technology constraints to create a pseudophysical design. Logical design is the basis for evaluating the feasibility of the physical design and deciding implementation alternatives.

Page 212   **4.   What are the benefits of logical design?**

- Logical design reduces the complexity of the solution.
- Logical design reflects and supports the requirements of conceptual design.
- Logical design provides a view of the solution as a single unit.
- Logical design acts as a point of contact for organizing cross-functional cooperation among multiple systems.
- Logical design acts as a starting point for the physical design.

Page 212   **5.   How do you identify services in a usage scenario?**

To identify services, examine a usage scenario to determine what the object is supposed to do, the kind of data the object must maintain, and the actions that the object must perform. If an object maintains information, it also performs the operations on the information.

Page 212   **6.   How do you identify attributes in a usage scenario?**

In a usage scenario, look for the words or phrases that further identify the object.

Page 212   **7.   What is a sequence diagram?**

A sequence diagram shows the actors and objects that participate in an interaction and the events they generate, arranged chronologically. It also identifies object dependencies in the system.

Page 213   **8.   How do you design the tables and columns in a data store for a solution?**

Each object that maintains data corresponds to a table in the data store. The attributes of the object form the columns in the table. Each row in the table stores values for various fields for a specific instance of the object.

Page 213   **9.   What is the purpose of refining the list of objects?**

You need to refine the list of objects because:

- Two objects might express the same information or control the same activity.
- Nouns in usage scenarios might be key attributes of another object.
- You might need a new object to control or coordinate a set of services.

Page 213   **10.   How do you verify the design by using individual object verification?**

In individual object verification, you identify an object's inputs and outputs and the capability or functionality that the object must provide. For any given input, you should be able to accurately predict the output and behavior and verify the independent parts of the object.

Page 213   **11.   What is the purpose of control in logical design?**

Control enables you to sequence objects. Control in logical design:

- Ensures transactional integrity of a scenario.
- Coordinates services across multiple objects.
- Identifies cross-object interdependencies.

Page 213   **12.   You are creating the logical design of a solution for a customer, and you discover a scenario that was not discovered in your previous analysis. What should you do with this new information?**

First, you should review all your current documentation to verify that the new information is not covered in your analysis. If the new information does not exist in your analysis, determine the effect of including functionality based on this new information in this version of the solution. Also determine the effect of omitting functionality based on the new information from this version. Once you have this information, you should notify the customer of the situation and work together to determine the best way to manage the new information. Be aware that the scope of the project might change depending on what you do with the new information.

Page 213   **13. What is the responsibility of the testing role during logical design?**

The testing role is primarily responsible for validating the logical design by measuring it against the conceptual design to validate that the logical design will cover the requirements. In addition, the testing role begins to define a high-level test plan.

Chapter 6   Creating the Physical Design
Review

Page 250   **1. What are the goals of physical design?**

The goals of physical design are:

- Transforming the logical design to specifications for a set of components
- Providing a baseline for implementing the design
- Identifying appropriate technologies for development
- Creating a structural view of the solution from the perspective of the development team

Page 250   **2. What is the difference between conceptual, logical, and physical designs?**

During conceptual design, the project team describes the solution from the perspective of the business and user communities. During logical design, the project team describes the solution from its own perspective. During physical design, the project team describes the solution from the perspective of the development team.

Page 250   **3. What does the development team do during physical design?**

During physical design, the development team evaluates technologies, creates prototypes, and prepares for development.

Page 250   **4. What does the deployment model include?**

The deployment model consists of:

- The network topology, which indicates hardware locations and inter-connections.
- The data topology, which indicates data store locations in relation to the network topology.
- The component topology, which indicates the locations of components and their services in relation to the network topology.

Page 250   **5. What does the project team do during the research step of physical design?**

During the research step, the team considers constraints such as enterprise architecture, business process, and infrastructure. In addition, the team identifies the requirements of the solution in terms of performance, availability, and scalability. The team then analyzes the differences between the requirements and constraints.

Page 250   **6. How does the project team handle the gap between requirements and constraints?**

To handle the gap between requirements and constraints, the project team:

- Identifies the areas in the infrastructure where the requirements might conflict with the constraints.
- Analyzes the gaps between the requirements and the constraints and determines whether they need to make choices to resolve conflicts.
- Identifies the requirements that are absolutely necessary for the project.
- Brainstorms solutions with all groups associated with the project.

Page 250   **7. During the analysis step of physical design, how does the project team use the list of objects and services created during logical design?**

The project team uses the list by:

- Categorizing services as user services, business services, data services, and system services
- Identifying hidden services

Page 251   **8. How does the project team refine the class diagrams during the analysis step of physical design?**

The project team refines the class diagrams by:

- Identifying objects that were not apparent during logical design
- Consolidating logical objects
- Categorizing objects into a services-based model
- Refining the methods by focusing on parameters
- Refining the attributes

Page 251   **9. How do you select the candidate technologies for the solution?**

In evaluating and selecting candidate technologies for the solution, you address business considerations, enterprise architecture considerations, and technology considerations.

Page 251   **10. What is the difference between the network topology and the data topology of the deployment model?**

The network topology is an infrastructure map that indicates hardware locations and interconnections. The data topology is a map that indicates data store locations in relation to the network topology.

Page 251   **11. What is the difference between the distribution strategy and the packaging strategy?**

The distribution strategy is a rationale for determining where the services will be located in the solution architecture. Distribution is services-based and not component-based.

The packaging strategy is a rationale for determining which services will reside in each component. You might have multiple strategies in a single solution.

Page 251   **12.   What is the difference between cohesion and coupling?**

Cohesion is the relationship among various internal elements of a component. Coupling is the relationship of a component with other components. A component should be tightly cohesive but loosely coupled.

Page 251   **13.   What is the purpose of a programming model?**

The programming model:

- Describes how the development team can use the selected technologies.
- Specifies standards that will be followed during the implementation of the project.
- Sets specific guidelines to provide consistent component implementation.

Page 251   **14.   What is a component interface?**

A component interface:

- Is a contract that represents the supplier and consumer relationship between components
- Is a means to access the underlying services
- Represents one or more services
- Includes underlying object attributes

Page 251   **15.   What are the various types of users of the user services layer of an application?**

There are two types of users of the user services layer of an application: human users who require an interface through which they can interact with the system, and other computer systems. A user interface provides visual means for humans to interact with systems. User services provide the navigation, validation, and error-processing logic.

Chapter 7   Designing the Presentation Layer
Review

Page 283   **1.   What is the function of the presentation layer in the business application architecture?**

The presentation layer is the part of the business application that provides a communication mechanism between the user and the business service layer of the application. The presentation layer contains the components that are required to enable user interaction with the application. The most simple presentation layers contain user interface components, such as Windows Forms or ASP.NET Web Forms. For more complex user interactions, you can design user process components.

Page 283   **2.   What are the features of a good user interface?**

Some of the features of a good user interface design include:

- Intuitive design
- Optimum screen space utilization
- Ease of navigation

- Controlled navigation
- Input validation
- Menus, toolbars, and Help
- Efficient event handling

Page 283   **3.   What are the differences between a high-fidelity and low-fidelity design?**

- Low-fidelity designs show main features, structure, and navigation; high-fidelity designs show the detailed screen layouts and interface elements.
- Low-fidelity designs allow you to quickly and easily explore alternative designs; high-fidelity designs, although quick to implement and change, require a computer and software.
- Low-fidelity designs are great for brainstorming and quick feedback; high-fidelity designs are typically developed from a low-fidelity design.

Page 283   **4.   What are some of the options that application developers can use to design user assistance for an application?**

Some of the options for designing user assistance in applications include:

- Online Help
- ToolTips
- Wizards
- Status displays
- Accessibility aids

Page 283   **5.   What are the various types of user interface models, and when should you use them?**

- *Windows desktop user interfaces* are used when you need to provide disconnected or offline capabilities or rich user interaction, and maybe even integration with the user interfaces of other applications.
- *Web-based user interfaces* allow for standards-based user interfaces across many devices and platforms. Therefore, you should use Web-based user interfaces when an application must be used on a wide variety of client devices.
- *Mobile device user interfaces* need to be able to display information on a much smaller screen than other common applications and must offer acceptable usability for the devices being targeted.
- *Document-based user interfaces* are used in some applications so that users can enter or view data in document form in the productivity tools they commonly use.

Page 283   **6.   Describe the difference between a user interface component and a user process component. Describe a situation in which you would use a user process component.**

A user interface component makes up the interface to the application that the user will be interacting with. A user process component encapsulates a specific process that a user might perform while interacting with the application. An example of a user process component is the user logon process. A user might be able to log on by means of a Web browser or a Windows-based application. The interfaces will be different, but the process of logging on can be the same. Abstracting the process of logging on away from the interface promotes reuse and consistency within the application.

Page 284

7.   How do you separate user interface from user process?

To separate user interface from user process, perform the following steps:

a.   Identify the business process or processes that the user interface process will help to accomplish. Identify how the user sees this as a task. (You can usually do this by consulting the sequence diagrams that you created as part of your requirements analysis.)

b.   Identify the data needed by the business processes. The user process will need to be able to submit this data when necessary.

c.   Identify additional state you will need to maintain throughout the user activity to assist rendering and data capture in the user interface.

d.   Design the visual flow of the user process and the way that each user interface element receives or gives control flow.

Page 284

8.   Your design calls for the use of Windows Terminal Services. What kind of user interface will you create to implement this design?

The remote computer will contain a Windows Forms user interface. The local computers will simply use Remote Desktop as a thin client to access the remote computer.

Page 284

9.   During the envisioning and planning phases, you determined that the users of the solution will be using a wide variety of hardware, will be located at various remote locations, and will not all have access to the company's intranet. What type of client lends itself to these constraints?

A Web-based client would be most appropriate. Because the users will not have a consistent hardware configuration, and because some might not have access to the company intranet, a secure Web-based solution would be appropriate.

Page 284

10.   After your design of the user interface is complete, what are some of the ways you can validate the design before implementing it?

The design of the UI will be derived from interviews with the users, the requirements that the customer has identified and approved, and the various use cases, usage scenarios, and activity diagrams that you created during the conceptual and logical design processes. After the user interface design is complete, you compare it to each of the sources to ensure that the user interface meets all the requirements.

Chapter 8   Designing the Data Layer
Review

Page 317

1.   How is the data model designed during the planning phase?

During the conceptual design process, the team researches and analyzes data requirements. These requirements help determine what actually must be stored and processed by the business solution. During logical design, the project team derives a set of data entities that are derived from the data requirements. At this stage, the team defines the relationships between various entities and creates a database schema.

Page 317   **2.   What is the purpose of the database schema?**

A database schema specifies how data is organized in a database. In the logical design process, the members of the project team create a database schema so that they can focus on what must be built before they focus on how to build it.

Page 317   **3.   What are the characteristics of attributes?**

The characteristics are:

- Attributes describe an entity.
- Attributes must be attached to the entity that they most closely describe.
- Attributes define the columns in database tables.

Page 317   **4.   What is the purpose of specifying data types in a database?**

Specifying data types in a database fulfills the following purpose:

- Data types specify how data will be stored in a database.
- Data types specify how data will be formatted.
- Data types help enforce data validation.
- Appropriate data type choices optimize data storage.

Page 317   **5.   How do most DBMSs support a many-to-many relationship?**

Most DBMSs support a many-to-many relationship by using a join table to hold information that maintains the relationship between the entities.

Page 317   **6.   How do you optimize transactions for good system performance?**

The transaction should be short-lived, incorporate only what is required, and should not be distributed.

Page 317   **7.   What is the impact of indexing on data access?**

Queries performed on indexed data are much faster and more efficient than queries performed on data that is not indexed. Rather than scanning an entire table each time a value is needed, the DBMS can use the index to quickly lead the query directly to the location of the required data because the index records the location of the data in the table.

Page 318   **8.   What is the difference between horizontal and vertical partitioning?**

In horizontal partitioning, you segment a table containing a large number of rows into multiple tables containing the same columns. In vertical partitioning, you segment a table containing a large number of columns into multiple tables containing rows with equivalent unique identifiers.

Page 318 **9.** **What are the benefits of normalization?**

- Minimized duplication of information
- Reduced data inconsistencies
- Reduction of empty fields (improved storage)

Page 318 **10.** **What is denormalization?**

Denormalization is the process of reversing normalization to generate tables with more fields that require fewer joins.

Page 318 **11.** **What are the three types of data integrity that can be enforced in a database?**

The following three types of data integrity can be enforced in a database:

- Domain integrity specifies a set of legitimate data values for a column and determines whether null values are to be allowed.
- Entity integrity requires that each row in a table has a unique identifier, known as the primary key value.
- Referential integrity ensures that the relationships between the primary keys (in the parent entity's table) and foreign keys (in the child entity's table) are always maintained.

Page 318 **12.** **How do you identify data integrity requirements?**

To identify data integrity requirements:

- Examine data requirements for uniqueness or limits and constraints that might be specified to ensure that entities can exist and be implemented correctly.
- If limits and constraints have been specified, determine whether the limits and constraints are bound to an entity or to a relationship between entities.
- Implement referential integrity requirements to ensure that all relationships are maintained.

Page 318 **13.** **What are the criteria for identifying business rules?**

The criteria for identifying business rules are:

- Identify conditions that must be satisfied for data to be considered valid.
- Identify conditions that must be avoided.
- Identify sequences in which events must occur.

Page 318 **14.** **How do keys implement referential integrity?**

Primary and foreign key relationships from the physical model directly correspond to the database engine's key settings. These key settings automatically enforce referential integrity between linked tables.

Page 318 **15.** **What are the benefits of using components to implement business rules?**

The benefits are:

- Easier maintenance because the code is stored in only one or a few locations and can be easily updated
- Scalability because additional application servers can be added to distribute the increased processing load

Chapter 9   Designing Security Specifications
Review

Page 352   **1.   What are some of the drawbacks of traditional security models?**

Some of the drawbacks of traditional security models include:

- They are based on user identity and not on code identity.
- They are highly prone to virus and worm attacks.

Page 352   **2.   What are some of the principles of secure coding?**

The following are some of the principles of secure coding:

- Rely on tested and proven security systems.
- Never trust external input.
- Assume that external systems are insecure.
- Apply the principle of least privilege.
- Reduce available components and data.
- Default to a secure mode.
- Do not rely on security by obscurity.
- Follow STRIDE principles.

Page 352   **3.   Which of the following statements about buffer overruns is true? (Select all that apply.)**

- **Type safety verification was designed to eliminate buffer overruns.**
- **A buffer overrun can cause an application to stop responding or to malfunction.**
- **A buffer overrun can be exploited by a malicious user to run arbitrary code.**
- **The error message that results from a buffer overrun can pose a security threat.**

All of these statements are true.

Page 352   **4.   During which MSF phase should the threat model be created?**

- **Planning**
- **Developing**
- **Stabilizing**

The threat model is created during the planning phase.

Page 352   **5.   What is the STRIDE model?**

The STRIDE model is a threat model that allows application designers to predict and evaluate potential threats to an application. Each letter in the STRIDE acronym specifies a different category of security threat: spoofing identity, tampering, repudiation, information disclosure, denial of service, and elevation of privilege.

Page 353   **6.   Read the following security attack scenario, and then decide which elements of the STRIDE model are implicit in the attack.**

Carl sees that Bob has left his workstation unattended and unlocked. Carl sits down at Bob's workstation and opens Bob's e-mail application. Carl, pretending to be Bob, sends an e-mail message to Alice. Carl quits the e-mail client and then walks away unobserved.

Four types of attacks—spoofing identity, tampering, repudiation, and elevation of privilege—are possible in the above scenario.

Page 353   **7.   What is code-access security?**

The .NET Framework provides code-access security to help protect computer systems from malicious code and to provide a way to allow mobile code to run safely. Code-access security allows code to be trusted to varying degrees, depending on the code's origin and on other aspects of the code's identity.

Page 353   **8.   What is role-based security?**

Role-based security applies mostly to the spoofing identity security threat by preventing unauthorized users from performing operations that they are not authorized to perform. Role-based security allows code to check the identity and role membership of the user. The .NET Framework includes classes to check Windows users and groups, in addition to classes to help implement role-based security for other authentication schemes.

Page 353   **9.   Which are the authentication providers supported by ASP.NET?**

ASP.NET supports three authentication providers: forms, Microsoft Passport, and Windows.

Page 353   **10.   What are the three types of security provided by Web services?**

The three types of security are:

- Platform/transport-level (point-to-point) security
- Application-level (custom) security
- Message-level (end-to-end) security

Page 353   **11.   What are the steps for designing an authorization and authentication strategy for an application?**

To design an authorization and authentication strategy for an application, you perform the following steps:

a. Identify resources.

b. Select an authorization strategy.

c. Select the identities used for resource access.

d. Consider identity flow.

e. Select an authentication approach.

f. Decide how to flow identity.

Chapter 10   Completing the Planning Phase
Activity, Exercise 1

Page 383   **1.**   **Review the test plan and then list three ways that use cases and usage scenarios are used in the testing process for Adventure Works Cycles.**

Adventure Works Cycles uses use cases and usage scenarios in the following ways:

- Use cases and usage scenarios define the actions to be tested for user functionality.
- Use cases and usage scenarios define the actions to be tested for adminstrative functionality.
- Use cases and usage scenarios will be used to write the specific test script scenarios.

Page 383   **2.**   **How will bugs be approved and documented for action for the solution?**

Change requests will be issued for bugs meeting the change criteria.

Page 383   **3.**   **Which user accounts must be configured on the test environment servers?**

- Network Administrator
- Sales Representative 1
- Sales Representative 2
- Sales Manager
- Web Customer 1
- Web Customer 2
- Reseller
- Production Clerk

Page 383   **4.**   **Why is the following threat important to list under threats to testing?**

Availability of sales staff for testing. The test team should be overseen by at least one sales representative. Mitigation: Gain prior agreement from the vice president of sales for two sales representatives to be assigned to test the application.

Because the bulk of the functionality is defined by usage scenarios with a sales representative as at least one of the actors, this requirement will greatly increase the validity of the testing. It will also ensure approval from the sales staff (provided the two selected representatives feel that their input is responded to by means of change requests). It can also provide the benefit of creating two representatives that are able to be very productive in the training and implementation of the application.

Chapter 10   Completing the Planning Phase
Activity, Exercise 2

Page 384   **1.   What are the parameters for the *addOrderDetail* method?**

The parameters are: ProductID and Quantity.

Page 384   **2.   Will two types of client interfaces be available in the application?**

Yes, Windows Forms and Web Forms.

Page 384   **3.   Why is the Interfaces section still to be determined?**

The interfaces cannot be documented until they are developed and validated. Although pseudocode could be written, it should not be left permanently in the technical specification, but replaced with the code when it is developed.

Chapter 10   Completing the Planning Phase
Review

Page 388   **1.   How do you scale up an application?**

You scale up an application by adding more memory, more or faster processors, or by migrating the application to a single more powerful machine.

Page 388   **2.   What do you need to take into consideration while designing for scalability?**

- Design processes so that they do not wait.
- Design processes so that they do not fight for resources.
- Design processes for commutability.
- Design components for interchangeability.
- Partition resources and activities.

Page 388   **3.   What do you need to take into consideration while designing for availability?**

Designing for availability includes anticipating, detecting, and resolving hardware or software failures before they result in service errors, event faults, or data corruption, thereby minimizing downtime.

Page 388   **4.   How does clustering enhance the availability of an application?**

Clustering allows two or more independent servers to behave as a single system. In the event of a failure of a component such as a CPU, motherboard, storage adapter, network card, or application component, the workload is moved to another server, current client processes are switched over, and the failed application service is automatically restarted, with no apparent downtime. When a hardware or software resource fails, customers connected to that server cluster might experience a slight delay, but the service will be completed.

Page 388   **5.   How do you reduce planned downtime of an application?**

One of the best ways to avoid planned downtime is by using rolling upgrades. For example, assume that you need to update a component on a clustered server. You can move the server's resource groups to another server, take the server offline for maintenance, perform the upgrade, and then bring the server online. During the maintenance, the other servers handle the workload and the application experiences no downtime.

Page 388   **6.**   **Why is reliability an important design consideration for an application?**

- Unreliable systems are very costly. Users bypass unreliable Web sites, resulting in lost revenue and reduced future sales.
- The expense of repairing corrupted data increases the loss due to application failure.
- Unreliable systems are difficult to maintain or improve because the failure points are typically hidden throughout the system.

Page 389   **7.**   **How do you design for reliability of an application?**

To design for reliability of an application, you need to perform the following tasks:

- Document reliability requirements in the specification.
- Use a good architectural infrastructure.
- Include management information in the application.
- Use redundancy.
- Use quality development tools.
- Use reliability checks that are provided by the application.
- Use consistent error handling.
- Reduce the application's functionality instead of completely failing the application.

Page 389   **8.**   **How do you define a performance requirement?**

To define a good performance requirement, you must identify project constraints, determine services that the application will perform, and specify the load on the application.

Page 389   **9.**   **Why do you need to design for interoperability?**

- Reduces operational cost and complexity
- Enables optimal deployments
- Uses existing investments

Page 389   **10.**   **How do you prepare an application for globalization?**

- Identify the cultures and locales that must be supported.
- Design features that support those cultures and locales.
- Write code that functions equally well in all the supported cultures and locales.

Page 389   **11.**   **What is the purpose of a monitoring plan?**

A monitoring plan describes what will be monitored, how the application will be monitored, and how the results of monitoring will be reported and used. Customers use automated procedures to monitor many aspects of a solution.

Page 389   **12.   What is the purpose of the migration strategies section of the migration plan?**

The migration strategies section describes the strategy or strategies that will guide the migration process. These strategies do not need to be mutually exclusive but can describe different parts of the overall migration. Strategy could be organized around releases (related to the business or to development or technology maturity) or organized around solution components. These strategies also need to take into account the migration of earlier systems into the new solution environment. You might have multiple migration strategy sections if you need to migrate both business objects and data.

Page 389   **13.   Why do you need to provide licensing specifications for both the development and the deployment phase?**

- During the developing phase, the team will work with selected technologies and software products. You must ensure that there are sufficient licenses for the required products.
- For the developing phase, you need to specify the number of licenses needed · for any software that might be used. The number of licenses needed depends on the type of solution and the number of users who will use the solution.

Page 389   **14.   What is the purpose of the development plan?**

The development plan describes the solution development process used for the project. This plan provides consistent guidelines and processes to the teams creating the solution. Having the development process documented indicates that the team has discussed and agreed on a consistent structure and direction to be used during the development process. It also facilitates reuse among different groups and minimizes the dependency upon one individual or group.

Page 389   **15.   What is the purpose of the test plan?**

The test plan describes the strategy and approach used to plan, organize, and manage the project's testing activities. It identifies testing objectives, methodologies and tools, expected results, responsibilities, and resource requirements. This document is the primary plan for the testing team. A test plan ensures that the testing process will be conducted in a thorough and organized manner and will enable the team to determine the stability of the solution.

Page 389   **16.   Who creates the deployment plan?**

The release management role of the MSF Team Model is responsible for designing and implementing the solution's deployment plan. Release management is also responsible for specifying the solution infrastructure and ensuring that the solution continues to run as expected after it has been deployed.

Page 389   **17.   What is a technical specification?**

The technical specification is a set of reference documents that usually includes the artifacts of physical design, such as class specifications, component models, metrics, and network and component topologies. During the developing phase, the technical specification becomes the method for documenting the actual implementation of the developed solution.

Chapter 11   Stabilizing and Deploying the Solution
Review

Page 424   **1. What are some of the specific goals of the stabilizing phase?**

The goals of the stabilizing phase include:

- Improve solution quality
- Address outstanding issues to prepare for release
- Make the transition from building features to focusing on quality
- Stabilize the solution
- Prepare for release

Page 424   **2. How does ongoing analysis of bug convergence provide warning signs about the stability of the project?**

If the numbers of reported and fixed bugs are not converging over time, the team is reporting as many new bugs as it is fixing. Solution stability is no closer than it was on the first day of the project. The team must treat this lack of convergence as a serious issue and resolve it quickly.

Page 424   **3. Why is zero-bug bounce a positive indicator for the project?**

Zero-bug bounce indicates that development has caught up with the backlog of active bugs needing resolution. It indicates that the quality of the build is improving.

Page 424   **4. What is a release candidate, and what are some of its features?**

After the first achievement of zero-bug bounce, a series of release candidates are prepared for release to the pilot group. Each of these releases is marked as an interim milestone. The purpose of the release candidate is to make the product available to a preselected group of users to test it. The users provide feedback to the project team, and the project team in turn continues to improve the product and resolve bugs that appear during the pilot.

Page 424   **5. What is a pilot, and what are its goals?**

A pilot is a test of the solution under live conditions, such as a subset of production servers, a subset of users in a users group, or a trial period for the entire production environment (with the ability to roll back). The goal of a pilot is to take the next step in the ongoing stabilization process and reduce the risks associated with deployment.

Page 424   **6. Why should pilot testing not be too easy?**

A pilot should test every case and situation that will arise in production, including operations tasks. A pilot that is too easy will not reveal enough information to select the strategy for moving forward. Intentional crashes of the pilot should be included to test rollback procedures, disaster recovery, and business continuity planning. The results of a rigorous pilot that is completed by proactive users will tell the team whether it should stagger forward, roll back, suspend the pilot, patch and continue, or proceed to the deployment phase (the ultimate goal of the pilot).

Page 424   **7. What are the deliverables of the deploying phase?**

The deliverables of the deploying phase are: operations and support information systems, including procedures and processes, knowledge base, reports, and logbooks; a repository of all versions of documents, load sets, configurations, scripts, and code; and a project closeout report, including project documents and customer surveys.

Page 425   **8. Which person or group is the best candidate to deploy the solution?**

This varies with the organization and the project. Sometimes the project team is the best candidate, and sometimes a specific deployment feature team should assume the responsibility. In some cases, an outside group should handle deployment. Ultimately, it is most important to develop a solid deployment plan and provide it to the person or group that is able to deliver a solid deployment.

Page 425   **9. What are some examples of core components? What are some examples of site components?**

Core components are such things as domain controllers, mail routers, remote access servers, and database servers. Site components include such things as local routers and file print servers.

Page 425   **10. What is the quiet period, and what are some of its features?**

The quiet period begins when deployments are complete and the team begins transferring responsibilities to operations and support. The quiet period generally lasts from 15 to 30 days.

Page 425   **11. What type of documents result from completing closeout activities?**

Closeout activities usually produce a customer satisfaction survey, a closeout report (including formal project closure, final deliverable versions, a customer survey result compilation, and a summary of next steps), a project review document, and a customer sign-off document.

Page 425   **12. Which MSF role handles the final sign-off from the customer?**

Product management typically obtains final sign-off from the customer for release of the solution. This signals the customer's approval of the solution and permission to disengage from the project.

Page 425   **13. What are the two types of project reviews that MSF advocates at the end of the deployment phase?**

Two types of project reviews are team reviews and customer reviews. In a team review, the core team assesses what it did well and what could have been improved. In a customer review, the team discusses with sponsors and stakeholders the project's outstanding issues, the level of quality and customer satisfaction, and the next steps following the project.

Glossary

A

accessibility aids Specialized programs and devices that help people with disabilities use applications more effectively.

activity diagram A UML diagram used to represent the state transition and flow of an application.

actor An entity in a use case that interacts with the system to be developed for the purpose of completing an event.

actors catalog An artifact that contains information about all the actors that will be used in use cases. See also *artifact*.

aggregation A special type of association that represents the relationship between a whole and its parts.

alpha code All code produced during the developing phase of the MSF Process Model. See also *beta code*.

analyzing risk The process of converting risk data into information that can be used to make risk decisions.

application architecture A set of definitions, rules, and relationships that form the structure of an application.

applications interoperability The infrastructure required to ensure interoperability between new *n*-tier applications and existing applications, business logic, and data.

architecture A design and plan for building something. Also the style of that plan or design. See also *application architecture*.

artifact An item that is physically available in the business environment and that describes an element or core business process.

association A structural relationship that describes a connection among objects.

asynchronous communication services Services that provide a message-based form of execution in which the requesting application is not dependent on a response within any given period of time.

asynchronous control The situation in which a client can submit a request and then continue performing other tasks.

attributes The names of data values that an object holds. Also known as *properties*.

authentication The process of positively identifying the clients of your application. Clients might include end users, services, processes, or computers.

authorization The process of defining what authenticated clients are allowed to see and do within the application.

availability A measure of how often an application is available to handle service requests as compared to the planned run time.

B

behavioral view A UML view that represents the dynamic or changing state of a system.

beta code All code tested during the stabilizing phase of the MSF Process Model. See also *alpha code*.

buddy testing A type of testing that involves developers who are not working directly on the creation of a particular code segment, employing them to perform coverage testing on their colleague's code.

buffer overrun A type of error that occurs when more data is written to a buffer than the buffer was programmed to contain.

bug Any issue arising from the use of the product.

bug convergence The point at which the team makes visible progress towards minimizing the active bug count.

build verification testing A type of testing used to identify errors during the build process. It can be thought of as the identification of compilation errors, as opposed to run-time errors, of all solution components.

business goals Goals representing what the customer wants to achieve with the solution. Business goals form the basis for determining the success criteria of the solution.

business requirements Requirements defining what the solution must deliver to capitalize on a business opportunity or to meet business challenges.

business rules catalog An artifact in internal team documentation that lists the business rules for a solution. This is a living document.

business services Units of application logic that enforce business rules in the correct sequence.

C

cache architecture A version of the client/server architecture in which the application provides a means for processing some client requests without forwarding the requests to another device.

check-in testing A type of testing performed by developers or testers before the code is checked into the change control system. This testing is performed to ensure that tested code is behaving correctly.

class diagram A UML diagram that depicts various classes and their associations.

Class-Responsibility-Collaboration (CRC card) A modeling tool that indicates all the classes with which a class must interact and identifies the relationships between classes.

client/server architecture A two-tier architecture that is based on a request-and-provide strategy. The client initiates a session with the server and controls the session, enlisting the server on demand.

clustered index A type of index that physically reorders the rows of data in a table to match the order of the index.

clustering A technology for creating high-availability applications. A cluster consists of multiple computers that are physically networked and logically connected by cluster software.

code signing The process of providing a set of code with credentials that authenticate the publisher of the code.

code-access security A technique that allows code to be trusted to varying degrees, depending on the code's origin and on other aspects of the code's identity.

cohesion The relationship among different internal elements of a component.

collaboration diagram A UML diagram that represents a set of classes and the messages sent and received by those classes.

commutative processes Two or more operations that can execute in any order and still obtain the same result.

compatibility testing A type of testing that focuses on the integration or interoperability of the solution under development with existing systems.

component and data topology A map that indicates the locations of packages, components, and their services in relation to the network topology. It also indicates data store locations.

component diagram A UML diagram that represents the implementation view of a system. This diagram is used to represent the dependencies between components or component packages.

conceptual design The first design process of the planning phase, during which the project team views the problem from the perspective of the users and business requirements and defines the problem and solution in terms of usage scenarios.

conceptual schema design procedure (CSDP) A methodology in ORM that focuses on the analysis and design of data. The conceptual schema specifies the information structure of the application, including the types of facts that are of interest, any constraints on these facts, and the rules for deriving some facts from others.

configuration testing A type of testing used to conduct solution tests in each of the possible solution configurations.

constraints Parameters to which the final business solution must adhere. They are aspects of the business environment that cannot or will not be changed.

coupling The relationship of a component with other components.

coverage testing Low-level technical testing.

CRC card See *Class-Responsibility-Collaboration.*

CSDP See *conceptual schema design procedure.*

customer One or more individuals who expect to gain business value from a solution.

D

data integrity The consistency and accuracy of data.

data interoperability The ability for applications to access and use data stored in both structured and unstructured storage systems such as databases, file systems, and e-mail stores.

data services Units of application logic that provide the lowest visible level of detail for manipulating data.

data type A definition used to specify the kind of data that is stored in a field.

database A collection of data values that are organized in a specific manner.

database schema A description that specifies how data is organized in a database.

delegation An extended form of impersonation that allows a server process that is performing work on behalf of a client to access resources on a remote computer. See also *impersonation.*

denial of service (DoS) Any attack that attempts to shut down or prevent access to a computing resource.

denormalization The process of reversing normalization to generate tables with more fields that require fewer joins.

dependency A relationship between two objects in which a change to one object (independent) can affect the behavior or service of the other object (dependent).

deploying phase The final phase of the MSF Process Model. During this phase, the team deploys the solution technology and site components, stabilizes the deployment, transfers the project to operations and support, and obtains final customer approval of the project.

deployment diagram A UML diagram that represents the mapping of software components to the nodes of the physical implementation of a system.

deployment model A model that represents the mapping of the application and its services to the actual server topology.

deployment view See *environment view*.

design goals A type of project goal. These goals focus on the attributes of the solution.

design view See *structural view*.

developing phase The third phase of the MSF Process Model. During this phase, the project team creates the solution, creates the code to implement the solution, documents the code, and develops the infrastructure for the solution. The developing phase culminates in the *scope complete* milestone.

development An MSF Team Model role that is responsible for developing the solution according to the specifications provided by the program management role.

distribution strategy A rationale for determining where services will be located in the solution architecture.

documentation and Help file tests A type of testing that focuses on testing all developed support documents or systems. The documents and Help files are compared with the solution to discover any discrepancies.

domain integrity A type of data integrity used to specify a set of valid data values for a column and determine whether null values are to be allowed.

DoS See *denial of service*.

E

elementary fact Refers to the fact that an object has a property, or that one or more objects participate in a relationship.

elevation of privilege An attack in which a malicious user gains access to greater privileges than the administrator intended, creating the opportunity for the user to launch attacks of every other category of security threat.

encryption The process of disguising data before it is sent or stored.

end user One or more individuals or systems that interact directly with a solution.

entity integrity A type of data integrity that requires each row in a table to have a unique identifier, known as the primary key value. See *primary keys*.

environment view A UML view that represents the distribution of the physical elements of a system. Also known as the deployment view.

envisioning phase The first phase of the MSF Process Model, during which the project team is assembled and comes to agreement with the customer on the project vision and scope. The envisioning phase culminates in the *vision-approved* milestone.

F

fact instance An individual observation about the relationship between two or more data values.

fact type The set of fact instances that share the same object types and predicate relationships.

flat-file database A type of data store in which all data in a single file is stored as a set of rows and columns.

focus group An information-gathering technique in which individuals discuss a topic and provide feedback to a facilitator.

foreign keys Keys used to link two tables.

forms authentication A system by which unauthenticated requests are redirected to a Hypertext Markup Language (HTML) form by means of Hypertext Transfer Protocol (HTTP) client-side redirection.

functional specification A virtual repository of project and design-related artifacts that are created during the planning phase of the MSF Process Model.

functional tests Tests that are specified by the users of the solution and created by the testing team.

G

generalization A relationship between a general thing (called the parent) and a specialized or specific thing (called the child).

globalization The process of designing and developing an application that can operate in multiple cultures and locales.

glossary One of the artifacts in internal team documentation that contains a list of terms used in artifacts and their meanings.

granularity A measure of the number of services and objects packaged in a single component.

H

hashing The process of matching data of any length to a fixed length byte sequence.

hierarchical database A database that stores a wide range of information in a variety of formats.

high-fidelity design A design that provides detailed information about screen layout and interface elements.

horizontal partitioning A method of partitioning tables in which a table containing many rows is divided into multiple tables containing the same columns.

I

identity A characteristic of a user or service that can uniquely identify the user or service.

impersonation A technique used by a server application to access resources on behalf of a client application.

implementation view A UML view that represents the structure of the logical elements of a system.

index An ordered list of rows in a table that a database management system (DBMS) can use to accelerate lookup operations.

information disclosure A security error in which an unauthorized user views private data, such as a file that contains a credit card number and expiration date.

instance An item of interest in the universe of discourse.

interchangeable component A component that is designed to release its resources, move into a pool managed by a resource manager, and be re-initialized for use by a new client application.

interface A means for requesting that a service perform an operation and a means for receiving information about the resulting attributes.

interim milestone A point in time that signals a transition within a phase and helps to divide large projects into manageable pieces. See also *milestone*.

interviewing An information gathering technique that involves a one-on-one meeting between a member of the project team and a user or stakeholder.

K

key A value used to uniquely identify each instance of an entity.

L

layered architecture A version of the client/server architecture in which various services in the application are clearly positioned in specific layers.

layered-client-cache-stateless-cache-server architecture A version of the client/server architecture that combines the layered-client-server, client-cache, and cached-stateless-server approaches by adding proxies throughout the system as necessary.

living documents Documents that are used and updated throughout the life cycle of the project.

localization The process of adapting a globalized application to a specific culture and locale, using separate resources for each culture.

logical design A process in the planning phase during which the solution is described in terms of its organization, its structure, and the interaction of its parts from the perspective of the project team.

low-fidelity design A design that shows the main structure and features of the user interface (UI) and illustrates the navigation path.

M

manageability The ease with which a system can be managed on all levels.

management interoperability The tasks of user account management, performance monitoring, and tuning for heterogeneous applications.

master project plan A collection of plans that addresses tasks performed by each of the six MSF team roles to achieve the functionality described in the functional specification.

master project schedule The schedule that applies a time frame to the master plan. The master project schedule synchronizes project schedules across the teams. It includes the time frame in which the teams intend to complete their work.

master risk assessment document A document used to describe the risks associated with developing the solution. The master risk assessment document that is developed during the envisioning phase is reviewed and updated regularly, but particularly at the milestones.

meaningful sample population Instances of information in the UoD, and the real-world problem that the project team is trying to solve.

messaging service A type of service used to route information and deliver information that is not time-dependent to many individuals.

Microsoft Solutions Framework (MSF) A structure developed by Microsoft that is a set of models, principles, and guidelines for planning, building, and managing business solutions.

milestone A point at which the team assesses progress and makes mid-course corrections. Milestones are review and synchronization points, not completion points.

mitigating risk The practice of predicting risks and then taking steps to eliminate them from a proposed course of action.

MSF See *Microsoft Solutions Framework*.

MSF Process Model A phase-based, milestone-driven, and iterative model that describes a generalized sequence of activities for building and deploying enterprise solutions. The MSF Process Model combines the waterfall model's milestone-based planning, and the resulting predictability, with the spiral model's beneficial feedback and creativity.

MSF readiness management process A process to help teams develop the knowledge, skills, and abilities (KSAs) needed to create and manage projects and solutions.

MSF risk management process A discipline that advocates proactive risk management, continuous risk assessment, and decision making throughout the project life cycle.

N

navigation map A map in user interface (UI) design that shows which component is called for each UI event.

network interoperability The ability of multiple vendor systems to communicate with each other without having to use common protocols.

network load balancing (NLB) A technique used to distribute traffic evenly across available servers.

network topology An infrastructure map that indicates hardware locations and interconnections.

NLB See *network load balancing*.

nonclustered index A type of index that maintains a small table of index information about a column or group of columns.

normalization The process of progressively refining a logical model to eliminate duplicate data from a database.

O

object diagram A UML diagram that depicts various objects in a system and their relationships with each other.

Object Role Modeling (ORM) A rich modeling methodology that allows you to analyze information at the conceptual level and model complex fact-driven, data-related business requirements.

object type The set of all possible instances of a given object.

object-oriented database A data storage system in which database objects appear as programming language objects in one or more existing programming languages.

objects People or things described in usage scenarios.

Online Help Refers to any help that is immediately available upon user request while the user is interacting with the system.

operations requirement A type of requirement that the solution must deliver to maximize operability and improve service delivery with reduced downtime and risks.

operations team The organization responsible for the ongoing operation of the solution after delivery.

ORM See *Object Role Modeling*.

P

packaging strategy A rationale for determining which services go into each component.

parallel testing A common usage testing strategy in which both the current solution and the solution under development are tested side-by-side at the same time.

Passport authentication A centralized authentication service provided by Microsoft that offers a single logon and core profile services for member sites.

performance testing A type of testing that focuses on predicted performance improvements to the solution under development.

physical design The final design process of the planning phase. During this process, components, services, and technologies of the solution are described from the perspective of development requirements.

pilot A test of a solution in the production environment, and a trial of the solution by installers, systems support staff, and end users.

pilot plan A plan that describes how the team will move the candidate release version of a solution to a staging area and test it.

planning phase The second phase of the MSF Process Model, during which the team determines what to develop and plans how to create the solution. The team prepares the functional specification, creates a design of the solution, and prepares work plans, cost estimates, and schedules for the various deliverables. This phase culminates with the *project plan approved* milestone.

population The group of all combined instances of a given type of item of interest in the UoD.

preliminary deployment model A model that includes network, data, and component topologies and enables the project team and other stakeholders to review the design.

primary keys Keys that uniquely identify each row of data in a table.

problem statement A short narrative describing the issues the business hopes to address with the project. It relates primarily to the current state of business activities.

process A collection of activities that yield a result, product, or service; usually a continuous operation.

process model A model that guides the order of project activities and represents the life cycle of a project.

process view See *behavioral view*.

product management An MSF Team Model role that is responsible for managing customer communications and expectations. During the design phase, product management gathers customer requirements and ensures that business needs are met. Product management also works on project communication plans such as briefings to the customers, marketing to users, demonstrations, and product launches.

program management An MSF Team Model role that is responsible for the development process and for delivering the solution to the customer within the project constraints.

programming model A model that describes how the development team can use the specific technologies and that sets guidelines for providing consistent component implementation and increasing the maintainability of the components.

project sponsor One or more individuals responsible for initiating and approving the project and its result.

project structure document A document that defines the approach a team will use to organize and manage a project. It describes the team's administrative structure, standards and processes, and project resources and constraints.

project tradeoff matrix A tool that helps identify the project features that are considered essential, the features that are not essential but that would be good to include, and the features that can be eliminated or added to the next version to accommodate the other two variables.

prototyping A technique in which information is gathered by simulating the production environment. Prototyping is a validation technique in which a prototype is used to provide details of processes, process flow, organizational implications, and technology possibilities.

R

realization A relationship, between classes, in which one abstract class specifies a contract that another class needs to carry out.

regression testing The process of repeating identical actions or steps that were performed using an earlier build of a product on a new build or version of the product.

relational model database A database in which data is stored in multiple tables and columns.

relationships A description of how objects are linked to each other.

release management An MSF Team Model role that is responsible for defect-free deployment and operations of the solution. Release management validates the infrastructure implications of the solution to ensure that it can be deployed and supported.

release readiness milestone The major milestone at the end of the stabilizing phase that represents the point at which the team has addressed all outstanding issues and releases the product.

reliability The ability of the application to provide accurate results.

repeatability A variable that measures how repeatable an issue or bug is. Repeatability is the percentage in which the issue or bug manifests itself. It is expressed as a percentage in the range of 10 percent (integer value 0.1) through 100 percent (integer value 1), where 100 percent indicates that the issue or bug is reproducible on every test run.

repudiation A situation in which a system administrator or security agent is unable to prove that a user—malicious or otherwise—has performed some action.

risk The possibility of loss or injury; a problem that might occur.

risk probability The likelihood that a risk will occur.

risk source Where a risk might originate.

role playing A validation technique in which a set of selected users performs multiple versions of a process to evaluate it and identify areas of potential refinement.

S

scalability The capability to increase resources to produce an increase in the service capacity.

scaling out Distributing the processing load across more than one server.

scaling up Achieving scalability by improving the existing server's processing hardware.

scope A guideline used to define what will and will not be included in a project. The scope corresponds to the project vision as defined in the vision statement and incorporates the constraints imposed on the project by resources, time, and other limiting factors.

secure communications A generic term used to describe the process of ensuring that messages remain private and unaltered as they cross networks.

security context A generic term used to refer to the collection of security settings that affect the security-related behavior of a process or thread.

sequence diagram A UML diagram that describes the interaction between classes. A sequence diagram shows the actors and objects that participate in an interaction, and a chronological list of the events they generate.

service A specific behavior that a business object must perform.

set Any group of instances. A set is not necessarily the same as a population. It can be part of a population, or a combination of instances from more than one population.

severity A variable that measures how much impact an issue or bug will have on a solution, on code, or on users. Severity is an integer in the range of 1 through 10, where classification 10 issues or bugs present the most impact.

shadowing An information gathering technique in which you observe a user performing tasks in the actual work environment and ask the user any questions you have related to the task.

signed data A standards-based data type that consists of any type of content combined with encrypted hashes of the content for zero or more signers.

solution concept A description of the approach the team will take to meet the goals of the project. Provides the basis for proceeding to the planning phase.

spiral model An iterative process model in which the stages of application development are characterized as inception, elaboration, construction, and transition. Each stage has five activity phases: requirements, design, implementation, deployment, and management. The spiral model's process is a continual cycle through the stages of development, with each stage requiring multiple cycles through the five phases.

spoofing identity An attack involving a malicious user posing as a trusted entity.

SQL injection A type of security error that can occur when developers dynamically build Structured Query Language (SQL) statements by using user input.

stabilizing phase The last of four distinct phases of the MSF Process Model. During this phase, all team efforts are directed toward addressing all issues derived from feedback. No new development occurs during this phase. The stabilizing phase culminates in the *release readiness* milestone.

state diagram A UML diagram that describes how a class behaves when external processes or entities access the class.

state management A process by which the solution maintains state and page information over multiple requests for the same or different pages.

stateless architecture A version of the client/server architecture in which each client request contains all the information that is required by the server to process the request. No information is stored on the server.

stored procedures Named collections of SQL statements that are stored on the DBMS. They are precompiled, eliminating the need for the query analyzer to parse the statement every time the stored procedure is called.

stress test A type of test specifically designed to identify issues or bugs that might present themselves when the solution under development is operating under extreme conditions.

STRIDE threat model A technique used for identifying and categorizing threats to an application. Each letter in the STRIDE acronym specifies a different category of security threat: spoofing identity, tampering, repudiation, information disclosure, denial of service, and elevation of privilege.

structural view A UML view that represents the static or idle state of the system. Also known as the design view.

surveys An information gathering technique in which sets of questions are created and administered to specific sets of users.

synchronous control The situation in which object services are invoked and the calling object waits for control to be returned.

system requirement A type of requirement that specifies the atomic transactions and their sequence in a system. System requirements help the project team define how the new solution will interact with existing systems.

system services Units of application logic that provide functionality outside the business logic.

T

tampering An attack in which a user gains unauthorized access to a computer and then changes its operation, configuration, or data.

technical specification A set of reference documents that usually includes the artifacts of physical design, such as class specifications, component models, metrics, and network and component topologies.

test plan A plan that describes the strategy and approach used to plan, organize, and manage a project's testing activities.

testing An MSF Team Model role that is responsible for identifying and addressing all product quality issues and approving the solution for release. This role evaluates and validates design functionality and consistency with project vision and scope.

top ten risk list An identification of the ten top priority risks, taken from the risk assessment document.

tradeoff triangle A tool that shows that any change to any one component represented in the tradeoff triangle implies that a corresponding change might need to be made to other components. The tradeoff triangle helps to explain the constraints and present the options for tradeoffs.

transactional service A type of service that provides the mechanism and environment for a transaction-based application.

type-safe code Any code that accesses only the memory it is authorized to access.

U

UML See *Unified Modeling Language*.

Unified Modeling Language (UML) A standard modeling language that is used to model software systems of varying complexity.

unit test A type of developer-performed internal coverage testing that takes advantage of automated testing.

universe of discourse (UoD) An application area in ORM that you create to design a solution.

UoD See *universe of discourse*.

usage scenario Specifies the activity performed by a particular type of user and provides additional information about the activities and task sequences that constitute a process.

usage testing A type of high-level testing that is often performed by potential users of a solution or by subsets of this group.

use case A description of high-level interactions between an individual and a system. A use case specifies the sequence of steps that a user will perform in a usage scenario.

use case diagram A UML diagram that represents the functionality that is provided to external entities by a system.

user experience An MSF Team Model role that is responsible for analyzing the performance needs and support issues of users and for considering the product implications of meeting those needs.

user instruction An information gathering technique in which users train the project team on the tasks that they perform.

user interface components Components that manage interaction with the user, display data to the user, acquire data from the user, interpret events that are caused by user actions, change the state of the user interface, and help users view progress in their tasks.

user profile A document that specifies the various users of the solution and their roles and responsibilities.

user requirement A type of requirement that defines the nonfunctional aspect of a user's interaction with a solution.

user services Units of application logic that provide the user interface in an application. The user services of an application manage the interaction between the application and its users.

user view A UML view that represents the part of the system with which the user interacts.

V

vertical partitioning A method of partitioning tables in which a table containing many columns is divided into multiple tables containing rows with equivalent unique identifiers.

visibility A variable that measures the situation or environment that must be established before an issue or bug manifests itself. Visibility is a percentage in the range of 10 percent (integer value 0.1) through 100 percent (integer value 1), where 10 percent indicates that the issue or bug is visible under only the most obscure conditions. Issues or bugs that manifest themselves in environments with under common conditions are said to be highly visible.

vision statement A short, concise statement used to establish a common vision and reach consensus among team members that a project is valuable to the organization and is likely to succeed.

vision/scope meeting A meeting during which the team and the customer arrive at a shared understanding regarding how the proposed solution will address the business challenge and how it is applicable to the current business scenario, given the scope that has been defined.

W

walkthrough A validation technique in which a facilitator guides users through a scenario and asks questions to determine whether the users agree with the description of individual actions and events.

waterfall model A linear process model that has the following well-defined development steps: system requirements, software requirements, analysis, program design, coding, system test, and operations. This process model has fixed transition and assessment points. All tasks for a particular step must be completed before proceeding to the next step.

Windows authentication A system used by Microsoft ASP.NET in conjunction with Internet Information Services (IIS) authentication.

wizard A user assistance device that guides users step by step through a procedure.

Z

ZBB See *zero-bug bounce*.

zero-bug bounce (ZBB) The point in the project when development resolves all the bugs raised by testing and there are no active bugs. More bugs might be logged after this point.

zero-defect mindset The goal for project teams in which the team commits to producing the highest quality product possible.

Index

A

At Microsoft Press, we use tools to illustrate our books for software developers and IT professionals. Tools very simply and powerfully symbolize human inventiveness. They're a metaphor for people extending their capabilities, precision, and reach. From simple calipers and pliers to digital micrometers and lasers, these stylized illustrations give each book a visual identity, and a personality to the series. With tools and knowledge, there's no limit to creativity and innovation. Our tagline says it all: *the tools you need to put technology to work*.

Expert guidance for anyone who develops with *Visual Basic .NET!*

Microsoft® Visual Basic® .NET Step by Step
ISBN 0-7356-1374-5

Graduate to the next generation of Visual Basic at your own pace! This primer is the fast way for any Visual Basic developer to begin creating professional applications for the Microsoft .NET platform by unleashing all the power of the .NET-ready version of Visual Basic. Learn core programming skills by selecting just the chapters you need—with code, optimization tips, advice, and samples straight from the experts. Upgrade your Visual Basic 6 applications quickly using "Upgrade Notes" sidebars, a special upgrading index, and practical advice about the Visual Basic .NET Upgrade Wizard.

Programming Microsoft Visual Basic .NET (Core reference)
ISBN 0-7356-1375-3

Accelerate your productivity with Visual Basic .NET! Building on the success of Programming Microsoft Visual Basic 6.0, this core reference equips new and veteran developers with instruction and code to get them up to speed with the Web-enabled Microsoft Visual Basic .NET environment. The book demonstrates best practices for porting and reusing existing Visual Basic code in the Microsoft .NET environment, as well as exploiting the object-oriented capabilities of the new version—complete with code samples and the book's text on CD-ROM.

Designing Enterprise Applications with Microsoft Visual Basic .NET
ISBN 0-7356-1721-X

Learn how to put the power of Visual Basic .NET to work to build enterprise applications! Most books about Microsoft Visual Basic .NET focus on the language or development environment. This book provides the detailed guidance you need to make the right design choices as you build enterprise-level applications with Visual Basic .NET. The author, who has extensive experience in designing, testing, and optimizing enterprise applications, discusses the technical and architectural tradeoffs you'll face as you develop large, multitier, distributed applications with multiple developers.

Microsoft Press has many other titles to help you put the power of Visual Basic to work. To learn more about the full line of Microsoft Press® products for developers, please visit:

microsoft.com/mspress/developer

Get a **Free**
e-mail newsletter, updates,
special offers, links to related books,
and more when you

register on line!

Register your Microsoft Press® title on our Web site and you'll get
a FREE subscription to our e-mail newsletter, *Microsoft Press Book
Connections.* You'll find out about newly released and upcoming books
and learning tools, online events, software downloads, special offers
and coupons for Microsoft Press customers, and information about
major Microsoft® product releases. You can also read useful additional
information about all the titles we publish, such as detailed book
descriptions, tables of contents and indexes, sample chapters, links to
related books and book series, author biographies, and reviews by other
customers.

Registration is easy. Just visit this Web page and fill in your information:

http://www.microsoft.com/mspress/register

Microsoft®

Proof of Purchase

MCSD Self-Paced Training Kit: Analyzing Requirements and Defining Microsoft® .NET Solution Architectures, Exam 70-300

0-7356-1894-1

_____

CUSTOMER NAME

Microsoft Press, PO Box 97017, Redmond, WA 98073-9830

MICROSOFT LICENSE AGREEMENT
Book Companion CD

IMPORTANT—READ CAREFULLY: This Microsoft End-User License Agreement ("EULA") is a legal agreement between you (either an individual or an entity) and Microsoft Corporation for the Microsoft product identified above, which includes computer software and may include associated media, printed materials, and "online" or electronic documentation ("SOFTWARE PROD-UCT"). Any component included within the SOFTWARE PRODUCT that is accompanied by a separate End-User License Agreement shall be governed by such agreement and not the terms set forth below. By installing, copying, or otherwise using the SOFTWARE PRODUCT, you agree to be bound by the terms of this EULA. If you do not agree to the terms of this EULA, you are not authorized to install, copy, or otherwise use the SOFTWARE PRODUCT; you may, however, return the SOFTWARE PROD-UCT, along with all printed materials and other items that form a part of the Microsoft product that includes the SOFTWARE PRODUCT, to the place you obtained them for a full refund.

SOFTWARE PRODUCT LICENSE

The SOFTWARE PRODUCT is protected by United States copyright laws and international copyright treaties, as well as other intellectual property laws and treaties. The SOFTWARE PRODUCT is licensed, not sold.

1. **GRANT OF LICENSE.** This EULA grants you the following rights:

   a. **Software Product.** You may install and use one copy of the SOFTWARE PRODUCT on a single computer. The primary user of the computer on which the SOFTWARE PRODUCT is installed may make a second copy for his or her exclusive use on a portable computer.

   b. **Storage/Network Use.** You may also store or install a copy of the SOFTWARE PRODUCT on a storage device, such as a network server, used only to install or run the SOFTWARE PRODUCT on your other computers over an internal network; however, you must acquire and dedicate a license for each separate computer on which the SOFTWARE PRODUCT is installed or run from the storage device. A license for the SOFTWARE PRODUCT may not be shared or used concurrently on different computers.

   c. **License Pak.** If you have acquired this EULA in a Microsoft License Pak, you may make the number of additional copies of the computer software portion of the SOFTWARE PRODUCT authorized on the printed copy of this EULA, and you may use each copy in the manner specified above. You are also entitled to make a corresponding number of secondary copies for portable computer use as specified above.

   d. **Sample Code.** Solely with respect to portions, if any, of the SOFTWARE PRODUCT that are identified within the SOFT-WARE PRODUCT as sample code (the "SAMPLE CODE"):

      i. **Use and Modification.** Microsoft grants you the right to use and modify the source code version of the SAMPLE CODE, *provided* you comply with subsection (d)(iii) below. You may not distribute the SAMPLE CODE, or any modified version of the SAMPLE CODE, in source code form.

      ii. **Redistributable Files.** Provided you comply with subsection (d)(iii) below, Microsoft grants you a nonexclusive, royalty-free right to reproduce and distribute the object code version of the SAMPLE CODE and of any modified SAMPLE CODE, other than SAMPLE CODE, or any modified version thereof, designated as not redistributable in the Readme file that forms a part of the SOFTWARE PRODUCT (the "Non-Redistributable Sample Code"). All SAMPLE CODE other than the Non-Redistributable Sample Code is collectively referred to as the "REDISTRIBUTABLES."

      iii. **Redistribution Requirements.** If you redistribute the REDISTRIBUTABLES, you agree to: (i) distribute the REDISTRIBUTABLES in object code form only in conjunction with and as a part of your software application product; (ii) not use Microsoft's name, logo, or trademarks to market your software application product; (iii) include a valid copyright notice on your software application product; (iv) indemnify, hold harmless, and defend Microsoft from and against any claims or lawsuits, including attorney's fees, that arise or result from the use or distribution of your software application product; and (v) not permit further distribution of the REDISTRIBUTABLES by your end user. Contact Microsoft for the applicable royalties due and other licensing terms for all other uses and/or distribution of the REDISTRIBUTABLES.

2. **DESCRIPTION OF OTHER RIGHTS AND LIMITATIONS.**

   • **Limitations on Reverse Engineering, Decompilation, and Disassembly.** You may not reverse engineer, decompile, or disassemble the SOFTWARE PRODUCT, except and only to the extent that such activity is expressly permitted by applicable law notwithstanding this limitation.

   • **Separation of Components.** The SOFTWARE PRODUCT is licensed as a single product. Its component parts may not be separated for use on more than one computer.

   • **Rental.** You may not rent, lease, or lend the SOFTWARE PRODUCT.

- **Support Services.** Microsoft may, but is not obligated to, provide you with support services related to the SOFTWARE PRODUCT ("Support Services"). Use of Support Services is governed by the Microsoft policies and programs described in the user manual, in "online" documentation, and/or in other Microsoft-provided materials. Any supplemental software code provided to you as part of the Support Services shall be considered part of the SOFTWARE PRODUCT and subject to the terms and conditions of this EULA. With respect to technical information you provide to Microsoft as part of the Support Services, Microsoft may use such information for its business purposes, including for product support and development. Microsoft will not utilize such technical information in a form that personally identifies you.

- **Software Transfer.** You may permanently transfer all of your rights under this EULA, provided you retain no copies, you transfer all of the SOFTWARE PRODUCT (including all component parts, the media and printed materials, any upgrades, this EULA, and, if applicable, the Certificate of Authenticity), **and** the recipient agrees to the terms of this EULA.

- **Termination.** Without prejudice to any other rights, Microsoft may terminate this EULA if you fail to comply with the terms and conditions of this EULA. In such event, you must destroy all copies of the SOFTWARE PRODUCT and all of its component parts.

3. **COPYRIGHT.** All title and copyrights in and to the SOFTWARE PRODUCT (including but not limited to any images, photographs, animations, video, audio, music, text, SAMPLE CODE, REDISTRIBUTABLES, and "applets" incorporated into the SOFTWARE PRODUCT) and any copies of the SOFTWARE PRODUCT are owned by Microsoft or its suppliers. The SOFT-WARE PRODUCT is protected by copyright laws and international treaty provisions. Therefore, you must treat the SOFTWARE PRODUCT like any other copyrighted material **except** that you may install the SOFTWARE PRODUCT on a single computer provided you keep the original solely for backup or archival purposes. You may not copy the printed materials accompanying the SOFTWARE PRODUCT.

4. **U.S. GOVERNMENT RESTRICTED RIGHTS.** The SOFTWARE PRODUCT and documentation are provided with RESTRICTED RIGHTS. Use, duplication, or disclosure by the Government is subject to restrictions as set forth in subparagraph (c)(1)(ii) of the Rights in Technical Data and Computer Software clause at DFARS 252.227-7013 or subparagraphs (c)(1) and (2) of the Commercial Computer Software—Restricted Rights at 48 CFR 52.227-19, as applicable. Manufacturer is Microsoft Corporation/One Microsoft Way/Redmond, WA 98052-6399.

5. **EXPORT RESTRICTIONS.** You agree that you will not export or re-export the SOFTWARE PRODUCT, any part thereof, or any process or service that is the direct product of the SOFTWARE PRODUCT (the foregoing collectively referred to as the "Restricted Components"), to any country, person, entity, or end user subject to U.S. export restrictions. You specifically agree not to export or re-export any of the Restricted Components (i) to any country to which the U.S. has embargoed or restricted the export of goods or services, which currently include, but are not necessarily limited to, Cuba, Iran, Iraq, Libya, North Korea, Sudan, and Syria, or to any national of any such country, wherever located, who intends to transmit or transport the Restricted Components back to such country; (ii) to any end user who you know or have reason to know will utilize the Restricted Components in the design, development, or production of nuclear, chemical, or biological weapons; or (iii) to any end user who has been prohibited from participating in U.S. export transactions by any federal agency of the U.S. government. You warrant and represent that neither the BXA nor any other U.S. federal agency has suspended, revoked, or denied your export privileges.

DISCLAIMER OF WARRANTY

NO WARRANTIES OR CONDITIONS. MICROSOFT EXPRESSLY DISCLAIMS ANY WARRANTY OR CONDITION FOR THE SOFTWARE PRODUCT. THE SOFTWARE PRODUCT AND ANY RELATED DOCUMENTATION ARE PROVIDED "AS IS" WITHOUT WARRANTY OR CONDITION OF ANY KIND, EITHER EXPRESS OR IMPLIED, INCLUDING, WITHOUT LIMITA-TION, THE IMPLIED WARRANTIES OF MERCHANTABILITY, FITNESS FOR A PARTICULAR PURPOSE, OR NONINFRINGEMENT. THE ENTIRE RISK ARISING OUT OF USE OR PERFORMANCE OF THE SOFTWARE PRODUCT REMAINS WITH YOU.

LIMITATION OF LIABILITY. TO THE MAXIMUM EXTENT PERMITTED BY APPLICABLE LAW, IN NO EVENT SHALL MICROSOFT OR ITS SUPPLIERS BE LIABLE FOR ANY SPECIAL, INCIDENTAL, INDIRECT, OR CONSEQUENTIAL DAM-AGES WHATSOEVER (INCLUDING, WITHOUT LIMITATION, DAMAGES FOR LOSS OF BUSINESS PROFITS, BUSINESS INTERRUPTION, LOSS OF BUSINESS INFORMATION, OR ANY OTHER PECUNIARY LOSS) ARISING OUT OF THE USE OF OR INABILITY TO USE THE SOFTWARE PRODUCT OR THE PROVISION OF OR FAILURE TO PROVIDE SUPPORT SERVICES, EVEN IF MICROSOFT HAS BEEN ADVISED OF THE POSSIBILITY OF SUCH DAMAGES. IN ANY CASE, MICROSOFT'S ENTIRE LIABILITY UNDER ANY PROVISION OF THIS EULA SHALL BE LIMITED TO THE GREATER OF THE AMOUNT ACTUALLY PAID BY YOU FOR THE SOFTWARE PRODUCT OR US$5.00; PROVIDED, HOWEVER, IF YOU HAVE ENTERED INTO A MICROSOFT SUPPORT SERVICES AGREEMENT, MICROSOFT'S ENTIRE LIABILITY REGARDING SUPPORT SERVICES SHALL BE GOVERNED BY THE TERMS OF THAT AGREEMENT. BECAUSE SOME STATES AND JURISDICTIONS DO NOT ALLOW THE EXCLUSION OR LIMITATION OF LIABILITY, THE ABOVE LIMITATION MAY NOT APPLY TO YOU.

MISCELLANEOUS

This EULA is governed by the laws of the State of Washington USA, except and only to the extent that applicable law mandates governing law of a different jurisdiction.

Should you have any questions concerning this EULA, or if you desire to contact Microsoft for any reason, please contact the Microsoft subsidiary serving your country, or write: Microsoft Sales Information Center/One Microsoft Way/Redmond, WA 98052-6399.

System Requirements

To get the most out of this training kit and the Supplemental Course Materials CD-ROM, you will need a computer equipped with the following minimum configuration:

- Pentium II, 266 MHz or faster
- 128 MB RAM
- 4-GB hard drive
- CD-ROM drive
- Microsoft Mouse or compatible pointing device
- Microsoft Windows 2000 Professional with Service Pack 3 or Microsoft Windows XP Professional
- Microsoft Office 2000 Professional with Service Pack 3 or later
- Microsoft Visio 2000 Professional or later

Test with Pearson VUE–
and save 15%!

Get certified

You invested in your future with the purchase of this book. Now, demonstrate your proficiency with Microsoft® .NET and get the industry recognition your skills deserve. A Microsoft certification validates your technical expertise and increases your credibility in the marketplace.

- Microsoft Certified Solution Developer (MCSD) for Microsoft .NET is the only certification that targets advanced developers who analyze and design leading-edge enterprise solutions using Microsoft .NET architecture, tools, and technologies.

- MCSD for Microsoft .NET reliably validates your ability to lead successful software development projects.

- As you earn the MCSD credential, you will cultivate your skills at envisioning and planning solutions and increase your opportunities.

Test with Pearson VUE

Pearson VUE, a Microsoft authorized test delivery provider since 1998, has teamed with Microsoft Press for a special, limited-time offer. Use this voucher to save 15% on one MCSD exam fee at any Pearson VUE™ Authorized Test Center!*

Redeem your discount voucher

Uncover your discount voucher code on the back of this page, and go to **www.pearsonvue.com/mspress** to register for the Microsoft MCSD Exam 70-300.

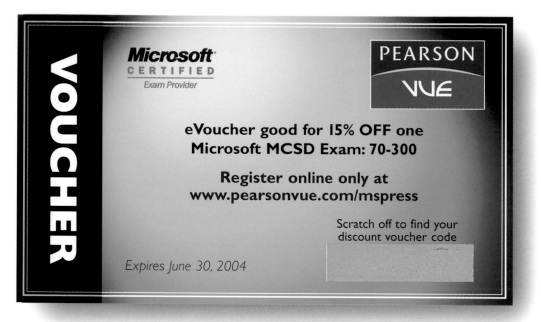

Schedule your exam online only at
www.pearsonvue.com/mspress

When you test with Pearson VUE, you get state-of-the-art testing technology and world-class service, resulting in an enhanced testing experience.

Convenient – choose from over 3,300 quality Pearson VUE test centers in more than 130 countries

Easy – real-time access to Web-based exam scheduling means you have 24 x 7 control over your exam schedule

Reliable – your exam will be ready when you expect it, and your exam results will be quickly and accurately reported to Microsoft

Secure – Only Pearson VUE has a Web Digital Embosser that helps protect your certification

For the location of a Pearson VUE test center near you, visit www.pearsonvue.com/mspress

Promotion Terms and Conditions:
• Voucher discount must be redeemed online at **www.pearsonvue.com/mspress**
• Exam must be taken at a Pearson VUE Authorized Center
• Voucher is available only in the English language version of these books
• Discounted exam must be taken on or before June 30, 2004
• Discounted exam registration must be made online at **www.pearsonvue.com**
• Promotion is limited to one discounted exam per candidate for each book purchased
• 15% discount is valid only on Microsoft MCSD Exam 70-300

Voucher Terms and Conditions
• Expired voucher has no value
• Voucher may not be redeemed for cash or credit
• Voucher may not be transferred or sold

Part No. X09-49339   0-7356-1894-1